Samuel Sharpe

The History of Egypt from the Earliest Times till the Conquest by the Arabs

Sixth Edition. Vol. I

Samuel Sharpe

The History of Egypt from the Earliest Times till the Conquest by the Arabs
Sixth Edition. Vol. I

ISBN/EAN: 9783744753210

Printed in Europe, USA, Canada, Australia, Japan

Cover: Foto ©ninafisch / pixelio.de

More available books at **www.hansebooks.com**

THE HISTORY OF EGYPT

*FROM THE EARLIEST TIMES
TILL THE CONQUEST BY THE ARABS*
A.D. 640.

By SAMUEL SHARPE.

IN TWO VOLUMES.
VOL. I.

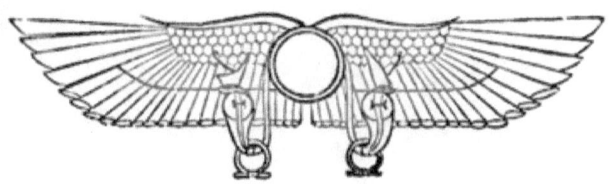

THE SIXTH EDITION.

LONDON: GEORGE BELL & SONS, YORK STREET,
COVENT GARDEN.
1885.

LONDON:
PRINTED BY WILLIAM CLOWES AND SONS, LIMITED,
STAMFORD STREET AND CHARING CROSS.

PREFACE.

Among the histories of the ancient world those of the Jews, of Greece, and of Rome, will always hold the first place in value; that of the Jews, because it contains the history of our religion; those of Greece and Rome for the poets and historians, the almost perfect works of art, and the quantity of knowledge that those nations have left us, and for the share that they have had in forming our opinions and guiding our tastes even in the present day. After these three histories, that of Egypt may certainly claim the next place, from the influence which that remarkable country has had upon the philosophy and science of the world. Even now the great stream of civilisation, after flowing through ages of antiquity and fertilising the centuries through which it has passed, is in its present fulness still coloured with the Egyptian opinions, as the Nile reaches the Delta red with Ethiopian soil. Architecture and sculpture, the art of writing and the use of paper, mathematics, chemistry, medicine, indeed we might add legislation, and almost every art which flourishes under a settled form of government, either took its rise in Egypt or reached Europe through that country. Many of our superstitions, and some of our religious truths, are here first met with; and above two hundred references to the Bible in these pages show how much light Egypt and the Scriptures may throw one upon another.

Much of the early portion of Egypt's history had been lost, and has latterly been regained; it had been hidden from us by the shade which time sooner or later throws over man's doings, and we are now delighted to find that it can be read by the light of modern science. Such further knowledge of the world's childhood brings with it some of the experience of age. An addition to the beginning of ancient history, without making our race older, gives us a longer life to look back to. We can thus more justly judge of the progress in science, in art, and in morals, with which God has already rewarded man's industry; we can more safely look forward to further improvement as a reward to our continued industry. The study of the past helps faith to lay hold upon the future.

The older monuments of sculpture teach us the names of numerous kings of Thebes, of Memphis, and of the Phenician shepherds; and though there may be doubts as to the order in which these early dynasties are to be placed, yet they leave us in no doubt as to the high antiquity which must be granted to this earliest of nations. Greek tradition begins with the Trojan war, when Egyptian Thebes was already falling from its high rank among cities. Jewish tradition begins a little earlier with the flight of the Israelites from Egypt, when the Egyptian kings already boasted of a long line of ancestors. Egypt was then a highly civilised country, the pyramids had been built near Memphis, the Egyptians had worked the copper mines on Mount Sinai, and the sculptured monuments which must have been seen by them, still prove the high state of the arts at that time. Even from before the time of Solomon the history may be traced with certainty through the reigns of Thothmosis, Amunothph, Rameses, and the other great Coptic kings, who for upwards of five hundred years made Thebes their capital, and usually held Lower Egypt as a province. It was during these reigns that Egypt, enriched by the Nubian gold mines, surpassed every country of the known world in wealth and power, and was foremost in all the arts of civilisation, of commerce, and of agriculture. Moses was there educated in all the learning of the Egyptians; and though Upper Egypt was at that time little known to the Greeks, Homer speaks of the armies and wealth of Egyptian Thebes as proverbial. No Theban historians, it is true, have recorded their great deeds; but the buildings are themselves the deeds, and the sculptures on the walls show that the nation was conscious of their greatness while performing them. The massive temples and obelisks covered with hieroglyphics, and the colossal statues, which have already outlived three thousand years, prove the high civilisation of the kingdom, even before the Jews had become a people, before the Greeks had got an alphabet; and they are among the causes of the lively interest with which we trace its history in the following ages. They marked these buildings with a serious gravity wholly their own. We have ourselves no national style in architecture, but we borrow from each what to our judgment or feelings seems most suitable for its purpose. We copy the buildings of the Chinese or Arabs for a summer house in the garden, those of the Greeks for a theatre, those of the Romans for a bridge, and for a triumphal monument, those of the Italians for a palace, those of our northern forefathers for a place of worship, and we go back to the early Egyptians for the models best suited for the solemnity of a tomb.

For about five hundred years more, beginning with Shishank the conqueror of Rehoboam, the kingdom was governed by kings of Lower Egypt, and the Thebaid fell to the rank of a province. The wars then carried on were chiefly in Syria, sometimes aimed at the conquest of Judæa and Samaria, and sometimes to save those kingdoms from becoming provinces of Babylon. The wealth and population of the country were as great or greater under these kings of Memphis and Sais, but the public spirit and virtue of the people were less; and much of that wealth which had before raised the great temples of Thebes was then spent in the hire of Greek mercenaries to surround a throne which native courage alone was no longer able to guard. The sovereigns were almost Greeks. It was then that Egypt was first open to Greek travellers, and the Greek philosophers eagerly sought from the Egyptian priests a knowledge of their famed science. The great names of Plato, who studied at Heliopolis, of Solon and Pythagoras, who had visited the Delta still earlier, and of many others of less note, prove how ready Greece then was to learn from Egypt.

During the next two hundred years, beginning with the conquest of the country by Cambyses, Egypt was mostly a province of Persia, and when not smarting under the tyranny of a foreign satrap was suffering as severely from its own half-successful attempts to regain its freedom. In these struggles between the Egyptians and their conquerors both parties trusted much to the courage of Greek mercenaries and allies; the Athenians were ranged on one side and the Spartans on the other; Persians and Egyptians had both placed the sword in the hands of the Greeks; and hence, when the power of Macedonia rose over the rest of Greece, when the Greek mercenaries flocked to the standard of Alexander, he found little difficulty in adding Persia, and its tributary province Egypt, to the rest of his conquests.

For three hundred years after the Macedonian conquest Egypt was an independent Greek kingdom, and nearly as remarkable for wealth and power under Ptolemy and his descendants, as it had been under its native sovereigns, and that at a time respecting which the faint traditions of consular Rome do not deserve the name of history. Though the Nubian gold mines were no longer worth working, the hoarded wealth of the country was by no means exhausted.

It is not as the birthplace of art and science alone that Egypt now claims our attention. No sooner did Greece itself sink than Greek literature took refuge in Alexandria. Philosophy then became coloured with the mysticism of Egypt, and literature was waited on by its criticism. To the Alexandrian copiers and libraries we mainly owe our knowledge of the great Greek writers and our earliest manuscripts of the Bible; while whatever help we have received from grammarians and critics, whatever in history we have gained from chronology, in poetry from prosody, in geography from mathematics, in medicine from anatomy, was first taught in Alexandria. Its public library was the admiration of the world. But Alexandria may be pointed to as a warning that it is possible to cultivate the intellect without raising man's moral worth; and after a reign or two we find that every public virtue was wanting among its citizens, while vice and luxury rioted in the palace. Every succeeding Ptolemy seemed worse than his father; till Cleopatra, the last sovereign of that remarkable family, unable to quell the rebellion of her Alexandrian subjects, yielded up her person and her capital to each Roman general who in his turn seemed able to uphold her power.

For nearly seven centuries more, to the end of this history, Egypt was governed by the Romans, or, to speak more strictly, for three centuries and a half by Rome, and for three centuries and a half by Constantinople, but always through the means of the Greek colonists in Alexandria. During most of these unhappy years, notwithstanding the introduction of Christianity, both the Alexandrian Greeks and the Egyptians were sinking in everything that makes a nation great or a people happy. The ancient learning fell with paganism, while the superstition still lived to mix itself with the religion of Jesus. Frequent rebellions and the inroads of the Arabs added to the weakness and misery of the province.

After the rise of Christianity, Alexandria no longer played that second part only in civilisation, nor furnished the handmaid sciences alone, but had its own schools in philosophy, and gave birth to sects in religion. In Alexandria took place that important union between Judaism and Platonism which should receive careful attention in the history of philosophy and of the human mind. Hence the Jewish Scriptures became first known to the pagans, and the doctrine of one God was perhaps less unwillingly listened to by them in consequence of its being united to some of their own philosophical opinions. The pagans were beginning to drop their polytheism, as Platonism appeared in the writings of the Jews; and both may thereby have been at the same time better fitted for the truths of Christianity. The later Platonists of Alexandria have perhaps hardly had justice done them by the moderns, either in regard to the improvement which they wrought in paganism, or the share which they have had in forming the present opinions of the world. Taking the doctrine of Plato as the foundation, borrowing something from the Jews and something from the other sects of pagans, they formed a philosophical religion, which we may think of little worth when offered as the rival of Christianity, but which we ought to admire as surpassing any other sect of paganism.

In Gnosticism we see another form of philosophy, an eastern mysticism, in which science was studied as a help to magic and divination; which had at the time, and no doubt still has, some share in moulding the opinions of Christians. It was common among the Jews at the time of the apostles; Paul censures it by name, and John indirectly. It was the parent, or perhaps the sister of Manicheism, and it has left its traces among several sects of Christians who seem to look for some other source for the origin of evil than the will of a benevolent Creator.

Among the three great families of Christianity, the Greek,

the Egyptian, and the Roman, the Egyptians often held the first place in importance. They were the first and chief corruptors of Christianity; and the history of wide-spreading error is hardly less important than the history of truth. The Egyptians were usually followed by the Romans as their pupils. The Egyptians long held the Nicene Creed against the Greek and Syrian churches; and though the opinions of modern Europe are in the first case to be traced up to Rome, yet, if we would carry back our search to their original source in Palestine, we must in most cases pass through Alexandria.

When the seat of empire was removed from Rome to Constantinople, and Alexandria lost its power over Egypt, the difference of religion between the two countries was the cause of a growing difficulty to the government. The Greeks of Alexandria, like the Protestants of Dublin, were of the same religion, politics, and blood as their rulers, and in a constant state of quarrel with their fellow-subjects. Sometimes an emperor like Zeno healed the disputes by treating both parties with equal justice. At other times, as under Theodosius, the country was governed according to the wishes of the less enlightened majority, and the Arian Greeks of Alexandria lost that ascendancy which they claimed as their birthright. But more often the emperors tried to govern the Egyptians by means of the favoured class; they goaded the people to rebellion by appointing to the churches and bishoprics and civil offices men whom the people hated as heretics and aliens; and at last the Egyptians, with an equal want of wisdom, threw themselves into the arms of their Arab neighbours, in hopes of regaining the government of their own church.

Thus Egypt, a country once the greatest in the world, but now to be counted among the least, gives us as many examples of what to shun as what to copy. On the banks of the Nile race after race has marked the high points to which it reached by its inventions, its buildings, or its literature, and in its turn has fallen back again to vice and littleness. The ruined temples and now unmeaning pyramids lead us to inquire, why arts decay and empires crumble, why Heliopolis is no longer a seat of learning, and why the papyrus rush ceased to grow in the Delta? They remind us that no wealth, no arts, no literature, can save a nation from ruin, unless it has the wish to check its own vices.

Thus also History amuses us while it teaches; it withdraws the mind from the cares of the present to live in the quiet of the past, where we hear of troubles without being made anxious, because the events that are to follow are already known.

Few of us would wish the thread of a story broken to be told where it disagrees with that of a former author, but it may interest the reader of Gibbon to learn in what points the writer of these pages has ventured to differ from that great historian. It escaped Gibbon's accurate eye that, on the death of Aurelian, part at least of the Roman world was governed for several months in the name of his widow Severina;—compare page 236 of vol. ii. with Gibbon, chap. xii. He also omits the name of Vaballathus Athenodorus as a Roman emperor, who reigned for one year as Aurelian's colleague;—see page 233. He seems mistaken in believing with Dion Cassius, that when the quarrels broke out between the Jews and pagans in several cities in the first century, the unhappy Jews were the assailants;—compare page 106 with Gibbon, chap. xvi. Again, he too hastily follows Procopius rather than Theophanes and Nonnosus at the end of his chapter xlii.; he thus confounds the embassy of Julianus in the reign of Justin, with that of Nonnosus in the reign of Justinian;—see pages 345 and 353. Lastly, he makes a needless difficulty of Elagabalus, who reigned three years and nine months, that is, three years and parts of two others, dating his coins in his fifth year.

With respect to the following pages, the author would add that he has thought it better not to treat of the literature and religion separately from the political events, but to throw the whole into the form of annals. Literature always takes its tone from the events of the day, and changes with the state of society; so also of religion. Although the idolatrous sculptures on the walls remain unchanged, yet the opinions about them change from century to century; and it is as necessary to note the passing of time when giving an account of a people's religion as when speaking of its government. Ecclesiastical history is very unfaithfully written when disjoined from the political quarrels which accompany the change of opinions. Again, he would remark that, from the scantiness of the materials, he has very often been unable to enlarge on an event as much as its importance seems to deserve. But he has in every case stated in the text or in the margin the works from which he has taken each piece of information, so that the inquiring reader may not only check his accuracy, but may at once see the sources in which further knowledge may be looked for.

He has to thank his learned friend, Dr. H. Jolowicz, of Koenigsberg, for the honour of having the Third Edition of his History published in a German translation; and though he differs widely from the chronological opinions of his German annotators, yet he has been enabled to correct several mistakes which are pointed out in the Notes to that edition, Leipsig, 1857-8.

Works by the Author.

- The Rosetta Stone, in Hieroglyphics and Greek, with Translations, and an explanation of the Hieroglyphical characters, and followed by an Appendix of Kings' names.
- Hebrew Inscriptions, from the valleys between Egypt and Mount Sinai, in their original characters, with translations and an Alphabet.
- Alexandrian Chronology.
- The Chronology of the Bible.
- The History of the Hebrew Nation and its Literature. Third Edition.
- The Hebrew Scriptures Translated; being a revision of the Authorized English Old Testament. Third Edition.
- Short Notes to accompany a Revised Translation of the Hebrew Scriptures.
- The New Testament, translated from Griesbach's Text. Sixth Edition; thirteenth thousand.
- Critical Notes on the Authorized English Version of the New Testament. Second Edition.
- Texts from the Holy Bible, explained by the Help of the Ancient Monuments. Second Edition.
- Egyptian Mythology and Egyptian Christianity, with their Influence on the Opinions of Modern Christendom.

DESCRIPTION OF THE WOODCUTS IN VOL. I.

On the title page.—The god Ra, in the form of the winged sun.

Fig. 1. The head of an Egyptian Fellah, or modern labourer. (H. Horeau.)

Fig. 2. The head of Rameses II., from a statue in the British Museum (J. Bonomi.)

Fig. 3. A stone which at the same time marked the boundary of the field, and the rise of the inundation on it. From a model in porcelain.

Fig. 4. An Egyptian crossing the river on a raft made of two bundles of rushes. (Denon, pl. 78.)

Fig. 5. The name of Labaris, spelt Ra, L, A, O, B. The syllable Ra is to be read last.

Fig. 6. The Bull Apis with a plate of metal between its horns. The horns represent the illuminated part of the moon when it is two days old, and the plate of metal represents the unilluminated part which may be also then seen on a clear night. On the forehead is a small model of the sacred asp or hooded snake. From a Bronze.

Fig. 7. The Basilisk or Uræus, the hooded snake, with a woman's head and a tall crown. From a tablet in the British Museum.

Fig. 8. The name of Osirtesen I. The characters in the first oval are perhaps, Ho-Ke-Ra, of which the sun Ra, though first in order, is pronounced last. Those in the second are, O, S, R, T, S, N, and spell the name that we here give to him, as the Greek authors usually call the Egyptian kings by the names in the second of the two ovals. The title over the first oval is Sot-nout, meaning *king of Upper Egypt, king of Lower Egypt*. That over the second oval is Se-ra, *son of the Sun*.

Fig. 9. A column in the tombs at Beni-hassan, with many flat sides, one of which is wider than the rest and carries a line of hieroglyphics. (J. Bonomi.)

Fig. 10. A view in the cave tombs of Beni-hassan. (Hector Horeau. This and most of the woodcuts with this name are from blocks kindly lent by this gentleman, belonging to his beautiful work, Panorama d'Egypte.)

Fig 11. The obelisk at Heliopolis. (J. Bonomi.)

Fig. 12. A granite needle standing on the bank of the Lake Mœris. (Burton's Excerpta Hieroglyphica.)

Fig. 13. The word Osiris.

Fig. 14. The word Amun.

Fig. 15. The four months of vegetation, distinguished by the half moon, a star, a numeral, and the character for growing herbs. (H. Horeau.)
Fig. 16. The four months of harvest, distinguished by the character for house. (H. Horeau.)
Fig. 17. The four months of inundation, distinguished by the character for water. (H. Horeau.)
Fig. 18. The words Month, Half-month, and Week.
Fig. 19. The name of Chofo, builder of the oldest pyramid, which is the second in point of size. It is spelt Ch, O, F, O.
Fig. 20. The name of Nefchofo, found in the largest pyramid. It is spelt N, F, Ch, F, O.
Fig. 21. Section of Chofo's pyramid. (Vyse's Pyramids.)
Fig. 22. Oxen drawing a block of stone on a sledge. From the quarries of Toora. (Young's Hieroglyphics, pl. 88.)
Fig. 23. Section of Nefchofo's pyramid. Two air-passages lead to the chamber in which the body was placed. The two lower chambers are of uncertain use. (Vyse's Pyramids.)
Fig. 24. Section of the chamber which held the body in Nefchofo's pyramid. There are five chambers of construction over it. (Vyse.)
Fig. 25. Plan of the pyramids, with the sphinx, the neighbouring tombs, and the great causeway. (Wilkinson's Map.)
Fig. 26. Restoration of the colossal sphinx, which lies in front of Chofo's pyramid. (J. Bonomi.)
Fig. 27. The name of Amunmai Thori I. The characters in the second oval are, A, M, N, M, T, R.
Fig. 28. The name of Amunmai Thori II. In the first oval Noubkora.
Fig. 29. The name of Osirtesen II. The characters in the first oval are, Ra, Mes, Ho, pronounced by the addition of the definite article Meshophra. The anvil is Mes, the beetle Ho, and the sun Ra.
Fig. 30. The name of Osirtesen III. The characters in the first oval are Mes, Ko, Ra. The single pair of arms is KAH; the three take the plural termination and become KO.
Fig. 31. The name of Amunmai Thori III.
Fig. 32. The name of Queen Scemiophra, spelt Ra, S, M, A, oB, O. Queens names have usually only one oval.
Fig. 33. Plan of the temple at Sarbout el Kadem. The older part is a cave hollowed out of the rock. (D. Roberts, R.A.)
Fig. 34. The name of Chebra, spelt Ra, K, B.
Fig. 35. The name of Chebra Amosis. The characters in the first oval are Ra, K, B; those in the second oval are A, M, S. The title over the first oval is NEB-TO, *lord of the world*; that over the second is NEB-MESO, *lord of battles*. This pair of titles is translated for us by Hermapion, in Ammianus Marcellinus. From the resemblance in sound between AMESH, *an anvil*, and MISHE, *a battle*, one character is used for both.
Fig. 36. The name of Amunothph I. The characters in the first oval are Ra-Seb, K, or Sebekra. Those in the second oval are A, M, N, O, Th, Ph, or Amunothph, *dedicated to Amun*. The harsh sound of this word is justified by our finding that the Greeks sometimes spelt it Amenophis and sometimes Amenothis. The position of the last

two characters is reversed in the woodcut by a mistake of the artist.

Fig. 37. The name of Mesphra-Thothmosis I. The three chief characters in the second oval are Thoth, M, S, the three smaller characters are Mes, Ra, H. If we put the definite article before the Ra it becomes Phra, as is required to make the name Mes-phra, given us by the Greeks. The anvil has the sound of Mes, as in Fig. 35, and its sound here confirms the meaning given to it there.

Fig. 38. An ear of the compound wheat with many spikes, the *Triticum Compositum*.

Fig. 39. The name of Thothmosis II. The three smaller characters in the second oval are MES, Ho, B. The beetle is Ho, the guitar is B, as we have made it in Fig. 5, Fig. 32, and Fig. 34.

Fig. 40. The name of Queen Nitocris. The characters in the first oval are Ra, Mi, K, or Mikera; those in the second are A, M, N, N, T, T, R, or Amun Neith Thor, or if the second T has a guttural sound, Amun Neith Gori.

Fig. 41. The god Amun-Ra, and Queen Nitocris on her knees, dressed as a man. From the obelisk of Thothmosis I.

Fig. 42. The obelisk as if upheaved by a mound of sand. (J. Bonomi.)

Fig. 43. The name of Thothmosis III. The characters in the first oval are Ra, M or Men, Ho, or Menophra, by putting, as in Fig. 37, the definite article Ph before Ra, and giving to the beetle the force of Ho, as in Fig. 39.

Fig. 44. The name of Mekora, or Menkera. The characters are Ra, M or Men, K. The three pair of arms only differ from the single pair by the vowel sound which follows.

Fig. 45. Section of the pyramid of Mekora, being the third in size in the plan Fig. 25. (Vyse's Pyramids.)

Fig. 46. Section of the fourth pyramid, being that which stands opposite to the middle of the third pyramid in the plan, and was built by the same sovereign. (Vyse.)

Fig. 47. The figure of Queen Nitocris with beard and man's clothes, but with feminine titles. "The good goddess queen of the world, Mykera, giver of life." From her obelisk at Karnak. (Burton's Excerpta, pl. 48.)

Fig. 48. Five figures, being a Nubian, a Copt, an Ethiopian, and an Arab, together with a Negro slave, selected from the four rows of men bearing tribute to Thothmosis III. The Nubian carries a tusk of ivory and a string of beads, probably amber. The Negro carries a stick of ebony. The Copt or Theban carries lotus flowers. The Ethiopian carries ostrich eggs and feathers. The Arab carries a pair of gloves. (Hoskins's Ethiopia.)

Fig. 49. The name of Amunothph II.

Fig. 50. A granite head in the British Museum, thought to be that of Thothmosis III.

Fig. 51. A brick arch at Thebes, bearing the name of Thothmosis III. (J. Bonomi.)

Fig. 52. A Map of the Peninsula of Sinai, showing the route of the Israelites from Egypt to the River Jordan.

Fig. 53. Three Egyptian soldiers in a war-chariot. The principal man or captain was called in Hebrew a chief of three.
Fig. 54. A view of hills which come to the edge of the sea near Mount Sinai and cause the route called, The Way by the Sea. (Bartlett.)
Fig. 55. An Egyptian tombstone from the burial-place of Taavah. (D. Roberts.)
Fig. 56. A view of Mount Serbal, and the Valley of Feiran. (Bartlett.)
Fig. 57. The letters of the Hebrew alphabet with their sixteen hieroglyphic originals. The other six Hebrew letters are copied, not from the hieroglyphics, but from other Hebrew letters, from which they differ by a slight distinctive mark. The hieroglyphic P, F, Th, K, and N, and T, which lie down, are turned up in their Hebrew copies.
Fig. 58. The name of Thothmosis IV. The smaller characters in the second oval are Mes, Meso, meaning *victorious in battles*.
Fig. 59. A view of the small temple built by Thothmosis IV., between the legs of the great sphinx. (Young's Hieroglyphics, pl. 80.)
Fig. 60. The name of Queen Mautmes, spelt Mo, T, M, Sh.
Fig. 61. A bas-relief at Luxor, representing in several groups the birth of this queen's son; 1st. The ibis-headed god Thoth, as a messenger, announces to the queen that she is to give birth to a child. 2nd. The god Knef, *the spirit*, and the goddess Isis, holding the queen's hands, put into her mouth the character for Life, meaning probably that of the coming child. 3rd. The queen while sitting on the midwife's stool has her hands rubbed by two of her maidens to ease the pains of child-bearing, while the child is held up by a third. 4th. The priests and nobles salute the new-born child, who is afterwards the King Amunothph III. (H. Horeau.)
Fig. 62. The name of King Amunothph III. The letters in the second oval are, A, M, N, O, followed by " Lord of Mendes." The O, is a contraction for the word Othph, seen in Fig. 49, showing that the last syllable of the name was not always clearly pronounced, and explaining why the Greeks sometimes thought it Amunoth, and sometimes Amunoph.
Fig. 63. A sitting colossus of Amunothph III., in the British Museum. (J. Bonomi.)
Fig. 64. The ground plan of the temple of Luxor. This court was added by Rameses II. to the older building by Amunothph III. (J. Bonomi.)
Fig. 65. A column formed of a cluster of eight stalks of the papyrus-plant tied together with bands; the eight buds form the capital. (J. Bonomi.)
Fig. 66. A column of a single papyrus-stalk and bud, of most unnaturally thick proportions. It is ornamented with bands, as if it were a cluster of several stalks. (J. Bonomi.)
Fig. 67. A column of a single papyrus stalk, with a full-blown flower for the capital. (J. Bonomi.)
Fig. 68. The name of King Amunmai Anemneb. The letters in the last oval are A, M, N, M, A, N, M, Neb.
Fig. 69. The hieroglyphics from which the Greek letters seem to have been copied. As we have seen in the case of the Hebrew alphabet, many of the Greek letters are set upright, which as hieroglyphics lie down. That the Greek Θ was copied from the Egyptian K is

DESCRIPTION OF THE WOODCUTS IN VOL. I. xvii

explained by the intermediate sound of the guttural. The older forms of the Θ and X were more close to the hieroglyphics than those in common use. If the Greeks gained their knowledge of letters from the Phenicians, as some historians tell us, it must have been from the Phenicians of the island of Cyprus, who owed their knowledge to Egypt.

Fig. 70. The name of Rameses I., spelt in the second oval Ra, M, S, S, O.
Fig. 71. The name of Oimenepthah I. It is spelt Pthah, M, O, I, N, but the order in which these letters are to be placed is learned from Manetho calling him Ammenophthes.
Fig. 72. The Abyssinian dog, the Feneck, with the hieroglyphic copy of it. A figure with the head of this dog was once the first letter in the name of Oimenepthah or Aimenepthah, as the letter A; but in most cases it was afterwards cut out to give place to the sitting figure of Osiris.
Fig. 73. Ground plan of the temple at Quorneh.
Fig. 74. A view of the portico of the temple at Quorneh in Thebes. (H. Horeau.) The spaces between the columns are open, and not filled up with low walls, as in the temples of a later time.
Fig. 75. A battle scene from Karnak, in which King Oimenepthah I. in his chariot is slaying the enemy. (H. Horeau.)
Fig. 76. Plan and section of the tomb of Oimenepthah in the hills on the west side of Thebes. (H. Horeau.)
Fig. 77. King Oimenepthah showing his love for the god Osiris. (Belzoni.)
Fig. 78. The god Anubis hanging up in heaven the lamp of the family of King Oimenepthah. (His sarcophagus in Soane's Museum.)
Fig. 79. The conquerors of the great serpent of sin, who carry it in procession. From the sarcophagus of Oimenepthah I., in Sir Jno. Soane's Museum. (Egypt. Inscript. pl. 64.)
Fig. 80. Mankind coming to judgment. (On the same sarcophagus.)
Fig. 81. The trial of a dead man by the judge Osiris. From a papyrus. (Denon, pl. 141.)
Fig. 82. The name of Amunmai Rameses II., spelt in the second oval Amun, M, Ra, M, S, S.
Fig. 83. View in the Hall of Columns at Karnak. (Owen Jones.)
Fig. 84. View of the portico of Luxor, before one of the obelisks was removed to Paris. (Denon, pl. 50.)
Fig. 85. A column from the Memnonium. Against it stands a figure of the king in form of a mummy. (J. Bonomi.)
Fig. 86. Section of the Hall of the Memnonium. Each of the taller columns in the middle avenue is copied from a single full-blown papyrus, each of the columns in the side avenue is from a papyrus in bud; as at Karnak. (J. Bonomi.)
Fig. 87. An ape on the top of a landmark, where he has taken refuge when the waters are out; the sign of the summer solstice. From the ceiling of the Memnonium. (Burton's Excerpta, pl. 58.)
Fig. 88. The Dog-star rising heliacally. Its name is S, T, T, S, or Sothis. (Burton's Excerpta, pl. 58.)
Fig. 89. The constellations of Orion and the Bull, with their names, Ori, A, N, and Mesora. (Burton's Excerpta, pl. 58.)

xviii   DESCRIPTION OF THE WOODCUTS IN VOL. I.

Fig. 90. Ground plan of the Memnonium.
Fig. 91. A column in the temple of Karnak. (J. Bonomi.)
Fig. 92. Rameses II. slaying his enemies in honour of the god Amun-Ra. He holds them by the hair of the head. The god encourages him with his gestures. Behind the king is his standard, carried by what should be a standard bearer, a stick with a pair of arms. (J. Bonomi.)
Fig. 93. The monuments on the face of the rock near Beyrout, one by Rameses II., and the other by an Assyrian monarch, probably Sennacherib. (J. Bonomi.)
Fig. 94. A troop of soldiers with bows, swords, spears, shields, and hatchets. They are addressed by a general, perhaps the king's son, with a single lock of hair, who holds an ostrich feather as a staff of office. (H. Horeau.)
Fig. 95. A war chariot with a pair of horses. (J. Bonomi.)
Fig. 96. The front of the temple of Abou Simbel, with four colossal statues sitting, two on each side of the entrance. The upper part of one is thrown down. (Owen Jones.)
Fig. 97. Plan of the same temple hollowed out of the rock. (H. Horeau.)
Fig. 98. Section of the same temple. (H. Horeau.)
Fig. 99. Plan of the temple of Assebona in Nubia, with the inner rooms hollowed out of the rock, and an avenue of sphinxes in front. (H. Horeau.)
Fig. 100. The name of Pthahmen-Miothph, or *approved by Pthah and dedicated to Truth.* The characters in the second oval are Pthah, M, N, Mi, O, Ph, I.
Fig. 101. The name of Oimenepthah II. The characters in the second oval are Osiri or O, I. M, N, Pthah. This name, like that of Oimenepthah I., is often written with a dog-headed Anubis in the place of the Osiris, for the first character.
Fig. 102. The name of Osirita Ramerer Amunmai. The order of the characters in the second oval is doubtful; they are Osiri, T, A, Ra, M, R, R, A, M, N, M.
Fig. 103. The statue of Pthahmen-Miothph. In the British Museum.
Fig. 104. The name of Rameses III. The characters in the second oval are Ra, M, S, S, with two others to which we do not here venture to give a force.
Fig. 105. Plan of the temple at Medinet Abou.
Fig. 106. View of the courtyard of Medinet Abou. The four smaller columns are of Greek work, and are a part of a Christian church which was built about the fourth century and dedicated to St. Athanasius. (H. Horeau.)
Fig. 107. Plan of the temple at Karnak.
Fig. 108. The lid of the sarcophagus of Rameses III. In the Museum at Cambridge.
Fig. 109. Plan of the city of Thebes, and of the hills in the neighbourhood, in which the kings, queens, and nobles were buried.
Fig. 110. Amun-Ra, his name is spelt A, M, N, R, A.
Fig. 111. Amun-Ra; Maut, *the mother*, his wife; and Chonso, their son. (H. Horeau.)

DESCRIPTION OF THE WOODCUTS IN VOL. I.   xix

Fig. 112. Chonso with the new moon on his head. Ch, N, S, O.
Fig. 113. Kneph. N, Ph, followed by the determinative sign.
Fig. 114. Seb. S, B.
Fig. 115. Chem. A, M, N, Ehe, Ch, M. The semicircle, usually a Th, here has the guttural force of the Ch. The whole is pronounced Amunehe Chem. From the word Amunehe comes the Greek word Mnevis, the name of the Bull of Heliopolis.
Fig. 116. Pasht. P, Ch, T.
Fig. 117. Athor. Her name is pictorial rather than spelt. It is a house containing the god Horus, or Ei, T, Hor, *the house of Horus*.
Fig. 118. Neith. The character for her name is followed by the feminine termination T, S.
Fig. 119. Thoth. His name is an ibis on a perch, of which the perch has the force of T, or Thoth.
Fig. 120. Hapimou, the Nile. H, A, P, I, Mo.
Fig. 121. Pthah. P, Th, H.
Fig. 122. Osiris. Is, Iri, followed by a sitting figure.
Fig. 123. Isis. Isi, followed by the feminine termination T, S.
Fig. 124. Horus. Or, I.
Fig. 125. Anubis. A, N, P.
Fig. 126. Typhon. T, P, O, followed by the feminine termination T, S.
Fig. 127. Nephthys. The character for her name is formed of two united, the dish NEB, and the house EI. Together they form the word Neb-t-ei, *lady of the house*.
Fig. 128. The goddess of the sacred tree of knowledge is pouring out of a jar two streams of water; one falls into the mouth of a man upon his knees, and the other into the mouth of his soul, in the form of a bird with human head and hands. (Egypt. Inscript. 2nd Ser. pl. 81.)
Fig. 129. The name of Amunmai Shishank. It is spelt A, M, N, Mi, Sh, Sh, N, K.
Fig. 130. Figures which may have been the origin of the Urim and Thummim of the Hebrews. 1st. A shrine containing the figures of the gods Horus and Truth, pronounced Ouro and Mei or Thmei. 2nd. A snake and a vulture each on a dish; they bore the same two names. 3rd. Another figure of Truth or Thmei on a dish. (J. Bonomi.)
Fig. 131. A metal cup in the British Museum which was brought from Nineveh. On the inside are engraved figures of the winged sun; the winged sphinx standing, and wearing the crown of Upper and Lower Egypt; and the beetle with outstretched wings, holding a ball or sun between its front legs.
Fig. 132. Four men carrying a religious ark in the procession of Rameses III. (Denon, pl. 134.)
Fig. 133. A standard or pole bearing the sacred asp, with the double crown on its head. (Denon, pl. 119.)
Fig. 134. A captive bearing the name of "The kingdom of Judah;" spelt J,U,D,H,—M,L,K,—land; from the walls of Karnak. (J. Bonomi.)
Fig. 135. The name of Amunmai Osorkon, spelt in the second oval A, M, N, Mi, O, S, R, K, N.

Fig. 136. The Egyptian title of Se-ra, *Son of the Sun*.
Fig. 137. The name of Rameses VII.
Fig. 138. The name of Takellothis, spelt in the second oval A, M, N, Mi, T, K, L, I, M, T, or Amunmai Takelimot, with four characters in the middle, meaning "the son of Isis."
Fig. 139. The name of Osorkon II., spelt A, M, N, Mi, O, S, R, K, A, N, followed by three characters meaning "the son of Isis."
Fig. 140. The name of Shishank II. or Amunmai Shishank, the son of Isis.
Fig. 141. The name of Bocchoris, spelt Ra, B, I, K. For the B, see Note on Fig. 39.
Fig. 142. A small pyramid with a doorway. From Meroë. (Hoskins's Ethiopia.)
Fig. 143. The name of Sabacothph, spelt S, B, K, O, T, P.
Fig. 144. The name of Sevechus, spelt in the second oval S, V, K.
Fig. 145. The name of Tirhakah, spelt in the second oval T, H, R, K, or Tiharak.
Fig. 146. An Assyrian sculpture, seeming to represent timber brought down from Mount Lebanon to the city of Tyre, and thence carried away in ships distinguished by the Phenician horse's head. They are accompanied by the winged bull of Assyria, and leave behind them Dagon, the fish-god of the coast of Palestine. They pass by the Island of Cyprus. (Botta's Nineveh.)
The next slab, not here drawn, tells us by the crocodiles that the timber is being landed on the coast of Egypt.
Fig. 147. Restoration of a colossal statue at Argo in Ethiopia. In its proportions it is shorter and stouter than nature. (Hoskins's Ethiopia.)
Fig. 148. Rameses II. suckled by a goddess. From a temple in the neighbourhood of Calabshe. (H. Horeau.)
Fig. 149. The name of Chemmis, spelt Ch, M, I.
Fig. 150. The name of Chephren, spelt Ch, M, R, N.
Fig. 151. The name of Mesaphra, spelt Ra, Mes, A, B.
Fig. 152. The name of Uchureus or Uchora, spelt Ra, Uch, O.
Fig. 153. The name of Asychis, spelt A, S, S, A.
Fig. 154. The name of Ammeres, spelt in the second oval A, M, N, A, S, R, U, or Amun Aseru. The name in the first oval may be Vophra, spelt Ra, B, O, B.
Fig. 155. The name of Psammetichus I., spelt in the second oval P, S, M, T, K. The name in the first oval is Vophra, spelt Ra, B, B. The name of Vaphres seems given to Psammetichus III. by Manetho, by a mistake, instead of to this king.
F.g. 156. The name of Necho, spelt in the second oval N, K, O. The name in the first oval is Vophra, spelt Ra, B, B.
Fig. 157. The name of Psammetichus II. That in the first oval may be read Okenra.
Fig. 158. The name of Psammetichus III. That in the first oval is Hophra, spelt Ra, H, B.
Fig. 159. Section of a tomb near the pyramids, called Campbell's tomb, from the name of the gentleman who opened it. It contains a true arch of three stones beneath a ruder brick arch. (Vyse's Pyramids.)

DESCRIPTION OF THE WOODCUTS IN VOL. L.   xxi

Fig. 160. King Hophra worshipping one of the punishing gods. British Museum.
Fig. 161. The four lesser gods of the dead interceding as mediators before the judge Osiris. A tablet in British Museum.
Fig. 162. The four lesser gods placed on the altar as a sacrificial gift to the judge Osiris. A tablet in British Museum.
Fig. 163. The name of Amasis, spelt in the second oval Io, M, Neith, S, T. The characters in the first oval are Ra, N, B, or Nephra.
Fig. 164. The name of Hanes-Vaphra, spelt O, N, S, B, B, Ra. The first half of her name may be the same as that of the wife of Shishank, from which the Egyptian town received its name Tape-Hanes, or Daphnæ.
Fig. 165. The head of Cyrus with an Egyptian head-dress. From a bas-relief at Persepolis. (Ker Porter's Travels.)
Fig. 166. The restoration of the temple at Sais described by Herodotus, by the help of five fragments in the British Museum, namely, two intercolumnar walls, two obelisks, and a capital. A third intercolumnar wall is in Rome.
Fig. 167. View of the mounds at Sa-el-Hagar, the ancient Sais.
Fig. 168. A small temple of a single block of stone at Tel-etmai near Mendes. (Burton's Excerpta.)
Fig. 169. Figures of three labourers and a musician. (H. Horeau.) The group is arranged by the artist.
Fig. 170. Figures of a king wearing the double crown, his queen, their son, and two bald-headed priests. One holds up his hands in the act of prayer before the ark which is standing on the ground; and the other, clothed with a leopard-skin, is placing fire and water on an altar. (H. Horeau.) The group is arranged by the artist.
Fig. 171. The model of a house in wood. From the British Museum.
Fig. 172. The crown of Upper Egypt, that of Lower Egypt, and the double crown formed of the two united.
Fig. 173. The statue of Amunothph III. in the British Museum. (J. Bonomi.)
Fig. 174. One of the colossal statues of Rameses II. in front of the temple at Abou Simbel. (J. Bonomi.)
Fig. 175. An Assyrian figure in bas-relief. In his right hand he holds a fir cone, with which, as with a sponge, he seems in the act of sprinkling water. The cone may have been filled with water out of the vessel held in his left hand. (J. Bonomi.)
Fig. 176. The figure of a woman in bas-relief, of the later Egyptian style. (J. Bonomi.)
Fig. 177. The fighting gladiator of Agasias. (J. Bonomi.)
Fig. 178. A column from the Memnonium, with the lotus flower from which it was copied. (J. Bonomi.)
  Page 197. An ornamental border formed of the flower and fruit of the lotus. From this, after several changes, the Greek border of the egg and spear pattern seems to be taken. It also resembles the fringe of bells and pomegranates worn in metal on Aaron's garment. (Monumens de l'Egypte, par Champollion.)
Fig. 179. The name of Cambyses, spelt K, N, B, O, Sh.

Fig. 180. The name of Darius, spelt in the second oval N, T, R, I, O, S. This is a good instance of the Asiatic mode of writing D, by means of N, T, as they wrote B by means of M, P. The first oval may be translated *beloved by Ra and Amun*.

Fig. 181 and 182. The earliest known coins that can be considered Egyptian. From the British Museum.

Fig. 183 and 184. Coins of Cyprus, with the bull Apis and the winged sun. The first has the Phenician characters S, A, for Salamis. From the Duc de Luynes' collection.

Fig. 185. The name of the satrap Amasis, partly illegible.

Fig. 186. The name of the satrap Nephra, spelt Ra, N, B.

Fig. 187. The name of Mandothph, spelt in the second oval M, N, D, O,—O, T, P, *dedicated to Mandoo*. The first oval is Ra, Neb, To, Ra, *lord of the world*.

Fig. 188. The god Mandoo, with a hawk's head and the crown of Amun-Ra.

Fig. 189. The name of Xerxes, spelt Ch, S, I, R, S.

Fig. 190. An Egyptian soldier with shield large enough to cover the whole body. From the Sculptures in Lycopolis. (Description de l'Egypte, vol. iv. 46.)

Fig. 191. The name of Artaxerxes, spelt A, R, T, Ch, Sh, Sh, S.

Fig. 192. The name of Inarus or Adonra-Bakan, spelt in the second oval A, T, N, Ra, B, Ch, N.

Fig. 193. The name of Amyrtæus, spelt Io, M, A, A, ?, T, K.

Fig. 194. The pigmy god Pthah. From a porcelain image of the same size.

Fig. 195. The goddess Ken standing between Chem and Rampo. Beneath is the Persian goddess Anaita and three worshippers. From a tablet in the British Museum. (J. Bonomi.)

Fig. 196. The pigmy Pthah, with his children, the Cabeiri, the punishing gods, and the bottomless pit guarded by apes. From a mummy case in the British Museum. (J. Bonomi.)

Fig. 197. The name of Thannyras, spelt in the first oval, after the upper characters, which mean Pharaoh, H, A, O, M, Ra. The characters in the second oval are divided into three groups, each following an M. Those in the first group are Ran—F, *his name*. Those in the second group are M, O, Ch, N, T, I, *successor to*. Those in the third group are Adon-Ra.

Fig. 198. The figure of Thannyras worshipping the sun. (Burton's Excerpta, pl. 6.)

Fig. 199. Thannyras in the form of a sphinx with a human head, presenting the figure of Truth to the sun. (Monumens Egypt. Prisse, pl. x.)

Fig. 200. Olmenepthah I. on his knees presenting offerings to Amun-Ra seated on a throne. Above the god is the sun with two asps, to which has since been added rays of light, each ending with a hand. From Cosseir. (Monumens Egypt. Prisse, pl. vi.)

Fig. 201. The name of Nepherites, spelt N, F, A, O, R, O, T.

Fig. 202. The name of Achoris, spelt in the second oval H, A, K, R, I.

Fig. 203. The name of Psammuthis, spelt in the second oval P, Si, Mo, T. The characters in the first oval may be translated *approved by Osiris and Pthah*.

DESCRIPTION OF THE WOODCUTS IN VOL. I.   xxiii

Fig. 204. The name of Nectanebo, spelt in the second oval N, O, Ch, T, A, Neb, Fo. The name in the first oval may be the same as that of the late king Achoris, spelt Ra, Ho, K.

Fig. 205. A mummy laid out upon a lion-shaped couch. The soul, in form of a bird with human head and hands, holds in one hand a sail, the character for wind or breath, and in the other hand the character for life. These it is putting into the mouth of the mummy to raise it from the dead, while the god Anubis is preparing to unwrap the bandages. (Wilkinson's Materia Hieroglyphica, i. 17.)

Fig. 206. The vault of heaven is represented by the goddess Neith coloured blue, who forms an arch by bending forwards till her hands touch the ground. Beneath this vault is the figure of a man falling to the ground in death. The red colour of his skin tells us that he is in his mortal or animal body, while beside stands upright a second body painted blue, which is his spiritual body, or angel, or ghost. On either side is the figure of Kneph-Ra seated. From a mummy-case in the possession of Dr. Lee at Hartwell.

Fig. 207. The name of Alexander the Great, spelt A, L, Ch, N, D—A, M, N, or Alechand Amun. (Egypt. Inscript. 2nd series, pl. 61.)

Fig. 208. The bust of Ptolemy Soter, from a bronze at Naples, found in Herculaneum. (Visconti, Iconographie Grecque.)

Fig. 209. The name of Philip Arridæus, spelt in the second oval P, L, I, P, O, S. The first oval means *beloved by Amun and approved by Ra*.

Fig. 210. The tomb of an Apis, being a chamber walled up in the tunnel under the hill near Memphis.

Fig. 211. The figure and name of Osiri-Apis or Serapis.

Fig. 212. The name of Alexander Ægus, spelt in the second oval A, L, K, S, A, N, T, R, S, Alexandros. The first oval means *beloved by Amun and approved by Ra*.

Fig. 213. The chasm in the rock by which the city of Petra is entered. (Bartlett.)

Fig. 214. The name of Ptolemy, spelt P, T, O, L, M, A, A, S.

Fig. 215. Silver coin of Ptolemy Soter, with eagle standing on a thunderbolt.

Fig. 216. The hieroglyphic word Pe-ouro, or Pharaoh, *the king*; from which the Greek artist copied the eagle and thunderbolt.

Fig. 217. Copper coin of Alexandria with the head of Jupiter or Serapis.

Fig. 218. A painting of Hippolytus in his chariot; his tutor following in alarm; the bull rising out of the water; and the fury of the bull, as a person, striking with a torch at the horses' heads. From a vase in the British Museum, which may be supposed to be copied from the painting by Antiphilus.

Fig. 219. The bust of Queen Berenice, from a bronze at Naples, found at Herculaneum. (Visconti, Iconographie Grecque.)

Page 302. An Egyptian landowner, holding his sceptre and staff of inheritance From the British Museum.

Fig. 220. The heads of Ptolemy Philadelphus and his first wife, Arsinoë, from a gem cut on sardonyx. (Visconti, Iconographie Grecque.)

Fig. 221. The name of Ptolemy Philadelphus; the characters in the first oval are, *beloved by Amun, to whom Ra gave victory*.

Fig. 222. A view of the temple of Isis in the island of Philæ, with the small

xxiv   DESCRIPTION OF THE WOODCUTS IN VOL. I.

temple of Athor behind; and a plan of the same. (Denon, pl. 72 and 70.)

Fig. 223 to 227. Five capitals formed of flowers and buds of the papyrus; from Philæ. (J. Bonomi.)

Fig. 228. A capital formed of palm branches; from Philæ. (J. Bonomi.)

Fig. 229. Statue of a priest, in the British Museum.

Fig. 230. Two figures drawn upon the wall with squares, showing the proportions used by the Theban sculptors. (J. Bonomi.)

Fig. 231. Coin with the heads of Soter, Philadelphus, and Berenice. (Visconti, Iconographie Grecque.)

Fig. 232. Coins with the heads of Philadelphus and his second wife, Arsinoë, on one side, and on the other Soter and Berenice, their parents. (Visconti, Icongraphie Grecque.)

Fig. 233. Coin of Arsinoë Philadelphus, dated in the year 33 of the king's reign, and with the mint mark ΠΑ, for Paphos in the island of Cyprus, where it was struck. (Visconti, Iconographie Grecque.)

Fig. 234. A small votive pyramid in stone, made to be presented to the temple as an offering. It bears the name of King Nantof, and his first name seems to mean "approved by the queen of Psammetichus III.," which would lead us to believe that this King Nantof was the sovereign priest of Memphis in the reign either of Hophra or Amasis. From the British Museum.

Fig. 235. The name of Ptolemy Euergetes; in the first oval, *Son of the brother-gods, approved by Ra, a living image of Amun*; in the second oval, *Ptolemy immortal, beloved by Pthah*.

Fig. 236. A doorway at Karnak, built by Ptolemy Euergetes in front of a small temple, which stands near the south-west corner of the sacred area which forms the great temple of Karnak. From a photograph.

Fig. 237. A figure of Mercury in the false antique style; from a slab in the British Museum, which was brought from Canopus.

Fig. 238. A diagram explaining how Eratosthenes measured the latitude of a place by the length of a shadow thrown by the sun on the equinoctial day at noon.

Fig. 239. A diagram explaining how Eratosthenes determined the angular distance between the towns of Syene and Alexandria by means of the shadows at those places on the longest day at noon, and then the length of the earth's circumference by means of the distance between those two towns.

Fig. 240. A coin of Ptolemy Euergetes. (Visconti, Iconographie Grecque.)

Fig. 241. A coin of his Queen Berenice. (*Ibid.*)

Fig. 242. The name of Ptolemy IV., *immortal, beloved by Isis*; and in the first oval, *son of the gods Euergetes, approved by Pthah, to whom Ra gave victory, a living image of Amun*.

Fig. 243. A coin of Ptolemy Philopator. (Visconti, Iconographie Grecque.)

Fig. 244. A coin of his Queen Arsinoë. (*Ibid.*)

Fig. 245. The name of Ptolemy V., *immortal, approved by Pthah*; and in the first oval, *beloved by the father-gods, approved by Pthah, to whom Ra gave victory, a living image of Amun*.

Fig. 246 A Roman coin of Marcus Lepidus crowning the young King Ptolemy

DESCRIPTION OF THE WOODCUTS IN VOL. I.   XXV

Epiphanes. The Roman has the title of guardian to the king. On the other side is a female head crowned with battlements, for the city of Alexandria. (From the Pembroke coins.)

Fig. 247. A coin of Ptolemy Epiphanes; his crown is formed like rays of light. (Visconti, Iconographie Grecque.)

Fig. 248. An Egyptian ship with one sail and several rowers, for navigating the Nile.

Fig. 249. The name of Ptolemy Philometor, meaning, *son of the two gods Epiphanes, approved by Pthah and Horus, like Ra and Amun.*

Fig. 250. The name of Ptolemy Euergetes II. In the second oval, *beloved by Pthah, living for ever;* in the first oval, *son of the gods Epiphanes, approved by Pthah, like Ra, a living image of Amun.*

Fig. 251. The elevation of the portico of the temple of Antæopolis. (Description de l'Egypte, iv. 56.)

Fig. 252. View of the temple of Apollinopolis Magna. (Denon, pl. 58.)

Fig. 253. Plan of the same. (J. Bonomi.)

Fig. 254. Side elevation of the same. (J. Bonomi.)

Fig. 255. Bas-relief of the Apotheosis of Homer in the British Museum. At the top is seated either Jupiter on Mount Olympus, or the poet on Mount Parnassus. Beneath him stands a figure of Memory. Then follow the Nine Muses and the female Apollo. On a pedestal stands the critic, holding a book in his hand. In the second division Homer is seated, and crowned by the king and queen, who are known to be Philometor and his mother by the queen standing before the king. The figures in front of the poet are, Fable, History, Poetry, Tragedy, Comedy, Nature, Virtue, Memory, Faith, and Wisdom.

Fig. 256. Hero's Steam Engine, copied from the manuscripts.

Fig. 257. Coin of Ptolemy Philometor. (Visconti, Iconographie Grecque.) The palm-branch, in Greek Phœnix, tells us that it was struck in Phenicia, probably in Cyprus, called in hieroglyphics, the Island of Phenicia.

Fig. 258. View of the small temple of Athor in the island of Philæ. (Hector Horeau.)

Fig. 259. The figure of the Nile-god as Aquarius, in the Zodiac of the temple of Dendera. (Denon, pl. 132.)

Page xxxvi. The collar, the badge of office, is being placed on the governor of a province. From a bas-relief in the British Museum.

Fig. 260. Hebrew writing from the rock at Wady Mokatteb (*Trans. R. Soc. Lit.*, 1832):

ל דכרן עבג דכרן רע זר :
דקן ניר דקא עם רק יהו
רן חהך : שלם רע ּ

For a memorial [offering] for Abeg, A memorial for his foreign companion [or concubine]. Keep alive the broken lamp of the rejected people, O Jehovah; Make [the nation] that has waited rejoice. A worthless peace offering.

CONTENTS OF THE FIRST VOLUME.

CHAPTER I.

INTRODUCTION; THE EARLY KINGS; THE INVASION BY THE SHEPHERDS, AND THEIR EXPULSION; THE RISE OF THEBES.

B. C.		PAGE
	Egypt, its boundaries	1
	Asiatic origin of the race, the ruling and lower classes	2
	The soil and climate	5
	Early civilization	8
	The sources of polytheism; the gods	9
	The several little kingdoms and first known Kings of This; of Thebes; of Elephantine	11
	Of Heracleopolis; the Lake of Mœris; the Labyrinth	12
	Of Memphis, of Xois	13
	The bull and other animals worshipped	ib.
	OSIRTESEN I.; early style of building; sculpture	15
	Obelisks of Heliopolis and of the Lake Mœris	17
	Hieroglyphics; their progress towards an alphabet	18
	The months; the language	19
	The art of making steel	21
1700 ?	SUPHIS or CHEOPS of Memphis, and his successor SENSUPHIS, conquer Thebes	21
	The Pyramids built; their size and use	22
	The Sphinx	26
	AMUNMAI THORI I.	27
	AMUNMAI THORI II.	ib.
	OSIRTESEN II.	ib.
1550 ?	OSIRTESEN III.	ib.
	AMUNMAI THORI III.	ib.
	Queen SCEMIOPHRA	ib.
	The copper mines and temple in Sinai	28
	Women in the priesthood, their condition	29
	The Phenicians settle in Lower Egypt	30
	The Shepherd kings make Egypt tributary	ib.
1600 ?	SALATIS	ib.
	BEON	ib.
	APACHNAS	ib.
	APOPHIS	ib.

B.C.		PAGE
1500 ?	JANAIS	30
	ASSETH	ib.
1450 ?	CHEBROS-AMOSIS of Thebes expels the Shepherd kings	31
	CHEBROS-AMOSIS, his son	32
	AMUNOTHPH I. by his marriage gains Ethiopia	33
	MESPHRA-THOTHMOSIS I.; his buildings, their grandeur	35
	Ethiopia less civilised	36
1400 ?	Joseph brought into Egypt as a slave	37
	He is made prime minister of Lower Egypt	38
	He changes the tenure of the estates	39
	The Israelites settle in Goshen	40
	MESPHRA-THOTHMOSIS II. and Queen NITOCRIS unite Upper and Lower Egypt; her palace, and obelisks	42
	The mechanical arts	43
	Chronological difficulties	45

CHAPTER II.

THE RISE OF THEBES; THE THEBAN KINGS OF ALL EGYPT.

	THOTHMOSIS III., or MENOPHRES, perhaps MYCERA	46
	The third and fourth pyramids built	47
	The several kingdoms united	48
1322	The calendar reformed; era of Menophres	50
	The buildings; the arch	51
	AMUNOTHPH II.	52
1300 ?	Moses leads the Israelites out of Egypt	54
	Their route described; passage of the Red Sea	ib.
	Hebrew alphabet borrowed from the hieroglyphics	64
	Hebrew names of months which do not belong to the same seasons with the hieroglyphical names	66
	THOTHMOSIS IV. He builds a temple to the great sphinx	67
	Mautmes, the birth of the son	ib.
	AMUNOTHPH III.; his musical statue	68
	The style of Egyptian statues, temples, and columns	69
	AMUNMAI ANEMNEB	72
	The Greeks driven out of the Delta; Erechtheus, Cadmus, and Danaus, founders of Greek cities	73
	The Greek alphabet copied from hieroglyphics	ib.
	RAMESES I.	74
1200 ?	OIMENEPTHAH I.; his name	ib.
	His palace at Quorneh, paintings, palace at Abydos, tomb near Thebes	75
	Love shown to the gods; the lamp in heaven	79
	The trial of the dead	80
	RAMESES II.; his palace of the Memnonium; of Karnak	85
	The Zodiac of the Memnonium	87
	His victories; colony at Colchis	91
	His march through Palestine and monument at Beyroot	92

B.C.		PAGE
	The art of war; soldiers, chariots	92
	Cave temples of Nubia	96
	The population; gold mines in Nubia	99
	Copper mines in Sinai	101
	The priesthood	ib.
	Pthahmen-Meiothph	ib.
1100 ?	Oimenepthah II.	ib.
	Osirita Ramerer	ib.
	Rameses III.; his palace at Medinet Abou	103
	March into Syria	105
	His sarcophagus	107
1000 ?	Rameses IV., V., and VI., at the time of the Trojan war. End of Theban greatness	108
	Thebes described	109
	The gods; the trinities; forefathers worshipped	111
	The Sacred Tree	117
	The Egyptian knowledge of geography	118
	The rise of the Hebrew monarchy; Solomon's trade on the Red Sea; gold from Ophir in Nubia	120

CHAPTER III.

RISE OF THE EAST OF THE DELTA; THE KINGS OF BUBASTIS AND TANIS; CIVIL WARS; INVASION BY THE ETHIOPIANS. B.C. 945-697.

945	Shishank of Bubastis; his alliance with the Jews	124
	Solomon's Egyptian Queen	125
	Superstitions and magical arts	126
	Intercourse with Judæa	128
	Shishank helps the Edomites to rebel against Judæa	129
932	Shishank conquers Rehoboam and takes Jerusalem	130
	The soldiers regain their privileges	131
	The city of Bubastis	ib.
	Osorchon I.; the unsettled state of Egypt	132
909	Zerah invades Judæa; perhaps Rameses VII.	133
	* * * *	
890	Takellothis of Bubastis	134
877	The Jewish trade on the Red Sea again attempted, but stopped	ib.
870	The Edomites revolt from Judæa	ib.
	* * * *	
	Osorchon II. and Shishank II. of Tanis	135
	Tyre, Sidon, and the Phenicians	ib.
	The island of Cyprus, its language and products	136
	Tanis in the time of Homer	137
	* * * *	
743	Bocchoris the Wise of Sais; his laws; Anysis of Memphis	138
	Conquest of Egypt by the Ethiopians; Isaiah's Woe against Egypt	139

CONTENTS OF VOL. I.

B.C.		PAGE
737	SABACOTHPH	141
729	SEVECHUS; his alliance with the Israelites	ib.
	Rise of Assyria	142
	Samaria conquered by the Assyrians	143
715	TIRHAKAH; his troops revolt	ib.
	Chronology fixed by the Babylonian eclipses	146

CHAPTER IV.

RISE OF THE WEST OF THE DELTA; THE KINGS OF SAIS.
B.C. 697–523.

B.C.		PAGE
	Memphis has fallen, its chief kings enumerated	148
697	AMMERES of Sais	149
679	STEPHINATHIS	150
672	NECHEPSUS; his learning	ib.
666	NECHO I.	150
658	PSAMMETICHUS I.; Greek mercenaries	ib.
	Egyptian troops desert into Ethiopia	151
	The inroad of Gog, or the Scythians	ib.
	The basalt quarries worked	153
614	NECHO II.; his fleet	ib.
	Begins the canal from the Nile to the Red Sea	ib.
	Circumnavigates Africa	154
610	Conquers Josiah; takes Jerusalem	155
	He is defeated by Nabopolassar	156
608	PSAMMETICHUS II.; the Ethiopians rebel	157
	Arbitrates among the Greek states	ib.
591	HOPHRA or PSAMMETICHUS III.; he conquers Palestine	ib.
	Defeats the Phenician fleet, takes Tyre and Sidon	158
	Nebuchadnezzar defeats the Egyptians and leads the Jews into captivity	ib.
	The prophet Ezekiel dissuades the Jews from alliance with Egypt	ib.
	Jeremiah warns them against settling in Egypt	159
	The remnant of Judah retreat there from the Chaldees	ib.
	The school of Heliopolis	160
	The arch invented	162
	The religion of Lower Egypt	ib.
	Egyptian army and Greek mercenaries	164
	The Egyptian soldiers dethrone Hophra	166
566	AMASIS	ib.
	The Greeks of Naucratis; their privileges and temples	167
	Thales, Solon, and Cleobulus visit Egypt	168
	Hecatæus; Pythagoras	169
	Xenophanes ridicules the lament for Osiris	170
	Cyprus conquered by Amasis	171
	Its alphabet borrowed from Egypt and carried to Greece	ib.
	Polycrates of Samos; his ring	173
	The rise of Persia	ib.

B.C.		PAGE
	Cyprus conquered by Amasis and reconquered by Cyrus	174
	Phanes deserts to Cambyses	175
	Cambyses marches through Arabia against Egypt	ib.
	The city of Sais	176
524	PSAMMENITUS defeated at Pelusium	178
	Memphis surrenders to the Persians; all Egypt follows	179
	Ezekiel's prophecy	180
	The Egyptian laws	181
	Clothing; mineral wealth	183
	The priesthood	187
	Tenure of the soil, its extent	189
	Sculpture, the styles compared	192
	Painting; Architecture	194

CHAPTER V.

THE REIGNS OF THE PERSIAN CONQUERORS, AND OF THE EGYPTIANS WHO REBELLED AGAINST THEIR POWER. B.C. 523–332.

B.C.		PAGE
523	CAMBYSES marches against Ethiopia and the Oases	198
	Plunders the Theban temples and tombs, breaks the colossal statue	199
	Wounds the bull Apis, and scourges the priests	200
	Cambyses goes mad, and marries his two sisters	202
521	DARIUS	ib.
	The Persians attack Libya unsuccessfully	203
	Aryandes, the satrap of Egypt	ib.
	Darius honours the sacred bull and the priests	ib.
	Aryandes coins money	204
	Coins of Cyprus	205
	Amasis an Egyptian made satrap or melek of Egypt	ib.
	Nephra melek of Egypt; good government under Darius	ib.
	The oases in the desert; the camel	206
	The canal, the taxes, the Ethiopian tribute	207
	Mandothph melek; (the battle of Marathon)	208
487	MANDOTHPH makes himself king	ib.
	The name of Amun-Ra cut out from the monuments	208
484	XERXES again makes Egypt a Persian province	209
	Achæmenes the satrap governs with severity	ib.
464	ARTAXERXES LONGIMANUS	210
460	INARUS [or PSAMMETICHUS] makes Lower Egypt independent; and probably Amyrtæus then reigns in Upper Egypt	ib.
	The Persians hold Memphis	211
454	Inarus killed, Amyrtæus holds out longer	212
	Hellanicus visits Egypt, ANAXAGORAS	213
	Herodotus, who wrote on manners and customs	ib.
	The Feast of Lanterns; a religious gathering of the people; a sham fight between the priests	214
	The fields under water during the inundation	ib.
	Memphis; the citadel of the White Wall, the camp of the Tyrians, the temple of Pthah, three Phenician temples, the hall of Apis	215

B.C.		PAGE
	The worship of Kiun, and Remphan	216
	The pyramids, their hieroglyphical inscriptions, the brick pyramid, the Labyrinth; Upper Egypt	218
	Curious customs, respect for animals, gravity in religion, intolerance, mummies at feasts, astrology	219
	National song, the Maneros	222
	ARTAXERXES LONGIMANUS conquers Egypt	223
	Sons of Inarus and Amyrtæus made satraps	ib.
	The sun-worship of the Persians	ib.
424	XERXES II. SOGDIANUS	225
423	DARIUS NOTHUS. Arxanes satrap of Egypt	ib.
	Democritus of Abdera, president of the temple of Memphis, writes on Hieroglyphics	ib.
404	ARTAXERXES MNEMON (his civil war with Cyrus)	226
400	NEPHERITES [or PSAMMETICHUS] of Mendes makes Egypt independent	227
	He allies himself to the Spartans	ib.
394	ACHORIS	ib.
	He helps Evagoras of Cyprus against the Persians	ib.
381	PSAMMUTHIS, NEPHERITES II., MUTHIS	228
379	NECTANEBO I.	ib.
374	Artaxerxes Mnemon attacks Egypt and is repulsed	229
	Eudoxus the astronomer, Chrysippus the physician, and Plato visit Egypt; their writings; Euripides	230
	Belief in a future state	232
361	TACHOS. The Persians attack him	233
	The Egyptians dethrone him	ib.
359	NECTANEBO II.	234
	Artaxerxes Ochus attacks Egypt unsuccessfully	236
349	He is successful on his second invasion	237
	Pelusium and Bubastis taken; Nectanebo flies	ib.
	ARTAXERXES OCHUS; ARSES; DARIUS CODOMANUS	238

CHAPTER VI.

EGYPT CONQUERED BY THE GREEKS. ALEXANDER THE GREAT; CLEOMENES. B.C. 332–322.

	ALEXANDER unites the Greeks against Darius Codomanus; defeats him in Asia Minor; takes Tyre	240
332	Marches on Egypt; Gaza conquered	ib.
	Pelusium taken; Memphis taken	241
	Alexander visits the Oasis of Ammon	243
	The city of Alexandria planned	ib.
	The government of the province; Egyptian judges	246
	Samaritans settle in the Thebaid	ib.
	Cleomenes left in command; his dishonesty	247
	Hephæstion made a demigod in Egypt	248
	Ptolemy the son of Lagus, or of Philip	249

B.C.		PAGE
	Alexander's death; Ptolemy made governor of Egypt as lieutenant of Philip Arridæus	250
	Eratosthenes, Manetho, and the Tablet of Abydos compared	252
	Table of chronology	256

CHAPTER VII.

PTOLEMY SOTER, AS LIEUTENANT OF PHILIP ARRIDÆUS, OF ALEXANDER ÆGUS, AND AS KING. B.C. 322–284.

B.C.		PAGE
322	Ptolemy aims at making himself independent	258
	He puts Cleomenes to death	260
	He conquers Cyrene	ib.
	He brings the body of Alexander to Memphis	261
	Perdiccas invades Egypt; passing by Pelusium, he marches against Memphis	ib.
	Perdiccas killed; Philip Arridæus and Alexander Ægus taken	262
	Ptolemy conquers Jerusalem, Phenicia, and Cœle-Syria	ib.
	Egypt well governed; Theban temples rebuilt	263
	Funeral of the sacred bull; its burial-place	ib.
	Children of mixed marriages held to be Egyptians	266
	Alexandria built and ornamented	267
	Its buildings; the god Serapis	268
	The Museum of philosophy; the use of papyrus	269
	The King Philip Arridæus put to death	271
	Alexander Ægus declared king of Macedonia and the provinces	ib.
	Antigonus invades Egypt; his forces	ib.
313	Cyrene rebels; and is conquered	272
	Cyprus conquered by Ptolemy	ib.
	Greek and Egyptian troops compared	273
	Demetrius son of Antigonus defeated at Gaza	274
	Antioch built as the capital of Syria and Babylonia	ib.
	Antigonus attacks Petra	275
312	Peace between Alexander's successors	277
	The state of the Greeks in Egypt	278
	Hecatæus visits Upper Egypt; the Theban temples and tombs; the Memnonium	ib.
	Greek mistakes about Egypt	279
	Jews settle in Alexandria; Hezekias the priest, and Mosollam the archer	280
311	Alexander Ægus put to death; Hercules proclaimed king of Macedonia and put to death	281
308	Ptolemy proposes to marry Cleopatra; she is murdered	283
	Demetrius destroys the Egyptian fleet	284
306	PTOLEMY takes the title of king of Egypt	ib.
305	Antigonus marches against Egypt; is stopped	285
	Demetrius besieges Rhodes	286
	Cœle-Syria and the island of Cos conquered	ib.
	Silk-weaving in Cos	287

Ptolemy's coins	288
His literary dinners	290
Apelles the painter; Euclid the mathematician	ib.
Diodorus Cronus the rhetorician; Stilpo	ib.
Theopompus the historian	291
Erasistratus and Herophilus the anatomists	292
Hegesias lectures on philosophy	293
The Cyrenaic sect of philosophers, Theodorus	ib.
Antiphilus the painter quarrels with Apelles	295
Apelles's picture of Calumny	ib.
Ptolemy's manners and opinions	296
His wives and children	297
He resigns the throne to his son	300
Remarks	ib.

CHAPTER VIII.

PTOLEMY PHILADELPHUS. B.C. 284–246.

B.C.		Page
284	PTOLEMY PHILADELPHUS; his education, tutors, and prospects	303
	Grand procession on his accession	304
282	Ptolemy Soter dies	307
274	The rise of Rome; embassy to Egypt	308
	Berenice dies; the feast of Osiris	ib.
	Magas, the king's half-brother, rebels at Cyrene	309
	Gallic mercenaries put to death	310
	The son of Philadelphus marries the daughter of Magas	ib.
	Philadelphus puts two brothers to death	311
	The Eleusinian Mysteries taught	ib.
	The Pharos lighthouse finished; Alexander's tomb; new cities	312
	Roads opened for trade to Berenice, to Cosseir, and to Suez; the canal finished; the gold trade	313
	Dionysius travels through Bactria to India	314
	Ethiopian elephants employed in war	315
	The island and temple of Philæ	ib.
	The Museum; its library	318
	First librarian Demetrius Phalereus; his character and writings	ib.
	Zenodotus; he edits Homer	319
	Euclid; his Elements of mathematics	320
	Ctesibius writes on hydrostatics; the water clock	ib.
	Theocritus the poet	321
	Callimachus, professor of poetry; his hymns	ib.
	Philætus; his poetry; Menander sent for	322
	Strato writes on physics	ib.
	Timocharis, Aristillus, and Aristarchus, astronomers	323
	Aratus; his astronomical poem, and his translators	324
	Sosibius, the rhetorician	325
	Apollodorus Gelotis and the Greek wines	ib.
	Manetho and Petosiris the Egyptian authors	ib.

xxxiv CONTENTS OF VOL. I.

B.C.		PAGE
	Colotes the Epicurean philosopher	327
	Homer and Herodotus read publicly in the theatre	ib.
	Zoilus the rhetorician, Timon the tragic writer	328
	Philadelphus collects pictures	329
	Helena the painter; drawing by squares	ib.
	The Septuagint translation of the Old Testament; its style; disapproved of by the Hebrews	331
	Philadelphus helps the Achaian League	334
	His wives and children; his coins	335
	Arsinoë; her tomb, and praise	337
	Ergamenes king of Meroë makes himself absolute	338
	Antiochus marries Berenice	339
	Extent and wealth of the kingdom	340

CHAPTER IX.

PTOLEMY EUERGETES, PTOLEMY PHILOPATOR, AND PTOLEMY EPIPHANES. B.C. 246–180.

B.C.		PAGE
246	PTOLEMY EUERGETES; he marches against Syria	343
	The queen's hair made into a constellation	344
	The poets praise her beauty	ib.
	Seleucus flies to Egypt from his brother	345
	Euergetes regains the booty of Cambyses; his popularity	ib.
	The Decree of the priests at Canopus	346
	His buildings at Thebes, in the Oasis, at Esne, at Canopus	347
	He invades Ethiopia; inscription at Adule	349
	The Jewish tribute delayed	351
	Greece helped against Antigonus	352
	Aristophanes the grammarian; accents invented	ib.
	Eratosthenes the geographer and chronologist	353
	Carneades and the New Academy	356
	Apollonius; his Argonautics. The Ibis	ib.
	Lycophron; his Alcandra; foretells Roman greatness	357
	Conon; Apollonius of Perga; conic sections	ib.
	Character of the Alexandrian authors	358
	The coins	360
221	PTOLEMY PHILOPATOR, puts to death his mother and brother	361
	The extent of his kingdom	362
	Antiochus the Great regains all Syria; invades Egypt; battle of Raphia	363
	Ptolemy tries to enter the temple at Jerusalem; the alarm of the Jews	365
	The Jews of Alexandria lose their privileges	366
	Egyptian troops; large ships	ib.
	Ambassadors from Rome, and from the Jews	368
	Philopator's vices, follies, and luxuries	ib.
	Alexandria supplied with corn at the public expense	369
	Sphærus and Eratosthenes	370

B.C.		PAGE
	The coins	371
204	PTOLEMY EPIPHANES, a minor	372
	Rebellion against the ministers; their murder	373
	The Alexandrians beg the Roman senate to guard the kingdom.	376
	Rome rises as Egypt sinks	377
	The Greek phalanx	378
	Rebellion of Lycopolis; the king's cruelty	380
196	The king declared of age; the Rosetta Stone	381
	His vices and follies	383
192	He marries Cleopatra daughter of Antiochus	384
	A second rebellion of the Egyptians	ib.
	The foreign provinces lost to Egypt	386
	Preparations for war	387

CHAPTER X.

PTOLEMY PHILOMETOR, PTOLEMY EUPATOR, AND PTOLEMY EUERGETES II.   B.C. 180–116.

B.C.		PAGE
180	PTOLEMY PHILOMETOR, a minor	388
173	His coronation when of age	ib.
	Antiochus Epiphanes conquers Egypt	389
169	The younger Ptolemy declares himself king, as Euergetes II.	ib.
	The foreign embassies	ib.
	The brothers join their forces against Antiochus	391
	Antiochus again enters Egypt; retreats at the command of Popilius	ib.
	Judas Maccabeus makes Judæa independent	392
	He asks the Jews of Egypt to join him in celebrating the feast	ib.
164	Philometor goes to Rome for help against his brother, and is replaced on the throne; Cyrene given to Euergetes	ib.
	Euergetes goes to Rome to complain	393
	Philometor refuses to obey the senate	394
	He conquers Euergetes in Cyprus and forgives him	ib.
	The Jews build a temple at Onion	396
	Their dispute with the Samaritans	397
	They bear high offices in Egypt	398
	Temples built at Parembole, at Antæopolis, at Ombos, and at Apollinopolis Magna	399
	Monks in the temples	400
	Offerings made for the dead	401
	The state of slavery	ib.
	Aristarchus the critic; Moschus his pupil; Bion	402
	The critics correct the text of Homer	403
	Pamphilus the physician; Nicander	406
	Hipparchus the astronomer; his discoveries	407
	Opinions on the length of the year	ib.
	Hero the mechanic	ib.
	The coins	408
	Wars in Syria	409

CONTENTS OF VOL. I.

B.C.		PAGE
	Philometor's death; his family	410
145	PTOLEMY EUPATOR murdered by his uncle	411
	PTOLEMY EUERGETES II.; his cruelties	412
	His coronation; second marriage; his person	ib.
	Scipio Africanus the Roman ambassador; Panætius the Stoic	414
	The Jews of Judæa write to Egypt; the books of Maccabees.	415
132	Jesus the son of Sirach	416
	The Alexandrians rebel; Euergetes withdraws to Cyprus; murders his son	417
	He regains his throne; the wars in Syria	418
	The tyranny of persons travelling on the public service	419
	Agatharcides; cause of the Nile's overflow	420
	The voyage to India or Eastern Africa	421
	The king's writings; salaries in the Museum	423
	Learned men; library of Pergamus; parchment used	424
	Literary forgeries, Posidonius the Stoic	425
	Hebrew inscriptions in Wady Mokatteb	426
	Jewish pilgrims to Mount Sinai	427

The collar, the badge of office, is being placed on the governor of a province.

THE HISTORY OF EGYPT.

CHAPTER I.

INTRODUCTION; THE EARLY KINGS; THE INVASION BY THE SHEP-
HERDS, AND THEIR EXPULSION, THE RISE OF THEBES.

(1) EGYPT, during the greater part of its history, had the same boundaries as it has now. It is little more than the strip of country that is every year overflowed by the waters of the Nile, between its seven mouths at the Mediterranean Sea on the north, and the cataracts or rapids which stop the navigation at Syene, on the south. This valley is shut in on both sides by the desert, and divided into two gardens by the river. The eastern bank formed part of Arabia, and the western bank part of Libya; and, before rivers were crossed in wicker boats, the Nile may have been the boundary between the two tribes. But as soon as men were bold enough to trust themselves to a plank, rivers ceased to divide nations; and at the beginning of this history we find both banks of the Nile, or of the Ægyptus, as it was also called, held by a people who, taking their name from the river, are called Egyptians. The country was then naturally divided as it is now. Upper Egypt is that part of the valley which is closely pressed in between two ranges of hills; while Lower Egypt is the open plain, where the more level and less rocky soil allows the river to divide itself into several streams, and which, from its triangular form, was by the Greeks named the Delta. To this we must add a few ports on the Red Sea, which, as they were separated from the Nile by a three or four days' journey over the sands, had but few

Herodotus, lib. ii. 17.

Odyssey, lib. iv. 477.

advantages for trade, and also two or three green spots in the western desert, made fertile by their own springs, such as the Great Oasis, the Little Oasis, and the Oasis of Ammon. Egypt could only attack its neighbours, or be attacked, through narrow and difficult passes. Of these one is on the south, at the first cataract, where the valley above the granite rocks at Syene takes the name of Lower Ethiopia or Nubia. A second is on the west, between the desert and the sea, along the coast of the Mediterranean, where it was afterwards bounded by the little Greek state of Cyrene. And the third is on the east, also along the coast, towards Syria and Arabia Nabatæa, where the salt lakes and marshes almost join the Red Sea to the Mediterranean. When the kingdom, under its more powerful sovereigns, was lengthened southward, it was still limited by one or other of the granite ranges which cross the valley and cause the cataracts in Ethiopia. Of these the second, or first above Syene, covers a long district from Wady Halfa to the Island of Saye; the third is at the Island of Tombos; and the fourth above the city of Napata. Each of these ranges of granite in its turn formed the boundary of the kingdom.

(2) In endeavouring to make use of the early notices of history we are often puzzled at finding that a wandering tribe carried its name into the land to which it removed, as the name belonged to the people rather than to the country in which they dwelt. Thus a difficulty hangs over the names by which the several parts of Egypt have at various times been called. In every case the name changed its place from north to south, and so we must believe that the tribes had at some early time moved southward from the head of the Red Sea; which gradual movement may have formed part of a great migration from central Asia. Upper Egypt had once been called Meroë, which name was afterwards carried southward almost to Abyssinia. At another time, Upper Egypt was named Cush or Ethiopia, till that name was in the same way moved southward beyond the cataracts, and sometimes even to Abyssinia. In the language of the country, Egypt was named Chemi, a word the same as Ham or Cham; in Hebrew it was named the land of Mizraim, one of the tribes

Genesis, ch. x. 7.

Diogenes Laertius, Vit. Democriti.

Hesiodi Theog. 985.

of the children of Ham; and from the Greeks it received the name of Ægyptus, Egypt, or the land of Copts; and these last two names, having once meant the Delta, were afterwards stretched southward to include the whole of the country.

(3) We learn from the book of Genesis that the Egyptians were a tribe from Asia, called the children of Ham; and their physical character, and their habits of life, both show that they were more nearly allied to Asiatics than to the less civilised tribes of the Arabian and Libyan deserts. Like their corn and rice and cattle, they had arrived in the valley from abroad; the natives of the neighbourhood, whether men, animals, or plants, were badly suited for cultivation. From the colour given to the women in their paintings, we learn that their skin was yellow, like that of the Mongol Tartars, who have given their name to the Mongolian variety of the human race; the darker brown of the men may arise from their having been more in the sunshine. The single lock of hair on the young nobles reminds us also of the Tartars; while the religious dread of the sea, the sacred bull, and the refusal to eat flesh, are what we meet with among the Hindoos. Their worship of the bull reminds us also of the Chinese, for whom Confucius wrote: "Thou shalt not slaughter the labouring ox;" and they were like the Chinese in their syllabic writing, and in dutifully setting out food at the graves of their forefathers. Their pious custom of embalming the dead can hardly have had its rise in Egypt, as the mineral pitch which the priests used was brought by foreign traders from the Dead Sea. But the sculptures give us more exact information, and tell us of two races of men, known by the form of skull; one seen in the statues of Lower Egypt, and the other in those of the Thebaid. Of these we find good grounds for believing that the former skull belonged to the original inhabitants of the valley, and the latter, the Theban, to a race of foreigners who afterwards, though at some very early period, gained a settlement there. The older and less intellectual skull we note in the head of the Great Sphinx, the earliest sculpture existing, and in the head of the modern Fellah (see Fig. 1), the present labourer on the soil. Between these, the earliest and latest examples, we also note it in the intermediate time in the heads of the kings

who ruled in Sais when Lower Egypt made itself independent of Thebes, and even in the heads of Theban kings when sculptured in stone belonging to the lower country. This form of skull is distinguished by a retreating forehead, a forward mouth, and an undue length of line from the chin to the back of the head. A race of people with this form of skull, who bear the name of the Galla tribe, yet hold undisturbed possession of the country to the south of Abyssinia. Hence it would seem to have been originally peculiar to the whole of eastern Africa, between the Negroes on the south

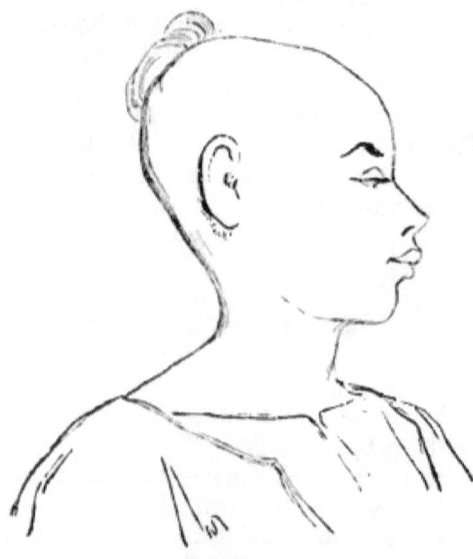

Fig. 1.

and the Arabs on the north. The more intellectual form of skull we note in the statues of Rameses II. (see Fig. 2), and the other great kings of Thebes, and in the statues of the gods of the same district. This is marked by a more upright forehead and a nose almost aquiline; and it seems to have belonged to a race of foreigners who brought into Egypt its language, its civilisation, and its religion. This diversity of race gave rise to a division of the people into castes, as long as they were under one sceptre; thus the nobles who owned the land were the soldiers and priests,

SOIL AND CLIMATE.

while the common people, the lower caste, were the labourers who tilled the soil and paid the taxes. The skulls of the mummies do not speak so clearly on these points, first because they belong almost exclusively to families of the priestly or upper class, and secondly because they are too modern to show us the Egyptians free from the mixture of Arabs, Phenicians, and Greeks, who freely settled among them. The inhabitants of Lower Egypt were further mixed with a large number of Phenicians, from the neighbouring parts of Syria, and not a few Greek traders on the coast. Indeed the difference of gods that they worshipped shows that the people of the Delta were not wholly the same in race as the Copts of Upper Egypt, while from the same reasons we see that the inhabitants of the oases were colonists from Thebes.

Fig. 2.

Diodorus Siculus, lib. i. 28.

Morton's Crania Ægyptiaca.

(4) The soil and climate of Egypt cannot but have had a large share in moulding the character of the people. It is a country almost without rain and wholly without brooks; in which every spot is barren that is not overflowed in the autumn by the waters of its one river, which scatters blessings along its banks, alike on the grateful and on the ungrateful, from Syene to the Mediterranean. The rains from the mountains to the south of Abyssinia, flowing through Meroë, Ethiopia, and Nubia, reach Egypt in the middle of June, when the Nile begins to rise at Syene. The little plains which fringe its banks through the Thebaid to a greater or less width are first overflowed, and, during the months of August, September, and October, the fields in the Delta become a sheet of water, leaving the villages on the raised mounds standing like so many islands in the ocean. The river is then red with Abyssinian soil, and when the fields are again left dry, in the beginning of November, they are found covered with a rich

Pliny, lib. xviii. 47.

mud, and need little or no labour from the husbandman. He values his land by the quantity of water upon it, and the sacred stone which bounds his field (see Fig. 3) measures at the same time the height of the overflow. No further manure is wanted, nor a sabbath year in which the ground may lie fallow. The husbandman has only to sow the seed and gather in the harvest; except indeed when his industry leads him to widen the valley and cultivate the borders of the desert, where he then has the more laborious task of watering, by means of trenches and hand pumps, the fields which the overflow would not otherwise reach.

Fig. 3.

As soon as the wheat and barley are gathered, the Indian corn and rice are sown, to grow during the inundation, and to be gathered before the former crops are again put into the ground. Vegetation is rapid in the winter months, when with us all nature is dead and our fields covered with snow; while in the months of our cheerful spring the climate of Egypt is painfully sultry and the fields parched with drought. The necessary clothes and houses are easily supplied in such a warm climate; and herds of cattle are not wanted in a country almost too hot for animal food and animal clothing. The two crops of grain and the supply of fish from the river, and yet cheaper onions and lentils, easily fed twice as many persons as could live in an equal space in Europe; and the same mud that manured the field was baked in the sun to form the hut in which the husbandman slept at night. There are few trees in the country, and wood is but little used; no seaworthy ships could be built till timber was afterwards brought from the forests of Cilicia or of Lebanon, though the Nile was safely navigated in barges built of the large rushes that grow on its banks. Building stone of several kinds is at hand; limestone from both sides of the river from Toora and Memphis up to Silsilis, sandstone from Silsilis and Heliopolis, granite from Syene, and transparent alabaster from Antinoopolis for works of greater delicacy; and such is the dryness of the air, that works of art, though uncovered from the weather, remain for ages untried by changes from hot to cold, or from wet to dry, and uninjured but by the hand of man. The wild birds and beasts are as peculiar as the climate and the surface of the country. The stunted shrubs and herbage of the desert furnish food to several kinds of deer; the river feeds the crocodile, the river horse, and numerous web-footed swimming birds; while the canals and marshes on its banks are frequented by a great variety of long-legged wading birds. Of the grass-eating animals, the buffalo seems the one most at home; of the grain-eating birds, there are very few beside the quail. The flesh-eaters, such as the eagle, the vulture, the hawk, the hyena, the jackal, and wolf, find their food wherever man or the other animals have been before them. When nations began to trade, the great source of wealth to Egypt was in the Nubian gold mines. By the help of these mines, the city of Thebes, which had the command of them, was for five hundred years the richest city in the world; and when this supply of gold ceased, Upper Egypt took the more natural rank of a province governed by the Delta.

(5) The Nile was not valued by the husbandman only; it was the longest inland navigation known to the ancients, and while the art of managing a vessel at sea was in its infancy, while ships were rowed timidly along the coast, the River of Egypt was a most important route for trade. The art of boat-building would be sooner learnt among the canals formed by the Nile's overflow than in the rocky creeks of Greece or among the breakers on the Tyrian shore. The husbandman who every autumn found the ditches round his fields too wide and too deep to be crossed on foot, would soon find out how

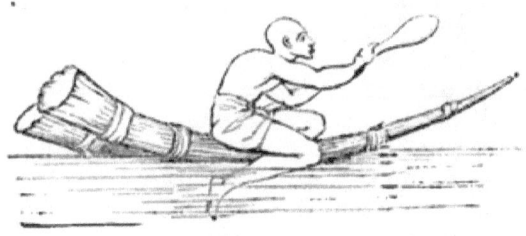

Fig. 4.

to make a bundle of rushes into a raft (see Fig. 4); and the rushes on which he crossed the overflow would afterwards carry him over the deeper river in equal safety. For nine months in the year the north wind blows strongly along the valley against the stream during the daytime, making it as easy for the large boats of burden to sail one way by day as to float the other by night. Thus even before the Nile became the route by which the wealth of India was exchanged for that of Europe, it enabled the husbandman to barter his corn for the manufactures of the city, and indeed enabled the people to live together in cities in greater numbers and in greater comfort, from the ease with which those cities could be fed. With these advantages, Egypt, like Mesopotamia, became one of the earliest countries civilised, one of the first in which a man thought it worth while to mark out a spot of land, and say, This is mine; and where his neighbours, while doing the same, acknowledged the justice of such a title to what he claimed. Men naturally settled, and multiplied, and cultivated the arts of civilisation, on a spot where food was so easily raised, and industry so much encouraged by the abundance with which it was rewarded. Being very much hemmed in on all sides by the desert, the population soon felt itself crowded, and found it necessary to study and improve the arts of producing food. Improvement in the other arts followed almost of course.

(6) While the neighbouring parts of Arabia and Syria were peopled with a few scattered herdsmen, who moved their flocks from valley to valley in search of wild pasture, Egypt was becoming crowded with tillers of the soil, and the banks of the Nile dotted with villages. While the trade of their neighbours was limited to light burdens on camels' backs, the Egyptian corn, and even building stone, floated easily from place to place in the largest quantities. Of course the advantages and rights of property, the science of law, and the arts of government, would be much sooner studied and better understood among a settled nation of husbandmen, than among the Assyrian hunting tribes, the descendants of Nimrod, or among the marauding shepherd races, such as the Arab children of Abraham, whose flocks would graze over the neighbouring corn-fields as over wild pasture; and though Israelites might quote the case of Cain and Abel, where it was the tiller of the ground that murdered the owner of the flocks, yet we may be sure that it was a more common case for the husbandman to be the injured

party; and we can well understand why the wandering shepherds were an abomination in the sight of the more settled Egyptians. Among their neigh- <small>Genesis, xlvi. 34.</small> bours, civilisation was checked by each man asserting the natural right of all men to all things, and claiming to enjoy and employ for himself his whole force, activity, and liberty; while the Egyptian was earlier in giving up a part of these for the greater advantages of a settled society.

(7) When letters first rose in Greece and Rome, the writers found a rich harvest of fable and tradition, out of which they wove those beautiful tales that we now read as the beginning of Greek and Roman history. The Egyptians were not favoured with historians who could thus fix and hand down to us their traditions; but then, on the other hand, they had from far earlier times carved the names and deeds of their kings on the walls of their temples, and thus have left us less of poetic fable and more of bald reality. In each case the history of the country begins with slight and scattered hints, which some minds seize upon as treasures and others overlook as worthless, but which the historian can neither safely lean upon nor yet wholly fling from him; and this is the case with the history of Egypt, before the reigns of Chofo in Memphis and Osirtesen I. in Thebes. These kings' monuments contain the earliest remaining records of the human race. They were sculptured even before the time when Abraham, according to the Hebrew writers, drove his herds into Egypt in search of food which the drought had made scarce in Canaan.

(8) There seem to be three sources from which the ancient polytheists drew their numerous objects of worship. First, the sun, moon, and stars, or host of heaven, as they are called by the Hebrew writers, were worshipped by men in the rudest state of society; secondly, the visible works of the Almighty, as reason advanced, gave them an allegorical god of the sea, god of fire, goddess of love; and lastly, in some few cases, the conqueror and law-maker, the scourge and friend of mankind, have been raised to that rank. In the first of these classes, were Ra, *the Sun*, from whose scorching rays the Egyptians hid themselves as from the anger of a powerful enemy; and the Moon, the lovely ruler of night, whom they

thanked for its cool refreshing beams; and the stars, in which, when the glare of daylight was removed, and the heavens opened before their eyes, they saw an evidence of the multitude of the divinities by whom this world is watched. In the same class was Chem, *the Land of Egypt*, and Hapimou, *the River Nile*, to whom the husbandman sacrificed for a good harvest; for which, in another climate, he would have prayed to heaven. In the second class were Kneph, *the Spirit*, Pthah, the god of fire, Thoth, the god of letters, or rather the very *pillar* on which the letters were carved; Athor, the goddess of love and beauty; and Pasht, the goddess of chastity. To the third class perhaps belonged the favourite goddess Isis, her sister Nephthis, and her husband Osiris, who after being put to death by the wicked Typhon, and avenged by his son Horus, was raised to life again, and made the judge of the dead. The later Egyptian historians begin with a certain number of cycles of fourteen hundred and sixty-one years each, during which they said that the gods governed Egypt; and of these Osiris and his son Horus were the last.

<small>Diod. Sic. lib. i. 13.</small>

<small>Vet. Chron. ap. Syncel.</small>

(9) Historians do not attempt to fix the year when the gods left off having children and living upon earth, but the first man who reigned in Egypt was Menes, or Mena, *the Eternal*, whose name would seem to prove that he was not wholly withdrawn from the region of fable; from him the later kings boastfully traced their lineage. According to the Egyptian chronologists, he came to the throne about fifteen hundred years before the Persian invasion, that is to say, two thousand years before the Christian era. He was probably the Menu of the Hindoos, their first of created beings, and holiest of law-makers; and at the same time the Minos of the Greeks, their earliest law-maker and their judge of the dead.

<small>Burton's Excerpta, pl. 2.</small>

<small>Herodotus, lib. ii. 145.</small>

Menes was followed by sixteen other kings who all reigned at This, a city which the Greeks called Abydos. The kingdom of This probably reached from Lycopolis, where the valley is broken and the river is hemmed in by the hills on each side, to Tentyra, where the hills again press in upon the banks and close the valley. The city stood at the foot of the Libyan hills, and was watered by a canal from the river. After these first seven-

<small>Manetho, Dyn. i. ii.</small>

teen kings the power of This fell, and Thebes rose to be the capital of Upper Egypt.

(10) During the first seven hundred years of our history, Thebes alone offers us an unbroken chain of reigns, by the help of which we may date the buildings, and the very few events which are known to us. The kingdom of Thebes may have reached, on both sides of the river, from Tentyra to Silsilis, where the sandstone rocks barely leave a passage for the water; and it held within these natural boundaries the largest plain in the valley of Upper Egypt, which is in some places twenty miles wide. On the east of the river it sometimes reached to Heliopolis. The city of Thebes stood on the east bank in the middle of a plain, and was opposite to a point where the Libyan hills on the other side jut forward to the river's edge. Hence it easily commanded the passage along the valley, whether by land or water, and was in part bounded and guarded by moats or canals. From the plain of Thebes a road, with here and there a spring of water, ran to Ænum on the Red Sea, and this gave to the capital the advantages of a port. From the mountains near this road were brought, at a later time, porphyry, and beautiful greenstone, which were so much valued by the sculptors. Emeralds and garnets were also there found; and what was yet more valuable, if the miners knew how to work it, there was some iron ore.

(11) The city of Elephantine, on an island in the Nile, just below the cataract at the southern boundary of Egypt, had also been the capital of a little kingdom; and we know the names, and nothing but the names, of nine kings who reigned there. Elephantine no doubt fell when Thebes rose over the city of This. The kingdom of Elephantine may have reached from Silsilis to the cataracts of Syene, or perhaps even to the second cataract at Abou-Simbel, and thus included part of Nubia. Its best known city, Syene, enjoyed the profit of carrying merchandise over the cataracts where the passage of the boats is stopped.

Manetho.

(12) A race of petty kings also reigned for two or three centuries at Heracleopolis, near Memphis; one of whom was Achthoes, who was said to have gone mad, and been killed by a crocodile. This story may have arisen from the warfare always carried on between the citizens of Heracleopolis

and those animals, which in earlier days were common even in the Delta, though they are now seldom seen below Lycopolis. The kingdom of Heracleopolis may have reached from Lycopolis to near Memphis. This is the least fruitful part of Egypt, as here the Libyan hills are so low as scarcely to guard the cultivated valley from the drifting sands.

(13) Joined to Heracleopolis is a rich valley in the western desert, which always receives part of the river's overflow, and was at one time made yet more fruitful by a large reserve of water called the Lake of Mœris. To the kings of Heracleopolis the country was no doubt indebted for that great national work, by which thousands of acres were artificially watered and brought into cultivation, and the Nile's overflow was in part regulated for the country on that side of the Delta. This useful work was formed by running a strong dyke or bank from north to south across the valley, through which a part of the waters would otherwise, and indeed does now, discharge itself nearly uselessly, into the Lake of Keiroun on the borders of the desert. By these means a tract of land two hundred and fifty miles round was, on the rise of the Nile, made into a lake, and, on the retreat of the water, was left fertilised by its mud. A royal fishery was established at the floodgates, which in a later age, while the water was running in, yielded a daily revenue of a talent of silver, or one hundred and fifty pounds sterling, and the smaller sum of twenty minæ, or fifty pounds, during those months in which the water was allowed to flow back again into the Nile.

<small>Herodotus, lib. ii. 149.</small>
<small>Linant, sur le Lac Mœris.</small>
<small>Pliny, lib. v. 9.</small>

(14) Labaris (see Fig. 5), who built the sacred building called the Labyrinth, near the Lake of Mœris, was probably a king of Heracleopolis, though Manetho calls him a king of Thebes. His name is on the tablet of Karnak, where a later king is worshipping his predecessors of the eight kingdoms into which Egypt had been divided; but it is not on the tablet of Abydos, which contains a list of one race of kings only. The Labyrinth, with its fifteen hundred cells, was rather a monastery for a college of priests than a palace for one chief. The rooms underground

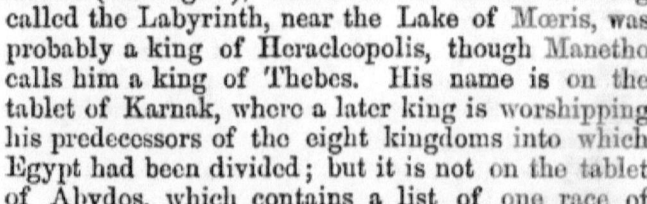
Fig. 5.
<small>Herodotus, lib. ii. 148.</small>

no doubt held the bodies after death and embalmment of the priests who had before dwelt in the upper rooms. On the death of Labaris, or one reign later, Heracleopolis sunk under the power of Thebes; and we find upon the walls of the Labyrinth the name of Amunmai Thori III. of that city, who added largely to the sculptures on that gigantic temple.

(15) Memphis was at the same time the principal capital of the level plains of Lower Egypt, where the river flows sluggishly through several large branches and countless canals, which water its cornfields and divide it into provinces. Sixty or seventy pyramids of various sizes on the edge of the desert remind us of the number and wealth of its kings or chief priests who sleep beneath them. Perhaps the tenth of those Memphite sovereigns whose names are known to us was reigning at the time at which the Hebrew writer placed Abraham's visit to Egypt.

(16) Xois, near the middle of the Delta, and about twenty miles from the sea, was another city whose priests were for a time kings over a small district. A chief priest, surrounded by a numerous priesthood, governed each city in Egypt; in those just mentioned he ruled as king, in the others as magistrate under a neighbouring king. They all alike held their rank by hereditary descent, and their power by the force of opinion founded on religion; and when several cities were united into one monarchy, this independence in the magistrate of each city was naturally a cause of weakness to the sovereign, and of freedom to the people.

(17) Before the fall of This the people of Memphis had already built a temple for the bull Apis (see Fig. 6), where they worshipped it as a god, and maintained Manetho, Dyn. ii. a college of priests to do it honour. In the same way the people of Heliopolis worshipped the rival bull, Amun-Ehe, called by the Greeks Mnevis, and the people of Mendes a goat, named Mando. One favoured animal of every sacred race received worship in its own city; while for the others the people respectfully stepped aside when they met them in the streets or fields. On the banks of the Nile it was easier, said the Greeks, to find a god than a man. It is not easy to understand the feelings which gave rise to this worship of the cats, dogs, crocodiles,

ibises, serpents, and the rest. In some cases perhaps it was the usefulness of the animal, and in some cases its strangeness. Thus the dog and jackal devoured the carcases

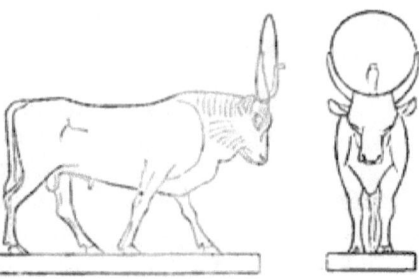

Fig. 6.

which, if left to rot in the streets, might bring disease upon the inhabitants. The cat kept the houses free from much vermin; the ibis broke the crocodile's eggs, and lessened the number of these dangerous animals; the hooded snake (see Fig. 7) may have gained respect because it stood upright on the strong folds of its tail and seemed to wear a crown; the ox ploughed the field, and its flesh was not wanted for food, as the people for the most part lived on vegetables; and it was perhaps worshipped the more zealously to mark their quarrel with their Arab neighbours, who did not know the use of a plough, and who killed and ate the animal by whose labour the Egyptians lived. But the very strangeness of this worship shows the need that we all feel for some religious belief.

Fig. 7.

While no better were thought of, it was easier to fancy the bull Apis a god, than to believe that this world, with its inhabitants, had no maker, and that our wants are supplied without means more powerful than our own. But, on the other hand, the Egyptians can have had no lofty notion of the wisdom, the power, and the goodness with which the world is governed, when they found the housing and feeding these animals a help to their devotion. They also carved stone statues of men for gods, or as images of unseen gods, and built temples for their dwelling-places, and appointed priests to take care of them, without, however, neglecting the worship of the animals. The more enlightened city of Thebes alone had no sacred animal. As the people themselves ate but little meat, they did not often offer flesh in sacrifice to their gods.

(18) The buildings were then much the same as those which afterwards rose in such calm and heavy grandeur. Venephres, a king of This, had already built pyramids at

Fig. 8.

Cochome, a town whose site is now unknown; and OSIRTESEN I. (see Fig. 8), a king of Thebes, who reigned over Upper Egypt and the Arabian side of Lower Egypt, had raised those buildings which are now studied by our travellers for the earliest known style of Egyptian architecture. He was the builder of the older and smaller part of the great temple of Thebes, now

Wilkinson, Thebes.

called the temple of Karnak, on the east bank of the Nile; and his unornamented polygonal columns (see Fig. 9) must be looked upon as the model from which the Doric column of Greece was afterwards copied. In this reign also, or earlier, were begun the tombs of Beni-Hassan, near Antinoopolis (see Fig. 10), which are grottos tunneled into the hills, and in which the older columns are of the same polygonal form. The walls of these dark tombs are covered with coloured drawings, the works of various ages, in which the traveller, by the light of the torch in his hand, sees the trades, manufactures, and games, indeed all the employments of life, painted, as if to teach us the great moral lesson that the habits of this early people were much the same as our own, and that three or four thousand years make less change in manners than we usually fancy.

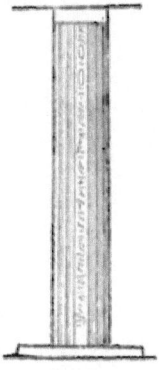

Fig. 9.

(19) Whether all the buildings that bear the name of Osirtesen were made in his reign may be doubtful; it is possible that some of them may have been set up in his honour by successors of a later age. Among these buildings must be mentioned the obelisk of Heliopolis, a square

tapering pillar of granite upwards of sixty feet high, dug out of the quarries at Syene (see Fig. 11). It has his name and titles carved in hieroglyphics on each of the four sides. Another tapering granite needle, which may be called an obelisk, stands on the western bank of the Lake of Mœris, and also bears his name. It was perhaps of use in raising and lowering the sluice gate by which part of the water of the lake was allowed to escape towards the desert.

Fig. 10.

It has a round top with a notch in it, on which may have rested and turned a beam to be used as a lever (see Fig. 12). Its front and back are wider than its two sides. Its four faces do not all lean back like a true obelisk, but its face is quite upright, while its back leans more than usual, as if there had been a danger of its being pulled backward. The mechanical purpose for which this stone was cut throws a doubt upon its great age; and as its inscription is nearly the same as that on the obelisk at Heliopolis, the doubt is carried to that stone. The doubt is further strengthened by the distance to which these blocks of granite were carried by their makers from the quarries of Syene, and by our knowing of no other obelisks earlier than the reign of Thothmosis I.

Fig. 11.   Fig. 12.

(20) For how many years, or rather thousands of years, this globe had already been the dwelling-place of man, and the arts of life had been growing under his inventive industry, is uncertain; we can hope to know very little of our race and its other discoveries before the invention of letters. But when the earliest remaining buildings were raised, the carved writing, by means of figures of men, animals, plants, and other natural and artificial objects, was far from new. We are left to imagine the number of centuries that must have passed since this mode of writing first came into use, when the characters were used for the objects only. The first great change in the art was to use the figures for the names of the objects, and not for the objects themselves, and thus they got a power of representing a sound or syllable; and then,

VOL. I.   C

by means of these monosyllabic sounds, they represented the names of thoughts, feelings, and actions, which cannot themselves be copied in a picture. The second great step followed upon the writers, or rather carvers, finding that twenty or thirty of these monosyllabic sounds came into use much oftener than the rest. These were vowel sounds, and vowels joined to single consonants, which, from their frequent use, were hereafter undesignedly to form an alphabet. And both these changes, each the slow growth of many centuries, must have taken place before the reign of Osirtesen I., in whose inscriptions we find some characters representing words or objects, others representing syllables, and others again representing single letters. Though the Egyptian priests had not then arrived at the beautiful simplicity of an alphabet, they must have made vast strides indeed before they wrote the word Osiris (see Fig. 13), with two characters for the syllables Os and Iri; and again, before they spelled the name Amun (see Fig. 14), with a vowel and two consonants. Afterwards, when easier characters came into use, this ornamental but slow method of writing received the name of hieroglyphics, or *sacred carving*.

Egyptian Inscript. pl. 86, 87, 88.

Fig. 13.

Fig. 14.

(21) The power of making our thoughts known to absent friends and after ages by means of a few black marks on the paper, and of thus treasuring up the wisdom of the world, is an art so wonderful in its contrivance and so important in its results that many have thought it must have been taught to the forefathers of the human race directly from heaven. But the wise Ruler of the world seems always to employ natural means to bring about his great ends; and thus in hieroglyphics we trace some of the earliest steps by which the art of writing has risen to its present perfection. And when we think of the kind feelings and the thirst of knowledge that have been both awakened and gratified by letters, and of the power that we now enjoy in our libraries of calling before us the wise of all ages to talk to us and answer our questions, we must not forget the debt which we owe to the priests of Upper Egypt.

(22) No monuments in Egypt are more interesting, and perhaps none more ancient, than the hieroglyphical names

for the months. They divide the year into three parts; the season of vegetation (see Fig. 15); the season of harvest (see Fig. 16); and the season of inundation (see Fig. 17); each of the seasons is divided into the first, second, third, and fourth month; and every month into thirty days. At some unknown time five additional days were added, called by the Greeks the *epagomenæ*. This civil year of three hundred and sixty-five days was certainly in constant use ever after the year 1322 before Christ, and fourteen hundred and sixty-one of these years were counted in the fourteen hundred and sixty natural years which followed that date. During that time, called a Sothic period, the civil new year's day, for

Fig. 15.

Choeac.   Athyr.   Paophi.   Thoth.

Fig. 16.

Pharmuthi.   Phamenoth.   Mechir.   Tybi.

Fig. 17.

Mesore.   Epiphi.   Payni.   Pachon.

want of a leap-year, wandered through the whole round of the seasons. But even at that early date, B.C. 1322, called the era of Menophra, the year of the calendar, we shall see, was no longer true to the names which the months bore. At that time the months had become a whole season too early for their names; and the month of Thoth, the first month of vegetation, began soon after Midsummer, or at the beginning of the inundation. Hence the question is naturally asked, when was the calendar formed, with the names of the months true to the seasons? This cannot be told, as we do not certainly know what was the length of the civil year before the era of Menophra. If, as Manetho says, the five additional days had been before added, with the help of astronomical knowledge brought from the east by the Phenician shepherds, and no after correction was made in the calendar, we may fix its date four hundred and eighty-seven years, or a third part of fourteen hundred and sixty-one years, before the era of Menophra. But even if this attempt to fix its origin be wrong, and the calendar had been several times reformed before the era of Menophra, at any rate we know of nothing in Egypt but the language which is older than the hieroglyphical names of the months. Besides dividing the year into months, the Egyptians made use of the half-month and the week as smaller divisions of time. The week is mentioned in many of the very oldest of the inscriptions. It is spelt U K, and may even be the original of our own word *week* (see Fig. 18).

B.C. 1808.

Egyptian Inscript. pl. 92, 6. pl. 104, 3. pl. 108, 3.

Fig. 18.

Month.　Half-month.　Week.

(23) The ancient hieroglyphics teach us that the Egyptian language was in its roots the same as the more modern Coptic, a language but slightly related to any other; and the Greek and Hebrew words which we now trace in it seem to have crept in at a later time. But in its manner of forming the tenses and persons of the verbs it is not unlike the Hebrew. As the people were at a very early period closely crowded together and less roving than their neighbours, because hemmed in by the desert, the language received fewer changes in each century than those of nations less fixed to the soil. When it becomes better known to us we find it divided into three dialects, the Thebaic of Upper Egypt, the Memphitic of the western half of the Delta, and the Bashmuric of the eastern half of the Delta. But before those dialects were observed, the kingdom had been in part peopled with foreigners. Arabs of various tribes had overrun Upper Egypt, while Phenicians, Jews, and Greeks had settled in the Delta; hence these dialects may perhaps in part be of modern growth; but of the three, the hieroglyphics teach us that the Thebaic is the most ancient, though afterwards equally corrupted by additions. Like all other early languages, it is full of monosyllables; but, unlike our own, these monosyllables are very much formed

with only one consonant, and thus increase the ease by which consonants came to be represented by characters which at the same time represented syllables. In pronunciation the Egyptian was strongly guttural, as we see by the confusion between Th, Ch, and K. For L, D, B, and G, they used the same letters as for R, T, P, and K, having in each case only one sound where we have two. The language agrees with the religion, and with the earliest buildings, in teaching us that the Thebaid was more closely joined to the eastern than to the western half of the Delta.

(24) Nothing in the art of war is more important than good weapons; and great indeed was the superiority of a nation like the Egyptians that had spears tipped with steel, while their neighbours had no metal harder than brass. In Greece iron was scarce even in the time of Homer, while among the Egyptians it had been common many centuries earlier. They probably imported it from Cyprus. It is not easy to trace its history; because, from the quickness with which this metal is eaten away by rust, few ancient iron or steel tools have been saved to clear up what the writers have left in doubt. The Greeks speak of hard iron from some countries, without knowing from what the hardness arose; like the Cyprian breastplate which Agamemnon wore at the siege of Troy; and, as the smelting furnaces were heated with wood, the iron must often have been made into steel by the mere chance of the air being shut out. But though we have not now the Egyptian tools themselves, we have the stones which were carved with them; and the sharp deep lines of the hieroglyphics on the granite and basalt could have been cut with nothing softer than steel. No faults in the chiselling betray the workman's difficulty. To suppose that the Egyptian tools were made of flint or highly tempered copper, is to run into the greater difficulty to escape the lesser. The metal which was best for the mason's chisel would be used for the soldier's spear. *(Iliad, xi. 20.)*

(25) Memphis, which had been governed for two or three hundred years by a race of kings or priests of its own, was strong enough under SUPHIS, or CHOFO, or CHEOPS (Fig. 19), and his successor, SENSUPHIS or NEF-CHOFO (Fig. 20), to conquer and hold Thebes *(Manetho. Eratosthenes.)*

a little before the time of Osirtesen I. These two kings
conquered the peninsula of Mount Sinai, the Tih or *hill-country*, as it was called, and have left their hieroglyphical inscriptions in the valley of Wâdy Mugareh on the north-west side of the range. There they worked mines, but of what mineral is doubtful. These

Bartlett's Forty Days.
Burton's Excerpta, pl. xii.

Fig. 19.   Fig. 20.

mines continued to be worked in the reign of the Theban King Amunmai Thori III.

(26) The fruitful rice- and corn-fields made Lower Egypt a place of great wealth, though from its buildings it would seem to be less forward in the arts than Upper Egypt. Industry and earnestness of purpose were equally great in each half of the country. While one race was hollowing its tombs out of the rock near Thebes, the other was building its huge pyramids on the edge of the desert near Memphis. The historian Manetho, who has the best claim to be followed in this part of our history, when so many of our steps are made in doubt, says that Suphis and his successor built the two greatest of these pyramids (see Fig. 21). Each of these huge piles stands upon a square plot of about eleven acres, and its four sides meet at a point about five hundred feet high. The stones were quarried out of the neighbouring hills, and some from the opposite side of

Pocock's Travels.

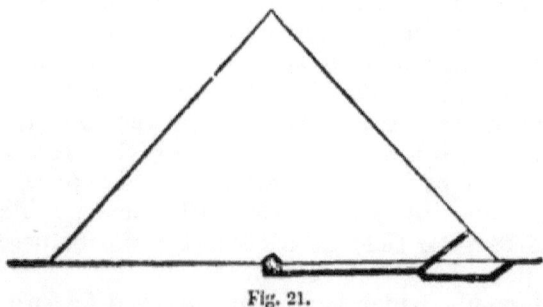

Fig. 21.

the Nile, and are all of a great size, and carefully cut into shape. The chinks between the stones are in some places filled with plaster of Paris and in others with the plaster mixed with mortar. In the limestone quarries of Toora, opposite to Memphis, the sculptures on the face of the rock tell us of the size of the stones there cut. In one place six oxen are dragging along a sledge with a block of stone on it, which measures eight feet by four; and the early date of the sculpture makes us suppose that this stone was to form part of the casing for the pyramids (see Fig. 22). We see in

Fig. 22.

these buildings neither taste nor beauty, but their size and simplicity raise in us a feeling of grandeur, which is not a little heightened by the thought of the generations which they have outlived. They take their name from the words Pi-Rama, *the mountain*, and though when compared with mountains they may perhaps seem small, when measured by any human scale are found to be truly gigantic. They are the largest buildings in the world. It is not easy to imagine the patience needed to build them; and we can well forgive the mistake of the vulgar, who have thought that in the early ages of the world men were of larger stature and longer lives than ourselves. They can only have been raised by the untiring labour of years; and they are a proof of a low state of civilization, when compared with the buildings of Upper Egypt. Yet the builders were men of great minds and lofty aim, and had not a little knowledge of mathematics and mechanics to shape and move the huge blocks, and to raise them to their places. The Temples of Thebes and the Pyramids of Memphis belong to different classes of the sublime in art. As we examine the massive roof, the strength of the walls and columns, and the sculptured figures of the Theban buildings, we feel encouraged in our efforts to overcome difficulties, and to do something great. As we gaze upon the huge simple pyramids, without parts and without ornament, we bow down in awe and wonder. The pyramids were built as tombs for the kings, and they may be taken as a measure of their pride. Each of these mountains of stone was to cover the body of one weak man, and to keep it after embalming till the day of his resurrection.

(27) Herodotus was told that each pyramid took twenty years in building, and that one hundred thousand men were unceasingly employed on the work, who were relieved every three months; while it was recorded in the hieroglyphical inscription then existing on the side of the largest pyramid, that sixteen hundred talents of silver were spent on the radishes, onions, and garlick, for the workmen, which was probably their only pay; and which, if the number of workmen is not exaggerated, was only eighteenpence a year of our money for each man. The wear of the last three thousand years has now removed from the sides of the pyramids the inscriptions which might have disclosed to us with greater certainty their builders' names and history; but that they were ornamented with hieroglyphics, we have the testimony of Herodotus, Dion Cassius, the Arabic writers, and other travellers till the fourteenth century. Of these two pyramids, that which was first built (see Fig. 21) is rather the smaller, and the more simple in its plan. The chamber in the middle, which held the sarcophagus with the king's body, is on the ground, and is entered by a passage nearly straight. Nothing that has been discovered in the stonework of the older pyramid proves that the builder, when he began, had made up his mind how large it should be. It may be that his ambition increased as the work grew under his hand. But it was otherwise with that

Lib. ii. 124.

Vyse's Pyramids.

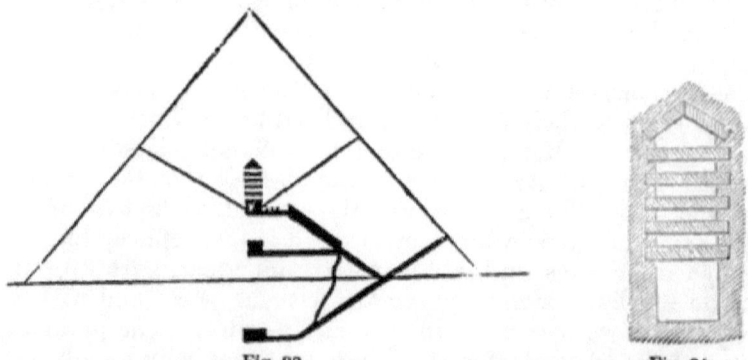

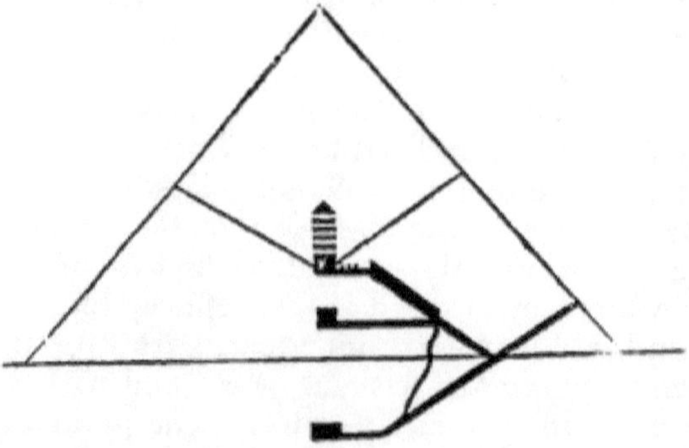
Fig. 23.

Fig. 24.

built by Nef-chofo (see Fig. 23). The second builder began with the intention that his pyramid should surpass the former, both in size and in safety against being opened. The chamber for the body (see Fig. 24) is not on the ground, but raised from it by 135 feet; it is curiously and carefully roofed, to save it from being crushed by the weight which was to be placed overhead. The passages were so arranged that the workmen, when they had placed the body in its chamber, could close its entrance by heavy stones let fall from within, and then as a method of escape let themselves down by a well into a second passage 90 feet below the surface of the rock, and thus return to the open air. The pyramids were built in steps, and casing stones were afterwards added to make the sides flat. The angle at which the sides slope seems to have been determined by the simple direction to the workmen, that, when a row of stones was five measures high, the row above was to be pushed back four measures. In order to bring the stones from the boats on the Nile to the rising ground on which the pyramids were to be built, it was found necessary to form a causeway over the low ground by the river side. This great work, which Herodotus thought little less gigantic than the pyramids themselves, was a thousand yards long, fifty feet broad, and

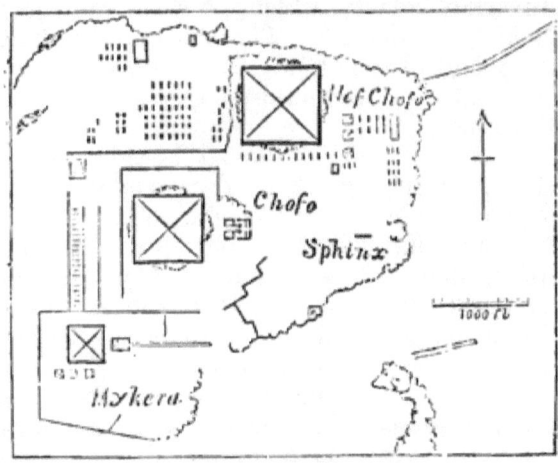

Fig. 25.—Plan of the Pyramids.

in some places forty feet high; and it was probably raised higher and higher as each row of stones was added to the pyramid, so that every stone was rolled to its place up this inclined plane. This great causeway, which led straight towards the older pyramid, was afterwards turned aside towards the larger (see Fig. 25); and thus clearly declares to us that it was first made for one purpose, and then used for a second.

(28) In front of the pyramid the second in size, lies the huge sphinx (see Fig. 26), a lion with a man's head, fifty

Fig. 26.

yards long, carved out of the rock, with its face to the rising sun. There were probably at one time two of these monsters, one on each side of the approach to the pyramid. So it is perhaps of the same age as the pyramid that it was meant to ornament. The sphinx had on its forehead the sacred asp, the usual mark of royalty, which the kings wore in gold tied on by the fillet or diadem. The shape of its skull is like that of the people of the Delta; it has a greater length from the chin to the back of the head than we see in the statues of the Theban kings.

(29) Many wise or bold men must have before ruled over the Thebans, gratifying their own ambition, while by keeping order they helped the people to improve the arts of life. They must have deserved our gratitude by fostering inventions in their infancy; but as they did not invent history they sleep unhonoured and unknown. Osirtesen is the first great king of Thebes that we meet with, the first of those whose monuments remain to us with their names carved upon the everlasting granite; but by a comparison of the tablets of kings at Karnak and at Abydos he seems to have been the last of his family. His descendants were only chief priests in the temple. If we follow Manetho, in writing by means of a G, K, or Ch, a character which in later times was a T, or Th, his name may have been Osiri-

gesen. He had a predecessor, whose name we may perhaps venture to pronounce AMUNMAI THORI (Fig. 27), or Amunmai Chori, *the conqueror beloved by Amun.* He again was followed by Noubkora, AMUNMAI THORI II. (Fig. 28), Meshophra, OSIRTESEN II. (Fig. 29), Meskora, OSIRTESEN III. (Fig. 30), AMUNMAI THORI III. (Fig. 31), and Queen SCEMIOPHRA (Fig. 32); but though we find their names on

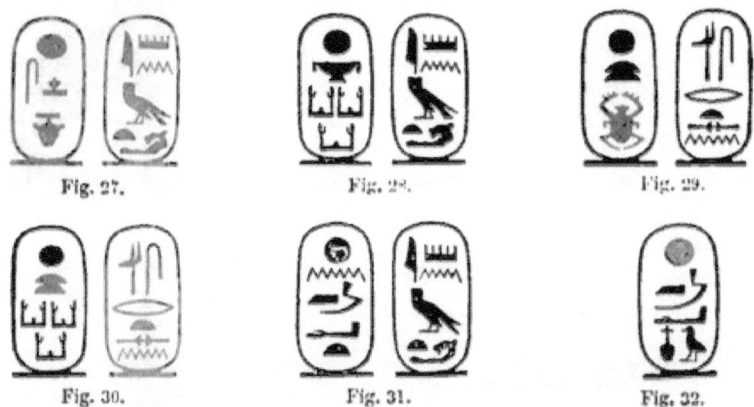

Fig. 27. Fig. 28. Fig. 29.
Fig. 30. Fig. 31. Fig. 32.

the tablet of kings at Abydos, in the list of the forefathers of the great Rameses, they are not mentioned in the genealogical table on the walls of the Memnonium at Thebes. It is doubtful how far the sway of each reached. But under them Thebes was every year rising in power, and the country marked as theirs by their sculptured buildings becomes in every reign wider than in the last. On the south we find that Osirtesen III. was master of part of Ethiopia as far as Samneh at the second cataract. To the east their names are found on the coast of the Red Sea, near the port of Ænum or Cosseir, which even at that early time enriched the kingdom of Thebes by its trade with Arabia. To the north, on the west of the Nile, the little kingdom of Heracleopolis falls under their sway; and the name of Amunmai Thori III. is found in the palace called the Labarinth, on the banks of the Lake of Mœris, which, according to Manetho, had been built two reigns earlier by Labaris.

Lepsius's Letters.

Wilkinson, Thebes.

(30) The strip of country on the whole of the Arabian

side of the Nile above the Delta belonged to these kings of Thebes; and they at last held the strip on the same side of the Delta; though this latter district seems more naturally to belong to Memphis. The Midianites or Arabs of the neighbouring peninsula of Sinai were usually in alliance with the Egyptians, or rather dependent on them; and they allowed the Egyptians to enrich themselves by working the copper mines in their range of mountains. At Sarbout el Cadem, near the mines, the Theban king, Amunmai Thori III., had a small room hollowed out of the rock as a temple to the Egyptian gods, for the use of the miners; and when a larger temple was built there, a few reigns later, this old rock-hewn temple remained as the inner sanctuary (Fig. 33). It reminds us

<small>Egypt. Inscript. 2nd Ser. pl. 36.</small>

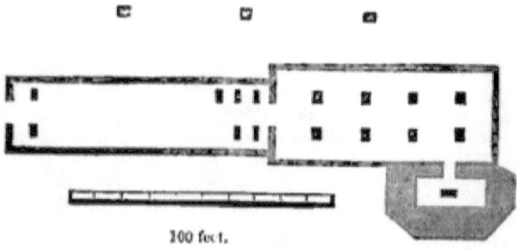

Fig. 33.

that the dark, low, small room which forms the sanctuary in every Egyptian temple is built in imitation of these early caves. This is perhaps the oldest temple in the world. The eastern side of the Delta was also enriched by the occasional arrival of caravans from the East, from Judea, and even, we are told, from Gilead beyond the Jordan, with their camels laden with spicery, and balm, and myrrh for the Egyptian market.

<small>Genesis, xxxvii. 25.</small>

(31) Scemiophra, one of these early sovereigns of Thebes, was a queen; and the country must have been long governed by monarchs before the custom of hereditary succession could have been so well established as to allow the crown to be worn by a woman. It is only in a settled state of society that the strong give way to the weak. Men would not form a monarchy in a very early stage. They must have united

together and resisted the usurpations of the strong, and felt the evils of anarchy, before agreeing to obey a king. And again, law must for many generations have gained the mastery over violence, before the peaceable regularity of the hereditary monarch could have been preferred to the turbulent vigour of the elected chief. Brute force must have long yielded obedience to mind, before a nation, or even a small state like Thebes, would risk its peace and safety by trusting the sword of justice to female hands, and before armies would obey one who could not lead them to battle. But in Egypt this would come to pass sooner than in most countries. Agriculture and trade early taught the Egyptians the rights of property and the advantages of civil laws, and they added thereto the sanction of religion, by making the monarch, whether man or woman, the head of the priesthood. Many of his titles were borrowed from the several orders of priests; and his crowns only differed in richness, but not in shape, from those worn by the priests, and those placed on the statues of the gods. Monarchy in some countries has been thought to be a patriarchal state, in which the people have been compared to the children, and the king to the father of a family; but in Egypt it was a religious community, in which the palace was a temple, the people worshippers at the gate, and the monarch the chief priest, who took upon himself the duty of making sacrifices to redeem his subjects from the punishment due to their sins. By the sovereign being the head of the priesthood, the people lost the political freedom which they might have gained from an opposition between the civil and ecclesiastical powers; and perhaps this union of the two powers in one head produced a government that was not stronger than necessary to keep order and check violence in this early stage of the world.

(32) The equal treatment which the women received in Egypt was shown in other circumstances beside their being allowed to sit on the throne. In the mythology, the goddess Isis sometimes held rank above her husband. We see on the mummy cases that the priestly and noble families traced their pedigrees as often through the female line as through the male; and, in the rudeness of their chronology, public records were sometimes dated by the names of the priestesses.

These are strong proofs of a high degree of civilisation, and they support the remark of Herodotus, that there were parts of Egypt, even in his time, where the debasing practice of a man having more than one wife was unknown to them. The increase of the population is a proof that the marriage vow was for the most part held sacred.

<small>Lib. ii. 92.</small>

(33) The journey of Abraham towards Egypt is represented as rather the movement of a tribe than that of a single family. There was at that early time a migration going forward of Phenicians, and other Arab tribes, moving out of their own country through Arabia into Lower Egypt, and thence along the African shore of the Mediterranean. They were peaceably driven out of Canaan by other troops of herdsmen, who were moving westward from Chaldæa and Mesopotamia, and who made the pasture land too crowded for their loose and scattered way of life. In the time when Abraham's journey is placed Lower Egypt was a well-tilled corn country, in which the harvest yielded more food than the people wanted for their own eating. Pharaoh, or *the king*, who probably dwelt at Memphis, was surrounded by princes and servants, and is by no means described as his equal, as the little kings of Canaan had been.

<small>Manetho.</small>
<small>Genesis, ch. xi.</small>
<small>Genesis, ch. xii.</small>

(34) The Phenicians, who had settled quietly in the Delta, soon got too strong for the people who had given them a home. They rose against the Egyptians, and attacked the cities and temples; and having defeated the king of Lower Egypt, they took Memphis. They then made SALATIS, one of themselves, king; and he stationed garrisons in several of the strong places, and made Upper and Lower Egypt pay him tribute, without, however, being able to put down the native kings. Salatis reigned nineteen years, and had a force, which, with the exaggeration which attends all numbers in ancient history, has been swelled into two hundred and fifty thousand men; and he was the first of the race of Phenician Shepherd kings, or Hycsos, who scourged Egypt for the next hundred years. He fortified a city called Abaris on the eastern frontier, said to be in the Sethroite nome, that is, in the neighbourhood of Pelusium; and from this fortress, and from Memphis, he sent forth his

<small>Manetho.</small>

soldiers, each year at harvest time, to gather in a duty upon corn, and the pay for his troops.

(35) Salatis was succeeded by BEON, APACHNAS, APOPHIS, JANIAS, and ASSETH. The Phenicians can hardly be said to have reigned over Egypt, they made its kings and people alike bend under their iron yoke for above one hundred years. But these cruelties taught the Egyptians the advantage of union; and at last the kings of Thebes and Memphis, and their vassals the kings of the other provinces of Egypt, made common cause against the Shepherds, and carried on a long and harassing war against them, till the foreigners were beaten by CHEBROS-AMOSIS, king of Thebes, the successor of Queen Scemiophra, already mentioned. He was already master of all Upper Egypt and part of Ethiopia from Samneh at the second cataract to the Lake of Mœris in the province of Fayoum. He drove the shepherds towards the frontier, and blockaded them in Abaris; and, on their surrendering, he allowed them to march out of the country in number not less than two hundred and forty thousand men. They left behind them no buildings or other traces of their power; and we remain in doubt as to which branch of the Arab family they belong to. They were, without doubt, the Philistines, those warlike enemies of Israel, who had thus gained a settlement in the southern corner of Canaan before the Israelites had left Egypt. The Israelites gave them the name of Philistines, or *foreigners*, a name which they not only fixed upon their place of settlement, Palestine, but left behind them at the place where they came from, Pelusium. As Shemmo is the Egyptian word of the same meaning, they probably also carried to the place of their settlement its second name of the district of the Simeonites. Their real name, however, would seem to have been Caphtorites; and Caphtor, the home from which they migrated into Palestine, was probably an island in the marshes on the east side of the Delta, where they had been living before the Egyptians had gained strength enough to drive them out. From their intercourse with the Island of Cyprus, they may have gained the use of iron, which made their soldiers so formidable to the worse-armed Israelites.

Manetho.

Gen. x. 14.

Deuteron. ii. 23.
Jeremiah. xlvii. 4.

(36) This war against the Phenicians had taught the several independent cities of Egypt the strength which is to be gained from union; it had accustomed them to act together, and had prepared the way for all Egypt to become one kingdom. Thebes was the chief gainer by the change. There was no great city on the east bank of the river to separate it from the seat of the Phenicians; and thus the territory near Heliopolis, from which the enemy was driven, fell to its share. Heliopolis, like Thebes, worshipped the god of the sun. From this time we find Upper Egypt rising in wealth and power, and its kings approaching to the rank of sovereigns of Egypt; and though we are still told the names of the kings of Memphis, these seem to have been sometimes under the sceptre of the kings of Thebes. With Amosis began that great family of Theban kings whose buildings have so long been the wonder of the world. Their temples and colossal statues are the models from which the Greeks copied, while their obelisks even now grace the cities of those nations which rose when Egypt fell. The walls of these buildings were covered, outside as well as in, with hieroglyphical inscriptions, containing the praises of their kings and gods; and the characters were always so large and clear, that anybody passing by in a hurry, even if he were running, could read them. It was a strong love of country and zeal for religion that thus ornamented the cities with temples; while the artists, looking beyond their own short lives, left monuments and records to be admired when they themselves should be forgotten. The paintings in the Theban tombs are the earliest known, and have outlived those of Greece and Rome; and we may yet hope to learn more of the lives and deeds of the kings from the hieroglyphics with which they are covered. Chebros-Amosis _{Manetho.} (see Fig. 34) was succeeded by a son of the same name (see Fig. 35).

Fig. 34.   Fig. 35.

(37) By this time Elephantine and This had sunk under Thebes, their more powerful neighbour, and ceased to be sovereign cities. Even if their chief priests had hitherto called them-

selves kings, they must have been entirely under the rule of Osirtesen III., and Amunmai Thori III., who have left us evidence in their buildings that their sway reached both to the north and to the south of these cities. The fall of This may in part be explained by comparing its position to that of Thebes. The city of This stands on high ground at the foot of the Libyan hills, separated from the Nile by a plain rich in groves and villages, which its fortified temple overlooks and ornaments; but Thebes is on the river's edge, and therefore better placed for trade. While This commands only the opening in the hills from the desert, through which now and then a few Arabs with their camels from the Great Oasis reached the valley of the Nile, Thebes commands the route which was every day becoming more important (with wells of water by the way), by which the trade of the Red Sea reached the boats on the river. Thus This bowed its head to Thebes, as Thebes was afterwards to yield to the cities in the Delta.

(38) AMUNOTHPH I. (see Fig. 36) reigned next; but by comparing together the lists of kings which have been preserved at Abydos, at Karnak, and in the Memnonium, he would seem to Burton's Excerpta. have had two sets of predecessors; one the series of kings whom we have already found reigning at Thebes, and the other perhaps his ancestors through whom he claimed descent from Osirtesen I. He probably added to his dominions a part of Ethiopia, which he may have gained by marriage; as his wife, Ames-athori, from her dark-coloured face among the red Egyptians, would seem to Wilkinson, Thebes. have been an Ethiopian. In some pictures her skin is painted black like a Negro. His first name, also, Sebekra, rather links him to Ethiopia, where the crocodile-god Sebek was chiefly worshipped. The increasing population of the Thebaid spread itself, either as conquerors or as traders, among their less civilised neighbours in the upper part of the valley of the Nile, and also on the coast of the Red Sea. Among the tombs which are tunnelled into the limestone hills on the western side of the river, opposite to Thebes, is one which was made in this

Fig. 36.

reign, and it seems to be the oldest in that neighbourhood. On the wall is carved a funeral procession by water, where the mummy of the dead man is lying in a boat, and is followed by other boats full of mourning friends and kinsmen; while in another place are some of his friends throwing dust upon their heads in token of grief. The water which they are being ferried across is most likely one of the lakes which are found near many of the temples, and which seem to have been dug for these ceremonies. Hence the Greeks afterwards borrowed their River Styx, the Lake of Acheron, Charon's boat, with other notions about the souls of the dead. The burial-places in the sides of the Theban hills are wide and lofty rooms, with their roofs upheld by columns, and their walls covered with paintings, which can be seen only by the dim light of the torch. These were meant to keep the embalmed bodies safe and undisturbed till the day of judgment; and, while the slight mud and wooden huts which sheltered the living reminded them of the shortness of human life, these massive buildings well deserved their name of the lasting abodes. The mummies which were buried in them have long since been broken to pieces in the search for gold and precious stones, which were often wrapt up in the same bandages with the body; and hence this sculpture in the reign of Amunothph I. is perhaps the earliest proof that can now be quoted of the Egyptian custom of embalming the dead. With the mummy were sometimes buried, not only treasures which the man valued when alive, but farming tools and corn for seed, for his use when he should come to life again; and the tombstone usually describes the buried man not as dead but as now living for ever. The days between the death and burial of a friend are always a most trying time for the grieving survivors; and this time the Egyptians lengthened to seventy melancholy days.

<small>Egyptian Inscriptions, plate 7.</small> (39) Amunothph, like most of the Egyptian kings, was worshipped as a god. On a stone in the British Museum we see him with his queen Ames-athori, with the sun upon his head, and before him is a table or altar on which a worshipper is pouring out a <small>British Museum.</small> libation. On another stone, made perhaps in the next reign, while he is styled the son of Amun, Ames-athori is styled the wife of Amun; as if the new king

denied that he owed his birth to his father, and claimed, as his father had done before him, to be the child of his mother and of the great god Amun-Ra.

(40) MESPHRA-THOTHMOSIS I. (see Fig. 37), who reigned next, enlarged the great temple or citadel of Karnak at Thebes, which had been begun by Osirtesen I., and he set up some obelisks in front of it. Of these early buildings every new temple or part of a temple was grander than the last. The architects were truly great men; they had been driven by the want of wood to work wholly in stone, and they made good use of that material. They can have borrowed thoughts from nobody. They drew from the storehouse of their own minds, and brought forth conceptions grand beyond all that had yet been seen. They discovered many of the rules by which is produced the sublime in art. They were above the use of trifling ornament. They felt the dignity of their calling; they had to do honour to their gods and to raise the thoughts of their fellow-worshippers towards heaven. Few of their buildings now remain; but even the later Egyptian temples, which were copied from them, are the world's models for solemn grandeur in architecture. At this time the granite quarries in the neighbourhood of Syene were busily worked, and the cutting out and removal of long blocks to be set up as obelisks at Thebes, proves the great skill of the engineers and the goodness of the workmen's tools. Of the statues and monuments carved out of this hard stone we know of none which were certainly made before this reign. There are reasons, as we have said, for thinking that the granite obelisks bearing the name of Osirtesen I. were made much later. But after the time of Thothmosis I. the use of granite becomes common for the royal works. Hence we may suppose that it was not till about this time that the knowledge of iron had encouraged the opening of quarries in the harder rocks.

Fig. 37.

Tablet of Abydos. Wilkinson, Thebes.

(41) Near Tombos, at the third cataract, are large quarries of granite where were made the statues and sphinxes for the temples between that town and the quarries of Syene. At

Tombos, the name of Thothmosis I. is found on the buildings; from which we learn that a part of that country had already been brought under the sceptre of Egypt, and this most likely took place at the marriage of Amunothph I. Thothmosis may even have held Napata, the capital of Ethiopia, and the whole valley of the Nile to the north of Meroë; but we find no monuments of his now remaining quite so far south. Ethiopia, however, as far as Tombos, and sometimes as far as Napata, remained joined to Egypt for many centuries; and the temples, with their paintings, statues, and hieroglyphics, prove that whatever may have been the original race of people, the Coptic blood, religion, and language had mixed largely with the natives. The temples, at the same time, teach us that the arts of civilisation were in every way less forward in Ethiopia than in Egypt; the Ethiopian temples are only like those of Thebes as bad copies are like the originals; and when the Greek historians tell us that Egypt was indebted to Ethiopia for its civilization, we have no difficulty in understanding that they were using both names in the more early sense, and that they should have said that the Delta received its knowledge of arts and letters from the Thebaid. The Ethiopian burial-places are small pyramids like those near Memphis, but with the addition of a portico borrowed from the Theban temples. The Thebans on the east side of the river had been tempted, by the nature of the rock, to form their underground tombs in the limestone hills on the left or western bank, and had thereby fixed in the language of their religion, Amenti, or the abode of the dead, in the west. So at Napata, the capital of Ethiopia, at the foot of Mount Barkal, situated at the limit of the tropical rains, the priests, following the Theban custom, built their little pyramids on the opposite or left bank of the river, though from the bend in the stream it placed their Amenti in the east. In the hieroglyphics the elephant, river-horse, and camelopard of Ethiopia are as little to be seen as the horse and camel of Arabia; while the temples at Napata, near the fourth cataract, are ornamented with the lotus of Lower Egypt.

Diodorus Siculus, lib. iii. 3.

(42) While these sovereigns were reigning in Upper Egypt, the race of kings or priests of Memphis was governing

Lower Egypt. While the kings of Thebes were hollowing their tombs out of the rock, the kings of Memphis continued that most ancient custom of building pyramids for their burial-places. The historian Manetho has told us their names; but the great temple of their chief god, Pthah, and any others that they raised, have long since been destroyed to furnish building materials for the modern city of Cairo, and hence their names remain an insulated and less useful piece of knowledge. It was during these reigns, after the Shepherd kings had been driven out of the country, and while the very name of a shepherd was hateful to the Egyptians, that the family of Jacob settled in Egypt. The account of Joseph's arrival there, Genesis, ch. xxxvii. and of his family following him, is related in the book of Genesis with biographical minuteness; and though criticism will not allow us to accept it all as history, yet the mention of Egypt and its customs, even if belonging to a later age, is too interesting to be omitted. It chanced that a company of Ishmaelite and Midianite merchants, travelling in a caravan from Gilead, with their camels laden with spicery and balm and myrrh for the Egyptian markets, had bought the young Joseph from his brethren for twenty pieces of silver, and on their arrival in Egypt they sold him as a slave to Potiphar, an officer of the king and a captain of the guard. Joseph's misfortunes all led to his own good. He soon rose by his good conduct to the head of his master's household; and when he was afterwards thrown into prison, by the wickedness of Potiphar's wife, it only led to his further advancement, and, by removing him to the capital, enabled him to rise in the king's service as he had before risen under the captain of the guard. It was not long ch. xl. before two of the great officers of state, the chief butler and the chief baker, were thrown into the same prison with Joseph, for some offence against the king; and he was able to bring himself into notice by a successful interpretation of these officers' dreams. It happened on the third day exactly as Joseph had foretold. That day was the king's birthday, and he dined with his nobles in grand state; and the chief butler was then restored to favour and to his high rank, and he handed the cup of grape-juice to the king in the presence of all the court; and on the same day the chief baker was beheaded, and his body hanged on a tree.

(43) After this, however, Joseph still lay two years in prison, till, fortunately for him, the king himself dreamed a dream. This may have been the king of Memphis, or more probably the little king of Bubastis, which was a city of some importance. He dreamed that seven fat cows came up out of the Nile, and fed in the meadows on the river's bank, and afterwards seven lean cows came out of the river and eat up the former. And he again dreamed that seven large ears of corn grew on one stalk (see Fig. 38), and afterwards that seven thin ears grew on a second stalk, and that the seven thin ears eat the seven large ears, as the seven lean cows had eaten the seven fat cows. In the morning the king sent for all the magicians and wise men of his capital, and called upon them to interpret his dream; but these learned priests could not help him to the meaning of it. The chief butler then told the king of the young Hebrew slave, who had so wisely interpreted the dreams in prison; and Joseph was sent for to the palace. Before entering on the task, he shaved himself like the priests of the country, and then showed the king that his dream was a message from God to tell him that the next seven years would be years of great plenty throughout Egypt, and that they would be followed by seven years of equally great famine. Joseph further advised that officers should be set over the whole land to gather into the royal granaries, during each of the years of plenty, one fifth of the crop, in store against the seven years of famine. This advice was well-pleasing to the king, and he employed Joseph to carry his own plans into execution. He made this Hebrew stranger the chief officer in the land, and put his own signet

Genesis, ch. xli.

Fig. 38. Triticum compositum.

ring upon his finger, as a token that the minister's command should have the same weight as his own. Joseph, who only a few days before had been in prison, was then dressed in the robes of state, with a gold chain round his neck; he rode in the second of the king's carriages, and as he drove through the streets of the city his servants ran before him crying out in the Egyptian language, "Ab-rek, Ab-rek," or *Bow the head, Bow the head*. He afterwards married Asenath, the daughter of Poti-pherah, the priest and governor of the city of On, or Onion, the capital of the district afterwards called the Nome of Heliopolis. But notwithstanding this marriage into the priesthood, and the favour of his sovereign, which was never withdrawn from him, Joseph's foreign birth was not forgotten by the Egyptians; and notwithstanding the titles with which he was honoured, they familiarly or reproachfully called him Zeph-net-Phœnich, or *Joseph the Phenician*.

(44) The years of plenty and of famine came to pass as Joseph had foretold. During the seven years of plenty he laid up in every city the fifth part of the grain grown in its neighbourhood, which he claimed from the landlords as a tax, when the abundance made it easy for them to pay it; and during the years of famine he unlocked the royal granaries, and sold his stores to the starving people at as high a price as he could get for them. Genesis, xlvii.
Their gold and silver, and even their herds of cattle, failed them by the end of the first year; and during the second year of famine, the unhappy Egyptians sold their lands, and even themselves, to the king, as the price of the food which the minister gave out for their families. Joseph bought up the whole land of Lower Egypt for the king; every man sold his field; and the whole soil, except that which belonged to the priests, into which class he had himself been adopted by marriage, then became the property of the crown. He then made a new division of the land, allotted out the estates to the husbandmen to cultivate; and gave them seed to plant, and required them for the future to pay one fifth part of the crop, as a rent, to the royal treasury. Thus did the Asiatic minister, copying the customs of the East, make the king the landlord of the whole country except the estates of the priests; and the land was then held by what is now known in Asia as the Ryot tenure. In Asia, however, the landowners are

tenants at a changeable rack-rent of about one half of the crop; whereas the Egyptians paid a fixed and lower rent of one fifth. The Egyptian landholder was therefore rich enough to have peasants or slaves under him, while the Indian ryot is himself the peasant-slave of his governors.

This rent was in the place of all direct taxes; and except the duties upon manufactures and upon the exports and imports, no other tax was laid upon the Egyptians till the country was conquered by the Persians. Thus from the history of Joseph and of his administration, we learn that Lower Egypt was governed by a despotic monarch. There was no aristocracy, as in Upper Egypt, in the form of an hereditary priesthood, to oppose a favourite slave and a foreigner being made the chief minister of the kingdom; or at least, though the body of priests were able to protect their own land from the land-tax, the chief priests were not strong enough to claim the chief offices of the state for themselves. Nor was the order of soldiers then strong enough to protect their privileges; but they were forced to yield up their lands with the husbandmen. Whatever little political freedom Lower Egypt had before possessed was then crushed, and Joseph assisted in reducing the whole of the people of the Delta to a more regular state of legal slavery.

(45) The Hebrew minister, encouraged by the favour shown by the Egyptians to himself, had sent for his father and brethren, who had been suffering under the famine in Canaan, and who had some of them before come down into Egypt to buy corn. They brought with them their herds and tents, and their families to the number of seventy souls, to settle there under the protection of the chief minister of the crown. When they were brought before the king they told him that by trade they were keepers of sheep; but by Joseph's advice they were careful not to call themselves shepherds, lest they should be understood to mean that they were *Shepherd* Arabs, the hated enemies of the Egyptians. The Egyptians had no difficulty in allotting to the new comers a place of abode and a tract of land for their numerous herds. The Valley of the Nile is surrounded with high land on the edge of the desert, which, though uncultivated, is not wholly barren and unprofitable. Here the Arab dwells in his tent, while his

k. Genesis, xlvi.

herds browse on the wild herbage. This strip of land, by a known and moderate degree of labour, may be watered by canals and wells, and thus made to yield a return to the husbandman. Such was the soil of those places in the land of Rameses or Heliopolis, where the Israelites were allowed to pitch their tents and tend their flocks; from the word Geshe, or *upper* lands, perhaps, they called it the land of Goshen. It was neither moistened by rain from heaven nor by the overflow of the Nile, but it was to be watered laboriously by means of trenches and hand-pumps and buckets. Thus the Egyptians gave up to the sons of Jacob an uncultivated tract of country, and gained a body of industrious thriving citizens well able to bear their share of the land-tax and the other state burdens. They were Shemmo, or *Strangers* in the land, and hence the Israelites called themselves the children of Shem. Their dwellings were probably fixed at Succoth, which we may suppose to be the village afterwards called by a name of the same meaning, Scenæ, or *the Tents*, situated between Rameses or Heliopolis and Thoum or Pithom. The land of Goshen had about the same boundaries as the Heliopolite nome, in which the chief towns were Onion, Babylon, Thoum, and Heliopolis. _{Itinerarium Antonini.}

(46) On the death of Jacob, Joseph's father, his body was embalmed after the Egyptian fashion. It was washed and anointed with spices by the sacred embalmers for the space of forty days, with the honours due to a man of rank, and the Egyptians mourned for the usual time of seventy days; and the body, when made into a mummy, was removed to Canaan, to be buried with his forefathers, as he had ordered on his death-bed. The Israelites soon got naturalised to Egypt. Some of the same race may have before settled in the neighbourhood of Heliopolis in the time of Abraham's journey, and others may have followed the steps of Jacob to share his advantages. They increased fast in numbers, and their industry added to the wealth of the nation, as their share of the land-tax added to the king's revenue. But they were a despised race of men, avoided by their neighbours as unclean: and no Egyptian would eat at the same table with an Israelite. _{Genesis, l.} _{Genesis, xliii. 32.}

THOTHMOSIS II.

(47) But to return to the history of Upper Egypt.

Tablet of Abydos.

MESPHRA- THOTHMOSIS II. (see Fig. 39) followed the first of that name on the throne of Thebes; but he is very much thrown into the shade by Amun - Nitocris (see Fig. 40), his strong-minded and ambitious wife. She was the last of the race of Memphite sovereigns, the twelfth or eleventh in succession from the builders of the great pyramids; and by her marriage with Thothmosis, Upper and Lower Egypt were brought under one sceptre. She was handsome among women, and brave among men, and she governed the kingdom for her husband with great splendour. She added to the temple of Karnak at Thebes, on the east of the Nile, and set up in one of the courtyards two great granite obelisks, each ninety-two feet high, which were there placed in honour of Thothmosis I. The obelisks agreeably break the line of the flat roof in a building which has too many horizontal lines. As being a sovereign in her own right, she is sculptured on the obelisks in man's attire; and at the top of the obelisk she is on her knees receiving the blessings of the god Amun-Ra (see Fig. 41). She also built the temple or palace of Dayr el Bahree, at the foot of the Libyan hills, being the first that was built on the west side of the river in the neighbourhood of Thebes. A straight road sixteen hundred feet long, between a double row of sphinxes, leads from the first gateway of this temple to the door of the court-yard; three hundred and fifty-five feet further, up a sloping paved road, is the granite doorway into the inner court, through a wall, in front of which stand sixteen polygonal columns, that once upheld the portico; and, three hundred and fifty feet further, is the second granite doorway into the small vaulted rooms and the chambers tunnelled into the side of the hill. The vaults of the ceilings were cut out of the flat stones, for though the form of the arch had been admired, its principle was not yet understood. The

Manetho.
Eratosthenes.
Wilkinson, Thebes.

Fig. 39.   Fig. 40.

building is dedicated to Amun-Ra, the Sun, whom the queen calls her father, the god whom the Thebans chiefly worshipped. As, by the fall of This and union with Memphis, Thebes was now the capital of all Egypt, it had no enemy to fear, and was no longer held within its old walls and moats.

Fig. 41.

(48) The buildings which were being raised by Queen Nitocris, at the same time in Upper and in Lower Egypt, prove the different degrees of civilization in the two people, and almost the difference in their political institutions. The temple-palaces of Thebes, ornamented with columns, obelisks, statues, sculpture without, and paintings within, were made by freemen who worked for their own religion and their own honour; but the pyramids of Memphis may have been made by slaves, driven by taskmasters, and working only for the vanity of their master. But we ought not to suppose any greater skill in the architects of either city than each case proves; and of the various ways in which the engineering difficulties might have been overcome, we may take it for granted that the rudest was that actually used. We know that when a town was to be stormed, the military engineers were often driven to the slow and laborious method of raising

against it a mound of earth of the same height as the city wall, and from this the besiegers attacked the garrison on equal terms. If the granite sarcophagus of a bull, weighing seventy tons without its lid, was to be let down into a well little more than its own size, within a chamber so narrow that machines could not be used, it could only be done by first filling the well with sand, then moving the sarcophagus on rollers on to the top of the well, and lastly lifting out the sand by handfuls while the sarcophagus standing on it was rocked from side to side on its arched bottom, and slowly sunk down into its resting-place. If an obelisk ninety feet long, or a statue fifty feet high, was to be placed upright, a groove or notch was first cut in the pedestal on which it was to stand, so that while it was being raised, one edge of its lower end might turn in that groove as on a hinge. The obelisk or statue was then brought by means of rollers till its lower end rested over this groove, and then its head was lifted up probably by means of a mound of earth, which was raised higher and higher, till the stone which leaned on it was set up on one end (see Fig. 42). If a huge block was to be placed on the top of a wall, it may have been rolled on rollers up a mound of sand to its place. Such labour will, in time, overcome difficulties which yield more quickly to a smaller force when skilfully directed. Of the six simple machines called the mechanical powers, the Egyptians used the wedge, the lever, and the inclined plane, but seem not to have known the screw, the pulley, or the wheel and axle. Though their chariots ran on wheels, they chose to drag a colossal statue on a sledge, rather than to risk the unsteadiness of putting rollers under it. Though their sailors pulled up the heavy sail by running the rope through a hole in the top of the mast, they had no moveable

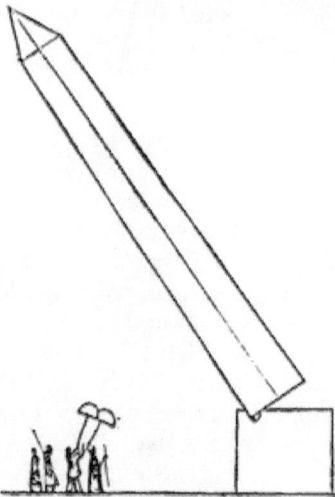

Fig. 42.

pulley fixed to the sail whereby a man can raise more than his own weight.

(49) Thus far we have traced a rather uncertain path through the reigns of twelve kings of Thebes, to whom Manetho has given names; and by mentioning the temples which they built we have been able to show both that they were real persons, and also what width of country they governed. Interpreting Manetho's disjointed lists by the help of the Tablet of Abydos, we have placed them in unbroken succession, and have put aside without notice the kings of the other cities, who have left us no records, believing that they were reigning at the same time, and were of a lower rank, and that thus their reigns add nothing to the time embraced within our chronology. This view of the case is very much supported by Eratosthenes, who in his list has nine kings in place of our eight, between Amunmai Thori II., the first on the Tablet of Abydos, and Queen Nitocris. But Eratosthenes, while agreeing with our chronology, does not agree with our history. He lets us know that our authorities are partial to Thebes, that the Theban kings were not always sovereigns; that the kings of Memphis sometimes governed Egypt, and at those times he leaves our Theban kings unnoticed. Nor does he always agree with us in the order of succession. Thus after Noubkora, our Amunmai Thori II., he places Chofo and Nef-chofo, the builders of the pyramids, as if Thebes were then under the shade of Memphis. After them he returns the sovereignty to the Thebans, and places Meskora, our Osirtesen III. He then again gives the sovereignty to Memphis in the person of Phiops, or to the Shepherds in the person of Apophis, who after two reigns is followed by Queen Nitocris. But the monuments seem not to support these opinions of Eratosthenes.

CHAPTER II.

THE THEBAN KINGS OF ALL EGYPT. B.C. 1322?—990?

(1) HITHERTO Egypt had been always under more than one sceptre. There had been many sovereign cities in which the chief priest of the temple, or head of the monastery, had at one time or other held the rank of king over the district of which that city was the capital. But we have hardly been able to note when these little kings sunk down to the rank of chief priest and magistrate in their several cities, and left the sovereignty to their more powerful neighbours of Thebes and Memphis. This great change in the political condition of Egypt was probably gradual; but the war which ended with the expulsion of the Phenicians, as it strengthened the power of the greater monarchies, so it left the others dependent on them. The most important union, however, was that between Thebes and Memphis, which took place by marriage in the last reign. This union, however, was not yet complete; THOTHMOSIS III. (see Fig. 43) on coming to the throne was a minor; Queen Nitocris, who had before governed for her husband, now governed for his successor; and even when the young Thothmosis came of age, he was hardly king of the whole country till after the death of Nitocris. We may remark that, on the buildings and tablets where we find her name joined either with that of her husband or of her successor, one or other of the names has in most cases, for some political reasons, been carefully cut out.

Fig. 43.

(2) Queen NITOCRIS, according to the historian Manetho, was the builder of the smallest of the three large pyramids near Memphis. The name of King Mecora, or Mencora, or Mencophra (see Fig. 44), has been found on the wooden mummy case in its underground chamber (see Fig. 45). The same name has also

_{Vyse's Pyramids.}

QUEEN NITOCRIS. 47

been found in the fourth pyramid (see Fig. 46), which was built beside it within the same enclosure and at the same

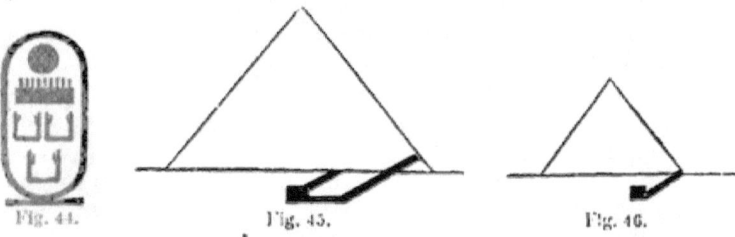

Fig. 44. Fig. 45. Fig. 46.

time. The largest of these two was no doubt meant for the king, and the smaller for somebody of less importance, probably Queen Nitocris herself. The name of King Mecora, which was used only at Memphis, and never at Thebes, was probably meant for her second colleague on the throne, Thothmosis III., whose first name, as written in Thebes, was Mehora, Menhora, or Menhophra. The guttural sound, written H or Th in Thebes, was written K or Ch in Memphis. Or it might even mean herself, as her full name was Mykera Amun-Neithchori (see Fig. 40); and in

Fig. 47.

her sculptures she is usually, though not always, dressed in man's clothes (see Fig. 47), to represent that she was a queen in her own right and not a queen consort. Herodotus says that, according to some, the third pyramid was built by King Mykerinus, and according to others, by a woman. At any rate, the agreement between the name in the pyramids and this queen's name, proves that Nitocris, who reigned at Thebes and was the last Memphite sovereign, was of the same family with the builder of the third and fourth pyramids. But she was probably the builder of them both, the smaller one for herself, and the larger one for the young King Thothmosis III.

Lib. ii. 34.

(3) The state of the arts was now changed in Memphis. Size was no longer valued so much as workmanship. This

third pyramid, like the two others which are so much older and larger, was built of the stone of the neighbourhood; but, unlike them, was beautifully cased with red granite from Syene, the most southerly part of Egypt, which stone was less likely before to have been brought to Memphis while the two kingdoms were under different sovereigns. This casing has unfortunately long since been carried off to form other buildings in the neighbourhood; and we have therefore lost the hieroglyphical inscriptions, which would have cleared up all doubt about the date and maker of this huge pile. The sarcophagus was found in an underground chamber beneath the middle of the pyramid, which was entered by a sloping passage from without, so that it was not made more difficult of approach by the pile of stonework raised overhead. It added to the monarch's glory, but not to the safety of his body. No second chamber has yet been found in the middle of the stonework, like that in the largest pyramid. So also the fourth pyramid, which accompanies this, seems to have had no chamber except that underground beneath it, and that also is entered from without.

(4) We have been able to note as many as six little monarchies within the limits of Egypt, and if to these we add Ethiopia, and perhaps the foreigners in the Delta, we may have eight monarchies which centred in Thothmosis III. Accordingly, when he added some new chambers to the great temple of Karnak, he was represented on the sculpture in one of the rooms as presenting offerings to his ancestors or predecessors of eight several dynasties, namely, the kings of Thebes, of Abydos, of Memphis, of Ethiopia, and of four other divisions of Egypt, perhaps Elephantine, Heracleopolis, Xois, and the district of the Shepherds. In one of the tombs near Thebes is a painting (see Fig. 48) of a grand procession of men of the four tribes bordering on the Nile, who are bringing their costly gifts in token of homage to this king. They together form the nation that pays him its willing obedience. First, there are dark-coloured men of Nubia, with Negroes in their company bringing skins, elephants' tusks, sticks of ebony, strings of beads—no doubt amber—ostrich eggs and feathers, apes, leopards, the ibex, and foreign plants carried in the earth in

<small>Burton's Excerpta, pl. 1*.</small>

<small>Hoskins's Ethiopia.</small>

which they grow. The granite obelisks from Syene are also counted as their tribute. Next, there are the Copts, men of a light-red colour, and long hair. Their gifts are large and tasteful vases of many shapes, but all beautiful, some holding plants of the lotus and lily kind, the usual emblems of the country. The Nubians and Copts are dressed alike, except that the Copts wear sandals, and the Coptic tunic is of a richer stuff. Then follow the dark Ethiopians, with less clothing, bringing ivory, ebony, ostrich eggs and feathers, dogs, oxen, leopards, apes, monkeys, and camelopards, with dishes full of gold rings. They also are accompanied with Negroes. The fourth are men with fair skins and beards, and warmer clothing, bringing long gloves, bows, chariots with horses, vases, bears, and elephants. They are people of Arabia and the Arabian side of the Nile, from whom the Egyptians got their supply of horses, and they seemed to be named Lydians, perhaps the tribe spoken of in the Old Testament as Lydians that bend the bow.

Fig. 48.

Genesis, x. 13.
Jeremiah, xlvi. 9.

(5) The tribute of gold rings brought by the Ethiopians was for the most part the produce of the hills in the desert between the Nile and the Red Sea. The sand at the foot of these hills was now enriching the whole country; not only

Napata, where the glittering grains first reached the river, but Thebes, that claimed the sovereignty over the district, and even the cities in the Delta, which by their trade spread the precious metal over the coasts of the Mediterranean. The gold was melted and worked into rings, as a form in which it could be kept most safely, by being strung upon a cord, or carried on a finger.

(6) There are two or three circumstances by which we may hope to fix the date of this king's reign. His full name at Thebes is Mehophra, or, as sometimes spelt, Menhophra Thothmosis (see Fig. 43); and Theon calls the beginning of the great Egyptian cycle of 1460 years, which began in the year B.C. 1321, the era of Menophres, and thus seems to fix the year in which either his reign began or he reformed the calendar. The observing man may note that every star rises to-day earlier than it did yesterday, and that every morning a fresh set peeps up from the horizon, to be seen only for a moment before they are lost in the brighter light of the daybreak. The day on which a star is thus first seen in the east is called its heliacal rising; and at the beginning of the era of Menophres, the first day of the month of Thoth, the civil new-year's day, fell on the day when the Dog-star first was seen to rise at daybreak, which was held to be the natural new-year's day, when the Nile began to rise, six weeks before the overflow. This agreement between the natural new-year's day and the civil new-year's day may have happened simply by the motion of the civil year; but it was possibly accompanied by a reform in the calendar, and by fixing the length of the civil year at 365 days, in the belief that the months would not again move from their seasons. Among the common names of the months, that of the last, Mesore, *the Bull*, was clearly brought into use at this time, when the year ended with the rising of that constellation. The months, however, were left with the mistakes in their hieroglyphic names, which had arisen from their former change of place. The four months which were named after the season of vegetation fell during the overflow of the Nile; the months named after the harvest fell during the height of vegetation; and those named after the inundation fell during harvest time. But if no alteration was

<small>Theon, ap. Cory.</small>

<small>B.C. 1321</small>

made at this time in the calendar, and the civil year already contained 365 days, the addition of the five days had probably been made 500 years earlier, when the first month of inundation would have begun with the Nile's overflow. The Egyptian year was never again altered. From the want of a leap year, 1461 civil years took place in 1460 revolutions of the sun; and in the beginning of the reign of the Emperor Antoninus Pius the new-year's day again came round to the season from which it moved in the reign of Menophres. Again, Plutarch says that the god Thoth, who in this case may be meant for Thothmosis, taught the Egyptians the true length of the year; and the figure of this king is often drawn with a palm branch, the hieroglyphic for the word year, in each hand; hence it is probable that he is the author of the change in the calendar, made in the year B.C. 1321. Censorinus, de Die Natali.

(7) Thothmosis III. was one of the greatest of the Egyptian kings. His buildings, which are scattered over all parts of the kingdom, prove the wealth and good taste of the people, while the sculptures on the walls recount the number of neighbouring tribes that owned his sway. He built or rather restored the temple of the Sun at Heliopolis, where Moses is said to have studied Egyptian learning; and he set up, perhaps, in front of it, the two granite obelisks which were afterwards removed to Alexandria, and of which one is now called Cleopatra's needle. He carved the obelisk which now ornaments the circus at Constantinople. He built a temple to Savak, the crocodile-headed god, at Ombos; and his buildings in Nubia, at Samneh, at Deer, and at Amada, prove that his sway over that country reached to the third cataract, and probably over the whole of Ethiopia north of Meroë. In this and the last reign the copper mines were again worked in the valley of Wady Mugareh, near Mount Sinai. The working of those mines must have been stopped as long as Egypt was at war with the Shepherd kings, and we find the names of no Egyptian kings upon the temple of Sarbout el Cadem, between the reigns of Amunmai Thor III. and Thothmosis II. During these years the little town of Paran near Sinai was perhaps not Egyptian Inscript. 2 Ser. 41. Wilkinson, Thebes. Laborde's Arabia. Egypt, Inscript. 2 Ser. 36.

free from the inroads of the Amalekites, or whatever Arab race it was whom the Egyptians had called the Shepherds. The kingdom of Thebes had now reached its full size. Thothmosis III. held Upper and Lower Egypt, and Ethiopia, and the peninsula of Sinai. It is true that some of his successors stretched their arms further, and won battles in Asia and, as they said, in Thrace; but these conquests were never long held. Several later kings were more wealthy and more powerful; but though their deeds were the greater, his were the earlier; and their glories never threw the reign of Thothmosis III. into the shade. Their names were never held in equal reverence with his. On the sacred beetles and other small images which were kept as charms, and often buried with the dead, we find his name oftener than that of any other king. We have a colossal head in the British Museum, which seems to have been of this king (see Fig. 50); and among the buildings in Thebes bearing the name of Thothmosis III., we find an arch built of brick (see Fig. 51), as well as a false arch made with advancing courses of stone.

<small>Egypt, Inscript. 2nd Ser. pl. 4e.</small>

(8) AMUNOTHPH II. (see Fig. 49), the next king, was the son of Thothmosis III. In his reign the arts of painting and sculpture made rapid strides, and gave promise of what they were to become a century later. Though his monuments are not numerous, yet the walls in some of the Theban tombs, made while he was on the throne, are covered with beautiful drawings of dancers, chariot-makers, leather-cutters, and other workmen, and of vases and borders, which equal any works of the same kind in Greece or Etruria. A rock-hewn temple at Ibrim, near Abousimbel, in Ethiopia, has a statue of this king, seated as one of a trinity between the god Thoth and the goddess Sate or Isis. He was most likely the Pharaoh in whose reign Moses led the Jews out of Egypt. When the Shepherds had been conquered by Amosis, and their army driven out of the country, many of the nation had been kept as slaves, and made to work in the

<small>Tablet of Abydos.</small>
<small>Wilkinson, Thebes.</small>
<small>Hereau, Panorama.</small>
<small>Manetho. Abul-Pharag., Hist. Dynast.</small>

Fig. 49.

quarries and at the buildings of the Delta. With these were mixed up the children of Israel, who in the eyes of the Egyptians were the same people. When Lower Egypt passed under the sceptre of Thebes, Joseph's services were forgotten or unknown; and the Jews who had increased in numbers in the three generations after his death, were treated as badly as the Phenicians. During Exodus, i. the last reign they had been employed on the fortifications of Pithom or Thoum, and Rameses or Heliopolis. The bricks for these buildings were made of mud from the Nile, worked up with chopped straw and then baked in the sun; and the Israelites were required to make the bricks without having the needful straw given to them.

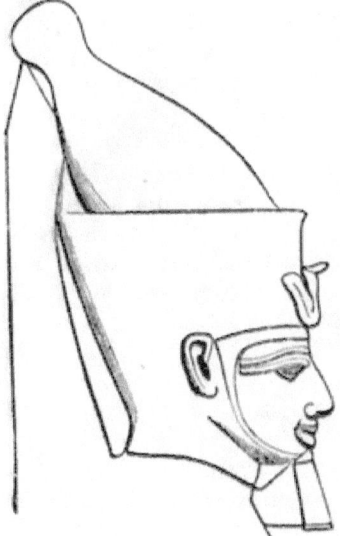

Fig. 50.

Fig. 51.

They were treated the more cruelly because their numbers made them feared. They had spread widely over Lower Egypt; but Amunothph, says the Egyptian historian, always confounding the Jews with the Phenicians, was warned by the priests to cleanse the country of these unclean persons, who were many of them lepers, and he sent them, to the number of eighty thousand, to live apart from the natives in the spot that had at first been allotted to them. They there chose Moses, a learned priest of Heliopolis, for their leader, who made a new code of laws for them, forbidding them to worship the Egyptian gods and sacred animals. Lastly, they took arms against the Egyptians, and were joined by troops from Canaan; but they were beaten in battle, driven out of the country, and many of them killed by Amunothph, who followed them in their flight to the borders of Syria.

<small>Manetho.</small>

(9) This is very unlike the well-known history in the Old Testament. However late may be the date of the writing, the march of the Jews under Moses is there recorded with strict geographical accuracy; and even now, if we correct the maps with the help of the measurements of the Roman roads in the *Itinerarium*, we may not only trace their route, but may fix with some probability the spot where they crossed on dry ground through the bed of the Red Sea, and where the Egyptian army was overthrown by the return of the waters (see Fig. 52). The interest which we feel in the journey would excuse even a search for their footsteps in the sand. Moses, on leaving *the City of the Sun*, called in Coptic Rameses, in Greek Heliopolis, marched the first day sixteen miles along the right bank of the Pelusiac branch of the river. He rested the first night at a village called *the Tents*, in Hebrew Succoth, in Greek Scenæ. The next day's march was of twenty-two miles, and passing by the town of Onion, called in the Roman Itinerary Vicus Judæorum, he encamped the second night at the edge of the desert, near the Egyptian fortified city of Etham. This city was named after the god Chem, there called Athom; and it has been also called Thoum and Pithom, and Patumos. It was ten miles from Bubastis. The number of followers of course increased as he passed through the land of Goshen. At Etham he left the northern

<small>Exodus, xiii. xiv.</small>

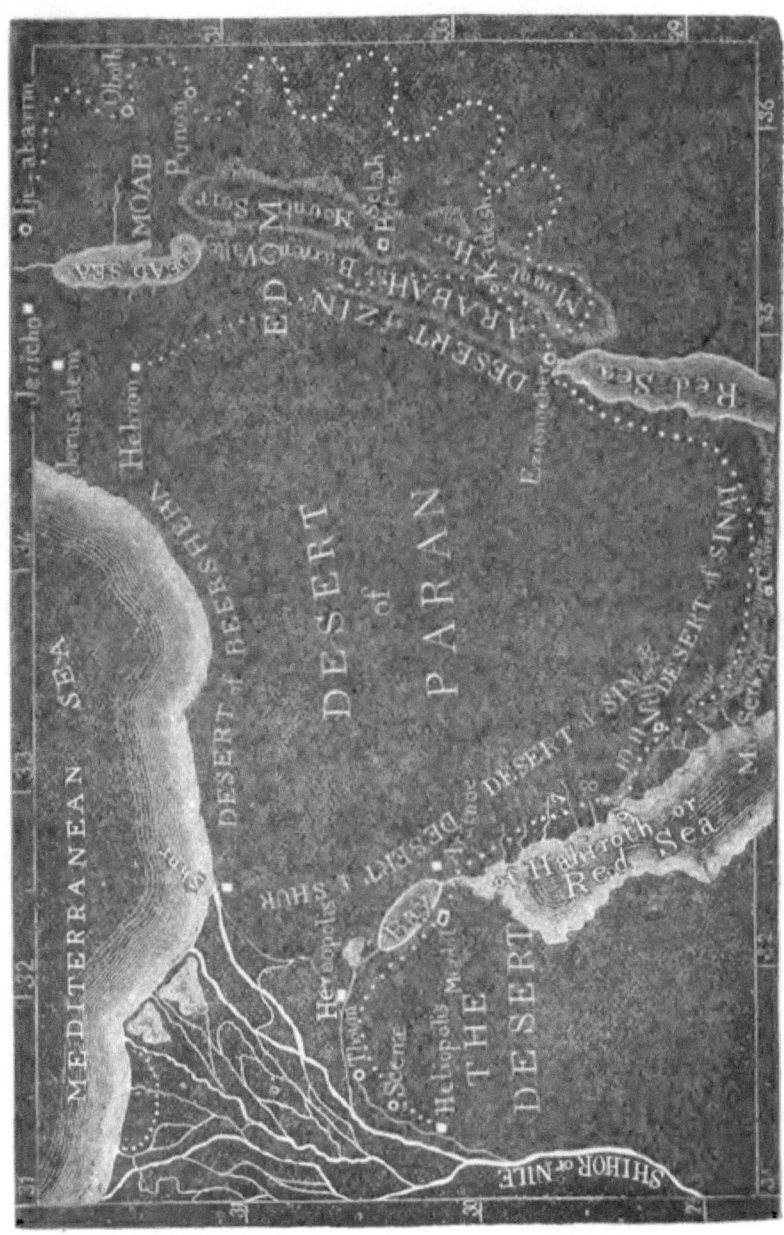

Fig. 52.—Map of the Peninsula of Sinai.

road to Pelusium; and his third day's march was eastward, towards Hiroth or Heroopolis, along a valley, through which the waters of the Nile sometimes flow during the height of the inundation, and through which Necho's canal was afterwards dug. From Hiroth the shortest way out of Egypt was on the north side of the Lower Bitter Lakes, and thence along the shore of the Mediterranean, through the desert to Gaza and the land of the Philistines. But the Egyptians were close in the rear, and the Israelites, to save themselves, had to quit the high road. They turned southward over the uneven sand-hills, and rested the third night, to their great disappointment, on the Egyptian side of the water. They encamped between the sea and a small hill fortress named Migdol, *the Tower*. This is perhaps the castle of Adjrud, on the shore of Pi-Hahiroth, *the Bay of Heroopolis*, or, according to modern maps, on the edge of the Upper Bitter Lake opposite to Baal-Zephon, the modern town of Arsinoë. On this southward march all doubt of their fate seemed at an end. They had lost all chance of finding fresh water. On one side was the salt sea, before them and on the other side was the boundless desert, and behind them were the Egyptian chariots, each carrying three soldiers (see Fig. 53). The

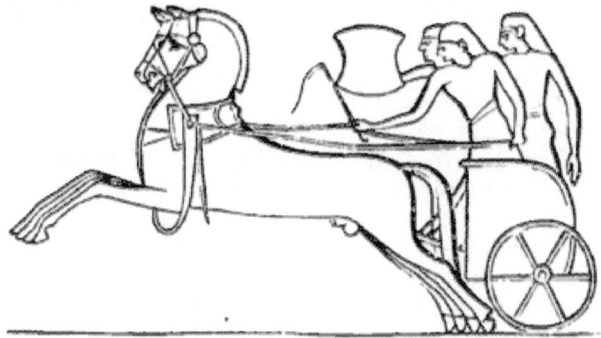

Fig. 53.

encroaching sands, which have since left the Greek towns of Arsinoë and Clysma at a distance from the head of the gulf, had not then divided the waters, and cut off the northern tongue of the Egyptian sea. Hence, when the Jews turned southward from Hiroth, which was then near the head of the gulf to which it gave its name, they seemed to the pursuing army to be hemmed in between the sea and the desert. But other destinies awaited them; they were a people for a purpose. Moses led them southward along the coast during the fourth day; and at night they found a way of escape which they had little hoped for. As they murmured in discontent against their leader, "the Lord caused the sea to go back by means of a strong east wind all that night, and he made the sea dry land, and the waters were divided. And the Israelites went through the sea on dry ground, and the waters were a wall to them on their right hand and on their left." The Egyptian army rashly followed in the morning. But the wind had fallen, perhaps the tide was rising; the waters suddenly returned, and their forces were overthrown and drowned. This most interesting place we recognise in a spot which, by the encroachment of the sand, has been left dry since the days of Isaiah. Here the hardened sand forms a bank which, though less than two miles wide, and only a foot or two above the high water, now blocks out the Red Sea, and divides the Bitter Lake from the gulf. From the situation of the town of Hiroth, the Israelites could not have appeared hemmed in, when half a day's march to the south of that city, if the lake had been separated from the gulf as it is now. The account of their march seems written with careful geographical accuracy; we have no more certain method of trying the truth of what an ancient historian relates than by examining his geography and natural history.

<small>Isaiah, xi. 15.</small>

(10) After passing the Red Sea the Israelites turned southward along the coast towards Mount Sinai, and the natural features of this desert peninsula are so unchanging that their path may yet be traced, and their halting-places fixed with much probability. The traveller now meets with the same springs of brackish water, the same clumps of stunted palms, the same spot where quails can live, and the same watered valley in which he can refresh himself after his thirsty journey over scorching sands and rocks. The road was well known to Moses, who had married a wife from the valleys at the foot of Sinai, and had thence come up to the rescue of his countrymen. After three days in the desert, part of

<small>Exodus, xv. xvi. xvii. Bartlett's Forty Days in the Desert.</small>

which time may have been spent at the little oasis now called the Wells of Moses, the Israelites came to some water, which from its bitterness they called Marah. [Exodus, xv. 23.] This may have been at Howarah, a bitter unwholesome pool, at which, however, a thirsty camel will not refuse to drink. The twelve wells and seventy palm-trees of Elim, the next resting-place on their [ch. xv. 27.] march, may be the valley of Ghurundel, which is not without some shade. Here they stayed several weeks. They then turned to the edge of the coast, and [Numbers, xxxiii. 10.] travelled for some time over the wet sands by the "way of the sea," at a place where the traveller now is pressed on to the shore by the head of the mountain range (see Fig. 54). They passed the little cove or port from which

Fig. 54.

the miners perhaps shipped their copper to Egypt, which has left its name in the Valley Taibeh. The road then turns from the coast; and it brought them to the watering-place of El Murkhah, where they met with [Exodus, ch. xvi. 13.] numerous quails or partridges of the desert, which still glad the hungry traveller in those barren regions. They then entered the narrow scorching valley of Mokatteb, [ch. xvii. 1.] which they called Rephidim, between bare granite rocks, without water and without shade. This is one of the most distressing parts of this thirsty journey, and it was here that they met with an enemy to bar their passage. They were in the region of the Egyptian copper-mines, which were chiefly worked in the valley of Mugharah. They then rested at Dophkah, or *the Bruising Place*, where the rock _{Numbers, xxxiii. 12.} may have been pounded by the miners in order to clear away the useless stone from the valuable ore. They next rested near the burial-place of the miners, a spot yet marked by the tablets dedicated to the Egyptian gods, and dated in hieroglyphical writing by the names of the Egyptian kings (see Fig. 55). This was a dreary place to

Fig. 55.

encamp in, and they may well have named it the Burial-place of Taavah, or of *pleasure*, by slightly changing its _{Exodus, ch. xvii. 8.} Egyptian name, Tau, *the hills*. Near this is the valley of Mokatteb. They were now in direct march towards Feiran, where the Egyptian miners had formed a little village. In this parching valley they were opposed by a body of armed men, perhaps the miners with some soldiers, under the command of Amalek, perhaps the Egyptian commander of the place. But the Israelites routed the enemy and marched on. They then encamped at Hazeroth, *the village* of Paran, within the district of Mount Sinai, and among the palm-groves in the fertile well-watered valley of Feiran, where Moses had before dwelt with his father-in-law, the chief of the tribe. The valley of Feiran is a delightful little oasis in the middle of a terrible desert of rock and sand. Here, at the foot of Mount Serbal, water is abundant palms, dates, figs, and pomegranates bend overhead in wild luxuriance. Here, the sweet-tasting manna drops like gum from the hanging bows of the turfeh-trees. Here flocks may be fed and corn grown. In this little valley, one hundred

Fig. 56.

and twenty miles from the passage of the Red Sea, the Israelites probably made their longest stay, and may have received the law. In sight is Mount Serbal (see Fig. 56), part of the range of Sinai; and the peak of Serbal, called Shepher by the Israelites, in the eyes of our more judicious travellers, has a better claim to be

Numbers, xxxiii. 23.

thought the holy mount, the Sinai from which Moses delivered the commandments to the people, than the point called Mount Sinai by the monks, which is about a day's march to the east of this, the only habitable valley in the neighbourhood.

(11) In this valley, at the foot of the holy mount, perhaps near the temple of Sarbout el Cadem, Moses set up an altar to the Lord, which he called the Altar of Jehovah Nissi. In so calling it, he either borrowed the name of the place, or gave to the spot a name for the future. And it remained a sacred spot in the eyes of the Egyptians, as well as the Jews. The Mount Sinai of the Jews was probably the Mount Nissa of the Egyptians, described as a lofty mountain in Arabia between Phenicia and Egypt, the fabled dwelling-place of the god Osiris when a child, and the fancied origin of his Greek name Dio-Nysus.

<small>Exodus, ch. xvii. 15.</small>

<small>Diod. Sic. lib. i. 15.</small>

(12) After the defeat of Amalek near the copper-mines, the Israelites were beyond the power of the Egyptians. They were in the land of the Midianites, a tribe of Ishmaelites or Arabs, who held the southern part of the peninsula. This tribe was entirely friendly, for Moses had married the daughter of their chief. Under their guidance the next portion of the journey was made; and the Israelites moved forward, halting at about twenty known springs or resting-places, without hindrance or loss of their way, till they reached Ezion Geber, at the head of the Gulf of Akabah. To a less encumbered body of travellers this would have been only a ten days' journey. From hence they marched northward along the Arabah, the Barren Valley which runs from the Red Sea towards the Dead Sea. They halted at a spot which they called Kadesh, or *Holy*, from the spring of water which there gushed from the rock to bless their aching eyes and allay their thirst. Here they were leaving the land of the friendly Midianites, and entering upon the country of another tribe. Their Midianite guide refused to go any further with them. They therefore sent forward spies or scouts from Kadesh to learn the way, and to examine the country which lay before them. On the return of the spies with favourable tidings, they asked leave of the Edomites, who

<small>Numbers, ch. xxxiii.</small>

<small>ch. x. 29.
ch. xiii. 2, 26.
ch. xx. 14.</small>

held the country to the north of Ezion Geber, that they might continue their march northward through Wady Arabah, and pass by their fastnesses. But they were refused. They had been able to send forward the spies; but they were themselves unable to follow, as the Edomites were too strong to be attacked. They had therefore to return from Kadesh to the Gulf of Akabah, and to proceed towards the Land of Promise by a longer route on the east side of Mount Hor, without a guide, through an unknown country, and through hostile tribes. The rest of their journey, till they reached the land of Moab, was a long and painful wandering, called the forty years in the desert; and we are unable to trace the path which their own historian has hardly attempted to describe. But it is beyond the bounds of our history. With them there had gone out of Egypt a crowd of others, who by the Egyptian historian are called Phenician herdsmen, but by the Hebrew writer are named Mixt people, or Arabs. Numbers, ch. xiv. 33.

(13) If we would form an opinion of how many were the Israelites who left Egypt under the guidance of Moses, we must not trust to the numbers mentioned in the narrative. The circumstances of the later history seem to prove that this little band of heroes, the bearers of laws, of letters, and of civilisation to the banks of the Jordan, became only the rulers, the judges, the priests of the Hebrew nation, and not the nation itself. After crossing the Jordan under Joshua, they were 150 years before they conquered and united the scattered tribes of natives. They then became their nobles and landowners; and the work of civilisation was helped by the whole nation at last adopting the traditions of their rulers, and believing that they were of the same family. At length, in the time of David, every soul in the Hebrew nation fancied that he was a descendant from the family of Jacob, that the two ruling tribes of Ephraim and Manasseh were descended from Joseph, the prime minister of Egypt, and that the other tribes were descended from his brothers.

(14) How little could an Egyptian philosopher then have foreseen the destiny which awaited the despised Israelites whom his countrymen were driving out of Goshen! They carried with them a knowledge of God's government, of his goodness and love of goodness, with those views of our duties

to Him and to one another which follow on the belief of one maker and ruler of the world. The polytheists, to get over the difficulty of the origin of evil, imagined bad gods as well as good gods, and thus felt their devotion weakened, their gratitude divided, and their duty doubtful; they thought their conduct blamed by one while approved by another of their objects of devotion. Though an attempt to explain the origin of evil by the war between the old serpent and the human race finds a place in the book of Genesis, it formed no part of the Jewish philosophy; it belongs to the legend on the Egyptian sarcophagus. That man fell from a state of innocence by tasting the forbidden fruit offered to him by woman, was an Egyptian, not a Jewish opinion. The Israelites knew no other cause for the origin of evil, as of good, but the Almighty's will. From a devout habit of tracing the hand of God in every event of life, the chronicles of their nation became religious lessons; and thus, while we owe to the Egyptians our first steps in physical science, we must grant to their Jewish servants the higher rank of being our first teachers in religion. Little could the Egyptian have perceived that the land of Goshen would possess an historic interest which Thebes and Memphis would want, and that the history of Egypt would be chiefly valued for the light which it throws upon the history of these persecuted Israelites.

(15) Among the sciences which the Israelites brought out of Egypt was the use of an alphabet and the art of writing, in which they soon surpassed their teachers, as far as in the more important matters of religion and philosophy. The Egyptian hieroglyphics, which were at first a syllabic method of writing, were never further improved than to add the use of letters to that of syllables. In their enchorial writing, their running hand, used on papyrus for less ornamental purposes, as they had a number of characters to choose from, they laid aside the more cumbersome, and made all the strokes of one thickness with a reed pen. Unfortunately their religion led them to forbid changes and attempts at reform, and hence they continued the use of the old hieroglyphics in all those ornamental and more careful writings which would be likely to improve the characters; and the enchorial writing was only used as a running hand. Nor

did this last ever reach the simplicity of a modern alphabet. The square letters of the Hebrews (see Fig. 57) are taken directly from the hieroglyphics; and it is to them that the world owes the great discovery that symbols should never be used, and that an alphabet is improved by having only one character for each sound. From the Egyptians also they borrowed the names of some of the letters, such as Teth, Nun, Pe, Tau, the Egyptian for *hand, water, heavens,* and *hill*. For others they copied the Egyptian plan of naming them after the objects which they seemed to represent, though without regarding what the Egyptian sculptors had meant them to represent. The Israelites had wondered at the vast Egyptian buildings, but made no attempt to copy them. They had lived within sight of the great pyramids, and might have learned when and why they were built; but they contented themselves with remarking that there were giants in those days. The Jewish philosophy and religion were not natives in the valley of the Nile. Among the Jews trade was discouraged and interest of money forbidden; women were not admitted into the priesthood; rewards for goodness and punishments for crime were looked for in this life, not after death; and mysteries in religion were as foreign to them as the notion that the earth could be flooded by rain from heaven was to the Egyptians. The Levitical threat that our crimes should be followed by misfortunes in this world may seem to fall short of the Egyptian trial of the dead, which told of an unseen reward or punishment awaiting every man after death; but it was no doubt wisely judged that coarser minds need the threat of speedier punishment, and indeed we all feel that our acts as certainly meet with their just rewards now as they will hereafter. But upon the whole,

Fig. 57.

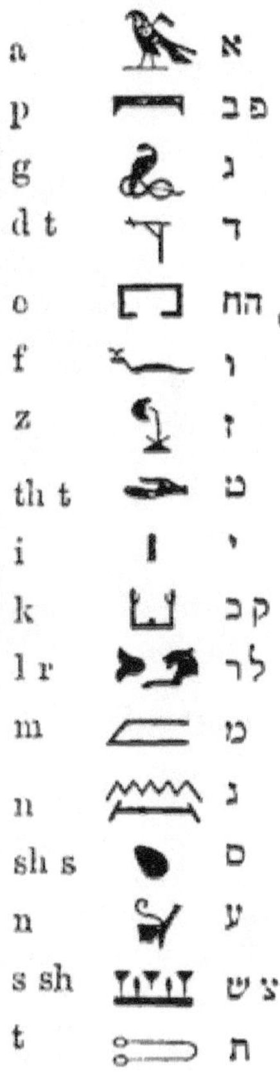

Hebrew Letters, with their Hieroglyphic originals.

VOL. I.   F

Heliopolis received as much science and philosophy from the east as it sent back.

(16) We must not hope to find among the Egyptians many traces of what they in return may have learned from the Israelites; the opinions and manners of a small and enslaved people would have little weight with a great nation. The Coptic language is indeed sprinkled with Hebrew words; but they may have been learnt from the Arabs, or from the Jews in after centuries. We are able to trace, from the names for several of the Egyptian months, that it was through the Hebrews or their language that the Egyptians gained some of their astronomical knowledge from Babylon, the birth-place of that science. Though the months Thoth and Athur are named after the Egyptian gods, and Phamenoth after King Amunothph, yet Pachon or Bethon, the month *of increase;* Payni or Beni, the month *of fruits;* Epiphi or Abib, the month *of corn in ear*, are clearly Hebrew names, and describe the seasons in which those months fell about the time of the reformation of the calendar; while Mechir or Mether, the month *of rain*, proves that these names were brought from Babylon, or Syria, as this last cannot have been a native of Egypt, where rain is nearly unknown. The names of the months do not, however, help us to fix the date of the Exodus.

Exodus, ch. xiii. 4; ch. xii. 2. The Israelites left Egypt in the month Abib or Epiphi, which was by the Mosaic law declared to be the first month of the Jewish year; but it was not till a few years before the reign of David that the first day of the month of Abib really became in Egypt so early as the spring equinox; so that this does not settle when the event took place, but only when that part of the narrative was written. Moses lived, say the genealogies of the Old Testament, three generations after Joseph, and seven before David, which is the best clue that we possess to the dates of these early events.

B.C. 1300.

(17) The hieroglyphical inscriptions, which enable us to determine the ages in which the various remains of early civilisation were made, disappoint us in telling but little more. It would seem that every other art and science had reached what must have been thought perfection before the art of history was invented; our pages during these years contain little more than a list of kings' names, and of the temples

which were built in their reigns. It may be that while, from the want of history, other deeds were to live only during the memory of one or two short-lived races of men, buildings seemed the chief means of gaining lasting fame and honour.

Fig. 58. Fig. 59.

(18) Thothmosis IV. (see Fig. 58) succeeded Amunothph II. He built the small temple between the forelegs of the huge sphinx near Memphis, which is now always buried in the sands except when the enterprise of an European traveller has it dug open to the light of heaven (see Fig. 59). Within the temple is the figure of Thothmosis worshipping the sphinx; so that in this reign at least, though probably much earlier, the rock had been carved into the form of that monster. He also built a temple, five hundred miles above the cataract of Syene, at El Birkel, or Napata, the capital of Ethiopia. On his death, his widow Mautmes (see Fig. 60) governed the kingdom during the childhood of her son. On the walls of the palace at Luxor we have a sculpture representing the miraculous birth of this son (see Fig. 61). In the first place, Queen Mautmes is receiving a message from heaven through the god Thoth, that she is to give birth to a child. Then the god Kneph, *the spirit*, takes her by the hand, and with the goddess Athor puts into her, through her mouth, life for the child that is to

Tablet of Abydos. Young's Hieroglyp. pl. 80.

Wilkinson, Thebes.

Fig. 60.

be born. She is then placed upon a stool, after the custom of the Egyptian mothers, as mentioned in the book of Exodus. ^{ch. i. 16.} While seated there, two nurses chafe her hands to support her against the pains of child-birth; and the new-born child is held up beside her by a third nurse. In another place the priests and nobles are saluting their future king. In this way the sculpture declares that the young king had no earthly father; and it explains what ^{Diod. Sic. lib. i. 47.} was meant by the royal title of Son of Amun-Ra, and also how the Greeks came to be afterwards told that the Egyptian queens were Jupiter's concubines.

(19) AMUNOTHPH III. (see Fig. 62), her son, though not one of the greatest Egyptian kings, is one of those best known, ^{Tablet of Abydos. Denon, pl. 44.} from his celebrated musical statue. It is one of two colossal figures, each above fifty feet high, sitting side by side in the plain opposite Thebes, having their feet washed

Fig. 61.—The Birth of King Amunothph III.

every autumn by the inundation, and every morning casting their long shadows on the white Libyan hills. They sit in front of a small temple built by this king. The most northerly of these is the sacred statue, and after the fall of the city it was visited by travellers as one of the chief wonders in that wonderful country, to hear the musical sounds which it uttered every morning at sunrise. As a work of sculpture it is not unlike the smaller statues in the British Museum (see Fig. 63), which

Fig. 62.

were made in the same reign; and from them we may learn the state to which the arts had then reached. Their attitudes are all simple, and, whether sitting or standing, they are in straight lines, and looking straight forward. If they are standing, their hands hang down on each side; if they are sitting, they rest on the knees. The bodies are without motion, and the faces without expression. The hands and feet are badly formed, the beard stiff, the limbs round, with only a few of the larger muscles marked, and the drapery is without folds. But nevertheless there is a great breadth in the parts, a justness in the proportions, and a grandeur in the simplicity. At a little distance the faults are not seen; and, as there is nothing mean or trifling to call

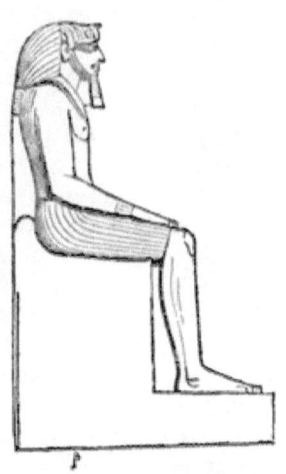

Fig. 63.

off the eye from judging the whole, they never fail to please the skilful beholder, and have at all times been praised by the best judges, ancient as well as modern. They teach us the superiority of rest over action, if we would represent the dignified and the sublime in art. But the sculptors wished their work to be lasting rather than beautiful; they made them not of white marble but of red granite or coarse gritstone. Amunothph III. also began one of the great temples of Thebes, now called the temple of Luxor (see Fig. 64), and made large additions to the older temple of Karnak, to which it formerly was

Wilkinson, Thebes.

joined by an avenue of sphinxes half a mile long. He built
the small temple of Kneph at Elephantine. His
_{Egypt.
Inscrip.
2nd Ser.
pl. 25, 26.} wars and victories on the south
of Egypt are recorded in a boast-
ful way on the pedestal of one of
his statues, where more than thirty Negro
prisoners with thick lips and bushy hair
stand with their arms tied behind, and each
bears the name of a conquered district of
Ethiopia. His name is found above the
granite district of the second cataract
oftener than that of any other Egyptian
king; and he ornamented the temple
of Soleb with statues and sphinxes of red
granite, worked by Egyptian sculptors in the
quarries near Tombos at the third cataract.

(20) The Egyptian columns were for the
most part formed like a cluster of four or
eight stalks of papyrus bound together by
cords, and having a capital formed by the
same number of buds of the plant. Such
are the columns in Amunothph's temples
in Thebes and in Soleb in Ethiopia (see
Fig. 65). But in the temples built by
this monarch we also find the earliest
instances of columns formed like one

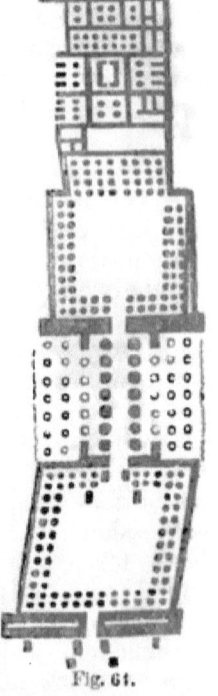

Fig. 64.

monstrously thick stalk of papyrus (see Figs. 66 and 67), small
at the base, and swelling wider from the ground, with a bud or
flower for the capital. The architecture of all nations shows
many of the peculiarities of their country, climate, and
customs. The Chinese palace is copied from the tents in
which the chief of the Tartar tribes encamps when with his
army; the Greek portico is copied from the wooden roof of
the cottage, upheld by trunks of trees; and the more pointed
roof of the Gothic cathedral is fitted to the rainy weather of
our northern climate. So the portico to an Egyptian temple
seems to be taken from the entrance to one of their tombs
quarried into the side of the limestone hills. The covered
part of the building is always low and solid; the walls are
thicker at the base, so that the sides slope inward like a
pyramid; and to point out more clearly to the eye this

strongest of forms, the door-posts are set upright. The hieroglyphics and sculptured figures, with which the face of

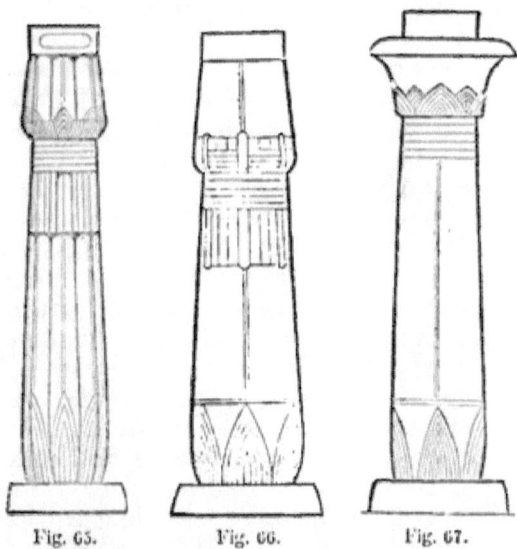

Fig. 65.　　　Fig. 66.　　　Fig. 67.

the walls is covered, are so slightly cut that they take nothing from the solidity, but rather remind us of it. To increase this massive look by means of contrast, two light and lofty obelisks are placed before the door. The thickness of the solid roof is shown by the overhanging cornice and its shadow; but on entering the door-way this mass of stone-work seems yet more heavy, when the eye measures the gigantic columns, which are set almost as thick as they can stand to uphold it. The aim of the builder was to produce grandeur by means of vast weight, and of yet more vast strength in the supports. A nation that made temples so grand, cannot have been blind to the grandeur of a good action. Men who allowed no false ornament in a statue, must have disliked the sight of meanness in behaviour. Such temples and such statues, whether standing or in ruins, raise high ambitious thoughts in the minds of many that see them, and they send some away with resolves to serve their country and their fellow-creatures, and with the wish to build for themselves a virtuous fame, by taking pains in some great work.

(21) By some tie or other, whether friendly or unfriendly, Amunothph III. of Thebes was closely allied to the cities in the eastern half of the Delta. He styled himself lord of Mendes, and ornamented his temple at Thebes with a row of colossal statues of the cat-headed goddess Pasht, who was more particularly the goddess of the city of Bubastis. On the base of each he is said to be beloved by this goddess, who is otherwise so little known in Upper Egypt.

(22) Amunothph's tomb is one of the oldest of the royal tombs near Thebes, and is a set of rooms, above three hundred feet long, tunnelled into the hill. The tomb of his wife Taia is also found in the valley of queens' tombs. They were both worshipped as gods, as we learn from a slab in the British Museum, where King Amunothph and his Queen Taia are seated with Osiris; while the goddess Isis is left standing beside them. In this reign, the quarries near Syene were actively worked for the hard black stone which, from the name of that town, is still called syenite. They had probably not been before opened. The quarries of red granite had been opened four reigns earlier, and had hitherto furnished the stone for the royal statues. But in this and the next reign a large number of statues were made of this very hard black stone; and to this time we may probably assign most of the syenite statues of gods and priests which have no king's name upon them; as in three reigns later, the better taste of the sculptors led them back to the granite quarries.

(23) The next king, AMUNMAI ANEMNEB, or Hor-nemneb (see Fig. 68), if we may thus venture to write his name, has left a large grotto among the sandstone quarries near Silsilis, on the walls of which he has recorded his victories over the Ethiopians. He is represented in a car, pursuing with bended bow the flying enemy, who after their defeat beg for peace; and in another picture he is leading home his prisoners in triumph. Near Abou Simbel, in Ethiopia, is a small temple dedicated to Knef and Amun-Ra, which was cut out of the rock by this king. We have two of his statues in

Fig. 68.

Tablet of Abydos. Wilkinson, Thebes.

the British Museum. One is in a group of the king with the god Chem, who holds his arm over him as his guardian; in the other, the king is himself in the character of Hapimou, the Nile god.

(24) As the neighbourhood of the Phenicians had a good deal changed the eastern half of the Delta, so the western half was not a little coloured by Greek civilisation. It would seem that there had been from the earliest times an important settlement of Greek traders, or pirates, near Sais, in the Delta, who carried on the Egyptian trade on the Mediterranean. They lived under their own laws and magistrates, and made themselves independent of the kings of Egypt; and Manetho, seeing that, like the Phenicians, they had gained a forcible settlement, calls them Greek shepherds, without noticing the difference in their way of life. He gives to their petty chiefs the name of kings; and says that they reigned in Egypt for upwards of five hundred years. The overthrow of this little state probably took place in the reign of Amunmai Anemneb, and the chiefs driven out of Egypt carried with them to Greece so much that was valuable of Egyptian science and civilisation, that many of the Grecian cities dated their foundation from their arrival. The fabulous or half-fabulous founders, Erechtheus of Athens, Cadmus of Bœotian Thebes, and Danaus of the whole Greek nation, were said to have then arrived from Egypt. But whatever may have been the names of the heroes driven away from Sais, they gave to Greece its architecture and some of its mythology, and the knowledge of an alphabet (see Fig. 69); and so willing were the Greeks at all times to look back to Lower Egypt as the birth-place of their civilisation, that, instead of seeing that a handful of Greeks had

Manetho.

Diod. Sic. lib. v. 58. lib. i. 23.

Fig. 69.

Greek Letters, with their Hieroglyphic originals.

in old times settled in the Delta, they thought Athens itself a colony from Sais. Thus, at this period of Egyptian history, when we have traced the chronology of the Theban kings for many hundred years, we are only entering on the fabulous ages of Greece, about four generations before the Trojan war, a war by which the Greeks of the Peloponnesus, who were then becoming more settled, undertook to punish the piracies of their neighbours on the coast of Asia Minor. From Egypt, the Greeks borrowed many of their religious opinions about the state of the soul after death, as we see from the Egyptian words which had been taken into the Greek language even before the time of Homer. From Charo, *silent*, they took the name of Acheron, the river in hell, and Charon, the boatman on that river; from Amenti, the place of the dead, Rhad-amanthus, *the king of the dead;* from King Menes, Minos, another judge of the dead; from Kabiri, *the punishing gods*, the dog Cerberus; and from Thmei, *justice*, Themis, the goddess of justice. The Egyptians, like the Hindoos, looked on the sea, and voyages by sea, with religious dread, and they held all seafaring persons in dislike as impious. This increased the natural jealousy with which they guarded the mouths of the river, and drove these foreigners, who were more often pirates than merchants, from their inhospitable coast, and it gave rise to the tradition that they burned all shipwrecked strangers upon the altar of Busiris. It was not till the seat of government was moved to Sais, that the people of Lower Egypt, who in blood, as in their prejudices, were half Phœnicians, ventured on foreign trade, or had any willing intercourse with their Mediterranean neighbours.

Diod. Sic. lib. i. 67.

Virgil, Georg. iii. 5.

Fig. 70.

Fig. 71.

(25) RAMESES I. (see Fig. 70) reigned next; but we know nothing of him but his tomb in the valley of kings' tombs near Thebes.

Tablet of Abydos. Wilkinson, Thebes.

(26) The name of his son and successor is variously written in the hieroglyphics. One of the more usual forms is Osirimenpthah, or OIMENEPTHAH (see Fig.

71); and it may be at the same time the name Osymundyas of the historian Diódorus, and Ammenephthes of Manetho, and Chomaeptha of Eratosthenes. At one time, the first letter in his name was a sitting Abyssinian dog, with large square ears and upright bushy tail (see Fig. 72). This was the vowel A or O. But later in his

Tablet of Abydos.

Fig. 72.

reign, on some change in religion or politics, this dog was ordered to be chiselled out of all his inscriptions from the south of Ethiopia to Tanis in the Delta. In its place was carved either a hawk for an A, or a sitting figure of the god Osiris for an O. Hence the difficulty about his name. In his tomb it is spelt with the sitting Osiris.

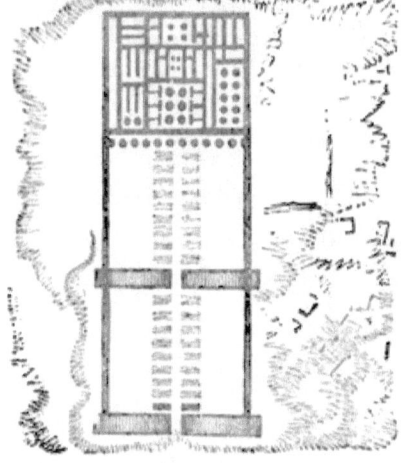

(27) Thebes being no longer the chief city of a province, but now the capital of the whole kingdom, was steadily increasing in size and magnificence. There Oimenepthah built a new temple at Rebek, now the village of Quorneh, which, though smaller than some of the Theban temples, is built upon what may be called the usual plan (see Fig. 73). In front of the roofed building are two square courts, one before the other. The doorway to

Wilkinson, Thebes.

Fig. 73.

each is between two lofty towers, which guard the entrance; and each court is crossed between double rows of sphinxes. This leads to the portico of ten columns (see Fig. 74),

Fig. 74.—The Temple at Quorneh.

behind which is a hall; and out of the latter are the passages into the several rooms on each side and beyond. The portico in this temple is open to the view of all who had been admitted into the courtyard, whereas we shall see in those built afterwards that the spaces between the columns were closed with a dwarf wall, so that the profane vulgar could no longer see what took place within. Oimenepthah also added the great Hall of Columns to the temple of Karnak; and the sculptures on its walls are in the best style of Egyptian art. We may there see painted in the liveliest colours the king's conquest of the people whom we have before called Lydians. He drives his chariot into the thickest of the fight (see Fig. 75). He storms their city

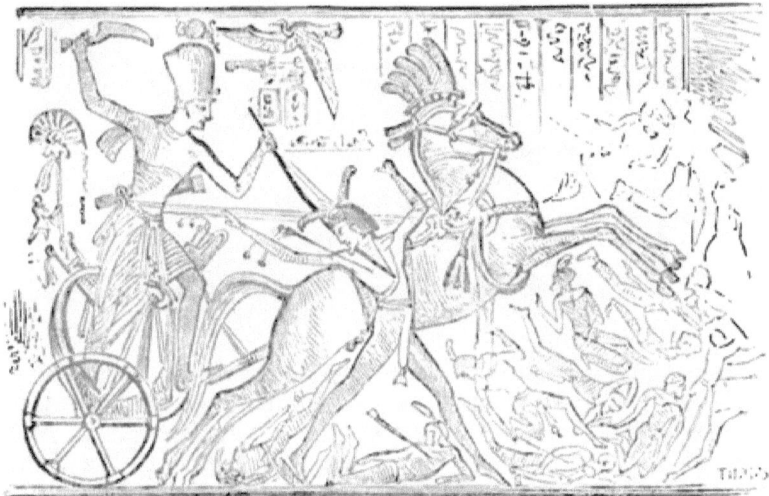

Fig. 75.

among the mountains, and leads back his prisoners in triumph to the temple of Amun-Ra. The River Nile is known in the picture by the crocodiles swimming about in it; and the bridge over it is perhaps the earliest met with in history. This king also built a temple and a palace at Abydos, once the capital and then the second city of Upper Egypt. Here he sculptured a list of the kings his predecessors on the throne, to the number of seventy-five, but of these the fifty-seven earlier can claim no place in history. They have left no monuments, and which of them ever reigned in Thebes, or even ever lived, must remain doubtful. The temple was dedicated to Osiris; and the palace, taking its name from the next king, who finished it, was by the Greeks called the

78 OIMENEPTHAH I. [CHAP. II.

Memnonium. Each of these buildings was at the same time a temple, a palace, and a convent for a body of priests.

(28) This king's tomb near Thebes is the most beautiful in Egypt; and as it escaped the search of the Greeks, Romans, and Arabs, it was, when opened by the enterprising Belzoni, in our own days, in the same state of freshness as when closed on the death of its owner. After entering the side of the hill with a torch in your hand, and passing down a staircase of twenty-nine feet (see Fig. 76), through a

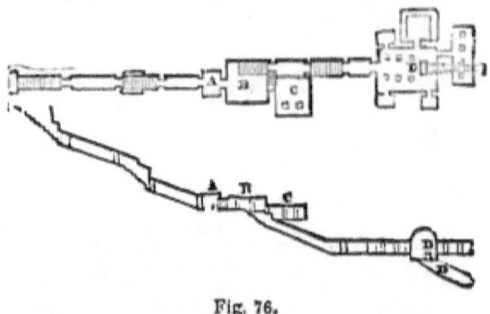

Fig. 76.

passage of eighteen feet, a second staircase of twenty-five feet, and a second passage of twenty-nine feet, you reach a small room (A), from which you enter the first grand hall (B), of about twenty-six feet square, having its roof upheld by four square pillars. A few steps then lead into a second hall of the same size (c). After returning into the first hall, then descending a third staircase, and passing through a passage and fourth staircase and a smaller room, you enter the third and largest hall, of twenty-seven feet square (D); and then, lastly, a small vaulted room beyond, in which once stood the alabaster sarcophagus of the king, which is now in Sir John Soane's Museum. With the sarcophagus had been buried a sacred bull and many hundred small images made of wood, in the form of mummies, which were there placed by the mourners at the funeral in token of their grief.

<small>Egyptian Inscript. pl. 71.</small>

(29) The walls of these caverns are covered with painted and highly-finished sculptures, and several curious fables. There are several groups of figures, each representing the

king embracing a god, placing his right arm in a loving manner round the god's neck (see Fig. 77). These are important, because unusual. Most pagan nations have boasted that they were beloved by their gods; but here we see the Egyptians, with a more religious

Belzoni, pl. 4 & 5.

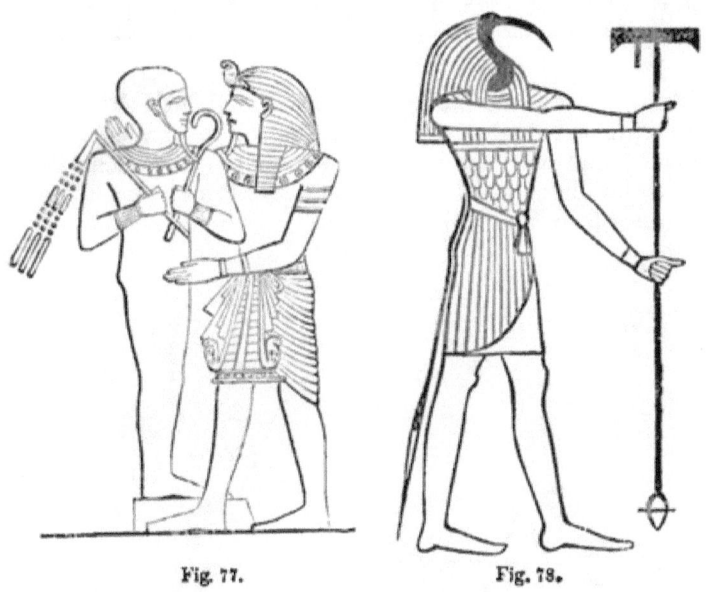

Fig. 77.   Fig. 78.

feeling, professing to love their gods in return. The Hebrew writers have explained to us the opinion of the ancients, that as long as a man's family was prosperous, his star remained in its place like a lamp hung up in the sky, only to be removed when his descendants came to ruin. On this king's sarcophagus we see the god Thoth, known by his ibis-shaped head (see Fig. 78), hanging up on the vault of heaven the all-important lamp, which was to give a light to the king's sons for ever. On the sarcophagus also there is the conquest of the Eternal Serpent, the great enemy of the human race, whose conquerors bear along his lengthy folds in solemn procession (see Fig. 79). There also within a garden are seen the river which divides life from death, and the bridge of life, and the keepers of that important bridge; there

2 Chron. xxi. 7.
Egyptian Inscript. pl. 61-67.

also are the tombs of the dead, their doors, and the keepers of those doors. The god Osiris is there sitting to judge

Fig. 79.

mankind, who are mounting up the steps of his lofty throne; before him are the great scales to weigh the conduct of the dead; and beneath his feet are the wicked men labouring with hatchets, as if condemned to work in the Egyptian gold mines (see Fig. 80).

Fig. 80.

(30) That solemn trial of every man for his conduct in this life, which was to fix his reward or punishment in the next, was enacted by the priests as part of the funeral cere-

mony (see Fig. 81). They put on masks distinctive of the several gods, and thus received the body in due form.

Osiris sat on a raised throne holding his two sceptres, and wearing the crown of Upper Egypt. Before him were placed the offerings, and near him were seated the four lesser gods of the dead. The deceased holds up his hands in prayer, and is introduced by two goddesses, each wearing on her head the emblem of truth. The wicked Typhon, as an hippopotamus, the Cerberus of the Greeks, accuses him to the judge, and demands that he shall be punished; while the four lesser gods of the dead intercede as advocates or mediators on his behalf. But a large pair of scales is set up, which is quietly adjusted by the dog-headed Anubis and the hawk-headed Horus. In one scale is placed the heart or conduct of the deceased, and in the other a figure of the goddess of truth. A small weight is moved along the beam by Horus, to make the two scales balance, and to determine how much the conduct falls short of the standard weight. Forty-two assessors are at hand to assist Osiris in forming his judgment, which when pronounced is written down by the ibis-headed Thoth. Thus are measured the goodness and the failings of the life lately ended. Those who were too uncultivated to listen to a sermon might thus learn wisdom from what they saw with their eyes, and this ceremony was a forcible method of teaching the ignorant

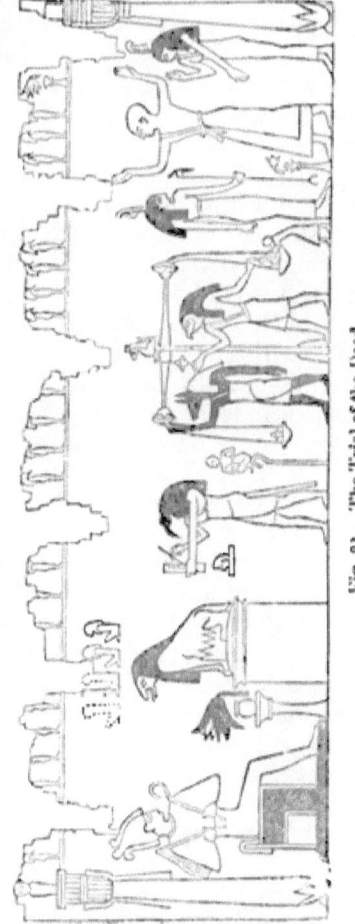

Fig. 81.—The Trial of the Dead.

Denon, pl. 141.

multitude that a day of judgment awaits us all after death, and that we should so regulate our lives that when weighed in the great balance they may not be found wanting. But unfortunately the Egyptians had no full trust either in the justice or the mercy of their gods; and the paintings which represent this trial, which is to take place on the day of judgment, always tell us that for their acquittal they in part trusted to some atoning sacrifices, which are there represented in the form of a flower laid upon an altar before the judge, and another flower before the assessors who are to advise him.

(31) The reader must be weary of meeting with so little beyond a list of the temples, statues, obelisks, and tombs which were made in each king's reign, and be looking for more of life and manners by which history teaches while it amuses, and be wishing to learn something of the poetry and philosophy. The Egyptians cultivated these branches of learning, as all civilised nations have done; but unfortunately we are not likely to gain many traces of them from inscriptions on stone. Letters were only known in the more cumbersome form of hieroglyphics; papyrus had not yet been used for writing; and tradition was almost lost before history fixed its fading lines. Hence the buildings and statues are all that now remain to prove the greatness of a race of kings, whose names, if they had been celebrated by the poet and historian, would perhaps have thrown those of many modern lawgivers and conquerors into the shade. The buildings and statues, indeed, which a bygone people have left are a living witness, not less certain than poems and histories, to prove their greatness; while the writings on them show a noble consciousness of greatness. In Greece, while we may still trace the walls of Argos and Mycene, which sent forth their warriors to the Trojan war, and whose bard sung their victories, no ruins mark the spot where the less poetical Troy then stood. We still admire and copy the temples and statues of Athens, whose historian has related the wars with the Spartans; though scarcely a stone remains to point out the city of Sparta, which had no such historians. We turn with equal pleasure to the buildings and to the histories of ancient Rome; while Carthage is equally without ruins and without writings. Hence, if

Fig. 83.—The Hall of Columns at Karnak.

the Thebans have not left us a Homer, a Thucydides, or a Livy to place them in the first rank among cities, at any rate their buildings prove that they can have been very little below it.

(32) AMUNMAI RAMESES II. (see Fig. 82), the son of the last king, was the monarch under whom Upper Egypt rose to its greatest height in arms, in arts, and in wealth. Manetho calls him Sethos, *the king*, thus giving him as his proper name the royal title, which is written in hieroglyphics by means of a twig and half-circle. He finished the palace of the Memnonium or Miamunei, at Abydos, so called from his own name, Miamun or Amunmai. He also finished the temple of Osiris in the same city; and on one of the walls he carved that list of his forefathers and predecessors on the throne of Thebes which is now in the British Museum, and is known by the name of the Tablet of Abydos, a monument which has guided us safely in this history through seventeen reigns. He placed a second such list of kings' names in the temple of Pthah at Memphis. He added several large parts to Osirtesen's old temple at Karnak, and particularly he finished the great hall which had been begun by his father (see Fig. 83). Of this the roof is upheld by one hundred and thirty-four gigantic columns, of which the largest are forty-seven feet high. This is called the Hall of Columns. The larger columns have capitals copied from the full-blown papyrus plant, and the smaller columns from the unopened buds of the same plant. In front of the hall he built the large courtyard, with its two large towers which guard its entrance. He added also a new courtyard and two lofty obelisks (see Fig. 84) to Amunothph's temple at Luxor, and he finished his father's temple at Rebek or Quorneh. Thus Thebes had already four large fortified temples or palaces—the three just mentioned and that of Queen Nitocris at Dahr el Bahree; and to these Rameses II. added a new palace, which had been begun by his father, and, like that at Abydos, was by the Greeks called the Memnonium. Diodorus calls it the tomb of his father Osymundyas or Osirimenpthah, in whose honour Rameses dedicated it to the god

Fig. 82.

Tablet of Abydos.
Wilkinson, Thebes.

Diod. Sic. lib. 1. 47.

Amun-Ra. In the first courtyard was a colossal statue of himself, larger than any other in Egypt, which measures twenty-two feet across the shoulders, and in the second yard were two smaller statues, from one of which was taken the colossal head now in the British Museum (see Fig. 2, page 5). The spacious rooms with the columns which once upheld the roofs, against each of which stands a mummy-shaped

Fig. 84. Fig. 85.

statue of the king (see Fig. 85), are still gazed on with wonder by our travellers, and were standing in all their glory when Hecatæus travelled in Upper Egypt; and he praises the inscription over the library door which called the books the medicine of the mind. In the Hall of Columns, as in that of the temple of Karnak, the larger columns have capitals copied from the full-blown papyrus plant, and the smaller columns from the unopened buds of the same plant (see Fig. 86). The largest columns in this temple, the Memnonium, are however only half the height of the largest in the temple of Karnak. On the ceiling of one of the rooms is carved a zodiac, divided into twelve parts, which

Diod. Sic. lib. i. 49.

Burton, pl. 58, 59.

THE ZODIAC IN THE MEMNONIUM.

bear the same names as the twelve months. Under each is the figure of the god to whom it was sacred. The place of the

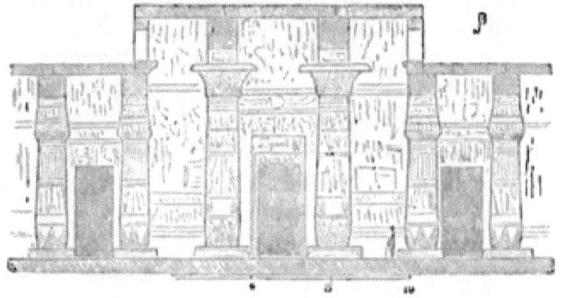

Fig. 86.

summer solstice is marked by an ape sitting on a boundary stone, to which he is driven by the rising waters (see Fig. 87). A little before this solstice is a star called the Bull's Eye—our Aldebaran—rising heliacally; and the beginnings of the four portions that follow the summer solstice are marked by the risings of the Dogstar (see Fig. 88) and three others— probably Regulus and Deneb in the Lion, and Spica Virginis. The figures of Typhon for the Great Bear, and of Orion throwing his dart at the Bull (see Fig. 89), were already used in

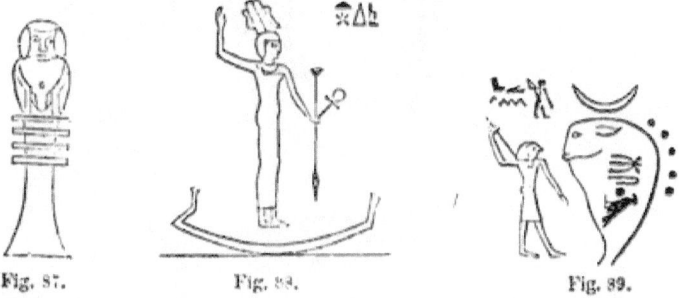

Fig. 87. Fig. 88. Fig. 89.

mapping out the stars. If this sculpture could be quoted to prove that the moving new-year's day of the civil year was the day of the Dogstar's rising, it would fix the date when it was made; but no such exactness can be seen in it; it rather proves the rudeness of the observations by which the astronomers learned the length of the year. They noted the longest day, and the days when the great stars were first seen to rise at daybreak. They had not yet learned the use of a gnomon in the line of the earth's pole, and the more exact observation of noting the time of the equinox.

(33) The temple of the Memnonium is surrounded at the back and at the two sides by vaults built of unburnt bricks, which would seem to have been each a dwelling for one of the priests of lower rank. They are about 130 in number (see Fig. 90). A smaller number of priests of higher rank,

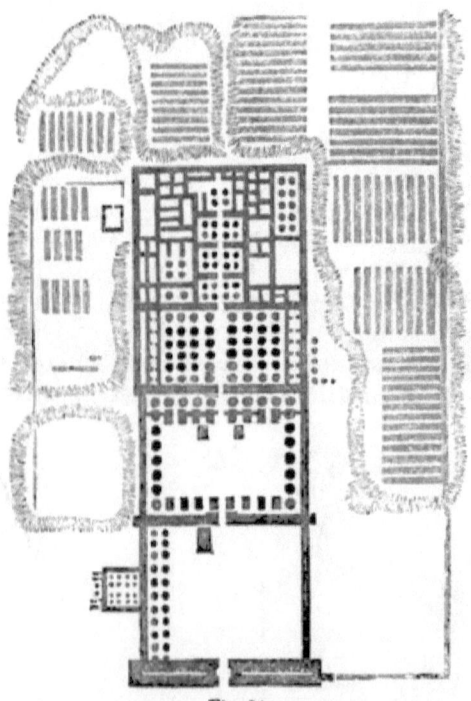

Fig. 90.

perhaps twenty, may have lived within the temple, in the small rooms around the sanctuary. The duty of these priests, who were maintained at the public expense, was to make sacrifices and offer prayers on behalf of the nation, in order to win the favour of the gods. The king, as head of the priesthood, also took the same duty upon himself. The sculptures on the columns and walls are chiefly employed in declaring the king's unwearied attention to the duty of making offerings to the various gods (see Fig. 91). Many of his statues represent him on his knees holding up either a shrine, the model of a temple, or a basin to receive the offerings and libations. In this way he was supposed to return the nation's thanks for blessings received, and to make atonement for the sins of the people; and the sculptures may be said to state his claim to the gratitude of the nation for so doing.

(34) Besides the temples and colossal statues of this king, we find a countless number of smaller works bearing his name, such as statues of priests, votive basins, and funereal tablets from the tombs. Of no other king whatever is the name so often met with on the monuments. This, however, partly arises from the nation continuing his series of dates for some few years after his death; as we must suppose that tablets dated in the 62nd year of Rameses II. were made

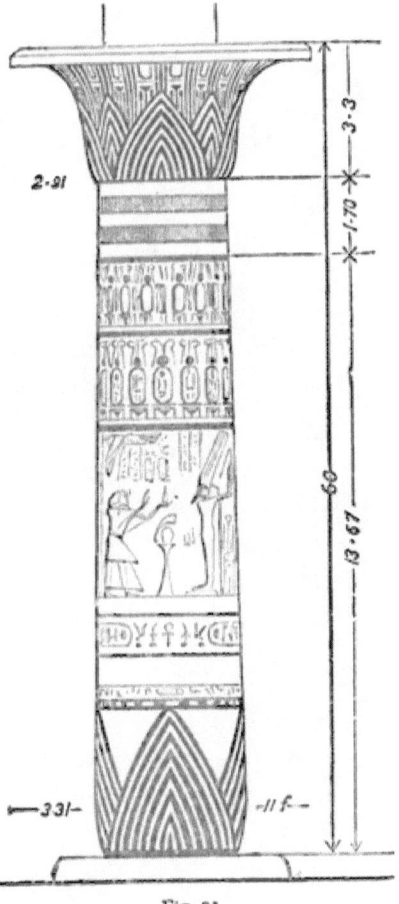

Fig. 91.

under one of his successors, more particularly as Rameses is therein said to be beloved by Osiris, the judge of the dead. The only works remaining at Memphis of this king are his overthrown colossal statue, which stood forty-five feet high, and a smaller statue of his son. The former is of limestone, and the largest known statue of that softer material. It may perhaps have been sculptured in Lower Egypt in the quarries of Toora. The latter is of granite. The yet larger granite statue which once stood in Memphis, of which

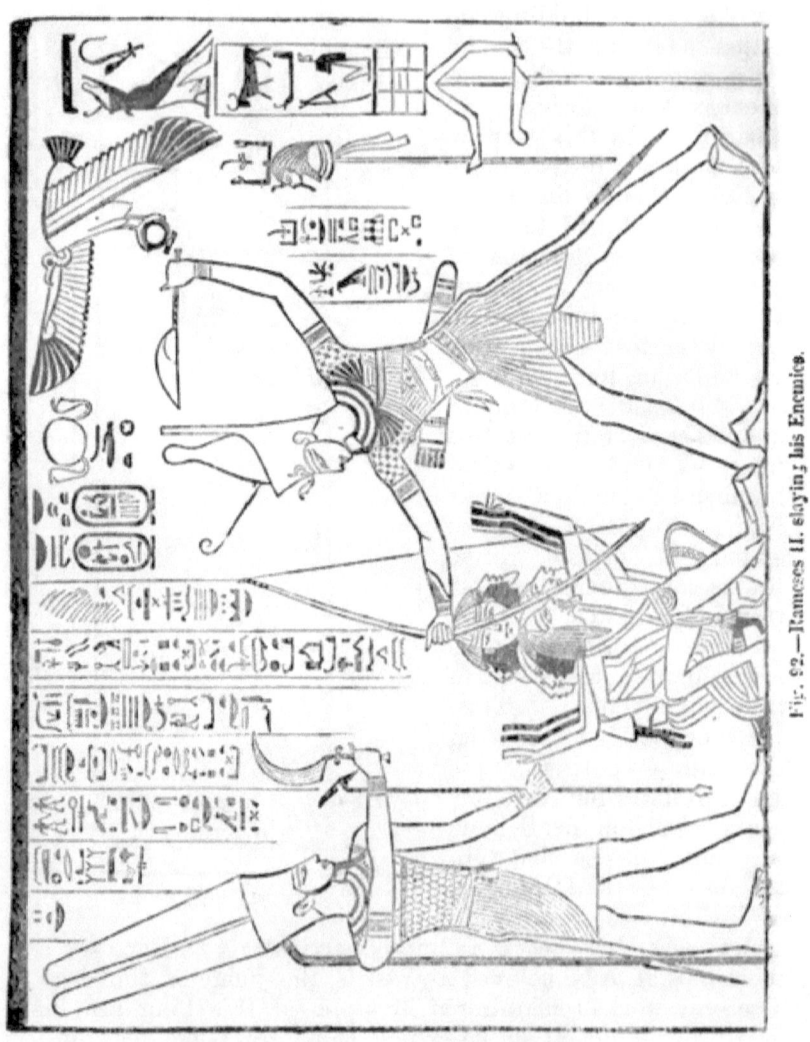

Fig. 82.—Rameses II. slaying his Enemies.

the fist is in the British Museum, was also probably of this king, though no name now remains to prove it.

(35) The Egyptian wars were now carried on, not as before, only against their neighbours of the desert and the southern part of the valley, but also against distant nations in Asia. Carved and painted on the walls of the temples of Thebes are the king's victories over Negroes and Ethiopians, over Arabs, and over a people whose single lock of hair on a shorn head proves that they were of a Tartar or Scythian race; he slays them to the honour of the god Amun-Ra (see Fig. 92), and the artists, not content, like Homer, with making the hero a head and shoulders taller than the soldiers around him, paint the conqueror many times as tall as the pigmy enemy whom he is destroying at a single blow (see Fig. 75). The hieroglyphics which were read to Germanicus in the reign of Tiberius re- Tacitus, Ann. ii. counted the Egyptian victories over the Libyans and Ethiopians of Africa, the Medes, Persians, Bactrians, Scythians, Syrians, and Armenians of the East, and the Cappadocians, Bythinians, and Lycians of Asia Minor, together with the weight of gold and silver, and the other gifts which these nations sent to Thebes as their yearly tribute. This inscription teaches at least that these nations were known by name in Thebes, though we cannot believe Rameses had overrun the lands of all. The more distant may have been allies in the service of those who were nearer to him; his battles with the Persians and Bactrians may have been fought on the banks of the Tigris. But the Egyptians in the pride of strength were raising up an enmity with the nations on the Tigris and Euphrates, which was to be the cause of unceasing wars, till the invaders were themselves invaded, and then Egypt sank under the struggle.

(36) The march of Rameses through Palestine, and the battles that he must have fought with the warlike Philistines, are not mentioned in the Old Testament; this may have arisen from his keeping close to the coast—a part of the country not then held by the Jews. The Hebrew nation was in its infancy, ruled over by its Judges, or living in servitude under the Canaanites. They had not yet gained possession of Jerusalem, their future capital, nor conquered the Philistines of the coast; and probably the march of the Egyptian army weakened the power of these enemies of the

Jews, and helped the latter to the conquest of Canaan. The overthrow of the iron power of the Philistines took place at about this time. Their forces may have been scattered and their strength broken by the Egyptian arms. The heroic struggles of Samson were made against the stragglers of a routed army, or a people whose soldiers were wanted in another quarter. The blank in the Hebrew writers, during the fifty years before the reign of Saul, may be partly filled by this passage from Egyptian history. Herodotus was told that the people of Colchis on the eastern shores of the Euxine Sea, to the south of the great chain of the Caucasus, were Egyptian in their language and manners, and that they were colonists who had been left behind there on the River Phasis by the Egyptian hero Sesostris on his return home from the conquest of Thrace. It is by no means unlikely that Rameses II., the widest of the Egyptian conquerors, should have marched to the foot of the Caucasus, even if the Colchians should not be allowed to have been Egyptians; but that he should have crossed into Europe and fought in Thrace is very improbable. On his return home he left behind him boastful monuments in the countries which he

Fig. 93.

conquered; and one of these still remains in Syria near Beyroot (see Fig. 93).

(37) The art of war was less rude among the Egyptians

CHAP. II.] THE ART OF WAR. 93

Fig. 94.—A Selected Group of Soldiers.

than among the neighbouring nations. The cities were fortified with moats, and walls, and wooden towers. Their standards were figures of animals raised on poles. The foot soldiers were chiefly archers, but some were armed with spears, some with battle-axes, and some only with clubs (see Fig. 94). The spears and arrows were tipped with metal. The men marched some in loose ranks, and others in a close square phalanx with the locked step; and the chiefs, like Homer's heroes, fought in chariots before the rest. Their best troops also fought in two-wheeled chariots drawn by a pair of horses; for though unarmed men sometimes rode on horseback, the horses in Egypt had not yet been bred large enough and strong enough to carry armed soldiers into battle. The chariots usually held three men, one to drive, and two to fight (see Fig. in p. 57); but the king's sons rode with only one companion in the chariot, and the king always rode alone (see Fig. 95). These war-

Fig. 95.

chariots and war-horses were the best known; and a little later Solomon supplied his army with them from Egypt. An Egyptian chariot cost him six hundred shekels of silver, or about eighty pounds sterling. An Egyptian horse cost him about a quarter of that sum.

1 Kings, ch. x. 28.

(38) The sculptured walls explain to us not only the art of war, but also the unhappy moral feelings with which it was carried on and brought to a close. There was little or

THE CRUELTY OF WAR.

no law of nations to soften its horrors. The only maxim agreed between them was, Woe to the conquered. We see no ceremonies of proclaiming war before it was begun; but the ceremony with which it was closed was counting out before the monarch the hands or other mutilated limbs to prove the number of his foes that had been put to death. On the Assyrian monuments we see that during the siege of a fortress, when a prisoner is taken, he is impaled alive on a stake, to warn the garrison of the fate that awaits them. The Egyptians were perhaps not so cruel. Among all nations slavery, with its accompanying horrors, was the lot of a

Fig. 96.

weaker neighbour; but even in the case of an enemy conquered in battle it was by the Egyptians sometimes allowed to stand in place of the more triumphant cruelty of slaughter.

(39) The temples, obelisks, and statues of Rameses II. are found in all parts of Egypt and Ethiopia. Egypt now ranked by means of its buildings as far before all other nations, as Greece did, ten centuries later, by means of its writings. A temple at Napata, at the foot of Mount Barkal, dedicated by him to his patron god, Amun-Ra, assures us that the kingdom of Egypt now reached southward to the fourth cataract. The large temple at Abou Simbel, in Nubia, near the second cataract, was hollowed out of the sandstone rock in this reign. The sculpture there is the grandest of any to the south of Egypt, but the Ethiopian artist did not give to the human figure the just proportions that we admire in the Theban statues. Four broad-limbed colossal statues of the king sit with their backs against the rock, and ornament the doorway (see Fig. 96). The inside is wholly dark. The figures in the great hall are dimly lighted up when the morning gleam is thrown in by the golden sand without; but the painted sculptures in the rooms beyond were never seen but by torchlight. It was dedicated to Amun-Ra, *the Sun*, and it sheltered the priests from the scorching rays of the god, while with their prayers they endeavoured to turn aside his punishment from the parched land (see Ground Plan, Fig. 97, and Section, Fig. 98). In these temples at Abou Simbel, Rameses is sometimes represented as worshipping the god with the head of the square-eared dog, a divinity who was still respected in Ethiopia, although in Thebes his worship had been discontinued in the middle of the last reign. But even here he was soon to lose his honours, and his name and form were to be chiselled off the wall. This probably took place before the end of this king's reign.

<small>Lepsius's Letters.</small>

(40) In Egypt the priests had long since left off using caves in the side of the mountain for their temples; such caves were now only used for burial-places, as at Benihassan (see Fig. 10). But the Ethiopians still followed the old fashion; and this larger temple at Abou Simbel is the finest work of the kind. Other Ethiopian temples are partly built, and partly hollowed out of the rock, like the old temple at Sarbout el Cadem, near Sinai (see Fig. 33). The older and more holy part is a dark cave, while the newer and larger part is built of squared stones, and copied from the

TEMPLE AT ABOU SIMBEL.

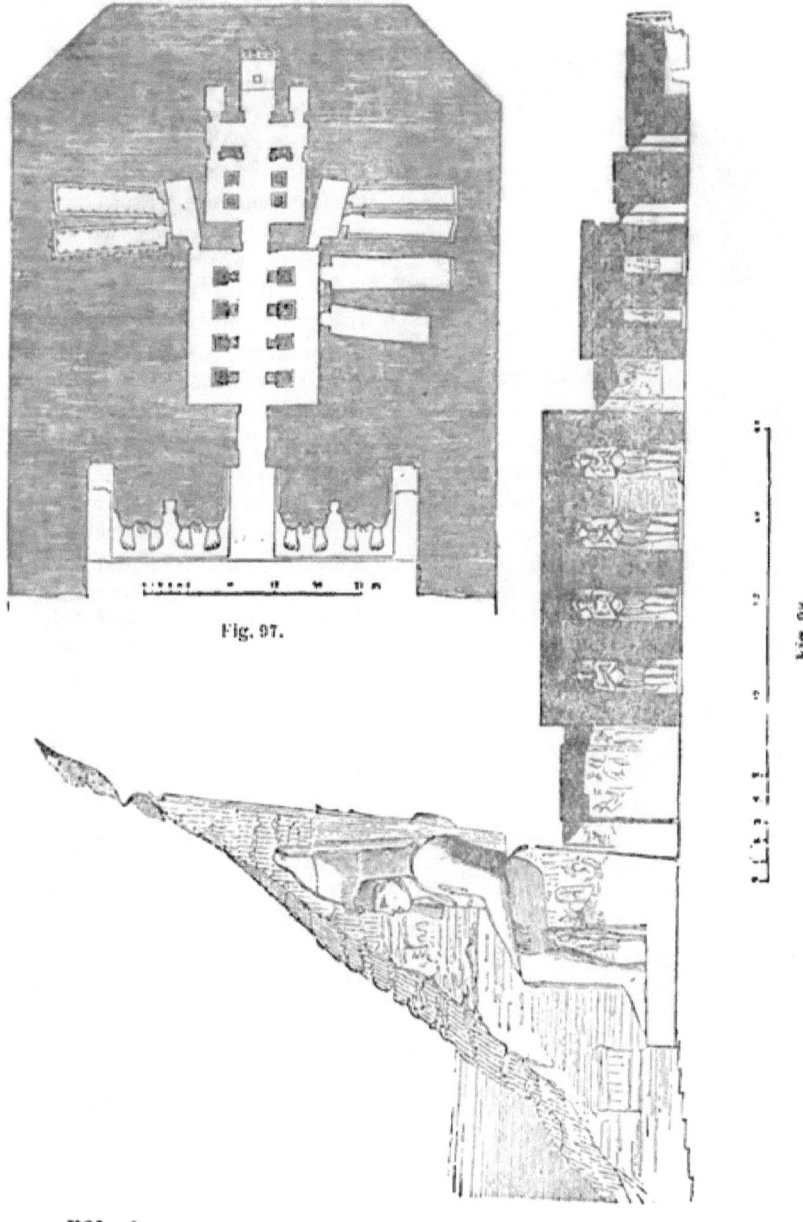

Fig. 97.

Fig. 98.

Theban temples. Such, among many, is the temple of Seboua, half way between the first and second cataract (see Fig. 99). It was built in this reign. The traveller, as he approaches, first meets with two colossal standing statues of Rameses II. He then passes along an avenue between two rows of sphinxes, eight on each side. This brings him to the entrance, a narrow door between the usual two solid square towers. On each side of the door is another colossal statue of the king. Beyond this gateway is the large courtyard, and from this a second door leads into the hall, with a stone roof, upheld by twelve columns. Beyond the hall are the dark and more sacred chambers, tunnelled into the side of the hill. These rock-hewn temples explain the origin of Theban architecture. The solid front of every temple is copied from the face of a hill, which has been cut smooth for the entrance. The sides slope like the hill, though in a less degree. The inner sanctuary of the temple, when built, is as dark as if hollowed out of the hill. In each case it is a set of dark rooms. And if the roof of the cave is sometimes carved as if formed of masonry, it is only the

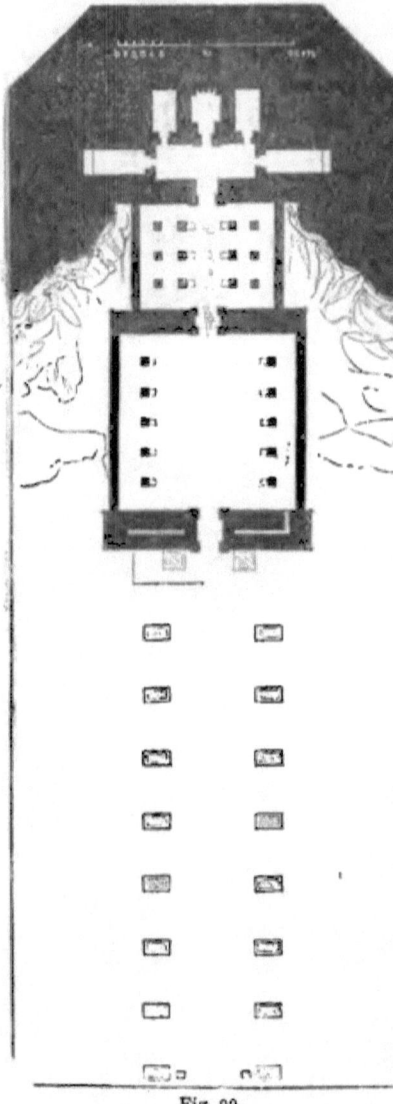

Fig. 99.

cave then borrowing back again something from the building for which it had first served as a model.

(41) Egyptian art had now reached its greatest beauty, and it was not yet overloaded with ornament. But the artists still copied the old stiff models of the human figure; and, while their birds and beasts are usually true to nature, every drawing of a man or woman upon the wall shows a front eye on a side face, and a front chest with legs walking to the side. Their religion and policy alike forbad change in this as in so many other matters. The population of the country may be reckoned at five millions and a half, as there were seven hundred thousand registered tenants of the crown of the military age. If the term of military service were three years, as we afterwards find it, this might allow a standing army of perhaps fifty or sixty thousand men, a number quite large enough to weaken the state and to endanger liberty. Tacitus, Ann. ii.

(42) By the late conquests in Ethiopia, the gold mines had fallen into the hands of the Egyptians. Though hitherto the metal may have been only picked up by the unsettled tribes of the desert, it had yet been a source of great wealth to Ethiopia; but when the mines were worked by Egyptian skill, the produce seemed boundless. The gold was found in quartz veins within a slaty rock, at various spots in the Nubian desert, between Derr on the Nile and Souakin on the coast. By taking possession of Napata, at the fifth cataract, Rameses had a town yet nearer to these mines than the former kings. They were said to bring in, each year, the improbable sum of thirty-two millions of minæ, or seventy millions sterling, as was recorded in the hieroglyphics under the figure of the king in the Memnonium, who is there offering the produce to Amun-Ra. To these mines criminals and prisoners taken in war were sent in chains, to work under a guard of soldiers; and such was their unhappy state, banished from the light of heaven, and robbed of everything that makes life valuable, that the Egyptian priests represented this as the punishment of the wicked souls in the next world. No other known mines were so rich. From the word Knoub, *gold*, the country has received the name of Nubia, or *the land of gold*. By the Hebrews it was called Cub. A port on the Red Sea, the Diod. Sic. lib. i. 49.

Ophir of the Hebrews, was afterwards by the Ptolemies named the Golden Berenice. Gold was henceforth more abundant in Egypt than in any other country in the world; and food and every natural product must have been dearer. Under these circumstances, while they may have imported iron and copper from Cyprus, oil and silver from Greece, with a few other articles from Arabia and Palestine, they could have exported very little beyond gold. The gold mines helped the people's industry in performing their great works in building and in war; but after a time it undermined that industry, and made the country an easier and richer prey for its neighbours.

(43) The European traveller who now visits Ethiopia, and admires the ruins of the highly ornamented and costly temples between the first and second cataracts, some built, but more hollowed out of the rock, and mostly of the reign of Rameses II., naturally asks what could have supported a population numerous enough either to make or to enjoy such great works. The gold mines must furnish the answer. The valley of land which could be cultivated is too narrow for more than a handful of poor villagers. A larger number could only have lived by the help of foreign trade or home manufactures. And Nubia enjoyed both of these while Egypt was well governed. The gold mines in the desert towards the east brought a highly paid carrying trade to the banks of the river, and particularly to those towns where the boats or their freights had to be helped over the cataracts. The home manufacture was not so profitable; it was in the sandstone quarries. These employed unskilled labourers, who sent off the building stone to Syene and Philæ, and to all towns higher up the stream than the sandstone of Silsilis; and they also employed sculptors, who made the statues and carved the hieroglyphics on small slabs, and scribes, who drew the hieroglyphics for the sculptors to cut. The sculptors, who were all of the priestly order, and their labourers the quarrymen, following the religious custom of Egypt, made some of the caves out of which the blocks were cut into temples to Amun-Ra, and Athor, and Knef, and Pthah; and as they were servants of the crown, they cut upon the face of the rock the colossal statues of the king and queen; while the pillars which they left within the cave to

uphold the roof they also shaped into statues of the monarch. In this way, and in this way only, can we explain how and why these cave temples were made in a tract of land seemingly so little able to support any beyond a poor and scanty population. But Thebes, as the seat of government, had the larger share of this wealth. Like Nubia the breadth of its productive soil was not enough to support the expenses of the wars and buildings which it at this time carried on. Its great prosperity was in part accidental, arising from these gold mines, as that of England from its coal and iron; and when, after a few centuries, these were worked out, and its greatness rested only on its agriculture, and other branches of industry, it was brought within very narrow limits.

(44) The copper mines on the range of Mount Sinai were still worked by the Egyptians. Those opened in the reigns of Chofo and Nef-chofo, the builders of the great pyramids, were in Wady Mugareh, a desert valley without water, not far from the route followed by the caravans. These were worked as late as the reigns of Thothmosis II. and Thothmosis III.; but latterly the miners had opened other veins on the side of the mountain of Sarbout el Cadem, in the same neighbourhood; and the remains of a small temple and of tombs ornamented with hieroglyphics prove that the Egyptian settlement there, in the reign of Rameses II., was rather a town than an encampment. But the supplies of food must have been brought from Egypt. The quantity of copper produced must have been small, from the scarcity of fuel, which was charcoal made from the acacia-tree; and the working of the mines must have ceased with the fall of Thebes and the opening of the Mediterranean trade, which then brought the metal in larger quantities from the island of Cyprus. The modern names enable us to distinguish the Egyptian halting-places; and Tabo, *the city*, a spot on the coast, to the west of Sarbout el Cadem, was probably the port from which the copper was shipped to Egypt.

Laborde's Arabia.

(45) We now possess but few traces of the Egyptian laws and customs, by which to explain the form of government; but there are two circumstances which throw some light upon it, and prove that it was of a mixed form, between a monarchy

and an aristocracy. First, every soldier was a landowner, and arms were only trusted to those who had such a stake in the country as would make them wish to guard it from enemies abroad and from tyrants and tumults at home. These men formed a part of the aristocracy. A second remarkable institution was the hereditary priesthood. Every clergyman, sexton, and undertaker, every physician and druggist, every lawyer, writing-clerk, schoolmaster, and author, every sculptor, painter, and land-measurer, every magistrate and every fortune-teller, belonged to the priestly order. Of this sacred body the king, as we learn from the inscriptions, was the head; he was at the same time chief priest and general-in-chief of the army; while the temples were both royal palaces and walled castles of great strength. The power of the king must have been in part based on the opinion and religious feeling of the many; and however selfish may have been the priests, however they may have kept back knowledge from the people, or used the terrors of the next world as an engine for their power in this, yet such a government while more strong must also have been far more free than the government of the sword. Every temple had its own hereditary family of priests, who were at the same time magistrates of the city and the district, holding their power by the same right as the king held his. The union between church and state was complete. But the government must have been a good deal changed by Rameses II. and his father. After all Egypt was united under one sceptre, the power of the monarch was too great for the independence of the several cities. The palaces built by these kings were not temples; the foreign tributes and the produce of the gold mines were used to keep in pay a standing army; and by a standing army alone could Rameses have fought his battles so far from home as in Meroë, Asia Minor, and on the banks of the Euphrates. The military landholders were wholly unfitted for foreign warfare.

<small>Diod. Sic. lib. I. 73.</small>

(46) Rameses II. was followed by three kings of less note, whose hieroglyphical names we may venture to read Pthahmen-Miothph (see Fig. 100), Oimenephtah II. (see Fig. 101), and Osirita Ramerer (see Fig. 102). Of Pthahmen-Miothph we have a colossal statue

<small>Wilkinson, Thebes.</small>

in the British Museum with the name of his father Rameses II. cut upon his shoulder. He wears an apron round his waist,

Fig. 100.

Fig. 101.

Fig. 102.

which is made to stick out by a frame fastened under it like a modern lady's hoop (see Fig. 103). Of Oimenepthah II. we have a seated statue in the same museum, which shows a change in the sculptor's art from the grand simplicity of Rameses II. to a greater attempt at detail in the anatomy, and to a weakness in expression.

(47) These kings were followed by RAMESES III. (see Fig. 104), whose long reign recalled the glory of the great Rameses. He built a new temple or palace in Thebes on the western side of the river, in a spot which now bears the Arabic name of Medinet Abou, or more correctly, Medina Tabou, *the city of Thebes* (see plan, Fig. 105). The courtyard now in ruins is one of the finest in Egypt (see Fig. 106). The portico of this new temple betrays a change in religious opinions, and a wish to mark more strongly the separation between the priesthood and the people, between the clergy and the laity. The portico of the earlier temple

Fig. 103.

Fig. 104.

at Rebek was open to view (see Fig. 74). Whatever ceremonies were performed under it could be seen by all who stood in front of it. But it was not so in this temple of Medinet Abou. Though it was in other respects on the same plan, it was closed in front by a low wall, which ran from column to column, so that the doings of the priests within could no longer be seen by the less holy laity without. Here the painted sculptures on the walls proclaim the king's victories over distant and neighbouring nations, and his triumphal and religious processions at home. In one of the sculptures we see the king sitting in his chariot, after his victory over the Arabs, while his attendants are boastfully counting and writing down the thousands of hands that they have brought home as trophies of the enemies that they had slain in battle. The handcuffed prisoners who stand by are guarded by the Egyptian bowmen. In another place the king under a canopy, the god Chem, the bull Apis, and the ark, are borne along on men's shoulders, in a religious procession, accompanied by priests and soldiers. The procession of Rameses III., sitting under a canopy, and carried along on men's shoulders, helps us to the derivation of an English word. This canopy, we learn from a remark of Horace, was the frame upon which was stretched a gauze net to keep off the gnats and flies; though the gauze is not shown by the sculptor because of its transparency. Horace mentions the shame felt by the Roman soldiers in the service of the luxurious Antony and Cleopatra, at having the royal gnat-gauze carried among the military standards of Rome. From Conops, *a Gnat*, it was named Conopium, and hence the word *Canopy*. The little regard which the Egyptians paid to regularity in their buildings is well shown by an addition which Rameses III. made to the great temple of Karnak. He broke down part of the wall on the west side of the front courtyard, and in the gap he built a small temple, half within the court and half outside (see Fig. 107). It has square towers, a courtyard, a portico, and inner

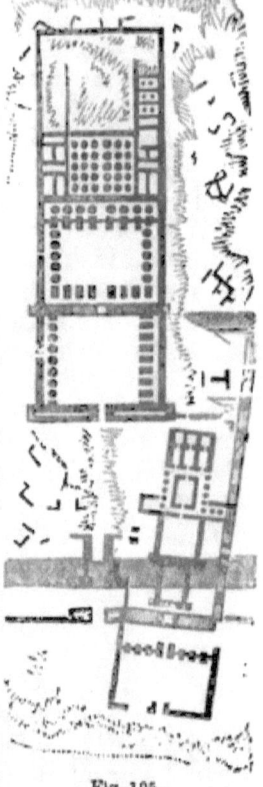

Fig. 105.

rooms of its own, but is in size only one twenty-fourth part of the temple of Karnak itself.

(48) By the inroads of Rameses III. through Palestine

Fig. 106.—Courtyard of Temple at Medinet Abou.

into Syria and other parts of Asia, the power of the Philistines must have been again weakened. These warlike and well-armed people on the coast had hitherto been able to debar the Israelites from the use of iron for weapons; but during the reign of Saul they

^{1 Samuel, ch. xiii. 19.}

were no longer too powerful to be met in battle. If the Egyptian army now occupied any part of the country, no other mention of it is made in the Bible than the quarrel of one of the soldiers with a Hebrew peasant, though a little earlier we meet with a poor Egyptian as slave to an Amalekite and a starving wanderer in the land. The Egyptian troops, indeed, were probably often wanted at home. We gather from a few hints among the inscriptions that the sway of these great Theban kings was not wholly undisputed by the rest of Egypt. The trouble seems to have come from the cities on the eastern half of the Delta, where the Phenicians settled freely for purposes of trade, where the Phenician Shepherds may have left behind them a mixed race, and where the language spoken and the gods worshipped were not wholly the same as those either of the Thebaid or the western half of the Delta. Thothmosis III. styles himself conqueror of Mendes, showing that he was called upon to enforce obedience in that city within his own dominions. That was followed by the ill-treatment of the Israelites under Moses in the same district. Then Thothmosis IV. styles himself Lord of Mendes. Amunothph III. also says he is Lord of Mendes, and particularly favoured by Pasht, the cat-headed goddess of

2 Samuel, ch. xxiii. 21.

1 Samuel, ch. xxx. 11.

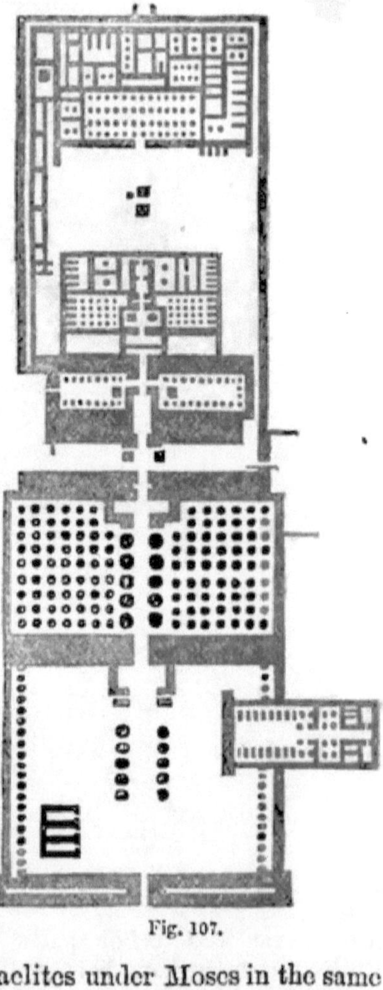

Fig. 107.

Bubastis. A little later the Greek settlers are driven by force of arms out of the west of the Delta. Then Oimenepthah I. styles himself Lord of San or Tanis, as if that city had claimed to be independent; and afterwards Rameses III. uses the same title. These notices are slight, but they are the only forerunners that we can find of the successful rebellion of the eastern cities a century later, when Thebes yielded its unwilling obedience to Bubastis. For the west of the Delta it is even yet more clear that the people bore no love to the Theban kings. In the numerous tombs of the priests and nobles of Memphis, which have been opened in the neighbourhood of the pyramids—tombs of all ages—in none of them are the inscriptions dated by the reigns of the great kings of Thebes.

(49) The calendar on the walls of Medinet Abou shows that the Egyptian knowledge of astronomy had as yet arrived at very little exactness. We there read that the festival of the day of the Dog-star was the first day of the month of Thoth, as it had been declared to be on the walls of the Memnonium one hundred years earlier, in the reign of Rameses II. Hence we see that they had not yet discovered the want of a leap year, or remarked that the new year's day had become a month earlier between these two reigns; and we must not trust to either calendar as the foundation of an exact calculation in chronology.

Egypt. Inscript. 2nd Series, pl. 57.

(50) The lid of the sarcophagus in which Rameses III. was buried is now in the museum at Cambridge. It is a slab of syenite, from the quarries near the first cataract. On it (see Fig. 108) is the king's figure sculptured in the form of a god between two goddesses, Isis and Nephthys; and as if he had himself on his death been changed into a god with three characters, he has on

Fig. 108.

his head the sun of Amun-Ra, and the horns of Athor, and he holds in his hands the two sceptres of Osiris. He is thus a trinity in himself, while he is also the first person in another of the Egyptian trinities, of which the two other persons are Isis and her sister Nephthys.

(51) Rameses III. was followed by three sons of his own name, RAMESES IV., RAMESES V., and RAMESES VI.; the first or second of whom was reigning at the time which the Alexandrian chronologists fixed on as the date of the Trojan war. In Thebes they carved their names upon the temples which had been built by their forefathers; but as their sculptures are never to be seen out of Thebes, we must suppose that their power was for the most part limited to that city, or at least to the Thebaid. These were followed by seven other Theban kings, of whom we know little but the names, and under whom Upper Egypt was falling, while Lower Egypt was rising in wealth and power. None of them held all Lower Egypt, and most of them were even vassals of the kings who then rose in Bubastis and Tanis. Here, as in other countries, on the growth of commerce the seat of government left the hills for the plains nearer the river's mouth. In Asia, Babylon was gaining in wealth and civilisation, what Nineveh two hundred and fifty miles further from the sea was losing; so henceforth the events in our history are to be traced, not among the hills of the Thebaid, but on the open plains of the Delta. Some nations have sunk when the framework of society has been undermined by vice and irreligion. This was not the case with the Thebans; they continued after their fall to be an earnest and devout people. Others have been conquered when several neighbouring states became united under one sceptre. Neither was this the case with Thebes. New and better weapons and discipline among the armies of the Delta may have been part of the cause of its fall. A lessened yield in the gold mines, and loss of wealth on the rise of the Mediterranean trade, may have been another part of the cause. A further cause of weakness in the Thebans arose from their castes, from that fixed line, drawn by religion and prejudice, between the upper and lower ranks of society, between the privileged soldiers and priests, and the unprivileged millions. The lower caste, tho

Wilkinson, Materia Hierogl. Manetho.

B.C. 1050.

hewers of stone and drawers of water, the sinew and muscle of the nation, were hardly of the same blood and language as the Copts who furnished the mind. They were a race more nearly allied to the Arabs. This want of unity in the population was a fatal cause of weakness. In the Delta, on the other hand, the races were less separated, the Coptic blood was less pure; and in the history of mankind it may be noticed that the pure races have usually been less open to improvement, and have sunk before the greater strength and energy of those that are more mixed. The power of Upper Egypt and its race of kings end in obscurity; we are unable to fix the date when Thebes ceased to be the capital of Egypt; but we must suppose that its fall, and the want of records, were caused and accompanied by civil war.

(52) The city of Thebes was at first wholly on the east bank of the river; but by this time it covered the rising ground on both sides, in the form of a horse-shoe, open to the south-west, and embracing a plain two miles wide (see Fig. 109). Through the middle of this the river flows, cutting the city in two, and distributing its blessings on all sides. This open space is in winter and spring covered with green herbage or golden corn; but in the parching season of the Dog-star, the water pours over from the brimming river, makes its way through countless channels, and at length the plain becomes an inland sea, which refreshes the city while it washes the very feet of the massive temples ranged around, and the husbandman in his painted barge sails over his own fields. Beginning at the south, at the river's edge, there stand the long walls of Amunothph's temple of Luxor, with its huge square towers and the obelisks before the entrance. Thence runs an avenue of sphinxes up to the large temple of Karnak, which forms quite a group of towers and obelisks. This was at the same time the cathedral and citadel of Thebes. Between and around these temples were the older dwelling-houses, partly hid by the rustling palm groves which gave them shade. From Karnak the eye follows the range of buildings across the Nile to the Libyan suburb, and to Oimenepthah's smaller temple of Rebek at Quorneh, at the foot of the hills which there press upon the river. Next is the Memnonium, the palace of Rameses II., and then the temple of Rameses III. at Medinet Abou,

each with its tall pyramidal towers, its numerous columns and statues, and surrounded by the dwelling-houses of this suburb. As a background to the buildings on this side, rise the white Libyan hills, among which is seen the temple of

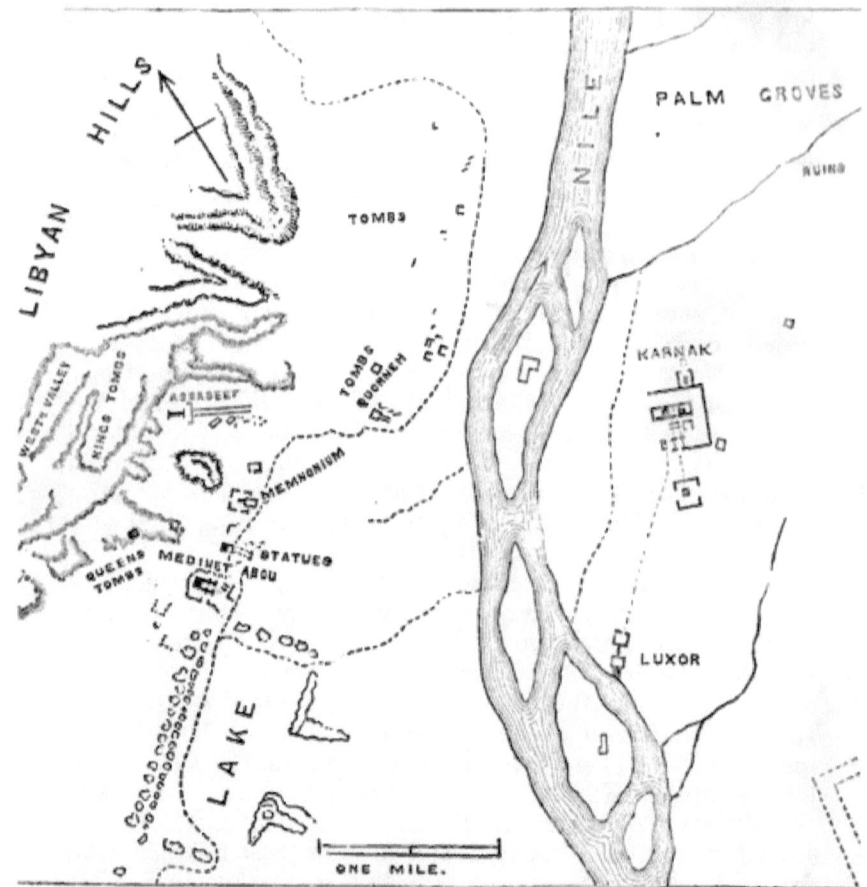

Fig. 109.—Plan of the City of Thebes.

Queen Nitocris, now called El Assaseef, the most northerly building in the city; and as a foreground the two colossal statues of Amunothph, sitting side by side in the plain, in solemn quiet grandeur, as if they alone were unchanging, while generations of busy mortals who peopled the city around were passing away. To the south, and opposite to this semicircle of temples and palaces, is the open plain, broken only by palm-groves and by the mounds of the sacred lake which was used in the ceremonies of burial. In the winding defiles of the Libyan hills behind the Memnonium are the Theban burial-places, between grand and most desolate rocks, where not a tree, nor a shrub, nor a blade of grass is to be seen. Here lie the remains of men whose

Fig. 111.—Amun-Ra, Maut, and Chonso.

stern virtues and lofty aim made Thebes a wonder among cities. The vaulted tombs of the kings are in one silent valley of this limestone range, and those of the queens in another; while persons of a lower rank were buried in a third spot not quite so far from the river, where the softer rock will not remain so many centuries without crumbling over the embalmed mummies.

(53) The history of error is often little less valuable than the history of truth. So would it be with the history of the Egyptian mythology, if we had the means of tracing it. But the paintings and sculptures in the tombs, which teach us the names and figures of the gods, and the offerings which were laid upon their altars, tell us very little of the feelings with which they were worshipped. Gods of the several cities perhaps often differed in name rather than character. They were very much worshipped in groups of three, without, however, confounding their persons; but at other times two or even three characters or persons were united so as to make only one god. The chief god of Thebes was Amun-Ra, *the Sun*, the king of the gods (see Fig. 110). He wears a

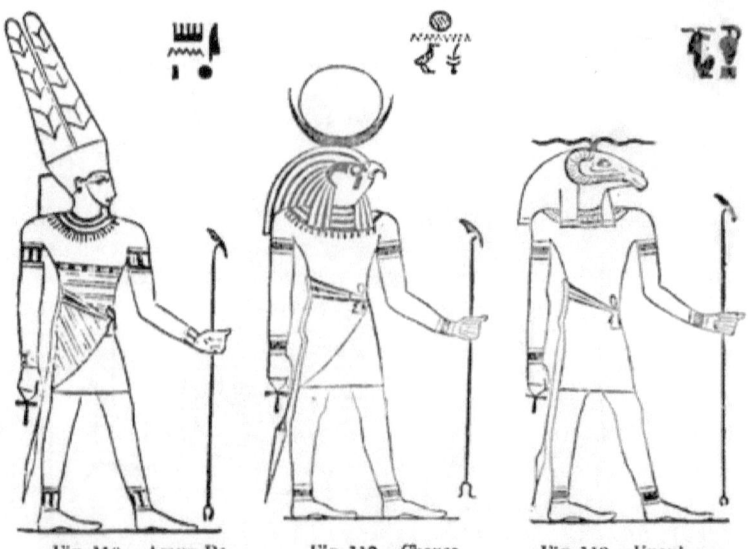

Fig. 110.—Amun-Ra.　　Fig. 112.—Chonso.　　Fig. 113.—Kneph.

crown more than half his own height. He forms a trinity with Maut, *the Mother*, and Chonso, their son, who both stand dutifully behind his throne (see Fig. 111). Chonso has a hawk's head and was one of the gods of the moon (see Fig. 112). Every king of Egypt was styled Zera, or *son of the Sun*, and he was often sculptured as the third person of the trinity, in the place of Chonso. With the spread of the Theban power, we note the acknowledgment of that power in the spread of the worship of Amun-Ra. In Nubia, and at Elephantine, to the south of Thebes, the chief god was Kneph, *the Spirit*, with a ram's head (see Fig. 113), who in imitation of the worship in the capital became Kneph-Ra. So Sebek, the crocodile, called also Seb (see Fig. 114), the father of the gods, became in due time Sebek-Ra. Chem, the god of generation, had his name from Chemi, *Egypt*. He is in form a mummy, with his right arm raised, and a whip in his hand (see Fig. 115). He also was sometimes joined to the gods

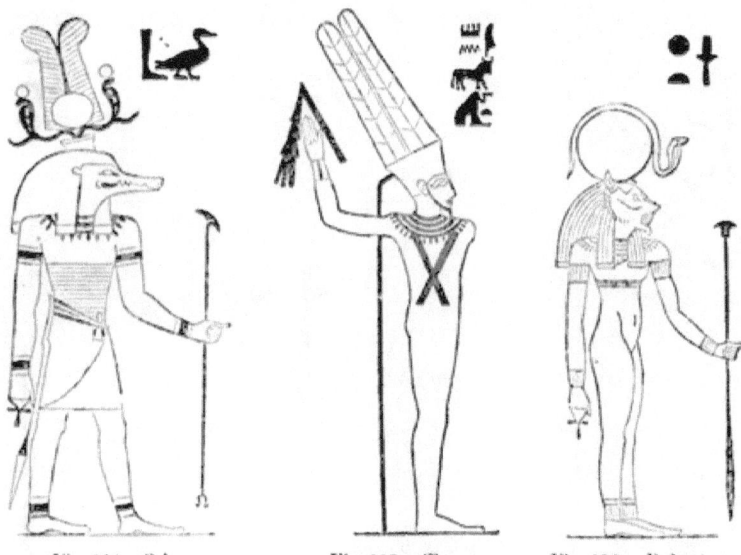

Fig. 114.—Seb.   Fig. 115.—Chem.   Fig. 116.—Bubast.

of Thebes and formed a trinity in unity, under the name of Amun-Ra-Chem. At Heliopolis and the neighbourhood this name of the god of the sun was pronounced Athom, and he gave his name to the city of Thoum. At Mendes in the Delta, and at Hermonthis near Thebes, the sun was called Mando, and became Mando-Ra. Bubast, goddess of chastity, was worshipped chiefly at Bubastis, and has a cat's head (see Fig. 116). Athor was the goddess of love and beauty (see Fig. 117); at Momemphis near Sais she was worshipped under the form of a cow. At Sais was worshipped Neith, the queen of heaven, the mother of the gods (see

VOL. I.   I

Fig. 118). She wears sometimes the crown of Lower Egypt. Thoth, the god of letters, has the head of an ibis, and holds a pen in his hand (see Fig. 119). He was one of the gods of the moon and lord of Hermopolis. Hapimon, the god of the Nile, has water plants on his head, and carries fruits and harvests in his arms, the river's gifts to his worshippers (see Fig. 120). Pthah, the god of fire, was worshipped in Memphis and little known in Upper Egypt. He is bandaged like a mummy (see Fig. 121), and was the chief god of the Lower country as Amun-Ra of the Upper.

(54) The only group of gods that was worshipped in every

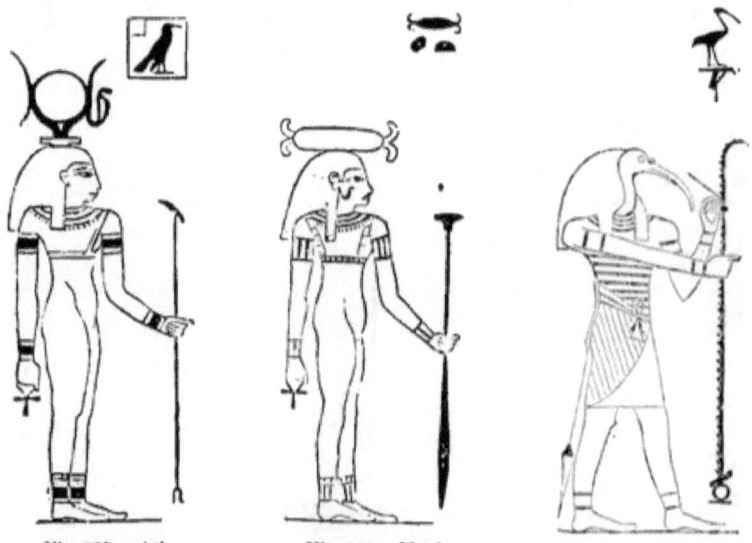

Fig. 117.—Athor.   Fig. 118.—Neith.   Fig. 119.—Thoth.

city alike was Isis, Osiris, and their family. They had once reigned on earth. They were feared less and loved more than the great gods, as being between them and the human race. Osiris had been put to death by his wicked brother Typhon, but raised again to life and to be the judge of the dead. He stands like a mummy, wearing the crown of Upper Egypt, and holding the whip in one hand and the crook in the other (see Fig. 122). Every good man, when dead, in some manner took upon himself the character of Osiris. Many cities claimed the honour of being his burial-

CHAP. II.]   THE EGYPTIAN GODS.   115

place, particularly Philæ, Sais, Busiris, and Taposiris. At Memphis he became united to Pthah, and was called Pthah-sokar-Osiris; and also to the bull Apis, and then became Osiris-Apis or Serapis, whom we shall hereafter see the chief god of Egypt. Isis, his queen and sister (see Fig. 123), was the favourite divinity of the country. She had the characters of all goddesses in turn; she was sometimes the mother, sometimes the queen of heaven, sometimes Hecate, the goddess of enchantments. Horus, their son, has a hawk's head, and wears the crown of Upper and Lower Egypt (see Fig. 124). He was the avenger of his father's

Fig. 120.—Hapimou.   Fig. 121.—Pthah.   Fig. 122.—Osiris.

death. But he sometimes appears with the sun on his head, as Horus-Ra, or Aroeris, the elder Horus; and he is not then the son of Isis. They had another son, Anubis, with a jackal's head (see Fig. 125), whose office was to lay out the dead body and to make it into a mummy. He was worshipped particularly at Ombos. The wicked god Typhon is in form a hippopotamus, walking on its hind legs (see Fig. 126). He was the author of evil, and he killed his brother Osiris. Nephthys was the sister and companion of Isis (see Fig. 127). Of this family the trinity is sometimes Isis, Osiris, and Nephthys, sometimes Isis, Nephthys, and Horus; and the love of mysticism soon declared that in each case the three characters formed only one god. The very names of their kings prove the nation's seriousness and religious earnestness. The name Amunmai Rameses, meaning, *Beloved by the god Amun and tried by the god Ra*, shows that the priests taught the gods' love towards man; and as he was also sometimes called Miamun Rameses, it reminds us they had already discovered the duty of man's love towards the gods. They spared no pains in lengthening the remembrance of the past by their monuments and inscriptions. Memory in a nation makes

Egyptian Inscrip. pl. 36, 4, 5.

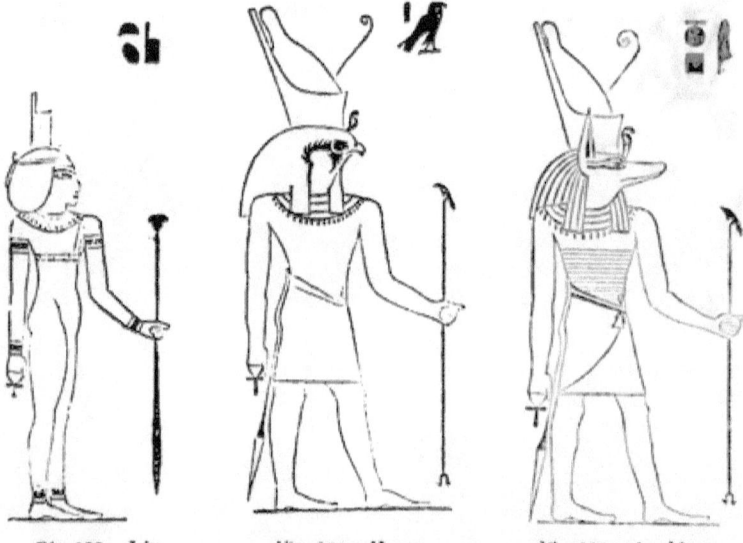

Fig. 123.—Isis. Fig. 124.—Horus. Fig. 125.—Anubis.

the difference between age and childhood. The fabric of society, like the form of government, is built on its recollections, and these they wisely cherished to the utmost. Guided by these feelings, every family worshipped its own forefathers, and on the monuments which record the piety of the deceased we usually see, that when one altar or table of food is set out for the immortal gods, a second is set out for his father and mother and their ancestors on both sides.

(55) Besides the gods in the shape of animals, and the

sacred animals themselves, the Egyptians had a sacred tree, though naturalists have not been able to determine which

Fig. 126.—Typhon.   Fig. 127.—Nephthys.

it was. It was probably one grown with difficulty, and not a native of the country. In some of the modern superstitions it seems to be a valuable fruit-tree, which it was criminal to injure; in others it is a sensitive acacia, which bows its leaves when they are touched, and thus greets the traveller who seeks its shade. We are told more of its supernatural doings than of its natural qualities. It showers down life and other blessings on the heads of the Theban kings; it pours learning into the mouths of philosophers (see Fig. 128), and speaks with a woman's voice, which was

Fig. 128.

understood to be that of the goddess Neith. Fifteen centuries later, we find this tree mixed up with Christian superstitions;

and yet later, when the early Italian artists represent Moses as listening to the voice which speaks to him out of the burning bush on Mount Sinai, they tell us that it was a woman's voice, by putting the Virgin Mary into the bush as the speaker.

(56) During the past centuries of Theban greatness, the country was little known to either Jews or Greeks, the two people in whose writings we naturally hope to find information. In the Hebrew scriptures Upper Egypt is scarcely mentioned, while by the Greeks it was only spoken of with ignorant wonder. In the Iliad Thebes is called the city of all the world in which gold was most abundant; having a hundred gates, through each of which two hundred warriors issued in their war chariots to battle and to victory. But it was to Homer wholly in the land of fable, far beyond the reach of knowledge; it was called the birthplace of some of the Greek gods; and it was with the righteous Ethiopians, or people of the Thebaid, that Jupiter and his family were said to be spending their twelve days' holidays, when the Greeks, fighting before the walls of Troy, thought their prayers were unheard. In the Odyssey we are told that Neptune visited the same country, and dined with these Ethiopians, while the other gods were at home in Jupiter's palace on Mount Olympus; but nothing is mentioned that shows that the poet knew anything of the places that he writes about. Hesiod also, when speaking of Memnon king of Ethiopia, by whom he meant Amunothph III., whose colossal statue was musical every morning at sunrise, calls him the son of the goddess Aurora. Everything in Egypt was seen by the Greeks enlarged through the mists of distance, and coloured by the poetic fancy of ignorance. But, with little help either from Greek or Hebrew writers, we have been able, by means of the kings' names on the sculptured buildings, to trace the gradual enlargement of the kingdom of Thebes, which was now the kingdom of Egypt. On the north side Amunmai Thori III. gained the province of Fayoum, and added to the temple called the Labarinth on the banks of Lake Mœris; and he also held the mines at the foot of Mount Sinai, where he left a temple for the use of the miners. Amasis drove out the Shepherds from the east of the Delta; and when the mines of Sinai had

been neglected because of this war, Thothmosis II. again built in that distant spot. Thothmosis II. also added to his kingdom Memphis and the west of the Delta. On the southern side Osirtesen III. moved the limits of his kingdom to the second cataract, and built at Samneh. Thothmosis I. pushed them yet further to the third cataract, and built at Tombos. And at last Rameses II. enlarged his kingdom to the fourth cataract, and built at Napata. After Rameses III. the power of Thebes began to grow less.

(57) The countries at this time known to the Egyptians were contained within very narrow limits. If we take either Memphis or Jerusalem as a centre, and draw round it a circle distant on every side by one thousand miles, it will contain every nation with whom the Egyptians had any dealings either by war or trade. It will contain on the south Egypt itself, Ethiopia, Meroë, and the Nubian gold mines; on the west Libya and the Greek isles; on the north the Trojans, Lydians, Lycians, Thracians of Asia Minor, Syrians, and Armenians; and on the east the Assyrians, Medians, and Babylonians. The geographer standing in Memphis or Jerusalem felt his knowledge of the world bounded by the Black Sea, the range of Mount Caucasus, the Caspian Sea, the warlike tribes of Scythians, Bactrians, and Persians, the Persian Gulf, the deserts of Arabia, the cataracts of the Nile, the Libyan desert, and the difficulties of navigating the Mediterranean Sea. Within that small space must be traced all the events of Ancient History before the improvement in navigation, which took place about the same time with the fall of Thebes, the rise of Lower Egypt, and the reign of Solomon in Judæa, and the Trojan war.

(58) At this time the Island of Meroë was the only state which bounded Egypt on the south that had any settled civilisation, the only spot in which we can suppose that the buildings had not been made by the Egyptians. Far less civilised were the other neighbours of the Egyptians. The Troglodytic Arabs, one of the chief tribes, held a strip of country of about four hundred miles in length on the African coast of the Red Sea, separated from Ethiopia by mountains and deserts. These were a wandering unsettled race of people, described by their neighbours as savages, whose wars arose for right of pasture rather

<small>Diod. Sic. lib. iii. 33.</small>

than for ambition or property. They fought with slings and darts, and outran horses in their speed. Some lived in caves, and killed the aged, the lame, and the sick; others, however, more civilised, afterwards traded with the men of Sheba of the opposite coast, and supplied the Egyptians with the myrrh, balsam, olives, topaz, and metals which their country or their trade produced. Like their neighbours the Egyptians, the Troglodytæ worshipped images and animals, particularly the turtles peculiar to their shores, while the more civilised tribes were worshippers of one God. During the earlier centuries all these Arabs were easily conquered by the Egyptians; but we shall hereafter find some of them inhabiting Ethiopia, under a settled form of government, and then conquering Nubia and harassing the Thebaid. The Egyptian name for Ethiopia was Ethosh, in which the first consonant had the doubtful guttural sound; and hence the Greeks softened it into Ethiopia, while the Hebrews hardened it into Cush.

<small>Pliny, lib. xii. 42.</small>

(59) During these years the Israelites had gradually defeated their enemies the Canaanites, and gained possession of a large part of their country. After various changes of fortune, sometimes masters and sometimes servants of the natives, they united their little states into one commonwealth, they changed their form of government and elected a king. Under Saul they defeated the Philistines; under David they conquered Jerusalem, and made that city the capital of the kingdom. The reign of Solomon was prosperous and peaceful. He strengthened his armies without having much occasion to use them; he built the temple; and was more powerful than any of the neighbouring sovereigns. Assyria, Babylon, and Media, had not yet risen to be great monarchies, and Egypt had been weakened by civil war.

(60) The desert coast of the Mediterranean Sea, between Gaza, the frontier town of Palestine, and Pelusium or Shur, the frontier town of Egypt, was called by the Hebrew writers the Desert of Shur. It was thinly peopled by a race of Arabs named Amalekites. They usually acknowledged the king of Egypt as their master; and thus the boundary of the Egyptian kingdom on the east lay between the towns of Raphia and Gaza. But during the disturbed state of Egypt Solomon conquered the Amalekites, and stretched his limits to the very

banks of the Pelusiac branch of the Nile. The Hebrew historians then boasted that his kingdom reached from the Euphrates, in the north of Syria, to the very river of Egypt. Solomon, by also making himself master of the Edomites, who held the desert country between Judæa and the Red Sea, with the rock-city of Petra, was able to command the route to a southern port, and thus to increase his trade with southern Arabia. The Edomites were a warlike unsettled race of Arabs, whose property was in their cattle, their waggons, and what their waggons could carry. They did not cultivate the soil, nor had they any respect for a landmark; and unless stopped by force were always ready to feed their cattle on the cultivated lands of their Jewish neighbours. But they were not without some sources of wealth. While the navigation of the sea was difficult, their country offered the readiest route for the passage of merchandise, both from the Persian Gulf to Egypt, and from southern Arabia to Jerusalem and Tyre. The caravans, or troops of camels laden with goods belonging to Midianites and other more civilised Arabs, paid a toll to the Edomites for a safe passage through their country, and for leave to drink at their wells. The caravan for Egypt came from Dedan on the Persian Gulf, through Teman on the borders of Edom, to Petra the capital, and thence on to the Jewish cities on the east of the Delta. But this trade must often have been stopped by war; and the Edomites were usually at war with the Jews. Saul, the first Hebrew king, drove back the Edomites from his frontier; and as the Hebrew kingdom grew stronger, David, after conquering the Philistines, the Moabites, and the Syrians, put garrisons in the chief cities of the Edomites to stop their inroads for the future. Solomon not only held the Edomites in the same obedience, but took possession of Eziongeber, a little port at the head of the Elanitic or eastern gulf of the Red Sea. This town more naturally belonged to the Midianites of Sinai, or rather to their friends the Egyptians. It was afterwards called Berenice by the Ptolemies; and its place is still pointed out by the Egyptian name of the valley in which it stood, Wâdy Tabe, *the valley of the city.*

(61) At Eziongeber Solomon fitted out a ship for the

Isaiah, xxi. 13.

1 Samuel, xiv. 47.

2 Samuel, viii. 14.

1 Kings, ch. ix. x.

southern trade. For this purpose he formed an alliance with
Hiram king of Tyre, who furnished him with Tyrian ship-
builders. The ship was of a size and class hitherto
unknown on the Red Sea, and called a ship of Tarsus, after
the city most famous for ship building. It was manned by
Tyrian sailors. The time passed on the outward and homeward voyages and in either port was three years; but of this,
in the infancy of navigation, a small part only was passed
under sail. They sailed only when the wind was in the
stern; and as in these seas it changes regularly twice a year,
we may fix with some certainty how far they could go in the
time. This was not far. They crept along the Egyptian
and Nubian shore to Abyssinia, bartering as they went; they
waited long before passing a headland; and therefore a
season's wind would hardly take them farther than Zanzibar,
a spot on the African coast where they would be stopped by
the promontory and the southerly wind and current. At the
limit to their voyage, as they had to tarry some time while
exchanging their goods, they must have waited a whole
twelvemonth during the return wind of that year and the
outward wind of the second year. The return wind of the
second year would bring them home again to Eziongeber.
There they spent the third year in port, while their foreign
goods were sent through Petra to Jerusalem and Tyre.
They brought home chiefly gold from Ophir, no doubt the
town known seven centuries later under the name of the
Golden Berenice, and not many miles from the modern
Souakin, where gold was more common than in every other
place of trade. From Ophir they also brought precious
stones and a rare wood named Algum, or Almug, probably
ebony. Other merchandise was silver and ivory from the
African coasts, with apes and rare birds named Tok, probably
parrots, from Abyssinia. Thus Tyre and Jerusalem now
enjoyed the wealth arising from bringing home by sea all
those costly articles which hitherto came on camels' backs
through the desert, and which Egypt received down the Nile
from Ethiopia, the articles which form the Nubian and
Ethiopian tribute to Thothmosis III., as painted on the wall
at Thebes. The Egyptians left this trade on their own
coasts to foreigners. Another voyage may have been to
Sheba and Hadramaut, on the coast opposite to Abyssinia,

where the spice merchants were to be met with from Muscat on the point of Arabia facing the mouths of the Indus. When not helped by the Tyrian sailors, the Jewish traders probably always ended their voyage at Hadramaut and at Abyssinia, as those were the spots afterwards marked by Jewish settlers. No vessels could overcome the difficulties of the winds on the southern coast of Arabia, and reach the coast of India, or even the Persian Gulf, from the Red Sea; for as yet the trade winds in those seas were not understood, by which, ten centuries later, vessels sailed southward along the African coast and crossed over to the peninsula of India. The Jewish historian tells us that Solomon received a weight of gold from these voyages equal in worth to two millions of pounds sterling. The king of Tyre must also have received a large sum. The figures may perhaps have been exaggerated; but the prosperity of Upper Egypt must have been seriously hurt by this discovery of a new channel by which the Nubian gold could reach the Phenicians without passing down the Nile. The rare wood which Solomon's ships brought home, named Almug or Algum, was not new to Jerusalem, though no such large pieces had yet been seen there. It was used to make musical instruments and rails for the palace and temple stairs. Hence its valuable quality was its hardness and power of receiving a polish. This quality, together with its country, are in favour of its being ebony, a wood always known to the Egyptians, and even grown in Egypt, though not so largely as in Abyssinia. The Jews gave to ebony its present name, from the Hebrew word Aben, *a stone ;* and if we would look for the origin of the word Algum, we may perhaps have it in the Coptic word Gom, *hard*, to which the Arabic traders would naturally prefix the article, and make it Al-gom. The name of the rare bird, the Tok, may perhaps be found in the Greek word Psit-tak-us, *a parrot.*

^{1 Kings, ix. 28.}

CHAPTER III.

THE KINGS OF BUBASTIS AND TANIS; CIVIL WARS; INVASION BY THE ETHIOPIANS. B.C. 945—697.

(1) THE fall of states is usually gradual, and often unnoticed. No monuments are raised to record defeats; no inscriptions are carved to recount a nation's losses; and thus we are unable to learn where the line of Theban kings ended. Some of the last that bore that title, together with the great name of Rameses, may have been little more than chief priests in the temple of Karnak. But the eastern half of the Delta was now rising in wealth and importance. The cities of Bubastis, Tanis, and Mendes equally claimed to be sovereign cities; and the first king of Lower Egypt who sat upon the throne of Rameses was SHISHANK of Bubastis (see Fig. 129), who raised his own city into independence and then conquered Thebes. Bubastis or Abou Pasht, *the city of the goddess Pasht*, was on the bank of the shallow Pelusiac branch of the Nile, about seventy miles from the river's mouth, and it was the chief city of the little district or *nome* of the same name. We may suppose that Bubastis had the willing help of all the eastern half of the Delta against the Thebans. The Bubastite nome also was next to that of Heliopolis, which the Jews called the Land of Goshen; and Bubastis was the nearest capital city to Palestine, being about sixty miles from the head of the Red Sea. Its sovereign priests had been able to ally themselves with the neighbouring Israelites, and thus to gain for Bubastis a higher rank among the cities of Egypt at a time when the power of Thebes was crumbling. Hence, in any struggle for power, the Jewish district of Heliopolis would of course join Shishank against the family of Rameses.

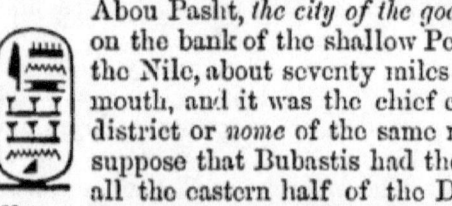

Manetho.
B.C. 945.

Fig. 129.

(2) The Jews also were great gainers by this alliance with the Egyptians. They owed them a debt greater than they

have owned, namely, the overthrow of the Philistines and Canaanites of the coast. The Jewish army was now able to obtain better arms; it was furnished with war-chariots and horses bought in Egypt. Solomon in his old age added to his other wives a daughter of the Egyptian king; and Shishank, as a dower, besieged and gave with her a town which the Israelites had been unable to take from their enemies. Gezer in Samaria, half way between Jerusalem and Joppa, had hitherto remained in the hands of the Canaanites. It was situated among the hills, and had defied the Hebrew arms. But the inroads of Rameses II. and Rameses III. had taught all parties the vast superiority of the Egyptian engineers; and Shishank sent an army two hundred and fifty miles from Bubastis, which stormed the walls of Gezer, slew the garrison, laid waste the place with fire, and gave its smoking ruins to Solomon as a dower with his daughter. None of Solomon's other wives were of equal rank with the Egyptian princess; one of the Hebrew Psalms was written in honour of this marriage, and the following lines were addressed to her:— *[margin: 1 Kings, ch. x. 28. ch. iii. 1. Joshua, ch. xvi. 10. 1 Kings, ch. ix. 16.]*

> "Hearken, O daughter, and consider; incline thine ear;
> Forget also thine own people and thy father's house.
> So shall the king greatly desire thy beauty;
> For he is thy lord; therefore worship thou him.
> The daughters of Tyre shall come with gifts;
> The rich among the people shall intreat thy favour.
> Instead of forefathers thou shalt have sons,
> Whom thou shalt make princes throughout the land.

[margin: Psalm xlv.]

(3) During this friendship between Egypt and Judæa, the Jews borrowed much from the arts and ceremonies, and also from the superstitions, of their more civilised neighbours. The priests wore the Egyptian ornaments, the Urim and Thummim, emblems of *royalty* and *truth* (see Fig. 130), and the people, forgetting their God, sometimes sacrificed to the brazen serpent. Many traces of this free intercourse between the two nations may be seen in the Hebrew writings. The whole history of the fall of man is of Egyptian origin. The temptation of woman by the serpent and of man by the woman declares the Egyptian opinion that celibacy is more holy than marriage. The sacred tree *[margin: 2 Kings, ch. xviii. 4.]*

of knowledge (see Fig. 128, page 117), the cherubs guarding with flaming swords the door of the garden, the warfare between the woman and the serpent, may all be seen upon the Egyptian sculptured monuments. The Mosaic laws are largely coloured by the Egyptian customs, some which they carefully forbid as being superstitious and idolatrous, and

Fig. 130.

some which they copy as being innocent. While the Egyptians worshipped statues not only of men but of birds, beasts, and reptiles, the Jews were forbidden to make the likeness of anything in the heavens above or on the earth beneath, in order to bow down and worship it. The Egyptian priests kept their heads shaved, but the Jewish priest was forbidden to make himself bald, or even to round the corners of his beard. The people of Lower Egypt marked their bodies with pricks in honour of their gods; and the officers of state marked their breasts and shoulders with the name of the king whom they served; but the Jews were forbidden to cut their flesh or make any marks upon it. The Egyptians buried food in the tombs with the bodies of their friends, and sent gifts of food to the burial-grounds for their use, and their funereal tablets show these tables of food set out for their forefathers; but the Jews were forbidden to set apart any food for the dead, and they are reproached by the Psalmist with having eaten of such sacrifices set out for the dead, when wandering in the desert. The Egyptians planted groves of trees within the courtyards of the temples, as the Alexandrian Jews did afterwards in the yards of their synagogues; but the Mosaic law forbade the Jews to plant any trees near the altar of Jehovah. The Egyptians

Exodus, ch. xx. 4.
Herodotus, lib. ii. 36.
Leviticus, ch. xxi. 5.
Herodotus, lib. ii. 113.
Leviticus, ch. xix. 28.
Deuteron. ch. xxvi. 13, 14.
Psalm cvi. 28.
Deuteron. ch. xvi. 21.

and Jews were alike in the practice of circumcision, and in refusing to eat the flesh of swine; except that the Egyptians, who reared these unclean animals to sacrifice to Isis and Osiris, indulged themselves in eating pork once a month, on the day of the full moon after the sacrifice. They were alike in their manner of reckoning the beginning and end of the day. Among the Greeks and Etruscans the day began at noon, among the Romans, as with ourselves, at midnight, among the Persians at sunrise, but among the Jews and Egyptians it began at sunset.

<small>Herodotus, lib. ii. 36. Lib. ii. 47 Servius, in Æneid, v. 738. Genesis, ch. i.</small>

(4) The wise men of Egypt added the vain studies of sorcery and magic to their knowledge of the physical sciences; and they made use of juggling tricks to strengthen that power over the minds of their countrymen which they gained from a real superiority of knowledge. When they opposed Moses before Pharaoh, whatever miracles he worked they attempted to work, and in some cases with an apparent success. Like him, they threw down their rods upon the ground, which then crawled about like serpents, and when they took them up in their hands they again became straight rods. And at the present day, after three thousand years, their successors are still performing the same curious trick. The Egyptian juggler takes up in his hand the *Naja*, a small viper, and pressing a finger on the nape of its neck, puts it into a catalepsy, which makes it motionless and stiff like a rod; and when it regains its power of motion, the cheated bystanders fancy that the magician's rod has been changed into a serpent. For the pretended arts of prophesying and looking into the secrets of nature, the Egyptians used drinking-cups made of silver and other metals, which were engraved on the inside with mystic lines and religious figures. Such was the popular belief in their power, that these magic cups were copied even in distant countries; and though no Egyptian divining-cups remain to us, we know them in the Assyrian copies (see Fig. 131). The Egyptian wizards and magicians had great and often mischievous power over the nation's mind; they spoke as with a voice from heaven, which even two thousand years later the law hardly ventured to check; the utmost that it

<small>Exodus, ch. vii. 11. Cuvier, Règne Animal. Genesis, ch. xliv.</small>

attempted was to punish those who consulted them. But the Jewish law called upon the mob to punish their own deceivers, and ordered them to stone to death anybody that practised magic or divination.

_{Leviticus, ch. xx. 27.}

Fig. 131.

(5) We may also mention a few among the cases in which the Jewish law seems to have borrowed something from the country which they had left. The Egyptians carved the praises of their kings and gods upon the walls of their buildings, both inside and out; and in the same way the Jews were ordered to write the words of their law upon their door-posts, and upon their gates. The Egyptians in their sculpture added wings to gods, to serpents, to crowns, and to the sun; and the Jews were ordered to place on each side of the mercy-seat a golden cherub, stretching out its wings. In the painting of a religious procession of Rameses III., an ark or box (see Fig. 132) is carried after the statue of the god Chem; it is represented as two cubits and a half long and a cubit and a half high,

_{Deuteron. ch. xi. 20; ch. vi. 9.}

_{Exodus, ch. xxv. 20.}

_{Denon, pl. 131.}

_{Exodus, ch. xxxvii.}

exactly of the size and form of the ark which they were ordered in their Law to make, and to carry with them till they found a spot whereon to build a temple to the Lord. In Jerusalem was a brazen serpent, said to be that which Moses had made in the desert and set upon a pole, that those who had been bitten might look on it and be healed; and among the Egyptian standards we often see the same serpent set upon a pole (see Fig. 133). And lastly, when the Israelites fell into idolatry, they made a golden calf to worship, the animal which, under the name of Mnevis, they had so often seen worshipped at Heliopolis.

2 Kings, xviii. 4. Denon, pl. 119.

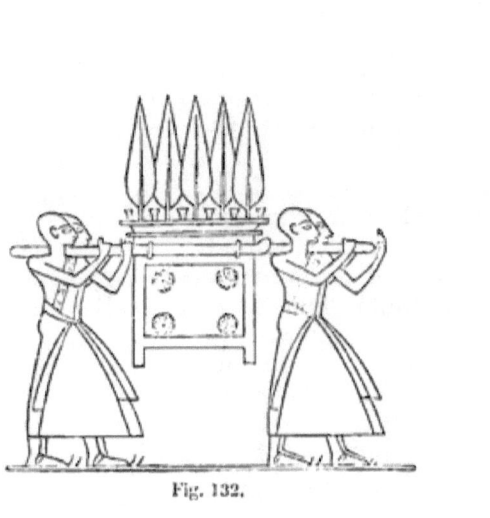

Fig. 132.

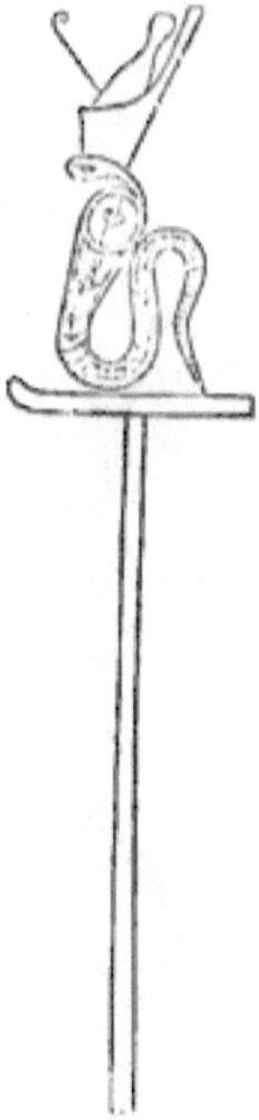

Fig. 133.

(6) But the friendship between Egypt and Judæa was not lasting; the Egyptian throne, now seated in Bubastis, was becoming stronger. Shishank now gave his countenance to the Edomites, and in Solomon's old age he encouraged them to rebel against the Israelites. He thus stopped Solomon's trade on the Red Sea, which could only have been looked upon by the Egyptians with

1 Kings, ch. xi. 19.

jealousy. Forty years before, when David conquered Edom, and put to death every male within his reach, Hadad, a child belonging to the chief's family, was carried away by his servants, and brought safely into Egypt. There he was educated; and when he grew up Shishank gave him the sister of Queen Tahpenes for his wife. Hadad's son lived in Shishank's palace at Bubastis with the Egyptian princes; and as Solomon's power grew weaker, Shishank sent Hadad home to raise the Edomites in rebellion against the Israelites. When Jeroboam, the prefect over the tribes of Ephraim and Manasseh, was in danger of being put to death by Solomon, he fled to Shishank for safety. On the death of Solomon took place the unfortunate division in the Hebrew kingdom. The two tribes in the neighbourhood of Jerusalem obeyed his son Rehoboam; while the northern and eastern tribes revolted, sent for Jeroboam from Egypt, and made him king. In the war which followed, Shishank, as is usual with those who interfere in their neighbours' quarrels, sided with Jeroboam, king of Israel, whose territories were furthest from him. Shishank then made a wanton attack on Judæa, and marched against Rehoboam at the head of a large army. His soldiers were not only Egyptians from

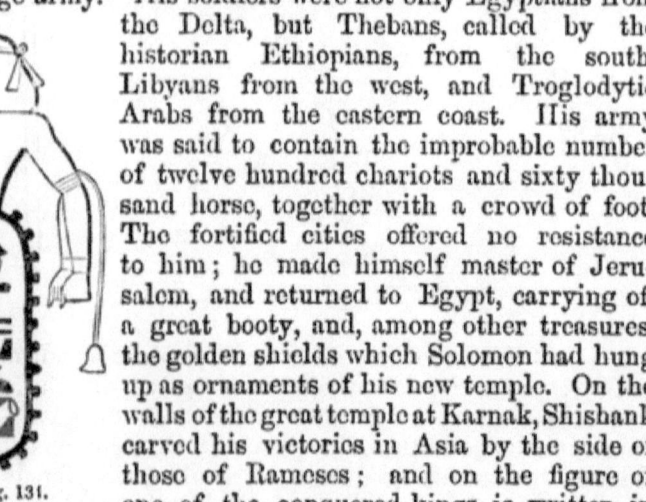

Fig. 134.

the Delta, but Thebans, called by the historian Ethiopians, from the south, Libyans from the west, and Troglodytic Arabs from the eastern coast. His army was said to contain the improbable number of twelve hundred chariots and sixty thousand horse, together with a crowd of foot. The fortified cities offered no resistance to him; he made himself master of Jerusalem, and returned to Egypt, carrying off a great booty, and, among other treasures, the golden shields which Solomon had hung up as ornaments of his new temple. On the walls of the great temple at Karnak, Shishank carved his victories in Asia by the side of those of Rameses; and on the figure of one of the conquered kings is written in hieroglyphics "The kingdom of Judah" (see Fig. 134). At

1 Kings, ch. xi. 40.

2 Chron. ch. xii. 2.

the same time, the alliance between Egypt and the revolting tribes was shown in the idolatry which Jeroboam then established in Israel. He set up two golden calves; one at Dan, at the northern end of his kingdom, and one at Bethel, at the southern end; and he established an order of priests to attend to their worship. This idolatry was the act of homage which the Egyptians made Israel pay for being spared when Judah was conquered.

(7) We have before seen that, under Joseph, the land owners of Lower Egypt lost their liberty; but it is reasonable to suppose that the great revolution by which the crown of Upper and Lower Egypt was removed to the Delta was not brought about without some advantages to the Lower country. It was probably at this time that the military of Lower Egypt gained the freedom from land-tax which had always been enjoyed by the order of priests, and probably by both orders in the less despotic Upper Egypt. Aristotle says that the military class was divided from the agricultural class by Sesostris; and, while some of the great deeds which the Greek historians have given to that fabulous name seem to belong to the great Rameses, we may perhaps give to Shishank some others, including this re-establishment of the military class in Lower Egypt. Another and a more important change which followed upon the removal of the seat of government was the separation of the temporal and spiritual powers. Their union had been a cause of strength to the Theban monarchy; and their separation caused the weakness of the several governments which succeeded to it in Lower Egypt. When the seat of empire left Thebes, the priesthood, whose power had centered in that city, can have had no longer that weight in the state which they before enjoyed. Shishank, indeed, bore the same priestly titles as the kings of Thebes; but the great body of the priests, of whom he claimed to be the head, looked upon him as an enemy. Though the soldiers of Bubastis made themselves obeyed in the Thebaid, the priests of Bubastis had no such claim to be listened to. They worshipped other gods, and spoke another dialect.

De republicâ, lib. vii. 10.

(8) The most flourishing time for the city of Bubastis was this reign, and its fortified temple was probably then built. When Herodotus admired it, five hundred years later, its great

age was proved by the height of the city mounds, which had been raised higher and higher each century, as the Nile's mud raised the soil of the Delta. He had seen larger and more costly temples in other cities, but he thought none so beautiful as this. It was dedicated to Bubast, a goddess, whom the Greeks called Diana. It was a strongly-walled grove in the middle of the city, two hundred yards square. Its entrance was guarded by two towers thirty feet high; and on the other sides its wall was surrounded by a deep moat or canal from the Nile, one hundred feet wide. The walls were ornamented with carved figures nine feet high, and the moat was shaded with overhanging trees. In the middle of this sacred grove, which was all called the temple, stood the covered building, containing in one of its rooms the statue of the goddess. The two tall towers at the entrance faced the east, and from them ran a paved road through the market-place to the temple of Thoth, at the other end of the city. But the arts did not flourish in these times of change and civil war. Many of the statues of gods in black syenite, which bear the name of King Shishank, seem from their style to have been made three hundred years earlier, in the reign of Amunothph III. Shishank gave the name of his queen, Tahpenes, to a city which the Greeks called Daphnæ, about twenty miles from Pelusium. But perhaps the lady's name was only Hanes, and hence the city would be called Tape-Hanes. Here was a royal palace; and from the name of the city we may suppose that it was one of those whose revenues were allotted to the maintenance of the queen's state and dignity.

(9) Shishank was not one of those great kings who have left a throne established for a long line of descendants. He was succeeded by his son OSORKON (see Fig. 135), and with him the power of the family ended. After his death the country was divided into several little kingdoms for two centuries; and as these years are marked by no national deeds abroad, and by no great works of art at home, we must fear that the energies of the people were chiefly wasted in their civil wars. Their lessened strength was shown

Fig. 135.

in their loss of territory; and Ethiopia, which had been subject to Thebes ever since the reign of Amunothph I., was now lost to Egypt, and became an independent state.

(10) The Hebrew historian tells us that a king of Ethiopia named Zerah, now led a large army of foot soldiers and chariots against Asa king of Judæa. He was defeated by the men of Judah at Mareshah, in the valley of Zephathah, on his march to Jerusalem. As he bore the common Egyptian title of Zerah, *Son of the Sun* (see Fig. 136), he of course reigned on the banks of the Nile. He may have been a king of Napata, who marched as a conqueror through Thebes and Heliopolis, leaving ruin and misery behind him, while he was too much of a barbarian to leave any lasting record of his power. But he was more probably one of the family of Rameses, who having inherited the sovereignty of Thebes, had for a moment re-established the power of that city over all Egypt. The Thebaid was sometimes called Ethiopia by the ancient writers; and as Rameses VII. (see Fig. 137), by leaving his name in the tombs of the sacred bulls near Memphis, has proved to us that his power reached as far north as that city, he may have been the Zerah of the Hebrew historian. The other kings of the name of Rameses, after Rameses III., are not known out of Thebes.

Fig. 136.

Fig. 137.

2 Chron. ch. xiv. B.C. 909.

(11) For the next two centuries no one city in Egypt had sway over the rest. In the absence of information we must suppose that Ethiopia, Upper Egypt, and in Lower Egypt, Bubastis, Tanis, Memphis, and Sais were each independent, and very probably some of them fighting against others. Thebes had lost the superiority, and no other had yet gained it. The city which now rose into importance was Tanis, called by the Hebrew writers Zoan. It was forty miles to the north of Bubastis, being half way between that city and the sea, and it gave its name to the Tanitic branch of the river. Its temple had been ornamented by the obelisks and sculptures of Rameses II. and his successors. The town was small; but on this break-up of the kingdom, its sovereign priests

Burton's Excerpta.

Manetho.

gained their independence, and held it for two hundred years. They even sometimes made themselves masters of Thebes, and sometimes fought against Judæa. In the Hebrew writings of this time Lower Egypt is called the plains of Zoan. Its rebellion and rise was so important an event to Jerusalem that the Hebrew writer uses it as a date. Thus the rebuilding of the town of Hebron by Rehoboam was said to have taken place seven years before the rise of Zoan. Manetho gives us the names of eleven kings of Tanis who governed that city for more than two hundred years. One is named Smendes, after the god Mando, and another Petubastus, after the goddess Pasht; but the monuments in the Delta, which they may have built, and upon which they may have carved their names and deeds, have been destroyed, and we know nothing more of them.

B.C. 920.
2 Chron. ch. xi. 10; Numbers, ch. xlii. 22.

(12) After a while TAKELLOTHIS of Bubastis (see Fig. 138) conquered Thebes, and governed all Egypt. It was at this time of Egyptian weakness that Jehoshaphat, one of the most prosperous of the kings of Judah, proposed again to enter upon the trade of the Red Sea which had brought so much wealth to Solomon. He had routed the Syrian war-chariots at the foot of Mount Bashan, and he had made the Edomites receive one of his lieutenants for their ruler. In a moment of pride and hope, his poet had declared in a triumphal psalm, that ambassadors would come to Jerusalem from Egypt, and that Ethiopia would soon stretch out her hands to God. But Jehoshaphat was not strong enough for such distant doings; he was not really master of the port on the Red Sea, nor of the route to it, and he would not accept help from the king of Israel, who offered to join him in the undertaking. His ships were therefore broken to pieces at Eziongeber, by some of the tribes who were unfavourable to Jewish power in that neighbourhood. A few years later the Edomites, who held Petra and the desert between the Dead Sea and the Red Sea, again revolted from the Jews, and for the future Egypt and Judæa were more separated than they used to be.

Fig. 138.

(13) The rule of Bubastis as the chief city in Egypt lasted a very short time. Then for a few years OSORKON II. (see Fig. 139) and SHISHANK II. (see Fig. 140) of Tanis were kings of Egypt; and though we have no knowledge of the means by which these rapid changes were brought about, we may be sure they were not peaceable. New dynasties were not

Fig. 139.   Fig. 140.

set up, and the seat of government four times removed, without civil wars. No temples were built, few hieroglyphical inscriptions now remain of these unhappy times, and the events that followed prove that the kingdom was much weakened by the changes. Thebes suffered severely on its conquest by the kings of the Delta. In the words of the Hebrew prophet Nahum, who wrote a century and a half later, "The great city of Amun, that was situate among canals and had floods round about her, whose moat was a sea and floods her defence; whose strength was Ethiopia and Egypt, and was boundless; whose allies were Africa and Libya; she was carried away and sent into captivity; her babes were dashed in pieces at the top of her streets; they cast lots for her nobles, and her great men were bound in chains."

<small>Ch. iii. 8.</small>

(14) The wealth of Tanis and Mendes and the other cities on the eastern side of the Delta arose from their foreign trade, which was carried on for them by the Phenicians. This active race of seafaring Arabs traced their origin from Muscat on the Persian Gulf, and they had carried their settlements from port to port along the eastern and southern shores of the Mediterranean, from Tyre to Carthage, and even further westward to the coast of Mauritania. Of these tribes the most civilised were the most easterly, particularly the people of Tyre and Sidon and Tarsus. These cities enjoyed the carrying trade of that end of the Mediterranean. The Egyptians, though they made great use of their own river, had no timber to build seaworthy ships, and thus had a religious dread of the ocean. Tarsus first entered on this course of usefulness and wealth, finding timber for its ships in the forests of Mount Taurus. Tyre and Sidon followed, cutting their timber on Mount

<small>Herodotus, lib. vii. 89.</small>

Lebanon, or using the better built and more famous ships of Tarsus. Their merchant vessels were as yet small and able to run up the shallow eastern streams of the Nile. The merchants there bought the corn and linen and drugs of Egypt, which they sold in Palestine, in Syria, and in Asia Minor, and even in more distant parts of the Mediterranean. The wealth that these cities gained, by having the foreign trade of Egypt in their hands, was boundless.

_{Ch. xxiii.} "Sidon," says Isaiah, "was a mart of nations, she carried the corn of the Nile over the wide ocean, and the harvest of the river was her revenue. Tyre was a maker of kings, her merchants were princes, her traders were the nobles of the earth." The Greeks had either not yet entered upon this commerce, or else, as Homer tells us, they were

_{Odyss. lib. xvii. 427.} too much of pirates to be trusted. He describes them as running into the mouths of the Nile in their little rowing galleys, and thence ravaging the fair fields of the Delta, killing the husbandmen whom they met with, and when the neighbouring cities were roused by the alarm, retreating hastily to their vessels with the Egyptian women and children whom they had seized as booty.

(15) The island of Cyprus, or at least its ports, were peopled with Phenician sailors, and it took its share of this carrying trade. The mountains on this island contained a good supply of timber for ship-building; and, what was equally valuable, its mines yielded a large supply of copper, which in the infancy of science was the most useful of metals. Iron was also worked there, and steel was probably made there even long before this time. The sharp deep lines of hieroglyphics on the basalt and other hard Egyptian stones could scarcely have been cut with any other than steel tools. The Cyprian breastplate in which Agamemnon fought

_{Iliad, xi. 20.} against Troy we must suppose was made of steel; because, at a later period, we find that the coat of mail made of Cyprian adamant, and worn by Demetrius the son

_{Plutarch, Vit. Demet.} of Antigonus, was so hard that no dart, even when thrown by a machine, could make a dent in it. The numerous little harbours in the mouths of the Nile and on the Phenician coast made Cyprus a place of great importance to the Tyrian merchants. Its language was Phenician; and the names of the towns Hamath, called by the Greeks Amathus,

and Hethlon, called Idalion, seem borrowed from towns of the same names in Syria; while the harbour of SecheImi, or *Happy Water*, called by the Greeks Salamis, tells us by its name that its people had brought their language from Phenicia. When the great nations of Assyria and Egypt, a few years later, struggled for power over the states which lay between them, Cyprus became important in politics. Afterwards, when the Greek ships were masters of the east end of the Mediterranean, Cyprus became almost a Greek island; but at this time it was Phenician, and as such shared in the trade with Egypt. We must suppose that Cyprus received from Egypt corn and gold in return for its metals and timber.

(16) Tanis was the ruling city of the Delta, and the seat of the Mediterranean trade, when Homer was writing his immortal poems in Greece; and it had the largest share of the wealth arising from this trade with the Phenicians. Homer certainly had very little knowledge of the country, but we may suppose that he knew something of the coast from the pilots in that trade. He tells us that the island of Pharos, where Alexandria now stands, was even then a shelter for ships, behind which they were pulled on shore in safety, and where they took in fresh water before again launching upon the ocean. This water they may have easily found in Lake Mareotis, which is only half a mile from the seashore. Homer was hardly writing nonsense when he says the island of Pharos was as far from Egypt as a ship could sail in a whole day, with a favourable wind on the stern. The pilots perhaps measured the voyage from the Tanitic or Mendesian mouths of the river, the only mouths that they were then allowed to enter. The north is a prevailing wind on that coast; and Homer adds that to return to Egypt from the island of Pharos was a long and tedious voyage. He tells us that medical herbs were among the products for which the valley of the Nile was celebrated; and we learn the same from the prophet Jeremiah, who, when he would taunt the Egyptians with their political weakness, tells them that they should go up to Gilead and get balsam, and that they multiply their own medicines in vain.

Odyss. lib. iv. 355.

Lib. iv. 483.

Lib. iv. 229.

Ch. xlvi. 11.

(17) After some time we find upon the Egyptian throne

BOCCHORIS (see Fig. 141), the son of Tnephactus, who had made the city of Sais independent. Sais was situated upon a mound on the right bank of the Canopic branch of the Nile, about forty miles from the sea. It was the capital of the western half of the Delta, and chiefly sought by the Greek merchants. It was now rising over Bubastis and Tanis, on the increase of the Mediterranean trade; as the foreign vessels found the deepest water in the Canopic branch. The mud which the Nile carries to the sea through its seven mouths does not there remain to make a bar in front of them all equally. The current on the coast, then as now, was clearing it away from the western and blocking up the eastern mouths with it. Hence the waters of the Nile, on which wealth floated to the Egyptian cities, were slowly leaving the eastern for the western half of the Delta; and Bubastis and its neighbours were being left like wrecked ships stranded on a sand-bank. The Greek traders at Sais were gaining the profitable carrying trade which had hitherto belonged to the Phœnicians. The Jews, who dwelt wholly on the east side of the Delta, hardly knew the Nile as a great river. The change then taking place has continued even to the present time; and travellers find it difficult to determine which were the old seven mouths of the Nile. And not wealth alone, but even religious honour followed the greater body of water; and the Egyptian priests declared that the deeper stream which flowed by Sais was the Agathodæmon, or great god of the country. In his honour the town at the mouth was named the city of Kneph, by the Greeks called Canopus. Thus Sais gained great advantages from its situation. Bocchoris the Wise, its first independent sovereign, was one of the great Egyptian lawgivers. His name was spoken of with gratitude for the next seven hundred years; and to him they gave the credit of many mild laws which may perhaps have been much more modern. Among these may be mentioned the law that nobody should be put in prison for debt, and no debt should be claimed without an acknowledgment in writing, if the debtor denied it on oath.

(18) The Jews at this time began to feel in danger from

their powerful and cruel neighbours the Assyrians, who, after carrying northern Israel into captivity, were coming down upon Judea. In their alarm the Jews looked around for help. They knew the Egyptians as more humane than the Assyrians; and they would willingly have paid a tribute to Egypt to escape Assyrian bondage. But though they received promises from that country, they received no help; and the prophet Isaiah calls Egypt " the Boaster that sitteth still " and doeth nothing. Isaiah ch. xxx. 7.

(19) The kingdom of Ethiopia was that portion of the valley of the Nile which is to the south of Egypt from the granite range of hills, which forms the cataract of Syene, to where the river receives its first tributary stream, the Astaborus. Like Egypt, it is bounded on both sides by the desert, but under a sunshine yet more scorching. Here the ostrich lays its eggs in the sands to be hatched, and when disturbed sails away before the wind, in scorn of the huntsman in his chariot; and here the camelopard browses on the branches of tall trees. The northern portion, between the first and second cataracts, which was afterwards called Nubia, is very barren, as the loftier and more rocky banks leave but a narrow strip of land to be watered by the overflow of the river. The southern part is more fertile and more populous. Two hundred miles above the Astaborus the Nile again divides into two streams of nearly equal size, the White River, which is the largest, and comes from the south, and the Blue River, which comes from Abyssinia on the south-east. Between this point and the Astaborus is the island of Meroë, a plain within the district of the tropical rains, in the land of acacia trees and ebony trees, a country too moist for the palm trees of Egypt and Ethiopia, and where the river-horse wades in the reedy fens, and tramples down the fields of rice and corn, and not far from the forests which give shelter to herds of small elephants. Meroë sometimes formed part of the kingdom of Ethiopia, but was probably at other times independent. The river within the bounds of Ethiopia makes two great bends, so that Napata, the capital, is separated on one side from Meroë by the Bahiouda desert, and on the other side from Egypt by the Nubian desert. The Nubians were of the same race as the Egyptians, though with a skin more copper-coloured, as living

under a hotter sky; but the Ethiopians or southern part of the population were of an Arabic race, or, in the language of the Old Testament, they were Cushites. But Ethiopia had for many years been ruled over by Egyptians; and the hieroglyphics and sculptured deities on the walls of the temples prove that the language and religion of their priestly rulers were the same as those of Thebes. Napata was built at the foot of a steep sandstone mountain on the right bank of the river. The burial places were small pyramids, differing in plan from those of Memphis by the addition of a portico (see Fig. 142).

Fig. 142.

The city had also a second field of pyramids in the desert on the opposite bank, eight miles up the river. The towns of Samneh, Tombos, Soleb, and Abou Simbel had been ornamented by the Egyptian taste and for the Egyptian religion of Amunothph, Thothmosis, and Rameses. The Egyptian arts even reached to Meroë, where we still trace the ruins of pyramids with a portico, and of temples covered with hieroglyphics in awkward imitation of those of Thebes.

(20) About two centuries before this time, soon after the death of Shishank, the Ethiopians had thrown off the Egyptian yoke; and now they marched northward perhaps a

ALLIANCE WITH JUDÆA.

second time, and conquered Egypt and put Bocchoris himself to death. SABACOTHPH the Ethiopian (see Fig. 143) then made himself king of nearly all Egypt. There was no league among the several cities to resist him, nor union in their councils. Anysis the king of Memphis fled from the danger. His blindness might perhaps be his excuse. He saved his life by escaping to the marshes of the Delta. The city of Tanis alone held out against the Ethiopians for a few years longer.

B.C. 737.

Herodotus, lib. ii. 137

Fig. 143.

(21) Ethiopia, though independent, was still a Coptic country; and when Sabacothph marched northward, the Thebans must have thought him more a native sovereign than Bocchoris of Sais. But not so the people of the Delta; to them he was a foreign conqueror. But he copied Bocchoris in making some new and milder laws; and henceforth criminals, instead of being put to death, were employed to raise the mounds of earth higher round the cities in the Delta against the overflowing waters of the Nile. On this invasion of Egypt, the working of the gold mines in Nubia, near the city afterwards called Berenice, was for a time stopped. The criminals and prisoners of war, who there worked underground beneath the lash of a taskmaster, and watched over by a guard of soldiers, would of course feel their situation changed on the defeat of the Egyptian army; and no doubt most of the violent revolutions in the country stopped the working of these mines. Sabacothph reigned eight years in Egypt.

Herodotus, lib. ii. 137.

Agatharcides, ap. Photium.

Manetho.

(22) SEVECHUS (see Fig. 144), the next king, was also of Ethiopia. His first name was Bokra, copied no doubt from that of the Egyptian king whom Sabacothph dethroned. He is known to us in the Old Testament under the name of Seve or So. During his reign Egypt remained a province, governed by a stranger, and he is little known on the Theban buildings. To him Hoshea, king of Israel, sent ambassadors with gifts, and with him he formed an alliance when he was threatened

B.C. 729.
2 Kings, ch. xvii. 4.

Fig. 144.

with an invasion by his neighbour, Shalmanezer, king of Assyria.

(23) The Assyrians had latterly been growing into a powerful monarchy, strong enough to be known to the Egyptians, without yet being so near them as to quarrel. We are told the names, and only the names, of a long line of Assyrian kings, sometimes called the earlier Assyrian monarchy. Of these names we can make no use, since they are unknown to Egyptian as to Hebrew history. But about the year B.C. 760 the Assyrians come to our notice under a king of the name of Pul. Their chief city, Nineveh, on the banks of the Tigris, was then the wealthy capital of an empire which included not only the upper part of the country watered by the Tigris and Euphrates, but the mountains of Kurdistan, and the plains on the further side of that range, which are watered by rivers running into the Caspian Sea. The kingdom was so well established by Pul, that his successor was able to indulge the ambition of widening it. Tiglath-Pileser, the next king, marched westward, and conquered Syria, and then took Galilee from the Israelites. His name teaches us that at that time Nineveh was on terms of friendship with Egypt, and was willing to borrow its fashions from that country as from a superior power; as, in addition to the two Assyrian words, Pul and Eser, his name is formed of the Egyptian name Takelloth, which we have seen borne by a king of Bubastis a century and a half earlier. It was no doubt at this time that some knowledge of Egyptian sculpture and architecture reached the banks of the Tigris. The sculptors ornamented the palaces at Nineveh with the Egyptian figure of the winged sun, and finding his name, Amun-Ra, not suited to their lips, they spelt it Obeno-Ra. At the same time, the more scientific city of Babylon adopted the Egyptian calendar with its year of three hundred and sixty-five days and its movable new-year's day, and called their months after the names of the Egyptian gods and kings.

(24) Assyria rose yet higher in power under Shalmanezer, the successor of Tiglath. By its conquests of the Israelites, it was becoming a near neighbour of Egypt, and was soon to be its chief enemy. While Shalmanezer's victorious armies were pressing upon the tributary kings of Samaria and Judæa,

they naturally looked to Egypt for help. Had these little Hebrew kingdoms been united, and had they allied themselves with their Syrian neighbours, who were of the same blood as themselves, they might perhaps have withstood the advance of the Assyrian armies. But since their quarrel they were unable to defend themselves; and Egypt could be of no service to them against Shalmanezer. To Egypt, however, many of the Israelites fled from the coming destruction, though the prophet Hosea warned them that they never would be able to return home. He tells them, that they would die among strangers, that Egypt would gather up their bones, and Memphis, so famous for its pyramids, would bury them. Shalmanezer soon conquered all the neighbouring countries, Sidon, and Acre, and the island of Cyprus. Tyre alone held out against a siege. The Assyrians therefore overran the rebellious Samaritans in spite of their Egyptian allies; they put down the kingdom of Israel, carried away the nobles as captives to the banks of the Caspian, and made Samaria a province of Assyria. Hosea, ch. ix. 6.
Menander, ap. Joseph.
2 Kings, ch. xviii. 10.

(25) The danger from Shalmanezer had threatened Judæa as well as Israel, and about the same time King Hezekiah seems to have hoped for succour from the Jews of Abyssinia, with whom his nation kept up some little intercourse by sea. The prophet Isaiah, though fearing an union with their Egyptian neighbours, saw no danger in receiving help from a people half way down the Red Sea, and he thus addresses Abyssinia: "O land of the winged Tsaltsal (or Spear-fly), beyond the rivers of Ethiopia, that sendest ambassadors by sea in reed boats upon the face of the waters." And he adds that at a future time the Abyssinian Jews will send gifts to Jehovah of hosts to the dwelling-place of the name of Jehovah on Mount Zion. Already, in their habits of wandering, many of the Jews had settled in Abyssinia; and when the prophet Zephaniah speaks of the piety towards Jehovah, which will be shown by the whole nation, he adds that even from beyond the rivers of Ethiopia his worshippers, the children of the dispersion, will bring their offerings. Ch. xviii.

Ch. iii. 10.

(26) TIRHAKAH (see Fig. 145), the third Ethiopian king

of Egypt, on coming to the throne, found Sennacherib, the next king of Assyria, pursuing these successes, and threatening the destruction of the kingdom of Judæa. The prophet Isaiah had warned Hezekiah, the Jewish king, that trusting in Egyptian help was leaning on a bruised reed; and so it proved. Sennacherib marched towards Egypt to attack Tirhakah instead of waiting to be attacked. He came to the walls of Pelusium, the frontier city, and laid siege to it in due form. He dug his trenches and raised his platforms to a level with the city walls, and was nearly ready for the assault, when he heard that the Egyptian army was marching from Memphis to the relief of the place. But the Egyptians were stopped by a revolt, arising perhaps from a jealousy between the priesthood and the soldiers. The governor of Memphis, the priest of Pthah, whom Herodotus calls by his priestly title Sethon, who was the general of the Egyptian army, had unwisely quarrelled with the soldiers about their allowance of land, at the rate of six acres a man, which they had been allowed to hold free of rent. He had treated them with great severity. So the soldiers refused to march with him. On this he encamped near Pelusium, with such citizens and volunteers as would join him, for the defence of the city. But the courage of these raw tribes was never tried. Before they met the enemy, the army of Sennacherib was no more. An unseen hand had routed or destroyed the Assyrians in the night; or the loss of their supplies by sea had left them without food with the desert in their rear; the prophet Isaiah gave glory to Jehovah for the destruction of the nation's enemy, and the Egyptians set up a monument in the temple of Memphis in gratitude to their god Pthah.

Fig. 145.

(27) Pelusium was one of the naval stations of the Egyptians; its population was made up of sailors. They were not Egyptians, but Phenicians and other seafaring Asiatics, who settled there of old. The place had to be attacked by sea, as well as by land, and for the siege of Pelusium, the Assyrians employed a fleet of

CHAP. III.] SIEGE OF PELUSIUM. 145

Phenician vessels, or ships of Tarsus, to meet the land forces with timber. This was cut on Mount Lebanon, and put on shipboard at the city of Tyre, as we see in a picture carved on the Assyrian monuments (see Fig. 146). But the timber ships were lost in a storm, and with them probably the other necessary supplies for the land forces; and when the Hebrew Psalmist speaks of the enemy retreating in fear from before the walls of Jerusalem, he also thanks God for breaking to pieces these ships of Tarsus with an east wind. Another Assyrian army, which, under the command of Tartan, had been sent against Ashdod, a

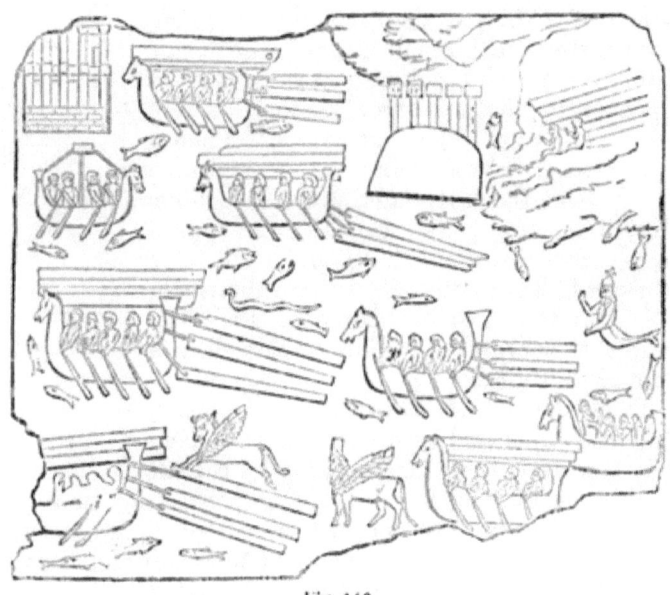

Fig. 146.

strong city of the Philistines, was more successful; it continued the siege of that place, and shortly afterwards took it.

(28) The kingdom of Ethiopia was now in its greatest prosperity. The Nubian gold mines added to its revenues; and kings who could hold Upper and Lower Egypt as a province did not forget to ornament their own cities with

taste formed in Thebes. The grand temple built at Napata by
Tirhakah was equal in size, though hardly in beauty,
Hoskins's Ethiopia. to those of Egypt. There the pigmy grotesque
figure of the god of Memphis stands against
the columns, and the king styles himself Beloved by the
Theban goddess Athor. Sabacothph had built on the large
island of Argo, or Gagaudes, as Pliny calls
it; and the colossal statues there still declare
its grandeur (see Fig. 147). And the kings
of these distant regions, eight hundred miles
to the south of Memphis, were now meddling
in the quarrels between the Assyrians and the
Israelites. Under Tirhakah Egypt was less a
province of Ethiopia than it had been under
the two former Ethiopian kings. Tirhakah
probably removed his seat of government from
the poorer to the wealthier part of his dominions. The priests of Thebes
Wilkinson, recorded on their walls his victories
Thebes.
over the Assyrians, as to the honour
of Egyptian arms; and thus Thebes again
Burton's gave laws to Ethiopia. The city
Excerpta, of Tanis now quietly submitted;
pl. 41. and we find the name of Tirhakah
among the sculptures which ornament the
temple of that city.

Fig. 147.

(29) Hitherto, the dates in our history,
during the thousand years which we have
hastily run over, have been settled by calculating backwards
from this reign along the line of Egyptian kings and Jewish
priests, by allowing about twenty years to a reign and thirty
to a generation. Hence, the error at the beginning may have
amounted to one or even two centuries, and must have grown
less as we approached this time. But here we have arrived
at certainty in chronology. Tirhakah, the Ethiopian,
Isaiah, reigned in Egypt while Hezekiah reigned in Judæa,
ch. xxxix. Sennacherib in Assyria, and Mardoch Empadus in
Ptolemæi Babylon; and with this last begins the series of
Syntax. recorded Babylonian eclipses on which the historian
Mag. now builds his chronology, while he acknowledges
his debt to the Alexandrian astronomers who have preserved

them for us, and to modern science which has calculated them. Henceforth the error in our dates ought not to be greater than twelve months, and is probably seldom twice as great; and with exactness in the dates follows greater certainty in history. The Egyptians kept no records of eclipses or of occultations of the stars.

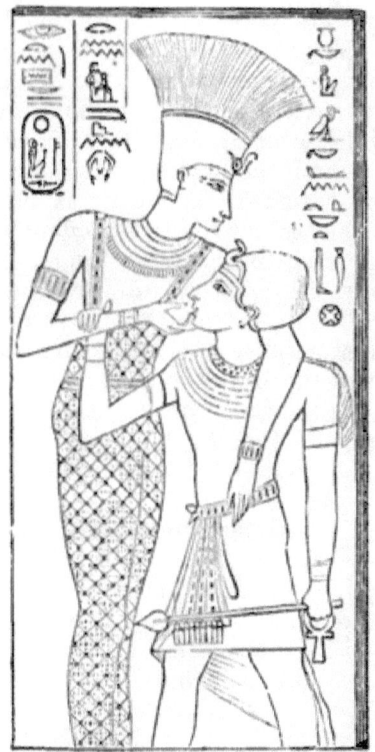

Fig. 148.—Rameses II. suckled by a goddess.

CHAPTER IV.

RISE OF THE WESTERN HALF OF THE DELTA. THE KINGS OF SAIS. B.C. 697—523.

(1) DURING the sixty years which follow the defeat of Sennacherib's attack upon Tirhakah, the Jewish annals are silent as to any wars between Assyria and Egypt. Of the two nations the Assyrians were the stronger; and whether from foreign conquest, or from other causes, Egypt was sinking in power. After the death of Tirhakah the kingdom fell to pieces; Thebes again lost its rank as the capital of Egypt; and the country was divided into several little monarchies. As many as twelve cities then found themselves the independent capitals of their several districts; and their twelve kings governed quietly without plunging the country into civil war. Memphis, though the largest city in the Delta, was not the governing city. Sethon of Memphis, who had commanded the army in the late reign, was the last of the kings or sovereign priests of that city that is known to us. But indeed of those who governed Memphis during the thousand years since Suphis, the builder of the pyramid, not many of their names have been saved. Manetho mentions none after Queen Nitocris. The kings who followed her when not kings of Thebes were subjects to the kings of Thebes. But though the kings or chief priests of Memphis after her time possessed little more than the title, and their sway may have been for the most part limited to the command over the temple services, yet they continued to add new buildings to their city. The ruins also of sixty pyramids on the range of Libyan hills show that they continued to build tombs for themselves of the same form, though not of the same lasting strength as before; and the brick pyramid of Asychis, which has been destroyed, was even larger than that of Nef-chofo, which has remained because built of stone. The tombs in the neighbourhood of the pyramids are as numerous as those near

_{Herodotus, ii. 147.}

THE KINGDOM BROKEN TO PIECES.

Thebes, and equally ornamented with paintings and sculpture, though not in equally good taste. But unfortunately we are very much left in doubt as to the age of these works of art; because the priests and nobles of Memphis never dated their inscriptions by means of a king's name. They had too little love for the Theban kings to count the years by their reigns and the names of their own chief priests or little kings were not important enough to answer the purpose. Herodotus and Diodorus mention some of these kings of Memphis, whose names they learnt during their inquiries in Lower Egypt; and the scanty ruins in the neighbourhood add few or none to the list. The chief names there found are Chofo (see Fig. 19), and Nof-chofo (see Fig. 20), the builders of the pyramids; Chemi (see Fig. 149), called by Diodorus, Chemmis; Chemren (see Fig. 150), called Chephren; Mesaphra (see Fig. 151), perhaps Thothmosis II., called Mœris; Mycera (see Fig. 44), perhaps Thothmosis III., called Mycerinus; Rameses, called Rampsinitus; Shishank, called Sesostris; his son Osorchon; Uchora (see Fig. 152), or Uchureus; Bokora (see Fig. 141), or Bocchoris; and Asisa (see Fig. 153), or Asychis. After

<small>Egypt. Inscript. 2nd Ser. pl. 38, 39, 41, 43.</small>

Fig. 149.   Fig. 150.   Fig. 151.   Fig. 152.   Fig. 153.

the time of Sethon the sovereignty of Egypt rested with Sais; and then the high priests of Memphis would of course have less power than when the more distant Thebes was capital of the kingdom. Herodotus did not find that any priest of Memphis after the time of Sethon was counted among the kings.

(2) During these years of confusion after the death of Tirhakah, the chief authority rested in a line of kings which may be traced as unbroken, though removing from Napata at the fourth cataract in Ethiopia, to Sais in the Delta. AMMERES, the successor of Tirhakah, was probably the same person as Amun Ascr

<small>Manetho. B.C. 697.</small>

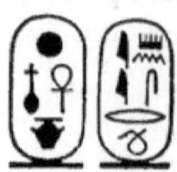

Fig. 154.

(see Fig. 154), whose name we find cut upon two noble lions now in the British Museum. They are of red granite from the quarries of Tombos at the third cataract, carved by the skill of Theban workmen for Amunothph III., perhaps for the temple at Soleb, but carried off by an Ethiopian king to ornament his temple at Napata. Ammeres, though an Ethiopian, reigned at Sais, where the chief strength of the nation was now to be found. There the Greeks had settled in large numbers, and had enriched the people of that district with their trade, and taught them higher skill in arms. Hence Sais quietly rose over its rival cities to be the capital of Egypt.

(3) STEPHINATHIS, the successor of Ammeres, was an Egyptian, as were his successors, and they all continued to reside at Sais. NECHEPSUS, the next king, has left a name known for his priestly learning; and astronomical writings bearing his name, though probably much more modern, are quoted by Pliny. They were in the Greek language, which was common in the western half of the Delta, where Greek arts and sciences were becoming known and copied, and were giving that half of the kingdom its superiority over Thebes; for in Upper Egypt the Coptic religion and prejudices so far forbad change as to stop improvement. Nechepsus was followed on the throne of Sais by NECHO I. and then by PSAMMETICHUS I., whose first name was Vaphra (see Fig. 155), and by this time the king of Sais was king of all Egypt.

Ausonius, Ep. 409, 20. Plin. lib. ii.

Manetho.

Fig. 155.

(4) We do not know by what troops Shishank and the kings of Tanis had formerly overthrown the family of Rameses; but the kings of Sais upheld their power by means of Greek mercenaries who made fighting the trade by which they earned their livelihood. The Nubian gold mines made wages higher in Egypt than in other countries; and Psammetichus had in his pay a large body of Carians and Ionians from the Greek settlements on the coast of Asia Minor. With these he carried on a long war in Syria, and, after a blockade of twenty-nine years, he took the city of Azotus or Ashdod, which had lately been

Herodotus, lib. ii. 152.

taken by Tartan the Assyrian general. To these Greek soldiers Psammetichus gave lands near Pelusium; and their settlement bore the name of the Camps. This was a space intrenched on that branch of the river, and within it were not only dwelling-places for themselves, but docks for their ships. It guarded the Pelusiac mouth of the Nile. He also had a standing army of Egyptians encamped on the three frontiers; at Elephantine, against the Ethiopians on the south, at Daphnæ near Pelusium, against the Arabs and Syrians on the east, and at Maræa on the Lake Maræotis, against the Libyans on the west. By his favours to the Greek mercenaries Psammetichus gave great offence to the Egyptian troops; and on his not complying with some of their demands, and refusing to relieve them when their three years' term of service was ended, the whole of the Elephantine guard deserted. They marched through Ethiopia, and settled at Ezar, seventeen days' journey beyond Meroë, in the country now called Abyssinia, where a people calling themselves their descendants were to be found three hundred years afterwards. Psammetichus marched in pursuit of the deserters. He did not himself go beyond Elephantine; but his Greek troops went much further, and they turned back after having passed through places wholly unknown, where the river was called by another name. Some of the soldiers cut an inscription, mentioning this distant march, on the shin of one of the colossal statues in front of the temple of Abou Simbel, at the second cataract; and if we do right in following Herodotus, and giving this event to the reign of Psammetichus I., when it seems rather to belong to Psammetichus II., this is one of the earliest pieces of Greek writing now remaining. The writer made use of the Greek double letters, Ps, Ph, Ch, and Th, and also of the long E, but not of the long O.

_{Herodotus, lib. ii. 30.}

_{Pliny, lib. vi. 35.}

_{Egyptian Inscript. 2nd Ser. 23.}

(5) In this reign the Medes, the Assyrians, the Jews, indeed all the west of Asia, were startled at hearing that a large army of Scythians was pouring down from Tartary over the cultivated plains of the south. The army of Medes, sent against them by Cyaxares, was wholly routed. No force could check their march. They spread in every direction over the whole country.

_{Herodotus, lib. i. 103.}

One body marched straight towards Egypt. They crossed Mesopotamia. They met with no resistance from Josiah, who then reigned in Judæa. They had passed the fortified cities. But they grew weaker as they moved further; and, when they reached the Egyptian frontier, Psammetichus was able, by gifts and prayers and threats, to turn them towards the coast of Palestine, and they plundered the city of Askalon as they marched northwards. Egypt escaped frightened but unhurt by this band of roving Tartars. They were routed and cut to pieces in their passage through the land of the Philistines, and many of them perished on the eastern shore of the Mediterranean. "It shall come to pass," says Ezekiel, writing a few years later about them, "in that day I will give to Gog," or the Scythians, "a burial-place in Israel, the valley of the passengers on the east of the sea. And it shall stop the noses of them that pass by; and there shall they bury Gog and all his multitude." We might have thought that distance would have made this people unknown in the Egyptian wars, but we seem to find them sculptured in the battle-scenes of the great Rameses.

Ch. xxxix. 11.

(6) Psammetichus made treaties of peace with the Athenians and other Greek states; he gave to his children a Greek education, and he encouraged the Greeks to settle in Egypt for the purposes of trade. Thus Egypt was no longer the same kingdom that we have seen it at the beginning of this history. It was no longer a kingdom of Coptic warriors, who from their fortresses in the Thebaid held the wealthy traders and husbandmen of the Delta in subjection as vassals. But it was now a kingdom of these very vassals; the valour of Thebes had sunk, the wealth of the Delta had increased, and Greek mercenaries had very much taken the place of the native landholders. Hence arose a jealousy between the Greek and Coptic inhabitants of Egypt. The sovereigns found it dangerous to employ Greeks, and still more dangerous to be without them. They were the cause of frequent rebellions, and more than once of the king's overthrow. But there was evidently no choice. The Egyptian laws and religion forbad change and improvement, while everything around them was changing as the centuries rolled on. Hence, if

Diod. Sic. lib. i. 6, 7.

Egypt was to remain an independent kingdom, it could be so only by the help of the settlers in the Delta. A granite obelisk, ornamented with sculpture by Psammetichus, now stands in the Campus Martius at Rome, where it was set up by the Emperor Augustus. On the pyramidal top, as usual, the king is represented in the form of a sphinx, and worshipping a god; but here, for the first time, we find the sphinx without a beard. The figures of the earlier kings, whether as men or sphinxes, all have beards; but the kings of this newer race in Sais followed the Greek fashion of shaving. There is also a broken statue of this king in the public library at Cambridge. It is in black basalt; and it was probably about this time that the quarries of basalt in the neighbourhood of Syene were first worked, at least, to any great extent. During the reigns of these kings of Sais, most of the statues were made of this very hard stone. It would seem as if the sculptors and their employers valued stones according to their hardness. The great kings of Thebes began with red granite, and then chose the harder dark syenite for their statues; and now the sculptors were ordered to cut their monuments out of this yet harder basalt.

(8) NECHO II. (see Fig. 156) succeeded his father Psammetichus, and made another great change in the military tactics of the Egyptians. Their habits and religion agreed in unfitting them for sailors, or for venturing on any waters but their own Nile; they thought all seafaring persons impious, as breaking through a divine law; and he was the first Egyptian who turned his attention to naval affairs. He got together two large fleets, built and manned by Phenicians, one on the Mediterranean, and one on the Red Sea. He also began to dig a ship canal which was to join these two seas, or rather to join the Nile to the Red Sea. It was to be led from the Nile near Bubastis, by the city of Patumos or Thoum, along a natural valley to Heroopolis, and then into the Lower Bitter Lake, which by this time had been cut off from the head of the Red Sea by a slowly increasing sand-bank. This change in the coast is spoken of by Isaiah. "The Lord," says the prophet,

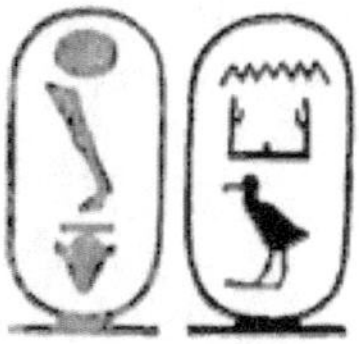

Fig. 156.

Herodotus, lib. ii. 158.
B.C. 614.

Ch. xi. 15.

"will cut off the tongue of the Egyptian sea;" and thus the spot where Moses marched between the waters, and where the Egyptians were drowned, became a bank that separated the sea from a new lake. From this lake, and through this bank, the canal was to be cut into the Red Sea. It was to be wide enough for two ships abreast. But the king was warned by the priests that he was working for foreigners, and gave up the undertaking. When it was determined that the canal should not be dug, Necho ordered his Phenician pilots to see whether the fleets might not be moved from sea to sea by some other channel; and for this purpose his mariners set sail on a voyage of discovery from the Red Sea coasting Egypt and Ethiopia, with a view to circumnavigate Africa. They spent nearly three years on the voyage. They twice landed and laid up their ships, sowed the fields and reaped the harvest, and then set sail again. In this way they came round to the well-known pillars of Hercules, the Straits of Gibraltar, and thus brought the ships safely into the mouth of the Nile, declaring to their disbelieving hearers, what to us is a proof of the truth of the whole story, that as they were sailing westward the sun was on their right hand. The voyage was too long to be repeated, but it was a noble undertaking on the part of Necho for the increase of commerce and geographical knowledge. The Carthaginians soon afterwards sent a fleet under the command of Hanno to follow the west coast of Africa; but, as Hanno's fleet was not victualled for a long voyage, it turned back before reaching the equator.

<small>Herodotus, lib. iv. 42.</small>

(9) Necho's ships were not all so innocently employed. By the help of his fleet he began to take part in the neighbouring Asiatic wars. He led a large army to attack the old enemies of Egypt, the Assyrians, whom we must now call Babylonians or Chaldees, since the seat of the Assyrian empire had been removed southward. Babylon, the capital of the plain through which the Tigris and Euphrates reach the Persian Gulf, had usually been subject to Nineveh, though ruled over by tributary kings. Latterly, however, the Kurds, or some other highland tribe that had also been subject to Nineveh, had rebelled and conquered Babylon. They then, with the new name of Chaldees, and under Nabopolassar as their

<small>Herodotus, lib. ii. 159.
B.C. 611.</small>

king, conquered Nineveh. Nabopolassar's kingdom therefore now reached from the Caspian to the Mediterranean, from the Persian Gulf to the Taurus and Caucasus. He was master of all the nations on the Tigris, the Euphrates, the Araxes, and the Orontes. Notwithstanding the neighbourhood of this mighty empire, Necho wished again to establish the Egyptian influence over Judæa, whose councils had latterly been wholly under that of Babylon. He landed his forces on the northern part of Palestine, to avoid the king of Judæa, with whom he was at peace, as he meant to march through Galilee towards the sources of the Euphrates. But Josiah king of Judæa distrusted his promises of friendship, and was faithful to the treaty with Babylon; and he led an army northward to stop Necho's march. The Egyptians and Jews fought a pitched battle in the valley of Megiddo, about sixty miles from Jerusalem. There the Jewish forces were routed by the Egyptian archers, Josiah himself was mortally wounded, and hurried off the field of battle in his chariot. He made good, however, his retreat to Jerusalem, as Necho without pursuing him marched northward towards Upper Syria. Necho found that that province, which is as far from Babylon as from Egypt, was badly guarded; and it yielded him an easy though useless victory. ^{2 Chron. ch. xxxv.}

(10) Necho then returned southward to punish the Jews for the resistance they had before offered to him. In the meanwhile King Josiah had died in Jerusalem of his wounds; and his son Jehoahaz had been king for three months, when Necho on his return from the Euphrates laid siege to Jerusalem. The Jews were then divided into two parties, a Babylonian party and an Egyptian party; and the latter, opening the gates to Necho, by his help deposed Jehoahaz, the late king's elder son, and made Eliakim, the younger son, king. Necho fined the city a hundred talents of silver, and a talent of gold, for its resistance; and he carried away Jehoahaz a prisoner to Egypt. On his return from these wars, the Egyptian king sent the armour which he wore at the battle of Megiddo to the temple of Apollo at Branchidæ, near Miletus in Caria, in gratitude to the god of his faithful mercenaries. Judæa then remained a

province of Egypt, paying tribute to Necho, and falling into some of the Egyptian idolatry. And when the prophet Urijah, the friend and follower of Jeremiah, raised his voice against the nation's forgetfulness of Jehovah, and had to flee for his life, and escaped into Egypt, Necho allowed Jehoiakim to fetch him back and put him to death.

<small>Jeremiah, xxvi. 20.</small>

(11) Nabopolassar, king of Babylon, however, was not long in sending his forces to regain the revolted provinces of Syria and Phenicia, and to punish his rebellious satraps, who had so readily joined the Egyptians. His son Nebuchadnezzar, who, as general, commanded the Babylonian army, defeated the Egyptian troops at Carchemish, on the Euphrates, and easily regained the whole of Syria. He drove the Egyptians altogether out of Palestine, and took away from Necho all that he had held between the Nile and the Euphrates. He conquered Jerusalem, and a few years later, in order to put a stop to all future revolts of the Jews, he led the Jewish king, Jehoiachin, and his nobles captive to Babylon. Thus the Hebrew nation, after weakening itself by the division into the ten tribes of Israel and the two tribes of Judah, in vain tried to maintain its independence between the great rival kingdoms of Egypt and Assyria. Shalmaneser had before put down the kingdom of Israel, and Nebuchadnezzar shortly put an end to the kingdom of Judah. Ever since the Assyrians in the reign of Sennacherib had defeated the armies of Tirhakah, they had claimed and sometimes received a tribute from Egypt as from a subject province. In this last war, the Babylonian historian speaks of Necho as the rebellious satrap of Nabopolassar.

<small>Berosus, ap. Josephum.</small>

<small>Jeremiah, ch. xlvi. 2.</small>

<small>2 Kings, ch. xxiv.</small>

<small>2 Kings, ch. xxv.</small>

<small>Berosus, ap. Josephum.</small>

(12) The weakness of Egypt and the strength of Babylon make it probable that about this time was made the military trench which joined the Lower Bitter Lakes to the Nile near Pelusium. It was dug for a fortification against eastern invasion, but was also useful for irrigation. There is always a natural drainage here of salt water from the Red Sea, through the lakes and through the sands, to the Mediterranean. Part runs into the Pelusiac

<small>Herodotus, lib. ii. 15, 113.</small>

marshes, where pits were formed for the manufacture of salt. Another part reaches the sea more to the east, and forms the Lake Serbonis, near Mount Cassius, the famed Serbonian bog, in which whole armies are fabled to have sunk on their march along the coast. Necho's canal, by bringing water from the Nile, made the Lower Bitter Lakes fresh, and they took the name of Crocodile Lakes; and from the Crocodile Lakes was dug the military trench to Pelusium, as a check to hostile inroads from Palestine and Arabia. Thus the whole eastern frontier of seventy miles from sea to sea was more or less guarded by lake or marsh or trench.

<small>Diod. Sic. lib. 1. 30.</small>

<small>Lib. 1. 57</small>

(13) PSAMMETICHUS II. (see Fig. 157), or Psammis, the next king of Egypt, was called off from these wars in Palestine by difficulties nearer home; and he was forced to lead his army into Ethiopia, to put down a rising of that nation. Palestine and all Syria remained in the hands of the Babylonians; the Egyptian power, during this reign of six years, was bounded on the east by the desert of Pelusium. The Grecian states, however, still looked up to him as their great neighbour, and when they quarrelled about the Olympic games they referred the matter to his arbitration. The several states complained that the Eleans, who acted as judges, often unfairly gave the prize to one of themselves; and Psammetichus wisely answered, that, as the Eleans had the management of the games, they should not allow their own citizens to enter the lists, lest their judgments should want impartiality.

Fig. 157.

<small>Manetho. B.C. 608.</small>

<small>Herodotus, lib. ii. 161.</small>

<small>Herodotus, lib. ii. 160.</small>

(14) HOPHRA, APRIES, or PSAMMETICHUS III. (see Fig. 158), as he is variously named by the historians and in the hieroglyphical inscriptions, succeeded his father, and was in the beginning of his reign as active and successful as the former was unfortunate. His first step was to send an army into Palestine, to the relief of Zedekiah, who, after having reigned for several years as the satrap of Nebuchadnezzar, had at last rebelled and

Fig. 158.

<small>Manetho. B.C. 591.</small>

<small>Jeremiah, ch. xxxvii.</small>

was being besieged in Jerusalem by the Chaldean army. On the approach of the Egyptians the Chaldees retreated, and left Palestine to be overrun by Hophra, who took the strong cities of Gaza and Sidon, and after defeating the naval forces of the Phenicians and Cyprians with his fleet, shortly took Tyre. But Nebuchadnezzar soon again marched upon Judæa with a larger force, and renewed the siege of Jerusalem. This time Hophra was unable or unwilling to help the Jews, and after a siege of fifteen months they opened their gates to the conqueror. Zedekiah was carried away prisoner by Nebuchadnezzar, the walls of Jerusalem were levelled with the ground, the nobles were carried away captive, and Judæa ceased to be a kingdom. Hophra had returned home with a great booty; but there his successes ended.

<small>Jeremiah, ch. xlvii.
Herodotus, lib ii. 161.
Diod. Sic. lib. i. 68.</small>

<small>Jeremiah, ch. xxxix.</small>

<small>B.C. 588.</small>

By his foreign wars he had weakened his kingdom, while he fancied he was strengthening it. Nebuchadnezzar, after conquering Jerusalem, took away from Egypt every possession that it had held in Arabia, Palestine, or the island of Cyprus.

<small>Berosus, ap. Josephum.</small>

(15) During these wars between Babylon and Judæa, the prophet Ezekiel, writing from the place of his captivity on the banks of the Euphrates, had warned his countrymen not to trust to the help of the Egyptians, nor then to aim at freedom or revolt against the power of Nebuchadnezzar. He foretold that Tyre and the other cities of Palestine, which had so readily joined the Egyptians, would soon be again conquered by the Chaldees; and he thus figuratively addresses Hophra: "Behold, I am against thee, Pharaoh, king of Egypt, thou great crocodile that liest in the midst of his waters; that hast said, My river is mine own, and I have made it for myself. But I will put hooks in thy jaws, and will cause the fish of thy waters to stick unto thy scales; and I will bring thee up out of the midst of thy waters, and all the fish of thy waters shall stick unto thy scales; and I will leave thee in the desert. . . . . Behold, therefore, I am against thee, and against thy waters; and I will make the land of Egypt utterly waste and desolate, from Magdolon to Syene on the borders of Ethiopia."

<small>Ezekiel, ch. xvii.</small>

<small>ch. xxvii.</small>

<small>ch. xxix.</small>

(16) After the death of Zedekiah, the Jews, smarting under the tyranny of the Chaldees, though they could no longer look to Egypt for help, turned to it as a place of refuge, and large bodies fled there for safety. *Jeremiah, ch. xlii. 15.* On the rebellion of Johanan, who had tried to make Judæa once more a free state, the prophet Jeremiah promised the Jews that if they remained in their own country God would take care of them; and he warned those who were removing into Egypt, that they would thereby sink deeper in the idolatry that they had lately fallen into. *ch. xliii.* But hunger and fear made them deaf to the prophet's eloquent warnings, and thousands removed quietly into Egypt; and when Johanan found himself unable to make head against the larger forces of the Chaldees, he also in despair led his little army along the coast of the Mediterranean through the desert, towards the Egyptian border, carrying with him the prophet and Baruch the scribe as well as his Chaldee prisoners. At the frontier Jeremiah again warned Johanan and the other Jews to turn back before entering the Egyptian city of Tahpenes or Daphnæ; but this little band of patriots, the remnant of Judah, as they proudly called themselves, had lost all heart; they saw no chance of success in battle; and, disbelieving the prophet, whom they accused of being a favourer of the Chaldees, they entered Egypt while their wives offered up their prayers and incense to the Egyptian goddess the queen of heaven. Hophra received these brave but unfortunate men kindly, and he allowed them to settle in the Land of Goshen, between Memphis and the Red Sea, the place where their forefathers had dwelt in the time of Moses, and which some of their nation had never quitted. Even before the arrival of these Jews there had been a small but continual stream of fugitives, both from northern Israel and from Judea, who moved southward to escape danger from the Assyrians. Some had paused at Beer-sheba on the edge of the desert, and had there raised an altar to Jehovah. But others had pressed forward into Egypt; Isaiah had strongly blamed this desertion of their country in its time of need. But his voice was little heeded. The inhabitants around Hebron, as being nearest to Egypt, flocked there in largest numbers.

(17) In one of these towns, perhaps Tahpenes, the first he entered after crossing the frontier marshes, or perhaps Heliopolis, the seat of learning, but in one of these towns, the prophet Jeremiah wrote his Lamentations. His friend Baruch the scribe probably held the pen for him. Whether they are the poems which we now possess under that name is doubtful. Here also he wrote some of his latter prophecies, in which he threatens destruction to Egypt, and that Nebuchadnezzar shall set up his throne in Tahpenes. He also gave a last warning to his countrymen, living at Migdol, at Tahpenes, at Memphis, and in Upper Egypt, to avoid the idolatry of the land. He reminds them that Jehovah's anger fell on Judah because they bowed down to strange gods. He warns them to leave off their sacrifices to the queen of heaven, or they shall be punished in Egypt as they have been punished in their own land. And, as a sign to prove that these threats shall hereafter come to pass, he tells them that they shall see Hophra, the powerful king of Egypt, put to death by his enemies, as they had seen Zedekiah, king of Judah, put to death by the Babylonians.

Jeremiah, ch. xliii.
ch. xliv.

(18) This settlement of Jews near Heliopolis must have existed very early, probably even from the time of Moses. Many may have remained behind at the time of the Exodus, though it was only on the rise of the Assyrian power that their numbers were much increased by those who fled there for safety. Here the Jews after a time lost the use of their own language, and adopted in its place the Greek, which was used by all strangers in the Delta. At the same time they gave some new words to the Egyptians. The native name for the river was Sihor, or Seiris, as the Greeks pronounced it, taken from the colour, *blue*. But it received its present name, the Nile, or *stream*, from the Jews. By this they at first meant the shallow Pelusiac branch, while they kept the grander name, *the river*, for the Euphrates. Some changes also in the pronunciation were probably brought from Chaldæa into the Bashmuric dialect, or that spoken in the neighbourhood of Bubastis. Such was using the letters L and B in the place of R and F, and Th in the place of the guttural Ch. Chaldæan science now entered

Jeremiah, ch. ii. 18.
Dionysius Perieg.
Isaiah, xxvii. 12.

the Delta. From this time the school of Heliopolis rose into notice. Here the Jewish rabbi was able to compare Babylonian science with Egyptian mystery. Here the Greek, Hebrew, and Egyptian languages were all understood; and those that came to learn might study the opinions of the three nations. Those who read the laws of Moses talked with those who read Homer, and those who read hieroglyphics. Here only did Egyptian learning feel a relief from the crushing weight of tradition and authority. The writings of many a Greek philosopher and Hebrew doctor afterwards took their colour from this school. Its fame reached, if not far over the globe, as far perhaps as the use of letters, to Thebes, to Babylon, and to Athens. And when our countrymen, on their hurried journey from England to Hindostan, now pass the village of Matarech, near Cairo, and look up at the obelisk there standing by itself among the low earth mounds, the remains of its temple and priestly college, they should not forget that they are on one of those remarkable spots, for a time the centre of the world's mind, whence Solon and Pythagoras borrowed their opinions and where Plato came to learn.

(19) The Hebrew law had required every Jew to present himself in the Temple of Jerusalem at each of the great feasts; but this was a burden too heavy for those that dwelt at a distance. Once a year, however, at the Feast of Tabernacles, this religious journey was still called for; embassies were looked for in Jerusalem with their gifts from the Pilgrims of the Dispersion in all the neighbouring countries; "and if the family of Egypt," says the prophet Zechariah, "go not forth, and come not up, they shall have no rain, they shall have the plague wherewith the Lord will smite the tribes that come not up to keep the Feast of Tabernacles." With the Egyptians the Jews readily mixed, as with the people nearest akin to themselves; and even the Hebrews of Judæa, while frowning on the less strict observances of these their Hellenistic brethren, still declared that an Egyptian was more closely allied to them than any other foreigner; and it was a part of their law that he might be admitted even into the

Ch. xiv. 18.

Mishna, De Levit.

priesthood after his family had obeyed the laws of Moses for three generations.

(20) Few buildings now remain which were raised in the time of the kings of Sais; a tomb, however, in the neighbourhood of Memphis, bearing the date of Hophra's reign, is remarkable for a stone arch built on mathematical principles (see Fig. 159). But the use of the graceful arch in the Egyptian buildings would have been very little suitable to their solemn feelings. They could look more quietly at a roof safely upheld by a row of thick closely set columns. The span of a wide arch moves us with rather an uneasy wonder; its stones seem overtasked; and the Arab happily remarks that an arch gets no rest. False arches made by advancing courses of stones are to be found of a much earlier date. In Thebes we find arches built of unburnt bricks, forming parts of vaulted rooms, as early as Amunothph I. and Thothmosis III.; but this is a true arch made of wedge-shaped stones, which stand because they all press to a common centre. This form of stonework, so beautiful, so useful for bridges and larger buildings, and now so common, was unknown in Greece, and we naturally look for the traces of its first employment.

Vyse's Pyramids.

Hoskins's Ethiopia.

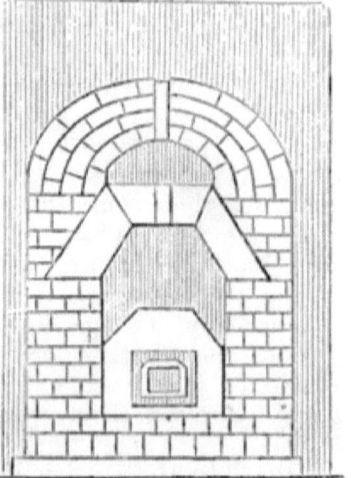

Fig. 159.

(21) The religion of Lower Egypt, under these kings of Sais, was not quite the same as that shown to us on the Theban monuments; and even when the gods had the same names, in the minds of their worshippers they may have been very different. In one word, the Thebans said that they were beloved by their gods, and the people of Lower Egypt thought of them very much as punishers. On the top of the Theban obelisk the god Amun-Ra is laying his hands on the head of the sovereign, in token of blessings bestowed (see Fig. 41), but on the temple of Sais, King Hophra

RELIGION OF LOWER EGYPT.

presents his offerings to appease a class of gods who threaten punishment with the sword of vengeance (see Fig. 160). These are the Cabeiri, of whom we find few or no traces in the religion of Upper Egypt. But as in the religion of the Delta the danger of punishment became greater, so also was there provided greater help in the person of advocates and mediators, on behalf of the worshipper. The

Fig. 160.

Fig. 161.

four lesser gods of the dead, who usually have the heads of a man, a hawk, an ape, and a dog, are these mediators, and are seen on the funereal tablets acting as friends of the dead man and interceding with the judge Osiris on his behalf (see Fig. 161). And not content with this, these four gods even consent to be sacrificed for the sinner; and he places them on the altar before the judge with other gifts as his atoning sacrifice

Fig. 162.

(see Fig. 162). The sculptures on the sarcophagus taken from the above-mentioned tomb of this reign contain a list of eighteen gods, which may be usefully compared with the gods of Thebes. They are, Selk, the scorpion-goddess, Mo, the god of Truth, a female Typhon, Thoth, lord of the city of Oshmoonayn, Seb, the father of the gods, Chem with the double crown, Osiris with the crown of Upper Egypt, Isis, the great mother, a second Isis named Sate, Anubis with a dog's head, a second Anubis with the same head, Nephthys, Horus with a hawk's head, Horus-Ra, or a second Horus, Thora, or a third Horus, distinguished by a scarabæus, Neith, the mother of the gods, a second Neith, and a goddess named Soneb. These were the gods chiefly worshipped in Sais. But in this long list we miss Amun-Ra, Athor, and Chonso, the gods of Upper Egypt, and even Pthah, the chief god of Memphis, and Knef, *the spirit*, and in their place find Selk, the scorpion, and Typhon, the accusing hippopotamus.

(22) The old Egyptian army was a body of landholders, who were each of them allowed about six acres of land, free of all rent and taxes, as their pay for doing military service when called out by the king. They were divided into two bodies, the Calasiries of Thebes and the eastern half of the Delta, amounting to two hundred and fifty thousand tenants of the crown, registered as of an age to carry arms, and the Hermotybies of Panopolis and the western half of the Delta, registered to the number of a hundred and sixty thousand men; thus, as the population was about four or five millions, these registered soldiers were about one in ten souls. But, as they were only called into service for three years at a time, and that most likely only once in a life, the number of men under arms was probably not more than a tenth of the soldiers, or a standing army of forty thousand men. This proportion of one unproductive soldier to each hundred of the population, is about the largest army that one of the European monarchies could now support without exhausting itself; but to this we must add an equal number for the Greek and Libyan mercenaries and the Phenician mariners, to measure the weight with which the Egyptian monarchy pressed on its subjects, and to show what a store of industry the trade and manufactures

Herodotus, lib. ii. 165.

had brought into being for the state to make use of. It was usual for the Calasiries and Hermotybies, each in their turn, to furnish a body of a thousand picked men to do duty as the king's body-guard, for which service they received a large daily allowance of bread, meat, and wine. The chief strength of an Egyptian army lay in its bowmen and chariots, and no difficulties arose as long as the mercenaries were only Arabs and Ethiopians, men worse armed and worse disciplined than themselves. Nor were the difficulties much felt when the kings of Lower Egypt engaged a large body of Greeks, the best soldiers in the world, as long as they were employed in active warfare. As long as the Egyptians enjoyed their privileges and the post of honour, they did not mind the Greeks being hired to fight their battles. But Hophra changed the established order of things, and employed the Carians and Ionians as his favoured body-guard in his palace at Sais; and the jealousy which thence sprung up between the native soldiers and the Greek mercenaries formed the chief difficulty of his reign. His conduct showed a wish to weaken the power of the military class; and this at last caused a rebellion and his own overthrow. Adicran, king of the Libyans, near Cyrene, had sent an embassy to Egypt to beg for help against Battus II., under whom the Dorian colony of Cyrene had latterly been growing more powerful. Adicran made an offer of his country to Hophra; and the king of Egypt, perhaps thinking it unsafe to employ his Greeks in this service, sent an army of Egyptians to check the power of his Greek neighbours. But the Egyptian troops were beaten in battle, many were put to the sword by the Dorians, and very few reached home after the rout. Upon the news of this disaster the Egyptian army declared that their brethren had been betrayed by their own king, and they raised the standard of revolt. Hophra sent Amasis, a popular general, to recall them to their duty; but while he was addressing the assembled rebels they placed a helmet on his head, and proclaimed him king, and his fears and his ambition joined in making him yield to their wishes. Hophra next sent Patarbemis, a man of rank, with orders to seize Amasis, and bring him before him alive. Patarbemis found Amasis on horseback at the head

Herodotus, lib. iv. 159.

Herodotus, lib. ii. 161.

of his troops, and, on delivering the message, was told that Hophra need not send, as Amasis would soon be with him. On the messenger's return, Hophra cruelly ordered his nose and ears to be cut off as a punishment for his want of success.

(23) Hophra, now seeing that the fate of his crown was to be determined by a struggle, got ready his forces for battle. He had about thirty thousand Greek mercenaries, chiefly Carians and Ionians; and Sais, his capital, was a well-fortified city. But he chose to march out, and cross the river, and give battle to Amasis near Momemphis, a few miles to the east of Sais; and though the Greeks as usual fought bravely, they were beaten by the larger number of the Egyptians, and by the difficulties which attend an army in an enemy's country. Hophra's pride is spoken of by Ezekiel. He had boasted that not even a god could shake his throne; but he was taken alive by Amasis; and, though kindly treated, was carried prisoner to Sais, deprived of his crown, and confined by his successful rival in what had once been his own palace.

<small>Herodotus, lib. ii. 169.</small>

(24) AMASIS (see Fig. 163), by this bold act of usurpation now king of Upper and Lower Egypt, was a man of high rank, though not of the royal family. He had originally gained the notice of King Hophra by a fortunate present of a crown made of spring flowers on the celebration of his birthday, entwined in the manner in which such garlands were usually placed on the statues of the gods. The king thereupon invited him to dinner, and was further pleased with his address, and admitted him into the number of his friends. Amasis rose rapidly in favour; he married the daughter of the late monarch Psammetichus; he won the love of the soldiers as of the king, and, as we have seen, ungratefully repaid the kindness of Hophra by dethroning him. But though he thus gained the crown by the overflow of the mercenaries, Amasis by no means withdrew his favour from the Greeks, who formed an important part of the population of the Delta. He even removed the Greek military colony from the frontier settlements, the Camps near Pelusium, to the very

<small>Hellanicus, ap. Athenaeum, cod. xv. 7. B.C. 566.</small>

Fig. 163.

<small>Diod. Sic. lib. i. 67.</small>

heart of the kingdom, and gave them dwellings near Memphis. He showed an unnecessary jealousy or forgetfulness of Tanis, Mendes, and Bubastis, the old rivals of Sais, his capital. He wholly stopped their trade on the Mediterranean, which had already fallen off on the overthrow of Tyre and Sidon, whose merchants had been the carriers from the eastern mouths of the Nile to the neighbouring and opposite ports. He thus hastened the ruin of the eastern half of the Delta. He made Naucratis, the city in which the Greek merchants chiefly dwelt, the sole port for the Mediterranean trade. It was situated about thirty miles from the sea and ten miles below Sais, on the Canobic branch of the Nile, which was then the deepest of the several channels into which the river was divided. No foreign vessel might enter any other than the Canobic mouth; and, if driven by accident or stress of weather into any other mouth of the river, it was either sent round to Naucratis, or the goods were carried there by barges. ^{Herodotus, lib. ii. 178.}

(25) Besides these advantages for their trade, Amasis gave the Greeks of Naucratis many civil and religious privileges. He allowed them to appoint their own magistrates and officers for the regulation of their commerce, and to build temples for the exercise of their own religion; and as these remarkable privileges were granted to this Greek city only ten miles distant from Sais, where were situated the seat of government and the king's own palace, instead of looking upon these foreigners with jealousy, he must have thought them the best support to his throne. And we are able to measure the naval power at this time of the several Greek states, and their activity in foreign commerce, by their buildings in this Egyptian city. The Greeks of the mainland, who had put forth their strength so successfully four centuries earlier, at the time of the Trojan war, were now no longer masters of their own seas. That high rank had for some time past been held by the seafaring inhabitants of the little islands of Ægina and Samos. Athens had not yet risen to be a naval power. The Greek merchants of Naucratis chiefly came from the islands and the west coast of Asia Minor, and few or none from the mainland of Greece. Those of three Greek states were numerous enough to have each a temple for themselves; while the other Greek merchants

had one temple in common. These temples of Naucratis were, that of Jupiter, built by the Æginetæ, that of Juno by the Samians, that of Apollo by the Milesians, and the large temple called the Hellenium, which last was built at the joint expense of the Ionians of Chios, Teos, Phocæa, and Clazomenæ, of the Dorians of Rhodes, Cnidus, Halicarnassus, and Phaselis, and of the Æolians of Mytelene. Thus Naucratis, in the appearance of its buildings, was a Greek city; and from the large temples on the islands of Ægina and Samos we may judge of the form of the smaller temples of Naucratis, which were copied from them.

B.C. 548.

Amasis also joined the Greek colonists in making gifts to their temples at home; and when the temple of Delphi was destroyed by fire, and the several Greek cities sent their presents towards the cost of rebuilding it, one of the largest presents was from the king of Egypt. To the temple of Minerva at Cyrene he sent a golden statue of the goddess; to the temple of Minerva at Lindus in Rhodes he sent two marble statues; while to the temple of Juno at Samos he sent two statues of himself, carved in wood. These kings of Sais acted as if they were as much Greek as Egyptian; and their liberality to the Greek temples is the more remarkable, because the Egyptians, unlike the Greeks, never admitted into their mythology the gods of their neighbours. The Greeks, on the other hand, were eager to copy the rites of the Egyptian religion; and after the sacrifice to Isis at Busiris, when thousands of votaries every year scourged themselves in token of the sufferings of Osiris, the Carian mercenaries were foremost in self-torture. They gashed their faces with their swords, and surpassed the Egyptians in fearlessness when using their weapons against themselves, as much as when using them against the enemy.

Herodotus, lib. ii. 182.

Herodotus, lib. ii. 61.

(26) Under the favour now shown by the kings of Sais to the Greeks, Thales, the first who had the title of Wise Man, travelled in Egypt in about the fiftieth Olympiad, perhaps in the last reign. He seems to have been chiefly in search of scientific knowledge, and did not forget to inquire into the cause of the Nile's overflow. He measured the height of the great pyramid by the length of its shadow. He is said to have been the first Greek that

Diogenes Laertius, lib. i.

foretold an eclipse; and to have learned from the Egyptians the valuable mathematical truth that the angle in a semi-circle is always a right angle; and he sacrificed an ox to the gods in gratitude for this increase of knowledge. But he has left no written works behind him. Soon afterwards, Solon, the Athenian lawgiver, came to Naucratis as a merchant, bringing the olive oil of Athens to exchange for the corn and other native products of Egypt and the more costly articles from India; and, while thus carrying on the trade of an oil-merchant, he studied the manners and customs of the country. The first duty and pleasure in life is to be useful, and the second is to improve ourselves and qualify ourselves for further usefulness. Solon had been in the highest degree useful to his countrymen in reforming their laws, and he was now in search of knowledge to qualify himself for further usefulness. From the Egyptians he copied the law that every man should be called upon by the magistrate to give an account of how he earned his livelihood. After selling his cargo, or leaving it at Naucratis to be sold by an agent, he visited Sais, the capital, where his character secured for him an honourable reception, and where he conversed with the priests of the temple of Neith, and inquired into their accounts of the history of their nation and of the world. They called the Greeks mere children of yesterday, and professed to have a knowledge of the events of the last nine thousand years. They gave him a marvellous account of the island of Atlantis, a country abounding in wealth of every kind, situated beyond the pillars of Hercules, but in the neighbourhood of Egypt, meaning perhaps part of Abyssinia. This account they must have gained from the circumnavigators in the reign of Necho. Solon returned to Athens with his mind enriched with knowledge; but had the pain of finding that his countrymen had already lost their zeal for the laws that he had left them.

Plutarch. Vit. Solon. Herodotus, lib. i. 30.

Plato, in Timæo.

Plato, in Critiâ.

(27) Solon was followed by his friend Cleobulus, a native of the island of Rhodes, who came to Egypt to study philosophy; and soon afterwards by Hecatæus of Miletus in Ionia, who went as high as Thebes, and wrote a valuable history of his travels. The Theban

Diogenes Laertius, lib. i.

priests showed Hecatæus the large wooden mummy-cases of their predecessors, standing upright round the walls of the temple, to the number of three hundred and forty-five; and when the Greek traveller boasted that he was the sixteenth in descent from Jupiter, they told him that those three hundred and forty-five priests had ruled Thebes in succession from father to son, each a mortal the son of a mortal, and that it was that number of generations since the gods Osiris and Horus had reigned in Egypt. Nations, like families, have usually been fond of claiming a long line of ancestors, but none have ever had a better right to that boast than the Egyptians. The Theban priest was speaking to Hecatæus in about the fortieth reign of this history, while his Greek visitor only pretended to be the sixteenth in descent from the gods. The Theban could then name with certainty more sovereigns of his country in the order of succession than we can kings of England. He was as far removed from the obscurity of antiquity as we English are in the nineteenth century. It is true that he boasted that the oldest of his mummies was ten times older than it was likely to have been; but, if he had confined himself to what we think the truth, his boast would still have been very remarkable, and he could probably have pointed to records standing around him which had existed some centuries before the time that the Hebrew historians give to Abraham.

_{Herodotus, lib. ii. 143.}

(28) While Solon and Hecatæus were studying the Egyptian customs, Pythagoras, of Samos, if we may trust to the slightest and most uncertain of traditions, was equally busy inquiring into the mystical philosophy of the Egyptians and Phenicians of the Delta, studying under Œnuphis of Heliopolis that learning which was the growth of the valley of the Nile, and that which had been brought from Babylon. But, well acquainted as we are with the sect of the Pythagoreans and their opinions ten centuries later, the life of their founder is wrapt in fable. He is said to have lived twenty years in Egypt, and on the conquest of the country by the Persians to have been taken prisoner and carried off to Babylon. The next Greek traveller was the philosopher Xenophanes, the Ionian, so famous for his just notions of the nature of God, as being one eternal infinite spirit. Here

_{Plutarch. De Isid. x. Jamblicus, Vit. Pythag.}

he made inquiries of the priests as to their religious opinions; and at the annual ceremony of the lament for the death of Osiris he was naturally puzzled with their grief for the sufferings of one whom they called a god. He did not understand how Osiris could have two natures, one human and one divine; and he wittily argued with them, that if they thought him a man they should not worship him, and if they thought him a god they need not talk of his sufferings. These inquiring Greeks came to Egypt to a people overflowing with wealth while at home they were only beginning to taste of luxuries, to a people who had been civilized at a time when Greece had been in barbarism, to a people who had taught them the first elements of much of their knowledge. The Greeks indeed had latterly made great progress in the arts and in civilization of all kinds; and they had moreover learned that they had the power of making further progress; while the Egyptians had not got that power, and were losing their rank in each succeeding century. But a forward movement in civilization is only to be insured by looking back to the steps that the world has already made; the knowledge of what has been done teaches us what may be done; and nowhere could the history of the past be studied so usefully as in Egypt (*vide p.* 427).

<small>Plutarchi Amatorius.</small>

(29) The island of Cyprus, though latterly sometimes in obedience to Egypt, and sometimes to Nineveh, had always been governed by its own kings; but Amasis made it subject to the Egyptian crown alike in name and in reality. It was peopled by a very mixed race. Greek and Phœnician traders had settled in some ports, Egyptians and native Cypriotes held other towns; and an Assyrian inscription tells us that that fifth race of people once held their island in subjection. Equally varied in style are the works of art throughout its cities. Their own Cyprian inscriptions have not yet been decyphered; the language and the letters are alike unknown. The Phœnician inscriptions are better understood. Of these the characters are borrowed from the hieroglyphics and enchorial writing of Egypt, and some of them are at the same time those from which the Greek letters were formed. Hence, while the Greeks may be right when they tell us that they owed their alphabet to the Phœnicians, they are

<small>Herodotus lib. ii. 182.</small>

certainly wrong when they tell us that the Phenicians were the inventors of letters. The Phenician letters, like those of all the other neighbouring nations, may be shown to be of Egyptian origin. The close intercourse of the Egyptians with the Phenicians of Cyprus, and the yet closer with the Phenicians of Pelusium, will explain how the knowledge passed from one nation to the other.

(30) The first wife of Amasis was Hanes-vaphra (see Fig. 164), if we may venture to spell her name from the hieroglyphical inscriptions.

<small>Egypt. Inscript. pl. 116, 24.</small>

She was the daughter of Psammetichus II., and sister of the last king, and her royal birth must have added to the strength of her husband's throne; she was probably the mother of his son Psammenitus, who succeeded him. When she died, though her husband was reigning in Lower Egypt, she was buried in the valley of queens' tombs on the west side of Thebes. We know her only in her beautiful Theban sarcophagus now in the British Museum, where she is named, in the usual style of Eastern compliment, the morning star, the evening star, the new moon, with other equally poetic names. Her sculptured figure, which lies upon the lid, has the crown of Amun-Ra, the sceptres of Osiris, and bears the name of the goddess Athor. The queen is thus made a threefold deity in her own person. Amasis had hitherto been supporting with his troops the party in Cyrene which was in rebellion against the family of Battus;

<small>Plutarch. Virtut. Mul.</small>

and on the defeat of the rebels he threatened to send an army against the young Battus, who then gained the throne. Battus sent to Egypt his mother and grandmother as ambassadors to plead his cause; and they were successful in appeasing the king's anger, and in uniting the two states by a friendly treaty. On the death of Hanes-vaphra, Amasis married a Greek lady, Ladica, the daughter of one of the chief men of Cyrene. The state and dignity of the Egyptian queen were maintained, not by a sum of money, but according to the Eastern custom of setting apart the revenues of certain provinces for her several wants. Thus the large income from the royal fishery at the flood-gates to the Lake of Mœris was allotted for the expense of her perfumes and

<small>Herodotus, lib. ii. 181.</small>

<small>Diod. Sic. lib. i. 52. Herodotus, lib. ii. 98.</small>

Fig. 164.

toilette; and a century later the taxes of the city of Anthylla were added to find her in sandal-strings.

(31) Amasis had been united by treaties and by friendship with Polycrates the tyrant of Samos, an island on the coast of Asia Minor; and Herodotus gives a curious account of the reasons which led to their quarrel. Amasis, considering the changes which are always happening in this mortal life, became alarmed at the continued prosperity of his friend, who was master of the largest naval force in the Grecian seas; and he wrote him word that he might be sure that some great calamity would soon befall him. To avoid the ruin which might be overhanging, he advised Polycrates to consider what treasure he possessed that would most trouble him by its loss, and to throw it away of his own accord, and to do the same again and again if his good fortune continued. Polycrates was pleased with his advice, and having an emerald seal beautifully engraved by Theodorus and set in gold as a ring, he threw it himself into the sea, hoping that the loss of this jewel might save him from the loss of his life or throne. But within a week of his doing so, a fisherman, having caught a fish of more than usual size, brought it to the palace at Samos, and when the cook cut it open the emerald seal was found in its stomach and delivered to the king. Polycrates then sent word to Egypt that he had regained his ring; and, according to the story, Amasis immediately withdrew from his alliance; he would have no treaty of friendship with a man who had been hitherto so fortunate, for it seemed certain that ruin would soon overtake him and all his friends.

Herodotus, lib. iii. 39.

(32) Hitherto Persia and Media beyond the Tigris had been little known to Egypt. They were separated from it not by natural boundaries only, but by the Jews, the Assyrians, and the Babylonians. When Assyria and Babylon were united, they conquered the kingdoms of Israel and Judah; they for a time held the cities of Tyre and Sidon, and the island of Cyprus, and drove back the Egyptian armies behind the shelter of their own desert. The Egyptians had been humbled at feeling themselves checked by an equal, but they were now to find their eastern neighbour their superior. In the course of this reign Cyrus came to the Persian throne, and, joining the kingdom of Media to

the country of his birth, founded the great Persian monarchy, the most powerful kingdom that the world had yet seen under one sceptre, and which threatened to trample down its neighbours on all sides. His armies were everywhere successful, and nations trembled at his approach. The Egyptians had good cause to be alarmed; to humble their power was the aim of his ambition, their wealth was the prize that his soldiers longed for. The coast and havens of Asia Minor were first to be conquered; and the larger part of that country was under the sway of Crœsus king of Lydia, the friend of Egypt. As the Persians moved westward against Crœsus, Amasis sent a body of troops to help his ally. The Egyptian forces were thought the best soldiers in the great battle in which the Lydians were defeated by Cyrus. These men or some of them may have been Greek in blood and language, as in military skill, though called Egyptian from the land of their adoption. They were drawn up in a square phalanx of ten thousand men—the form which was afterwards so celebrated when used by the Macedonians—and they refused Crœsus's request to fight otherwise than in their usual ranks, one hundred deep and one hundred wide. When the Lydians were routed, these allies made honourable terms for themselves, and were allowed to settle in Æolia, at Larissa, and at Cyllene, near Cyme; and these two towns continued for many years to be called Egyptian. The two Egyptian sculptured monuments on the face of the rocks near Ephesus and Smyrna, which Herodotus thought were the work of his favourite hero Sesostris, were probably cut by these soldiers of King Amasis.

<small>Xenophon, Cyropæd. vi. 3, 20.</small>

<small>Xenophon, Cyropæd. vii. 1, 45.</small>

<small>Herodotus, lib. ii. 106.</small>

(33) As each little kingdom fell one by one under the Persian arms, the danger to Egypt became more threatening. Cyprus was next to be conquered, and then, whether the Persian forces moved by land or by sea, no independent state would remain between Egypt and the coming storm. The island of Cyprus had hitherto been under several kings, each holding his own little kingdom; and Amasis had latterly made them do him homage and pay him tribute. Against Cyprus, Cyrus then sent a large force, and he defeated the Egyptian troops and conquered that island. The Jews, grateful to him for

<small>Herodotus, lib. ii. 182.</small>

<small>Xenophon, Cyropæd. lib. viii. 6, 8.</small>

the permission to return home from captivity and rebuild their temple, saw his troops march with pleasure, and with earnest wishes for their success. The writer of some of the latter chapters in the book of Isaiah, the most spiritual among the Hebrew prophets, assured his countrymen that God had given Egypt and Ethiopia and Nubia to the king of Persia as a ransom for the Jewish captives in Babylon. On his statue in Persepolis, Cyrus boastfully placed a head-dress copied from that of the Egyptian kings, as if he were already master of the valley of the Nile (see Fig. 165). But the successes of the Persians were for a time stopped by their king's death; and it was not until the fourth year of the reign of Cambyses, his unworthy son, that the Persians attacked Egypt, and the prophet's words were fulfilled.

_{Chap. xliii. 3; xlv. 14.}

_{B.C. 529.}

Fig. 165.

(34) Among the Greek mercenaries in the Egyptian service was a general named Phanes, a man able in council and brave in the field, who, having had a quarrel with Amasis, fled from Egypt about the time that Cambyses was preparing to march. Amasis, though he trusted chiefly to the native troops, saw how useful the deserter might be to the enemy, and he sent a galley in pursuit of him. The Egyptian officer actually overtook him and arrested him in Lycia, but Phanes again contrived to escape, and reached Persia in safety. Phanes not only disclosed to Cambyses the state of Egyptian affairs, but he did him the greatest service by explaining to him the difficulty of crossing the desert, and that the easiest way to enter Egypt was to send an embassy to the Arabs, and from them to obtain a supply of water for his army. But before Cambyses reached Egypt King Amasis was dead, after a reign of forty-four years.

_{Herodotus, lib. iii. 4.}

(35) Amasis was one of the most prosperous of the Egyptian kings; and the agreeable recollections of his sway, and of the Nile's generosity during his reign, were strengthened by its being the last to which the nation could look back with unmixed pride. He made many good laws; and many others were called by his name, merely to explain that they existed in the time of

_{Diod. Sic. lib. i. 95.}

the native sovereigns. Under Amasis the city of Sais had reached its greatest size and beauty. But it never was so large as either Thebes or Memphis, and could hardly be called the capital of the kingdom, although it was the seat of government for two hundred years. Its palace or citadel was dedicated to the goddess Neith, whom the Greeks called Minerva, and it was the largest in Lower Egypt. This was a plot of ground half a mile square, surrounded with a brick wall fifty feet thick. In the middle of this sacred area stood what we must call the temple of Neith, though by the Egyptians the whole area was named the temple. The covered building was entered through a portico, with columns formed like trunks of palm-trees, all built of stones of the greatest size, some brought from Memphis, and some even from Elephantine. It was ornamented with obelisks, colossal statues, and sphinxes. On one side of the temple were the tombs of the unfortunate Hophra, and of his ancestors who had reigned at Sais. Here, for want of natural hills, the embalmed bodies were placed in cells in the city walls, to keep them above the level of the waters when the Nile was at its height. On the other side was the lake, of a round form, lined with stone, on which the sacred mysteries of Isis were celebrated by torchlight. Behind the temple was the tomb of Osiris, for Sais would not yield the honour of being his burial-place to any city in Egypt.

(36) Not less remarkable than this large temple of Neith was a small temple, which, Herodotus was told, was of a single stone, twenty-one cubits long, fourteen wide, and eight high. This great block, if it was a single block, was dug out of the quarries near Elephantine, and two thousand boatmen were employed during three years in floating it down the Nile to Sais. Amasis meant to have placed it within the courtyard of the temple of Neith, and it was brought with great labour to the door, and had not been carried further when Herodotus visited the place. But it was more probably made of a small number of large blocks, of which some are in the British Museum; and we are able to judge of the whole from the parts which we now possess (see Fig. 166). Sais began to fall on the death of Amasis. It suffered with the rest of Egypt under the

Persian conquerors. It afterwards had fifty years more of prosperity when the Persians were driven out, but again fell on their return. It continued, however, to be a town of

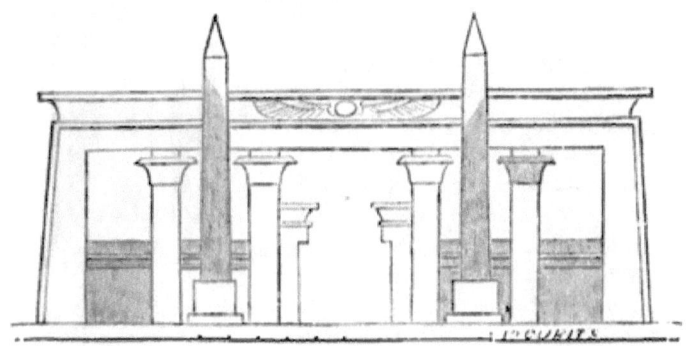

Fig. 166.

importance for some centuries longer, even after Alexandria was built, when its deserted temples were robbed to furnish building stones for the new city. It is now only a ruined wall, with a few mounds by the side of the river, over which the wolf and jackal walk at leisure, with here and there a broken granite column, or a block covered with hieroglyphics. It was built in a part of the country where originally there

Fig. 167.

was not a piece of stone larger than the grain of sand which is blown there from the desert, where not a pebble is to be found by digging; and these mounds now bear the name of Sa-el-Hagar, or *Sais the stony* (see Fig. 167). At Tel-etmai, near Mendes in the Delta, is another small temple or monument of this reign, of a single block of granite (see Fig. 168). It measures about twenty-five feet high by fifteen wide, and is mounted on a base which raises it fifteen feet higher.

Fig. 168.

(37) PSAMMENITUS succeeded his father Amasis on the throne, and in the difficult task of defending Egypt against Cambyses. He encamped with his Egyptian army and Greek mercenaries at the Pelusiac mouth of the river, to await the approach of the Persians, who, having made their way through Arabia, halted in the neighbourhood in preparation of battle. While the two armies were in sight of one another the Greeks learned, as they expected, that the deserter Phanes was at the head of a body of the Persians; so they led forth his sons before the camp, and had the cruelty to put them to death in the sight of their father; and mixing their blood with wine and water, the whole of the Greek mercenaries drank of it. On this the two armies joined in battle; and though many at various times have been fought under the walls of Pelusium, between the Egyptians and their invaders, none was ever so important as this. After a long and hard-fought day the Egyptians were driven from the field, and they fled in disorder towards Memphis. A large number of each army were slain, and their bodies were piled up in two heaps; and when Herodotus afterwards visited the spot, the people pointed out to him the difference between the strong skulls of the Egyptians and those of the Persians, which were weaker because their heads had always been covered with thickly folded turbans.

(38) After this victory Cambyses marched towards Memphis, as being the strongest city in Egypt, and the one whose surrender would be followed by the rest of the kingdom. He sent forward a messenger up the river by a vessel of Mitylene to invite the Egyptians to open their

gates; but, in violation both of the laws of humanity and of the custom of war, they put the Persian messenger to death and sunk the ship, with its crew of two hundred men. Cambyses therefore brought up his army and laid siege to Memphis in due form. The city did not long hold out, though garrisoned by the whole force that Psammenitus could command after his overthrow at Pelusium, and he surrendered to Cambyses within six months of his coming to the throne. On the tenth day after the citadel was taken, Cambyses made the conquered Herodotus, lib. iii. 14. king, with his nobles, sit in mock state at the city gate, while his daughter and the maidens of the chief Egyptian families were forced to carry pitchers for water in the dress of slaves; and his son, and two thousand other young men of the same age, were led forth to be put to death, as the Persian judges had ordered that ten Egyptians should die for every Persian that had been drowned in the ship of Mitylene. The unhappy Psammenitus bore these misfortunes in silent grief; but, on seeing an old man, who had been his friend, asking alms of the soldiers like a common beggar, he burst into tears. He had commanded his feelings at the death of his son, at his daughter's and his own disgrace, but at the unlooked-for grief of his friend in poverty he gave way to weeping. On the fall of the capital the conqueror met with no further resistance. The upper class, when defeated, received no support from the mass of the people; a nation is seldom strong when divided into two castes.

(39) At Memphis Cambyses received messengers from the neighbouring Libyans, from Barca, and from Cyrene, who brought gifts and promised submission without resistance. The offerings of the Libyans were graciously received, but the five hundred pounds of silver brought by the Cyrenæans were ordered to be given to the soldiers as unworthy of the king's acceptance. Cambyses then went to Sais, and took possession of the palace of Amasis. There he ordered the late king's embalmed body to be brought out of the tomb and flogged and insulted; and finding that the mummy was too strong to be easily broken, he had it burnt, as much in contempt of the opinions of the fire-worshipping Persians, as of the conquered Egyptians. Psammenitus himself was not long allowed to live. Had he submitted quietly to his altered lot, it is

possible that Cambyses, according to the Persian custom, might have made him melek or satrap of the country which had so lately been his kingdom; but Psammenitus was found planning resistance to the conqueror, and was therefore put to death.

(40) The prophet Ezekiel wrote in the reign of Hophra; but a few words afterwards added to his book describe this conquest of Egypt by Cambyses, and his then sending messengers up the Nile to invite the Ethiopians to submission. "The day is near," said the prophet, "the day of the Lord is near, a cloudy day, when the sword shall come upon Egypt and great pain upon Ethiopia. . . . . . The Ethiopians and Libyans and Troglodytæ, and all the Arabs, and the people of the land that is in league with them, shall fall by the sword. . . . . . From Magdolus to Syene shall they fall by the sword, saith the Lord God. . . . . . I will destroy their idols and make the images to cease in Memphis; and there shall be no more a prince in the land of Egypt. . . . . . I will make Upper Egypt desolate, and will set fire in Tanis, and execute judgment in Thebes. I will pour my fury upon Sais, the strength of Egypt, and will cut off the multitude of Memphis. . . . . Sais shall have great pain, and Thebes shall be cut asunder, and Memphis shall have distress daily. The men of Aven and of Bubastis shall fall by the sword, and their women shall go into captivity. At Daphnæ shall the day be darkened, when I shall there break the sceptres of Egypt; and the pomp of her strength shall cease." It was at Daphnæ, or Tahpenes, on the Pelusiac branch of the Nile that the battle was fought which put an end to the Egyptian monarchy, and made Egypt a province of Persia.

<small>Ezekiel ch. xxx. 1-9 and 13-19.</small>

(41) Thus ended the second great period of Egyptian history, during which the kingdom had mostly been governed by kings of Lower Egypt. Under these monarchs the trade and wealth of the country had very much increased by an increase of its shipping and by the employment of numerous Phenician mariners in coasting voyages, which the religion and habits of the Egyptians alike forbade them to undertake. Their wars had been chiefly carried on in the endeavour to uphold the Hebrew nation as a barrier against the encroachments of the Assyrians, or rather in the struggle for which of

those two great rival empires should hold Palestine as a province. The more neighbouring Assyrians wished to govern the Jews by means of a satrap, while the more distant Egyptians only aimed at protecting the kings of Samaria and Judæa as dependent allies. The formation of the Egyptian armies was very much changed from those which of old issued out of Thebes. The chief strength no longer lay in the landholders; the Greek mercenaries were found more obedient to discipline and more brave in battle. The employment of mercenaries made the king better able to carry on his foreign wars; but, while it made him stronger abroad, it made him weaker at home; it sowed the seeds of jealousy between the king and his subjects, and at last, as we have seen, helped to overthrow the monarchy. Often must the Egyptian statesman have wished that his countrymen were less wealthy or more brave, when he found that the gold with which he tried to guard the frontier was rather a booty that quickened the Persian attack, and a cause of luxury that weakened his own defence.

(42) There are but few Egyptian laws with which we are acquainted; and we have no knowledge of when these were enacted, or when they went out of use, or which were always in force. Those which related to crimes against persons were for the most part founded on the simple rule of revenge, an eye for an eye and a tooth for a tooth; an unhappy rule, by which the magistrate makes an apology for the guilty act that he wishes to check, and almost encourages it by imitating; amendment of the criminal was no part of its aim. These, like the common law of all countries, took their rise before the memory of man. When, however, from time to time, on the increase of knowledge and humanity, a new law was made to soften the severity of the old custom, the king was the lawmaker, and he received honour accordingly from a grateful nation. The king, however, was not the judge to administer the laws; but the highest judicial body was a court of thirty judges, who sat together to hear causes, and who were chosen, ten from Thebes, ten from Memphis, and ten from Heliopolis. For matters of less weight, each *nome* or district was governed by its own *nomarch*; but, as there was no wealthy and powerful aristocracy, either priestly or

Diod. Sic. lib. i. 94.

Lib. i. 75.

Lib. i. 73.

military, as there had formerly been in Upper Egypt, the king's will was nearly absolute. Death was the punishment for perjury, for murder, and for witnessing a murder without endeavouring to save the sufferer; but a woman with child was not to be put to death before she had given it birth. If a child killed his parent, he was cruelly tortured and then burnt alive; while the punishment of a parent for killing his child was only imprisonment for three days with the dead body. Killing a slave was also punished with death; for a man had more power over his children than over his slaves; the slaves had their rights secured to them by law, and thus were of very little worth in money. The informer who failed in making good his charge received himself the punishment which he was planning for his victim. The soldiers, who were a privileged body, were punished very slightly for deserting their post; they suffered some disgrace which they might if they pleased wipe off, and they easily regained their former rank. Forgers of deeds and of seals, and makers of false weights and measures, were punished with the loss of both hands. Those who betrayed a secret to the enemy were to lose the tongue. In all cases the punishment fell on the guilty limb. No debt could be recovered at law without a written acknowledgment, if the person from whom it was claimed denied it on oath; and to limit the accumulation of interest, by which the poor so unwisely put themselves in bondage to the rich, the debt was in all cases limited to double the sum originally lent, which limit has since been adopted in the bond debts of Europe. No debtor could be thrown into prison, his goods only could be seized; and the Egyptian lawyers laughed at the blunder of the Greek law which held every workman's tools sacred from seizure, but allowed the man himself to be imprisoned. All these laws are such as we should expect to find accompanied with a good deal of political liberty; and we may remark the same of the law that every man was required under pain of death to give an account to the magistrate of how he earned his livelihood: for tyrants fetter the actions of their subjects only to add to their own power; it is the free people that take care that no man shall be a trouble to his neighbours.

(43) The cruel punishment of burning a child to death for the murder of his parent was, from the nature of the crime, not likely to be often carried into execution, and it might have been little known in practice when still to be found in the laws. But unfortunately, we have the authority of Manetho, the Egyptian priest, for the fact that some criminals were openly burnt alive in the form of a sacrifice, every year at midsummer, in the city of Idithya. Nations less earnest in their religious feelings shuddered at the inhuman cruelty; but it had probably gone out of use long before the Egyptians were reproached by Virgil and Ovid with sacrificing human beings to the Nile to obtain a bounteous overflow. Since that time altars have seldom been lighted for human sacrifices but by men who, shame to say, have been struggling for theological opinions, in entire forgetfulness of the humility, mildness, and brotherly kindness for which such opinions are chiefly valuable. Plutarch. De Iside et Osiride. Georgic. lib. iii. 5. Ars. Amat. i. 617.

(44) The clothing of the Egyptians was mostly linen, made from flax, which grew abundantly in the Delta; and linen formed an important article of trade. Wool was but little used; they neither wanted its greater warmth, nor is the soil fitted for grazing sheep. A people that ate but little animal food was not likely to wear animal clothing. Some little cotton was brought from India, and it was afterwards grown in Upper Egypt; but the reign of Amasis is the earliest time that we find it mentioned, and then only as a great rarity. Amasis sent to Sparta as his royal gift a breastplate ornamented with gold, and fleeces from trees, as cotton was first called. The cotton may have been placed as wadding under a plate of metal, but more probably this piece of defensive armour was wholly made of strong twisted cords. At any rate, this is the first mention of a material for cloth which is now grown largely in Egypt as well as in Asia and America, and seems likely to become the chief clothing of the world. Another netted or woven breastplate was presented by Amasis to the state of Rhodes, with the magical number of three hundred and sixty-five threads in every cord; and even six centuries after his death it was shown in the temple of Minerva in the city of Lindus as a sacred Pliny. lib. xix. 2. Herodotus, lib. iii. 47. Pliny, lib. xix. 2.

184 THE CLOTHING. [CHAP. IV

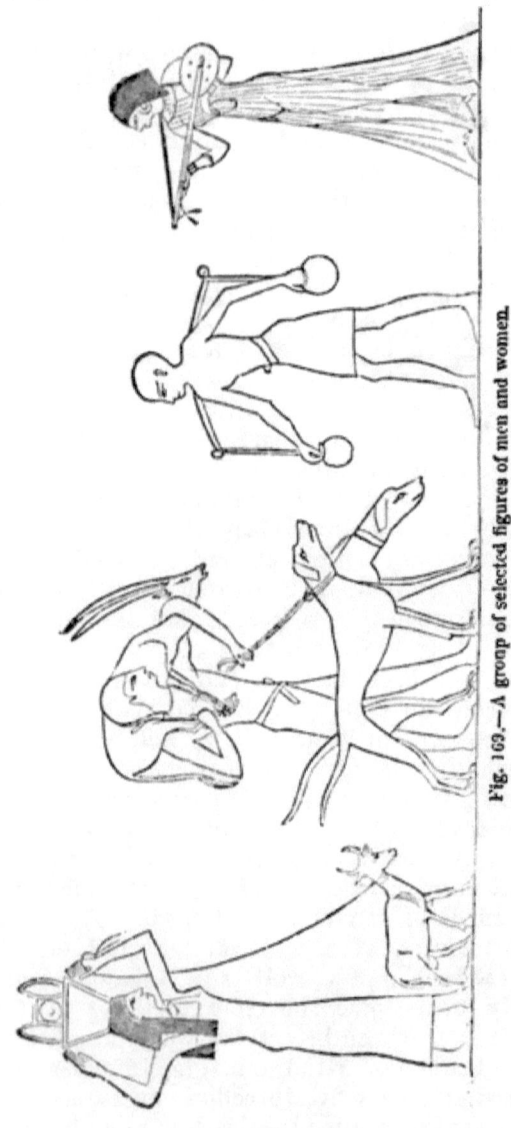

Fig. 169.—A group of selected figures of men and women.

relic, though almost pulled to pieces by the fingers of the numerous visitors who had amused themselves with counting.

(45) The ordinary dress of the people was very slight, as befits a warm climate (see Fig. 169). The women wore one single linen garment, which reached from the neck to the ankles. It was very thin, sometimes loose, and sometimes so tight that it only allowed a short step to be taken in walking. The men wore a loose and shorter garment of the same material, though coarser, which reached only to the knees, except in the case of grand persons, when this garment was as long as that of the women. Beneath this outer garment the men wore a yet shorter apron or petticoat tied round the waist. Of these two the outer garment was often so thin that the apron was seen through it; and it was thrown aside when they were engaged in labour; and then the apron was their only piece of dress except the shoes or sandals. Over these ordinary garments a cloak was worn in colder weather, and robes by the king, queen, priests, and officers of state (see Fig. 170). The robe was sometimes made of skin. Nothing was worn upon the head except the marks of royal and priestly rank, such as the striped linen shawl, the crown, and the helmet in time of war. The ordinary dwelling was a small plot of ground enclosed between four walls (see a model, Fig. 171). No roof was needed as a shelter against

Fig. 171.

rain or cold. The walls and the palm trees which surrounded the house afforded shade, and the inmates slept under the open sky. In the corner, however, of some of these dwellings was one and sometimes a second small dark covered room to

186 THE CLOTHING. [CHAP. IV

Fig. 170.—A group of selected figures of king, queen, and priests.

which the inmates could retire for greater privacy or for greater shelter from wind or sand or cold or sunshine. The mildness and dryness of the climate, which thus allowed the people to sleep in the open air and to move about with little or no clothing, brought on a sad looseness of morals. The corruption perhaps began in Lower Egypt. The sacred tie of marriage was neglected, and the women, not being held in honour, could not teach their children to aim at rectitude. After the loss of domestic virtue the nation could not hope to enjoy either public liberty or real happiness. The seeds of its decay were certainly sown. The priesthood alone held out against the general corruption. The priests were forbidden by law from marrying more than one wife. Other men had as many as they chose, and all children were held equally legitimate whatever woman was the mother. Diod. Sic. lib. i. 80.

(46) The priesthood was divided into four orders, the Soteno, the Nouto, the Othphto, and the Bachano. The first two wore crowns, and were probably at first distinguished as belonging, one to Upper Egypt and the other to Lower Egypt. The Soteno wore the Mitre or tall cap with a ball on the top, known as the crown of Upper Egypt. This was made of linen. The Nouto wore the flat ring or Plate of Gold with a tall piece before and behind. This was known as the crown of Lower Egypt. These two priestly crowns when united form the double crown of Upper and Lower Egypt (see Fig. 172); and the king usually bore the double priestly title, perhaps pronounced Sot-Nout, meaning *Chief* and *Holy*. Both the above-mentioned crowns, the one of linen and the other of gold, were copied by the Israelites, and worn one over the other by the Jewish high priest in the service of the temple. The Othphto, whose name means *Dedicated*, were probably those under monastic vows and vows of celibacy, a body of priests whom we find in later days confined within the temple walls, and only allowed to speak to a Egypt. Inscript. pl. 31, 32.

Exodus, xxviii. 36, 39.
Leviticus, viii. 9.

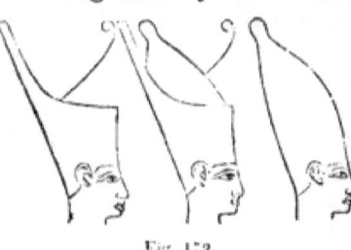
Fig. 172.

visitor through an iron grating. The Bachano were the hired servants.

(47) Among the causes of Egypt's wealth we must mention the distinction of its industrious classes into castes, which, whether upheld for economical or religious reasons, was the adoption of that well-known principle the division of labour. Not only were the priests, the soldiers, and artizans habitually separated, but every particular trade and manufacture was carried on by its own craftsmen, and none changed from one trade to another or carried on several. This gave them a skill in manufactures and trade that was quite unknown to the neighbouring nations. The names which Egypt has given us for the native products of the soil, such as ammonia from the Oasis of Ammon, syenite from the city of Syene, natron and nitre from Mount Nitria, and alabaster from the city of Alabastron, topaz and sapphire stones from the islands of Topazion and Sapirene in the Red Sea, emerald from Mount Smaragdus, prove not so much the native richness of the country as that the people were the first who had skill enough to discover and make use of these products.

<small>Plato, in Timæo.</small>

(48) They made use of the cubit measure divided into six hand-breadths, or twenty-four fingers; and also of the royal cubit, which consisted of this lesser cubit and a hand-breadth over. The royal cubit contained twenty English inches and two-thirds. The Jews made use of the same measures for length of a cubit and a hand-breadth. Longer distances the Egyptians measured by the schœnus of about six miles in length. Land was measured by the aroura or half acre, which, if square, measured a hundred cubits on each side. That measures nearly the same were in use from the earliest times we learn from the size of the pyramids. Exactly such was the cubit used in making the five smaller pyramids of Gezeh; while in the four largest it was about half an inch longer. The side of the base in the pyramid of Chofo measures four hundred royal cubits; in that of Nef-Chofo, the largest pyramid, it measures five hundred lesser cubits. In the others also the side of the base is always of an even number of royal cubits;

<small>Egypt. Inscript. 2nd Series. pl. 46.</small>

<small>Ezekiel, ch. xl. 5.</small>

<small>Herodotus, lib. ii. 168.</small>

<small>Vyse's Pyramids.</small>

and the three small pyramids near that of Nef-Chofo each stand upon an aroura of land, measuring one hundred royal cubits on each side.

(49) The land of the whole country was divided into three unequal portions. One belonged in name to the king, and was held by tenants of the crown, who paid a rent or land-tax of one fifth of the crop. A second portion belonged to the hereditary priesthood, who held it free of rent for their own maintenance and for the expenses of the temples and of the religious services. The third portion was held by the military order, on the tenure of serving three years in the army when called out, which was probably to be only once in each man's life. In this way two millions and a half of acres, or a quarter of the cultivated land of the country, was held by four hundred and ten thousand soldiers, at twelve *arouræ*, or six acres, a man. The whole cultivated land of Egypt may have been about eleven millions of acres, or perhaps a fourth part of that of England and Wales, of which part was watered by the natural overflow of the river, and part by means of canals and ditches. But from the climate and habits and vegetable diet of the people, life was supported more easily in Egypt than on most spots of the globe; and, at a time when the drachm of silver would purchase about a bushel of wheat, the maintenance of a child who could run about without shoes or clothes, did not cost his father twenty drachms in all from his birth till he was his own master; hence we need not be startled at the population being stated at various times at three and at seven millions. Indeed, an actual standing army of forty thousand native soldiers and forty thousand mercenaries, which we meet with a few years later, could hardly be supported by less than five millions of people. For purposes of government the kingdom was divided into nomes, which varied in number from thirty to forty, each of which was governed by its chief city; and again into smaller districts, which were called villages, but were less than our parishes, and varied from eighteen thousand to thirty thousand. Thus a village would be a space of about two hundred and forty acres, or forty such farms as were allotted to each registered soldier. But

Genesis, ch. xlvii.
Herodotus, lib. ii. 168.
Diod. Sic. lib. i. 80.
Lib. i. 31.

we have no Egyptian Domesday-book remaining to correct the blunders we may have fallen into in thus attempting to explain the tenure of the soil.

(50) The Egyptians gave full employment to the sculptor; and the sculptor's art in its highest branch, when portraying the human form in statues or on the wall, betrays as clearly as does that of the poet or historian the rise or fall of good taste and civilisation in a nation. Egypt had led the way in this art, but after a time ceased to improve. The statues were made, as it would seem, without the help of clay or soft models, by which alone ease and grace can be given to the figure. Indeed, the mud of the Nile will not answer for the purpose of clay. They were cut at once on the hard stone from measurements, or at best from small drawings. Hence arose their stiffness, the straightness of their lines, and hence also the correctness of the proportions in the larger parts, and the want of finish in the smaller parts. The nation's respect for a dead body forbad their studying anatomy; as at the embalmment they only cut so

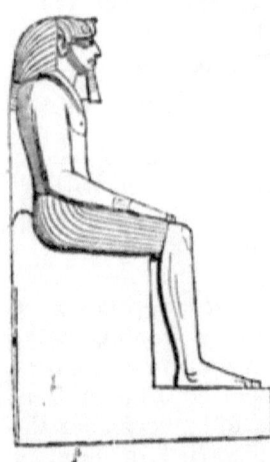
Fig. 173.

far as was necessary to take out the bowels and softer parts. Hence the bones and muscles are but slightly marked, and the veins not at all. The faces show very few marks of youth or age or of aim at likeness. The hieroglyphics show a style of art at Memphis was very different from that of Thebes, and not nearly so good. Of the statues made at Memphis we can form no opinion, as the smaller ones may have been moved from place to place; and the colossus of the Theban king, forty-five feet high, was of course made under the direction of a Theban artist. The Theban school produced its best statues as early as the reign of Amunothph III., whose sitting colossal figures are a model of quiet and noble grandeur (see Fig. 173). It continued to flourish without much loss of simplicity till after the reign of Rameses II., and we may distinguish as many as four schools to which it gave birth. These were the

Ethiopic, the Assyrian, the Greek, and the later Egyptian under the kings of Sais. Of these four one only, namely, the Greek, carried art forward to a higher degree of excellence. They were all children of the same rude but healthy mother; but the other three turned aside from the true path, as they were misled by false taste of one kind or another. Their works are of value to the antiquary and historian; but they can only help the artist, when by a comparison with those of early Egypt and Greece they teach him what temptations of ornament he has to fear, and what faults of exaggeration or weakness he has to shun. They offer also the same help to the critic when unable to find words wherewith to describe

Fig. 174.

Fig. 175.

the merits of the better works. He makes use of these as examples, in order to point out the faults from which others are free.

(51) The Ethiopian artist did not keep to the true proportion of the human figure. He made it too broad and thick (see Fig. 174). He mistook stoutness for grandeur, and strength of limb for dignity. The colossal figures of King Rameses II. at Abou Simbel are only six heads high. Though

certainly if ever such a fault could be excused, it is at the front of this temple, where four of these broad-limbed giants sit with their backs against the rock, as though to support it. But we must remember they were not meant for figures of Hercules or Atlas, but for the portraits of a king of a highly cultivated people.

(52) The comparison of the Assyrian sculpture (see Fig. 175) with the early Egyptian sculpture is yet more favourable for the Egyptians. The Egyptian artist, while every step was new to him, attempted very little action in his figures, and wisely placed them at rest, and more often seated. They are correctly balanced, and their limbs are suited to the weight that they have to bear. He did not give his chief attention to the less important, and overlook that which is more so. The proportions of the whole are always more correct than the proportions of the parts. He added no trifling ornaments, nor variety of folds in hair and drapery to cover the want of grace and beauty. From these faults the Assyrian sculptor is by no means free.

(53) The later Egyptian school, under the kings of Sais, bears the usual marks of a declining state of the art (see Fig. 176). The artist has more science and less judgment;

Fig. 176.   Fig. 177.

more eagerness to display his knowledge of anatomy and less fear of displaying his ignorance. In particular, when aiming at grace and beauty, his muscles are puffed with an unnatural swell. Such is the character of the statues made of basalt under the kings of Sais.

(54) When we turn to the Greek school (see Fig. 177) we are still further reminded that it is not easy to describe excellence except by mentioning the faults from which it is free. The Greek artist was able to attain to almost every end which the others had in view, because he was not misled as they were into false paths towards those ends. He could produce beauty without the help of ornament, grace and delicacy without affectation, strength without coarseness, and action without loss of balance. If he could give us his opinion about the other schools, he would probably say of the early Egyptian statues that the makers of them were beginners, who though they had not reached to high excellence, were in the right path towards it; that if their works do not show great skill, they show at least their good sense in not attempting beyond what they understood. Of the Ethiopic, the later Egyptian, and the Assyrian sculpture, he would probably say that they were the works of men who had already missed the true path, and were not in the way towards excellence.

(55) In one merit, and perhaps only one, was the early Egyptian artist superior to the Greek. The Greek statues have truth, muscular action, grace, beauty, and strength. They show pain, fear, love, and a variety of passions. But none of them are equal to those of Egypt in impressing on the mind of the beholder the feelings of awe and reverence. The two people were unlike in character; and the artists, copying from their own minds, gave the character of the nation to their statues. Plato saw nothing but ugliness in an Egyptian statue. The serious gloomy Egyptians had aimed at an expression not valued by the more gay and active Greeks. The Egyptians, however, had learned the superiority of rest over action in representing the sublime; and the artist who wishes to give religious dignity to his figures should study the quiet sitting Egyptian colossus of the reign of Amunothph III. In Michael Angelo's statues of Moses and Lorenzo we see how that great master in the same way made use of strength at rest when he wished to represent power and grandeur.

(56) The Egyptian statues were of various materials,

but none of these at all equal to the beautiful marbles of Greece and Italy. Many of the oldest statues were of wood, and these always had the features painted. Others were of soft limestone from Thebes and Toura, and some few of alabaster. But a great many were of granite and syenite from Syene, hard gritstone from Abou Simbel and Heliopolis; and during the reigns of the kings of Sais we meet with statues of yet harder basalt, from Syene, so hard indeed that it could not easily be cut with a flat chisel, and probably had to be chipped with a point. Yet these are all beautifully polished with sand, without a trace of the crystals or of the tool left on the surface. Porphyry, foreign marble, and bronze were not used till a later period. Under the kings of Sais also we meet with numerous small statues and images made of porcelain or baked clay, with the addition of a glazed surface coloured blue or green by the presence of a little copper. Many of them are models of mummies, made in large numbers, with long inscriptions written round the body, but wholly cast in a mould, not carved by hand; and sold cheaply, for grieving friends to bury in the tomb, or place under the bandages round the body. In earlier times these models of mummies used to be made of wood or stone and carved by hand.

(57) For painting, as the Egyptians had very little wood, and their stone walls were wanted for sculpture, and they had not invented any colours which would lie on canvas, they were limited to narrow strips of papyrus and a few wooden mummy cases. These were a poor field for the display of art; indeed, the mummy cases were mostly out of sight. Hence painting was not so much practised as sculpture, and progress in both was hindered thereby; for improvement, like a change in fashions, often is forwarded by the yielding and perishable nature of the material on which we work. The artist who in his stone statues, made by measurement, had taught his hand to give a hard stiffness to the human form, carried the same stiffness into his drawings and into his sculptures in relief, which were cut upon a drawn outline. When drawing the human figure, the pencil moved with no more freedom than the chisel; and the artist's eye looked to the statues instead of to nature. But this was less the case with birds and beasts, of which there were no statues. For

them the draughtsman looked only to nature; and when he had traced an outline on the flat stone, the sculptor often cut in low relief the figure of the animals with truth and variety of attitude. The colours used by the painters were few in number and of simple materials. The white was limestone, the red and yellow were ochres, the blue and green were copper, and the black was charcoal, all laid on by the help of gum and water.

(58) Though the Egyptian quarries did not furnish the sculptor with any stone equal to Greek marble, they gave to the architect everything that he could wish for. The stone was for the most part floated northward down the river, and very rarely carried southward against the stream; hence the temples of every city were made from the quarries next above. The nummulite limestone of Memphis was not so much liked as to be used out of its own neighbourhood; and the quarries of Toura on the opposite bank of the river supplied the better limestone of which the buildings in the Delta were made. The limestone of Thebes was also used for some few buildings in that city, but was not liked by the architect so much as the sandstone of Silsilis; hence Silsilis supplied the greater part of the stone for the beautiful temples of the Thebaid. Above Silsilis we come to the granite and syenite and basalt of the first cataract; but these stones are too hard for building purposes, and were only used for statues, obelisks, and smaller works; hence all the temples above Silsilis, such as those of Philæ, Syene, and Elephantine, are of sandstone from the quarries of Kardassy and Kalabshee in Nubia.

(59) The Egyptian architecture received a high acknowledgment of its excellence when it was copied by the Greeks; and we may gain much by noting when and how the Greeks altered and improved the art of which they had learnt something by observation in the Delta, during their intercourse with the kings of Sais. We shall thus see how the forms and ornaments which the Egyptians copied from nature, became yet more graceful in the hands of the Greeks, with whom good taste and simplicity were as inborn qualities of the mind. As there was little or no wood at hand, the Egyptians made a post by tying together with bands a number of strong rushes. This they imitated in stone; and one of their earliest columns is like a bundle of papyrus

stalks thus tied together with bands. When they further departed from nature, and made a column in imitation of a single over-thick papyrus stalk, they yet kept the bands round it, which then had no meaning. So the Greeks in their column also kept the graceful but unmeaning fillet. The Egyptian papyrus column, like the plant itself, is not thickest at the bottom, but swells as it rises from the ground. All that is good in this form is kept in the Greek column, which has a slight and pleasing swell about the same height from the base. The Egyptian papyrus column is naturally ornamented at the top with a bud, or flower, or flowers, and leaves of the same plant, which thus form a capital (see Fig. 178); and the Greek column, though not like the stalk of a plant, but like the trunk of a tree, is yet often headed with a capital ornamented with leaves and flowers. The capital of the Doric column may be the bud of the single papyrus column shortened into proportions which are more agreeable, as soon as the likeness to the plant is lost. The Egyptian square pillar with the Osiris-like statue standing quietly against it, was first copied in their own Isis-headed column, where the weight of the building rests upon the head of the goddess; and it may then have given to the Greeks the thought of their Caryatides, who so painfully support the same weight. The three-fold lines which alternate with the ovals of the kings' names on the curve of the Egyptian cornice become the triglyphs and metopes on the Doric temple.

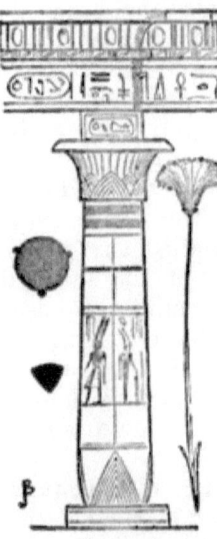

Fig. 178.

(60) When we have seen that in so many of its smaller parts the Egyptian temple was the model of the Greek, we shall have less difficulty in believing that the same is true of the whole, with only such change as the climate, the purpose, and the taste of Greece required. The Greek temple was not to be a castle or place of defence, and therefore the wall round the courtyard, and the two towers at the gateway, were not wanted; and it was raised off the ground on three or four steps, that the portico might be better seen and admired.

Instead of the roof being flat, as the climate of Egypt allowed, it was made sloping, to throw off the rain; but in appearance the flat roof is still kept, and the sloping roof looks like a second placed over it. Thus we get the Greek pediment; and the Greek columns remain of one height, as if the roof were flat. Unfortunately, the remaining temples of the two countries are so far apart both in place and in age, as the temples of Thebes and the temple of Ægina, that we could not hope to see any close agreement; but if we had any temples remaining in Lower Egypt, perhaps the agreement would be closer.

(61) In sculpture such was the superiority of the Greeks, that it is only in the lower branches of the art that any traces can be found of thoughts borrowed from Egypt. The Greek leg of a chair, formed of a lion's head and leg, was not copied from nature; the Egyptian lion-shaped couch was the original, or rather the middle link between nature and the Greek chair. So among the elegant Greek borders there are several for which we find the model not in nature, but in the Egyptian border of lotus-flower and fruit, which was also the original for the Jewish and Assyrian bells and pomegranates. The rude statue of Diana in Ephesus, which was so old that it was said to have fallen from heaven, was swaddled round the body and legs like a mummy, or rather like the Egyptian statues of Pthah and Osiris. The earliest Greek statues, sometimes called the works of Dædalus, such as the small bronze figures, often have the left leg forward and the arms hanging down by the side, like the Egyptian; and indeed Pausanias tells that some of the oldest of the Athenian statues were of the Egyptian style. The earliest Athenian coins have the full eye on the side face, like the Egyptian bas-reliefs. Lib. i.
ch. 42.

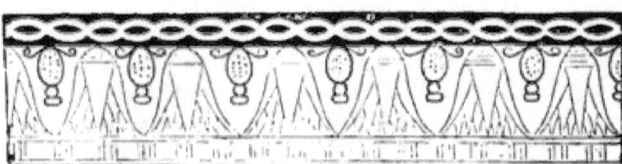

Border of Lotus Flower and Fruit.

CHAPTER V.

THE REIGNS OF THE PERSIAN CONQUERORS, AND OF THOSE EGYPTIANS WHO REBELLED AGAINST THEIR POWER.
B.C. 523—332.

(1) As soon as CAMBYSES (see Fig. 179) felt himself master of Egypt, he turned his thoughts towards the conquest of Ethiopia and the oases in the Libyan desert. He also gave orders for the sailing of an expedition against Carthage. But seamen have always a strong love of country; and his mariners, who were all Phenicians, refused to attack their countrymen who had settled on the coast of Africa; and, as the whole naval power of the Persians was in their hands, Cambyses had no choice but to give up that last undertaking. His messengers, whom he had sent forward with presents to the king of Ethiopia to require his submission, returned unsuccessful; and therefore, leaving his Greek mercenaries to guard the Delta, he led his Persian forces southward. But he set forward on this expedition more like a madman than a general.

Herodotus, lib. iii. 17.
B.C. 523.

Herodotus, lib. iii. 25.

Fig. 179.

He made no provision for the support of his large army, nor thought of the nature of the country into which he was marching, caring as little about the sufferings of his own soldiers as about the ruin of the villages on his route. When he reached Thebes he sent off a body of fifty thousand men westward, with orders to reduce, first the Great Oasis, one hundred and twenty miles to the west of the river, and then the Oasis of Ammon, nearly four hundred miles further, while he himself led the main body of his army forward towards Ethiopia. But before he had passed one fifth of the journey to Meroë his supplies failed him. The river's banks in Nubia are too lofty to be overflowed; hence the country was very barren, and could afford him but little food; and the army had nothing to live upon but the beasts of burden, and the roots and herbs at the water's edge. Cambyses then at last turned back, and reached Thebes after the loss of a great part of his army, and after the men had drawn lots for slaying one in ten to support the lives of their companions. From Herodotus's account we need not suppose that Cambyses passed beyond Nubia, or even reached the city of Abou Simbel. But later writers fancied that the Persian army had advanced till it was stopped by the sands of the great Nubian desert; and again, by the time of the geographer Ptolemy, a town on the further side of that desert had gained the name of the Treasury of Cambyses.

(2) The other army of Persians, which was sent against the oases, was even more unfortunate than the main body. They reached the Great Oasis in safety, after a journey of seven days through the Libyan desert. They then marched forward towards the Oasis of Ammon; but nothing more is known of them. They may have been ignorant of the distance, and been in want of water; they may have been betrayed by their guides; or they may have been overtaken by a hurricane from the south, which in the month of May often blows up a cloud of fine sand over the unadvised traveller, covers every trace of his path, blinds his eyes, makes his breathing painful, takes away at the same time his strength and his spirits, dries up his bags of water, and leaves him to perish in the desert. Not a man out of the whole body either returned to the valley of the Nile or reached the Oasis of Ammon; they all perished in the Libyan sands.

(3) Cambyses, on his return northward, carried off from Thebes a large booty of gold, silver, ivory, and precious stones, and among these treasures the golden zodiac from the Memnonium. He overthrew the massive walls of the temples, set fire to what would burn, and broke the statues with the zeal of a religious conqueror. He forced open the underground tombs of the Theban kings, to carry off the treasures that had been buried therein; and he afterwards enriched the palaces of Persepolis and Susa, and the temples of the fire worshippers, with the offerings which the piety of fifteen centuries had dedicated to the honour of Amun-Ra. One of the colossal statues of Amunothph III., above fifty feet high, though sitting, was then with a laborious wantonness broken

Diod. Sic. lib. i. 46.

Pausanias, lib. i. 42.

in half at the waist, the head and shoulders were thrown to the ground, while the remaining part was left in a sitting posture. This statue gained its celebrity by uttering musical notes every morning at sunrise, to the wonder of the surrounding worshippers; and it was to stop this miracle that the Persians broke it. But the zeal of the Egyptian priests was not so easily checked; and when the Persians left the country the broken statue uttered every morning the sounds as before. In looking at the numerous broken statues, we cannot fail to observe that most of them were broken on purpose, either in wantonness or in insult; and when they were of great size and hard stone this could only be done by a blow as from a sledge-hammer. Nor is it less clear that the principal blow was aimed at the beard. From this alone we might learn to which of the enemies of Egypt we owe the destruction of these works of art. The Persians held their own beards in such reverence, that they thought the greatest insult that they could offer to the Egyptians was to break off the beard from the statues of their gods and kings. In Nubia, above the cataract, the beards which remain upon the statues tell us that they were beyond the reach of the Persians.

(4) On this conquest by the Persians, as we have before seen on the conquest by the Ethiopians, the working of the gold mines near the Golden Berenice again ceased. The criminals and prisoners, the unhappy victims of Egyptian tyranny, labouring in the caverns under a guard of soldiers, must have heard with delight of the Persian success. Their chains fell from their hands as Egypt lost its liberties; the slavery of their masters was their freedom.

<small>Agatharcides, ap. Photium.</small>

(5) When Cambyses returned in disappointment to Memphis he continued in his course of tyranny and in his attacks upon the Egyptian religion. It happened that the bull Apis had been some time dead, and the priests, after a long search, had found a successor with the wished-for spots. It was black, with a square white spot on its forehead, and a second large spot in the form of an eagle on its back; it had double hairs on its tail, and the mark of a scarabæus under its tongue. Accordingly, instead of being put to the plough it was made a god. As we learn from its statues, it had a round plate of gold fixed between its horns

<small>Herodotus, lib. iii. 27.</small>

(see Fig. 6). The horns and the plate of metal were meant to represent the new moon, only one day old, when that planet, on a clear evening, appears like a pale round plate, embraced within a pair of horns of light, upon which it rests. To add to the animal's holiness, the priests said that it had no earthly father, but that a ray of light came down from heaven upon the cow its mother, and this was followed in due time by the birth of the god; and that the mother had no second calf. When it was brought to Memphis the whole city put on a face of rejoicing, the people received the lowing animal in their best clothes, and gave themselves up to feasting and every outward appearance of joy. Such was the face of the city when Cambyses returned from the Thebaid, dispirited at the loss of one large army, and at the other's want of success against the Ethiopians. He immediately declared that the people of Memphis were rejoicing at his misfortunes. He ordered the city magistrates into his presence, to ask the cause of the feasting; and when they said that it was for the arrival of the bull Apis, he had them put to death for telling him a falsehood. He then sent for the priests, and when they told him the same story he ordered them to bring this wonderful bull into his presence. When the animal was brought in he struck at it with his dagger, and wounded it in the thigh, and laughing told the priests that it was made of flesh and blood, and was no god. He then had the priests scourged, and ordered the rejoicing of the citizens to be stopped on pain of death. Thus ended this great Egyptian festival; and when the bull shortly afterwards died, it was buried privately without the usual pomp. Cambyses afterwards opened the tombs in the neighbourhood of Memphis, and broke up the mummies. He went into the great temple of Pthah, and made a joke of the dwarf statue of the god, which in this temple was rather a Phenician than an Egyptian deity. He also forced his way into the Phenician temple of the Cabeiri, the punishing gods, which none but the priests ever entered; he laughed at the ceremonies, and burned the statues.

Herodotus, lib. iii. 37.

(6) The mad and violent conduct of Cambyses was not shown only against the Egyptians. When his messengers had returned from Elephantine before his march towards Meroë, they had brought back from the

Lib. iii. 30.

Ethiopians a long bow, sent in mockery of the weakness of the Persians; and his brother Smerdis had won the respect of the soldiers by being able to draw it within two fingers' breadth of the full. Cambyses therefore in jealousy sent him back to Persia, and soon afterwards sent a messenger after him to murder him. Then, copying the Egyptian customs, and disregarding the laws of his own country, he married one of his sisters, and then another sister, putting the former to death. The physicians said that much of this violent conduct arose from an epilepsy, which he had laboured under from his birth; but the Egyptians said that his madness was sent from heaven as a punishment for his murder of the bull Apis. Thus men who have the misfortune to be brought up in a false religion fancy that there is one rule of justice for themselves and another for their Maker, and that the decrees of Providence are governed by even less wisdom than they feel in their own breasts. The Egyptians would have punished Cambyses, if they could, for the best of reasons; for crushing their country, for putting their king to death, and for murdering his own brother and sister; but they thought the crime that the gods punished him for was killing the sacred bull.

(7) Thus Cambyses wasted two years in Egypt, till he was recalled by a rebellion of the Magians at home. <small>Lib. iv. 167.</small> He appointed Aryandes prefect of the province, and then returned to Syria. There he soon died, and after an interregnum of a few months was succeeded by DARIUS (see Fig. 180), the mildest of the Persian rulers over the conquered Egyptians.

(8) It was about that time that the Princess Pheretima fled to Egypt from Barca, to beg for help from the Persians. She was the mother of Arcesilaus, king of Barca, which with Cyrene and three other little cities together made the Pentapolis; and when the people of Barca rebelled against the Greek nobles and put her son to death, she fled to Egypt for help.

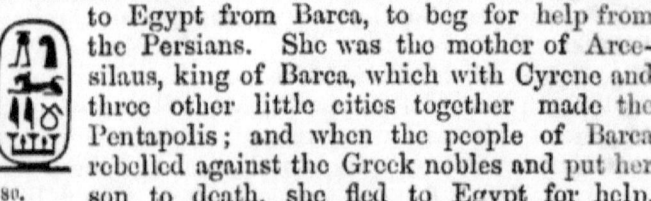
Fig. 180.

She was favourably received by Aryandes, both as an excuse for stretching the Persian power, and also on account of services rendered by her family to Cambyses; and he sent a large force to avenge her quarrel. The Persian army was commanded by Amasis, and the fleet by Badres, of the Persian royal race; and they laid siege to Barca in due form. During nine months the city was obstinately defended, the other four cities taking no part in the struggle. The open assaults of the Persians were driven back by the sallies of the besieged; their mines were met with countermines; and the city was at length only taken by treachery and falsehood. The Persians, as though in despair, made a treaty with the citizens; but when the latter opened their gates, the oaths were broken, the army rushed in, put the rebels to death, and gave up the place to Pheretima and the descendants of Battus the Dorian. The Persians would then have attacked Cyrene, but they were recalled by Aryandes; and during their whole march to Egypt they were harassed by the Libyans in the rear, who put all stragglers to the sword. Herodotus, lib. iv. 200.

(^) The quiet of the country was for a short time disturbed by a rebellion against Aryandes, whose government was marked with no little cruelty; and Darius thought it necessary to lead an army into Egypt through Arabia to check further mischief. On his arrival in Memphis, he found the people in grief for the death of the god Apis, the sacred bull. There was the same stir through the city and for the same cause as when Cambyses arrived there. But the behaviour of the two kings was by no means the same. Darius, instead of being angry, offered a large sum as a reward to any one who could find a new bull with the right spots. If the sum was as large as one hundred talents of gold, which is the amount mentioned, we must suppose that it was meant also to cover the two costly ceremonies of installing the new god and burying the old one. The feelings of the Egyptians in these matters were not new to Darius; he had been in Memphis before, when he formed part of the body-guard of Cambyses. And now that he was sovereign of the country, he yielded to the scruples of the priests of the temple of Pthah, who thought it wrong that his statue should be set up in front of that of Rameses II., because that great hero was said to have conquered the Scythians, a task which as yet Darius had been unequal to. Polyænus, Stratagem. vii. 11. Herodotus. lib. iii. 139; lib. ii. 110.

(10) It was in the reign of Darius that money was first

coined in Egypt. The well-known golden Darics had been lately coined by the king in Persia, and the ambition of the satrap Aryandes led him to coin silver in his province. The Aryandean money of Egypt was long highly valued; but it is not now known to us, perhaps only because we do not know how to distinguish it from the silver money of Persia. We find, however, in our cabinets some very early coins having on one side the dolphin and a small fish with a line of waves between them, or a man riding on a sea-monster in place of the dolphin; and on the other side the word "melek" written by means of an owl with the two sceptres of Osiris, and the sun with rays, in place of the hawk and thunderbolt, which are more usual on the later coins (see Figs. 181 and 182). These may possibly be the coins we are in search of. The dolphin, or the man on the sea-monster, may represent Arion, whose statue Herodotus so describes; and then the whole may be read Melek Ari-antebt, or the *satrap Aryandes*. The coinage of Aryandes, however, cost him his life; and his crime may have been his thus putting his own name upon them. For this and for some other acts in imitation of royalty, Darius charged him with rebellion and put him to death.

Fig. 181.

Fig. 182.

(11) The coins of Cyprus (see Figs. 183 and 184), also of these years, though engraved in good Greek art, show that that island was not beyond the reach of Egyptian opinions. The inscriptions are in Phenician letters, borrowed from the hieroglyphics. They bear on one side the bull Apis accompanied with the hieroglyphic character for life; and over it is the winged sun, sometimes as sculptured by the Egyptians, and sometimes in its more Persian form. On the other side is either the eagle or a flying dove. These coins perhaps belong to the towns of Salamis and Paphos; and the name of Apoi,

the bird, may, with the Egyptian article prefixed, represent the name of that latter city. In Cyprus we find Greek art united with Phenician language and Egyptian letters and superstitions.

Fig. 183.

Fig. 184.

(12) After the death of Aryandes, Darius gave the government of Egypt to Amasis (see Fig. 185), who had been before employed as general in the attack upon Barca. Amasis, by his name, and particularly by his titles in the hieroglyphical inscriptions, would seem to have been a native Egyptian, perhaps of the old royal family; and his appointment is a proof as it was a cause of the mild government under Darius. He bore the title of crowned melek, or satrap, of Upper and Lower Egypt, and called himself the son of the goddess Neith, as the kings of Sais had done; in the same way that the Theban kings had called themselves sons of Ra, and the Memphitic kings sons of Pthah. Amasis was succeeded in his high office by his son Nephra (see Fig. 186), with the same titles; and Egypt was quietly ruled over by these two meleks till about the twenty-ninth year of Darius. Thus under these native rulers Egypt was governed with mildness and justice. Temples were built, and the public worship of the gods performed as usual; and Darius, from his many new

Burton's Excerpta, pl. 3, 4.

Fig. 185.

Fig. 186.

Diod. Sic. lib. i. 95.

and wholesome laws, was counted by the Egyptians among their great lawgivers. He is the only one of the Persian kings who received from the priests the ancient religious titles.

(13) In the reign of Darius was built the oldest of the temples which now remain in the Great Oasis. It is dedicated to the god Amun. The Oasis is separated from the valley of the Nile by a desert without water, too wide to be crossed without a camel, which has a stomach that enables it to drink enough to bear a week's journey without need of a second supply. As this beast of burden is never mentioned in the hieroglyphical inscriptions, we may be sure that such a journey was usually performed by friendly Arabs, and not by Egyptians. Here are no springs on the road, at which the traveller and his beast may drink, as between Thebes and the Red Sea; and as well might a merchant attempt to send his goods across the ocean without a ship, as from Abydos to the Oasis without a camel. This animal is called the ship of the desert. The Egyptians had known it even from the time of Abraham, but had no need of its services on the river's bank. They did not busy themselves in journeys across the desert, or we should see it carved on the monuments and painted in the tombs. Nor is it among the foreign animals that ornament the nation's triumphs. The Ababdeh Arab is even to this day the owner of the camels with which the caravans cross the desert on either side of the river. He was of a subject race, and unclean in the sight of an Egyptian; and perhaps the patient camel fell into the same contempt as its master. To the north-west of the Great Oasis are the Western Oasis, the Little Oasis, and the Oasis of Ammon, with here and there a well of water between them. When these islands in the sand were colonised by Egyptians it was from the Thebaid, as we see by the gods to whom their temples were dedicated. These green spots find their moisture by being sunk like basins in the desert; and the traveller looks down into them with delight when his thirsty camel reaches the brink. They lie in an irregular line, along which the water drains through the sand, like a river underground, to the Mediterranean near Cyrene, either from the Nile's overflow in Ethiopia, or from the rains in Darfour. Along the

whole of this route some little trade was carried on with Thebes; but that any army, however small, should ever have reached Upper Egypt from the Mediterranean through the Oases seems impossible. There was a tradition, however, that at some early time the Phenicians had marched from Carthage and sacked Thebes; and the Theban priests told Herodotus that two of their priestesses had once been seized and carried off by the Phenicians of Libya.

Ammianus Marcellinus, xvii. 4, 3.

Herodotus, lib. ii. 54.

(14) Under these native meleks the great canal which was to join the Nile and the Red Sea, and which had been begun by Necho II., was again carried forward. It was dug from Bubastis as far as the Lower Bitter Lakes, about forty miles from the present head of the Red Sea; and though not at the time carried further, it had the effect of watering the land through which it flowed, and of making the waters of these little lakes sweet and full of water-fowl and fish. They were then called the Champsi or *Crocodile* Lakes.

Lib. ii. 158.

Pliny, lib. vi. 33.

(15) The tribute levied by Darius on Egypt and Cyrene amounted to only seven hundred talents of silver, or one hundred thousand pounds sterling, besides the crown revenues on the fisheries at the Lake of Mœris, and the hundred and twenty thousand measures of corn which were paid to the Persian garrison in the White Wall of Memphis and to their allies in the other fortified cities. There was a Persian saying that Cambyses governed like a lord, and Darius like a tradesman; but, though the army may have admired the former, the suffering people must have preferred the latter, for as long as the tribute was regularly paid, Darius left the Egyptians to the quiet enjoyment of their own laws and religion and of the rest of their wealth. The Ethiopians also, though they had been able to resist the rash invasion by Cambyses, could not now refuse to own themselves the subjects of a king who governed all Egypt quietly and firmly. But it would have been difficult for the Persians to levy any large tribute from so distant a country; and therefore a very small payment was thought enough to make it appear to the government at Susa as if the valley of the Nile to the south of Syene was an obedient province.

Herodotus, lib. iii. 91.

Herodotus, lib. iii. 89.

Lib. iii. 97

The Ethiopians, though owners of the Nubian gold mines, bought off all foreign tyranny by sending to Persia every third year the trifling gift of four pints of gold dust, two hundred logs of ebony, five negro slaves, and twenty large tusks of ivory.

(16) The melek Nephra was succeeded in his government by MANDOTHPH (see Fig. 187); and thus in this long reign Egypt had a third generation of native meleks.

<small>Burton's Excerpta, pl. 3, 5. B.C. 492.</small>

Fig. 187.

But goodness of government will not easily reconcile a great nation to the loss of its independence; and in proportion as the foreign chain is less felt it seems as if it might be the more easily thrown off. The great defeat of the Persians by the Greeks, which had lately taken place at Marathon, had done much to shake their power in Egypt, both by withdrawing all the Greek mercenaries from their service, and by teaching the world that even the Great King might be conquered by courage. During three years Persia and all its provinces were kept in a bustle by the levies of men, and by the supplies of ships, horses, and grain, which were being got together for a new attack upon Greece; and in the fourth year, as these forces were gradually drawn towards the Hellespont, the Egyptians raised the standard of revolt. The young Mandothph, who had already as satrap governed the country for five years, declared himself king of Upper and Lower Egypt, with all the usual titles, and succeeded in making himself master of the kingdom.

<small>Herodotus, lib. vii. 1. B.C. 490.</small>

<small>B.C. 487.</small>

(17) We see upon the statues and monuments of King Amunothph III. many cases in which the first half of his name, and also the first half of his god's name, Amun-Ra, have been cut out to leave room for other letters to be carved in their place. It seems probable that this was done at this time in order to make the one name into Mandothph and the other into Mando-Ra. It is true, indeed, that the removal of the word Amun out of the god's name is to be seen on some monuments of an earlier date, and on none of a later date than Amunothph, and this has led to a belief that it was done by one of his immediate successors. But we know of no change, but that here conjectured, which could have required the

removal of the three letters, A M N, neither more nor less, out of the two names, and of no earlier king that could have wished for it. Moreover the British Museum furnishes us with one monument in which both the name and figure of the hawk-headed Mando-Ra (see Fig. 188) have been clearly made to take the place of Amun-Ra, while the bad style of workmanship proves the late date of the usurpation.

(18) Egypt was now again independent, and its sacred soil no longer trod by the enemy; but its independence did not last long. The difference between being governed by Mandothph the Persian satrap and Mandothph the sovereign of Egypt did not rouse the Egyptians in his support. He was saved for one year by the death of Darius, and for another, perhaps, by Xerxes hardly feeling himself safe on the Persian throne; but in the second year of the reign of Xerxes (see Fig. 189),

Fig. 188.

Mandothph was easily conquered, and the country again reduced to a Persian province. We know little of the three years of Mandothph's reign; the historians who speak of the rebellion do not even mention his name, and it is only known to us on two or three hieroglyphical inscriptions. One tells us that he was Persian satrap of the country in the thirtieth year of the reign of Darius. Another is dated in the second year of his own reign. A third inscription is near the island of Philæ, and is a dedication to Mandoo, the sun, the god of Mendes, in Lower Egypt, of which city Mandothph was probably a native, and from whose god he took his name.

Burton's Excerpta, pl. 3, 5.

Fig. 189.

H. Horeau, Panorama.

(19) On this second conquest the Egyptians no longer found themselves under the mild government of a native melek; Xerxes appointed his brother Achæmenes to the office of satrap, and he ruled them with all the severity that the late rebellion seemed to call for.

B.C. 484. Herodotus, lib. vii. 7.

VOL. I.   P

To make the country more helpless, the Egyptian troops
were drafted into the Per-
sian armies, and even made
to fight on board the fleet.
In the naval battle of
Artemisium the Egyptian
Hermotybies and Calasiries distinguished themselves by their courage, and in the great battle of Platea
they held a post of honour. One
heavy-armed body of Egyptians in
the Persian service was remarkable
for their large shields, which
reached down to the feet (see Fig.
190).

<small>Herodotus, lib. viii. 17. Lib. ix. 32. Xenophon, Anab. i. 8, 9.</small>

Fig. 190.

(20) The latter years of the reign of Xerxes, and the
beginning of that of Artaxerxes, his successor (see Fig. 191),
are wholly without events in Egyptian
history, till, in the fifth of the latter, after
six-and-twenty years of slavery, on the
rebellion of Bactria against the Persians, when their
forces were called in another direction, the Egyptians
made a second struggle for freedom.
INARUS, the son of Psammetichus, who had
been reigning in the city of Marœa, not far from
where Alexandria was afterwards built, raised the Libyans in
rebellion against the Persians; and in a short time the greater
part of Egypt joined him. His name is written in the
hieroglyphics Adon-ra-bakan, meaning, *The servant of Adon-
Ra* (see Fig. 192). The Persians had few
troops in the province except their garrisons,
and the whole of the open country declared
for Inarus. The prefect Achæmenes
got together what forces he could;
and the two little armies met in battle
near the city of Papremis, in the nome of
Prosopites, near the head of the Delta. Here the Egyptians
were conquerors; the righteousness of the cause
added strength to their charge, and their tyrants
were routed and put to flight. But while the
two fortresses Memphis and Pelusium were held by the

<small>B.C. 460. Ctesias, ap. Photium.</small>

<small>Thucydides, lib. i.</small>

<small>Herodotus, lib iii. 12.</small>

<small>Thucydides, lib. i.</small>

Fig. 192.

Persians, the Egyptians had by no means gained their freedom; and such was the low state of warlike skill in the country, that no number of Egyptians could dislodge the Persian garrisons. Inarus therefore sought an alliance with the Athenians, who, after a long struggle with the naval forces of the island of Ægina, were at length masters of the sea, and had at that time at Cyprus a force of two hundred ships. The payment sent to Athens by Inarus, or Psammetichus, as the Athenians called him, was about seventy-two thousand bushels of wheat. The price of the Athenian friendship was five bushels for each citizen, but the payment hoped for by the Athenian fleet was the wealth of Egypt and the spoil of the Persians. Of course the force on its arrival was to be maintained by the Egyptians. The Athenians accordingly ordered part of their fleet to sail from Cyprus in order to help Inarus; to leave the more valuable conquest of Cyprus for the hope of present gain; and these allies entering the Nile with forty galleys, where the Persians had fifty, took twenty and destroyed the remainder, and made themselves masters of the river. They then sailed up the Nile towards Memphis, and again beat the Persians, and gained possession of two-thirds of that city. The Medes and Persians, with those of the Egyptians who had not revolted, withdrew into the other third of the city, called the White Wall, where the Greeks attacked them and kept them closely blockaded; and such was the unhappy state of Egyptian weakness that, while the whole of the Delta remained in the power of Inarus and the Athenian adventurers, the Persians were able to hold part of Memphis. Upper Egypt is not mentioned by the historian; it could add little strength to either party, but no doubt it sided with Inarus.

<small>Scholiast. in Aristoph. Vesp. 716.</small>

<small>Ctesias, ap. Photium.</small>

<small>Thucydides, lib. I.</small>

(21) While the Athenians thus held Egypt for Inarus, Artaxerxes sent to Lacedæmon to try to bribe the Peloponnesians to attack Attica, and thereby get the Athenian fleet recalled. But not succeeding in this, he sent a large army by land, under the command of Megabazus, who had no difficulty in defeating the Egyptians. Megabazus drove the Athenians out of Memphis; and, on their retreating, he blockaded them in the island of Prosopites, between two streams of the Nile. The nomes or districts within the Delta

are all islands. That of Prosopites, which is about twenty miles below Memphis, is twenty-seven miles long by fifteen broad. On three sides it is bounded by the deepest channels of the river; on one only is the river so shallow as to be easily forded. There the Athenians, after having lost their ships, held out for a year and a half more, till the Persians turned the river into another channel, and carried the place by storm. Inarus was betrayed and put to death by crucifixion; most of the Athenians perished; and the remaining few, crossing the desert, escaped to Cyrene, after having been masters of a large part of Egypt for six years. Fifty Athenian triremes, that shortly afterwards entered the Mendesian mouth of the Nile in ignorance of what had happened, were attacked by land and blockaded by the Phœnician vessels in the service of the Persians, and most of them were taken or destroyed.

<small>B.C. 454.</small>

(22) But even then all Egypt did not submit to the Persians. AMYRTÆUS (see Fig. 193), who had been fighting on the side of Inarus, still held out in some of the islands of the Delta, protected by the extent of the marsh land and by the more warlike character of the people. He sent to Athens for help, as Inarus had before done; and Cimon, who was at the head of the Athenian forces in Cyprus, sent him sixty ships; but they returned without being of much use to him, on hearing of the death of Cimon. But here unfortunately our history fails us. Amyrtæus reigned for six years. But whether he afterwards came out of the marshes and defeated the Persians, or whether, as is more probable, he had already been reigning in Egypt for the six years in which Inarus governed the Libyans to the west of the Delta, is doubtful. We now find, however, numerous hieroglyphical inscriptions all over Egypt bearing his name, from which it seems that he made additions to the great temple at Karnak, and repaired some of the ruin wrought by Cambyses, and also added to the temple of Amun in the Great Oasis. For Amyrtæus, also, was carved a beautiful sarcophagus, now in the British Museum, covered inside and out with hieroglyphics, from which it seems probable that he reigned many

<small>Fig. 193.</small>

<small>Manetho.</small>

<small>Wilkinson, Thebes.</small>

<small>Egypt. Inscript. pl. 24.</small>

years, and that he died in possession of his throne. But upon the whole we find but few sculptures on the walls, and yet fewer statues made during the Persian wars with Egypt. While Phidias was at work in Athens upon the frieze of the Parthenon, and Scopas was chiselling his group of Niobe's family, the Egyptian artists made no statues which were afterwards thought worth preserving.

(23) Egypt had latterly been closed against all Greek travellers. The states of Greece during these years were engaged in a constant struggle against the Persians; sometimes defending their own country from invasion, as in the ever famous battles of Marathon, Thermopylæ, and Salamis; and at other times sending their fleets to help the neighbouring states of Cyprus and the coast of Asia Minor to throw off the Persian yoke. At such a time no Greek could venture into Egypt. He would have been seized by the Persian governor as a spy, or as an agent employed to raise the province in rebellion. But during the few years that Egypt was independent under Inarus and Amyrtæus, when the Athenian mercenaries were helping them against the power of Artaxerxes, many philosophers and men of learning took advantage of the opportunity to satisfy a curiosity that had been raised by the accounts of Thales, Solon, Cleobulus, and Hecatæus, who had visited the country before the Persian conquest. Among the first travellers after this interval of sixty-three years was Hellanicus, who wrote an account of his travels, which was to be seen in the libraries of Alexandria six hundred years afterwards, though since lost. Anaxagoras, the tutor of Pericles and of Euripides, came to Egypt about the same time. By his wisdom and eloquence he had governed Athens for several years; but he afterwards withdrew from politics, and gave himself up to science. He wrote on Physics and on the cause of the Nile's overflow. But the writings of these scientific travellers have long been lost and forgotten; while those of Herodotus, who followed them, who wrote on manners and customs, on laws and religion, and studied human nature, are still read with the freshest feelings of curiosity.

Aulus Gellius, lib. xv. 23. Athenæus, lib. xi. 6.

Diodorus Siculus, lib. i. 38; lib. xii. 39.

(24) Herodotus came by sea, and most likely landed at Naucratis, the port to which the Greek merchant vessels

all sailed; and he visited with care the chief cities in Lower
Egypt, and then made a more hasty tour through
the Thebaid. He was at Sais at the Feast of
Lanterns, when all the houses were lighted up, inside
and out, in honour of the gods; and there he gained
much information from the learned scribe who had the care of
the treasures in the temple of Neith. In one of the rooms of
the royal palace stood a wooden statue of a cow in a kneeling
posture, with a round plate of gold between its horns, its
head and neck thickly overlaid with gold, and a purple
mantle over its back. Before this cow aromatics were burnt
every day, and a lamp stood burning every night in honour
of the goddess; and once a year it was brought out of its
chamber into public, to join in the lamentations for the death
of Osiris. He was in the Delta during the inundation of the Nile, which is at its greatest height in
September; and he describes in the style of a
painter the appearance of the country when under water,
when the vessels sailed over the fields from city to city, and
passed by the pyramids in the voyage from Naucratis to
Memphis. He was at Busiris during the great feast
of Isis, and saw the votaries scourge themselves by
thousands in token of what Osiris suffered and of
their own sinfulness, while the sacred ox that had been
sacrificed was roasting for their feast. This may have been
about midsummer, at the end of the natural year, but if it
took place in the last week of the civil year it was then in
the beginning of December. At Bubastis he examined
the great temple of the goddess Pasht, standing
in a grove in the middle of the town as at the
bottom of a basin, surrounded by the mounds which had been
raised higher and higher each century against the inundation
of the Nile, and on which the houses were mostly built.
There he witnessed one of the great religious
gatherings of the Delta. Men and women in
numbers came there in barges from the neighbouring cities
to be present at the sacrifice. During the voyage they sang
and clapped their hands, some adding to the noise by the
clatter of rattles, others by musical instruments; and as often
as they passed a town on the river's banks they bawled out
and taunted the people that came forth to look at them

Herodotus walked over the interesting field of battle near Pelusium, where Psammenitus was conquered by Cambyses, and the Persian power established; and then over that not less interesting field near Papremis, where it was overthrown on the defeat of Achæmenes by Inarus. At Papremis he also witnessed the sham fight which once a year took place between two parties of the priests at the door of the temple. At sunset one party, armed with wooden clubs, stood around the temple to guard the doorway; while a second party, also armed with clubs, were employed in drawing along a four-wheeled carriage, on which was placed the shrine and the image of the god within it. The one party claimed admission for the god, and the other refused it, whereupon a fierce battle ensued; blows were given in earnest, heads were broken, and blood flowed, and sometimes lives were lost in zeal for this religious duty. At Heliopolis, the chief seat of Egyptian learning, he made many inquiries respecting religion, and gained from the priests many particulars relating to the gods, which were not taught publicly to the world.

<small>Herodotus, lib. iii. 12.</small>

<small>Lib. ii. 63.</small>

<small>Lib. ii. 3.</small>

(25) It was at Sais and Memphis that Herodotus made his longest stay, and where he gained most of his information relating to Lower Egypt. It was founded on what he saw and on what he was told by the priests, and not, as it would seem, on writings. The priests did not quote to him any historic books. But at Sais he found many who were familiar with the Greek language; and his account of the kings of Sais seems thoroughly trustworthy. As far as his history is about Upper Egypt it seems very little to be relied upon, as we learn by comparing it with the more exact list of kings in Manetho and with the certain information on the monuments; and in particular he gives many of the great actions of Rameses and Shishank to a king of the name of Sesostris, whom we in vain search for in history. With the priests of Lower Egypt the chief hero was their own Shishank, who overthrew the family of Rameses, and made the unwilling Thebans carve his praise on the temple of Amun-Ra. And by putting together his actions and those of some others, and then spelling his name badly, Herodotus has created for us the great Sesostris.

(26) Memphis was then at its greatest size; it had been

rising on the fall of Thebes, and with its citadel and suburbs had a circuit of one hundred and fifty *stadia*, or sixteen miles. The chief building, after the citadel of the White Wall, was the great temple of the pigmy god Pthah (see Fig. 194), ornamented with stately porticoes and colossal statues of the gods and kings added by the piety and magnificence of successive sovereigns. On the south side of this temple was the Phenician quarter of the town, called the Camp of the Tyrians. Here stood the temple of a god whom the Greeks named Proteus, and also the temple of the foreign Venus, another Phenician deity. This latter we recognise in the goddess Kiun, the only unclothed goddess known upon the monuments. She stands upon the back of a lion, and presents flowers to Khem, the author of life, and snakes to Ranpo, the author of death, who like herself is a foreigner among the gods of Egypt (see Fig. 195). They are both mentioned in the book of the prophet Amos, one in the Hebrew and the other in the Greek. Kiun was perhaps made the wife of the pigmy Pthah. A third Phenician temple was that of the pigmy gods, the Cabeiri, into which none but the priests ever entered. These gods we recognise on the mummy cases as the torturers of the wicked after death. Their name, Kab-iri, means the *punishment-makers;* and for that purpose they carry swords, snakes, and lizards, while beside them is the lake of fire into which their victims were to be plunged.

Fig. 194.

Fig. 196.

They were the children of the pigmy Pthah (see Fig. 196). From their name and character the Hebrews borrowed those of the cherubs, who sat before the garden of Eden with a flaming sword turning in every direction, to guard the way to the tree of life against the approach of the sinner. From their name also the Greeks borrowed that of Cerberus, the doorkeeper of hell. On the same side of the temple of Pthah was the hall, or rather stable used for the bull Apis, whenever Egypt was fortunate enough

Fig. 195.

to possess an animal with the right spots. It was a small building, surrounded by a colonnade in which Herodotus, colossal statues eighteen feet high filled the place lib. ii. 176. of columns. The newest temple was that of Isis, Eustathius, which had been built in the reign of Amasis. On Alexandr. the hill of Sinopium, to the west of the city, stood a temple to Osiris, where the god had a bull's head, and was called Osiris-Apis, or Serapis; while on the hill of Sakkara, in the same neighbourhood, he had some of the attributes of Pthah, and was called Pthah-Sokar Osiris. The burial-places were in the west, on the edge of the desert, and chiefly in a plain between the hills, which is named the plain of mummies. Here lie the embalmed remains of the citizens of Memphis, among countless mummies of cats and ibises; but the kings and priestly nobles were buried on the hills, in pyramids built of brick or stone. The low Libyan hills, that separate the grass land from the glaring western sands, are fringed along their tops, as far as the eye can reach, with pyramids of all sizes, the burial-places of men who once owned the plain. The fields and gardens of the living, like life itself, are bounded by the tombs, and beyond lies the silent pathless desert.

(27) Herodotus visited the quarries on the east of the Nile, from which much of the stone was dug for the pyramids, and then the three large pyramids themselves on the west of the Nile, ten miles from Memphis; and his guide, translating the hieroglyphics on the largest pyramid, told him that it cost in building sixteen hundred talents of silver, or two hundred and thirty thousand pounds sterling. The brick pyramid of King Asychis, which Herodotus says was even larger than either of the three which are still the wonder of the world, is not now standing. It was probably built with unburnt bricks, and may have in part crumbled to dust in the course of so many centuries. Nor can we trace with certainty the ruins of the vast sepulchre and palace which Herodotus calls the Labyrinth, and which he thought more wonderful than the pyramids themselves. It was situated a little above the Lake of Mœris, and near the city of Crocodilopolis. It had twelve large courts surrounded by fifteen hundred rooms above-ground and fifteen hundred more under-ground, in which last were buried the bodies of the priests and of the sacred crocodiles. Herodotus wandered in admiration through winding ways and courts, from halls into passages, from passages into chambers, from those into closets, and from those again into other vaulted rooms, all of massive stone and covered with

Herodotus, lib. ii. 124.

Lib. ii. 136.

Lib. ii. 148.

sculpture; but he was not allowed to enter the chambers under ground. He afterwards made a hasty tour up the river to Thebes and Elephantine, but he tells us nothing of the wonders of Upper Egypt. The priests in the Delta had talked with him in the Greek language, but as he did not know a word of Egyptian he could gain less knowledge in the upper country; and perhaps the Theban buildings, which we now look upon with such interest, did not surpass those which in his days were standing in the Delta, and which he had already studied more at his leisure. He was told that from Elephantine to the river's mouth was eight thousand stadia. But the roads, where there were any, had never been measured; and as the tired traveller always thinks the way long, he did not find out the mistake; though when Eratosthenes afterwards measured the distance it was found to be only five thousand. Herodotus, lib. ii. 9.

(28) In their manners and customs Herodotus found the Egyptians unlike everything he had been used to in Greece. They wrote from right to left. They ate their meals in the streets. The women went to market on business, while the men sat at home at the loom. Daughters were forced to maintain their parents; sons were released from that duty. Men wore two garments, while women wore only one. The priests were shaven, while other men wore beards. Everything was remarkable and new to him, but perhaps nothing more remarkable than their respect for the sacred animals. Whoever killed one of these intentionally was put to death; and indeed whoever killed a hawk or an ibis even by accident was condemned to die. Whenever a house was on fire the chief care of the neighbours was to save the cats; the men and women might be burnt in the ruins, but the cats were to be saved at all risk. When a cat died a natural death every inmate of the house shaved his eyebrows, and when a dog died they shaved all over. The dead cats were carried to the sacred tombs at Bubastis, where they were embalmed and then buried. In the same way the hawks were made into mummies and sent to be buried at Butos, the serpents at Thebes, the crocodiles in the Labyrinth near Crocodilopolis, the ibis, that useful enemy of vermin, at Hermopolis, bulls and cows at Atarbechis, and the other animals in the other

cities. The priests noted down with great care all prodigies and events that followed, as part of the art of prophecy, judging that at a future time the same events would most likely follow the same prodigies. They studied astrology, undertaking to foretell the events of a man's life from knowing the hour of his birth; and they had numerous oracles to which they applied for information about the future, more particularly the oracle of Nephthys at Butos. They named the days after the sun, moon, and five planets, the seven gods who were thought to watch over them, and thereby divided time into weeks; and the names now in use in nearly every Christian nation are only translations of those used by the Egyptian priests.

<small>Herodotus, lib. ii. 82.</small>

(29) Among the Greeks, as afterwards among the Romans, religion was divided into three branches. The poet wrote on the persons and deeds of the gods; the philosopher taught the path of duty and offered consolation to the troubled breast; while the priest performed the sacrifices and ceremonies fixed by law. But among the Egyptians, as with ourselves, the priest took the whole upon himself; and thus the moral teacher, strengthening his persuasion by threats of punishment in the next world, ruled the mind of his hearers with a power unknown in Greece or Rome. But the widest difference between Greek and Egyptian was in their inward religious feelings. The sacrifice at a Grecian festival was a thank-offering by grateful hearts for blessings received from heaven; whereas the sacrifice in the Egyptian temple, in behalf of the crowds who were scourging themselves after a long fast, was meant as a sin-offering to appease the anger of gods before whom they trembled. The Egyptian temples and statues were as severe and their form as unchanging as the everlasting desert behind them, or the scorching sun overhead, and as little likely to raise in the mind any thoughts but those of awe and wonder as the sluggish river flowing below. The graceful works of art, the playful dance and song, which enlivened the Greek religion, were as foreign from the banks of the Nile as the cool valleys and the groves watered by gushing brooks.

(30) The Egyptian priests were the first to teach that a man does not wholly die when life leaves the body. They said that after death the soul dwelt in the bodies of other

animals, and was there imprisoned for its sins during a number of other short lives, and that after thus passing, for three thousand years, through the bodies of birds, beasts, and fishes, it was again allowed to take upon itself a human covering. Hence they carefully saved the dead body from decay, by embalming it as a mummy, that it might be ready for the soul to re-enter when the years of punishment were at an end. Unfortunately for the progress of knowledge and for the improvement of society, the priestly teachers of the nation taught for the most part only according to fixed rule and the unchanging traditions of their colleges. We hear of no opposing schools of philosophy, as in Greece, who brought out truth by their disputes; no dissenters from the established opinions, who by their rivalry kept one another's minds from stagnating. All teaching was according to law, and perhaps on the supposition that a perfect knowledge of truth had been already attained. Under these circumstances the nation remained stationary, while their neighbours, who had started later in the race of civilization, were rapidly overtaking them, and soon to pass them. Though professing a knowledge of astronomy, they still declared that the natural year was of the same length as their civil year, and of 365 days only. Though the new year's day, the first day of the month of Thoth, had slowly moved from midsummer to midwinter, they still said that their civil year needed no intercalary days.

<small>Herodotus, lib. ii. 123.</small>

(31) In everything relating to religion the Egyptians were grave, serious, and in earnest. Such was the solemnity of the temples and ceremonies, that though Herodotus disbelieved much that was told him of the gods, he often held it too sacred to be talked about. No Greek or Roman ever lost his life as a religious martyr from the earnestness of his belief in Jupiter and Juno; but on the several conquests of Egypt many of the believers in Isis and Osiris have laid down their lives in the pious defence of the bull Apis, the ibis, the cats, and the other sacred animals. The Egyptians never admitted into their religious scheme the gods of their neighbours. And, unfortunately, this religious earnestness was accompanied with the same fault that it carries with it in modern times, namely, religious intolerance, which the Greeks were more free from. The people of

<small>Lib. ii. 18.</small>

Marea and Apis, on the banks of the Lake Mareotis, who were Libyans, and did not hold the religious opinions of the Egyptians, saw nothing wicked in eating cow-beef, and did not like to be forbidden to kill a cow in their own cities. They pleaded that they were not Egyptians. But they could obtain no religious toleration from their rulers, because in drinking out of their lake they drank the sacred waters of the Nile. The Libyans of Parætonium and that neighbourhood, beyond the limits of the Nile's bounty, were not forbidden to eat cow-beef. This religious seriousness followed the Egyptians on all occasions, so much that at their feasts a small model of a mummy was presented to the guests, to remind them of the uncertainty of life. Their one poem, the national song, named the Maneros, or *Song of Love*, was a melancholy lamentation on the death of Osiris, of which Theocritus has left us a free translation, and Bion a beautiful poetical imitation. The chorus of the national song in Athens was the soul-stirring words,

<small>Theocrit.
Herodotus,
lib. ii. 78.</small>

<small>Theocrit.
Idyll. xv. 100.</small>

> I will carry my sword concealed in a myrtle branch,
> As Harmodius and Aristogiton did,
> When they slew the tyrant,
> And made the Athenians equal.

But the Egyptians were more ready to sympathise with grief than with joy, and when the melancholy Maneros was each year sung through their streets, the doleful chorus in which the people joined was,

<small>Bion,
Idyll. i.</small>

> Ah, hapless Isis, Osiris is no more.

The priests in the procession join in the lamentation, and console the goddess in the same strain; and the poem and the festival end every year with the advice, which to foreign ears, untuned to this mournful devotion, seems almost laughable,

> Cease, Isis, cease to-day, thy tears forbear,
> Reserve thy sorrows for another year.

(32) Herodotus left the country by sea, as he came, and thence sailed to Tyre; and very soon afterwards Egypt was again closed against all Greek travellers. On the deaths of Inarus and Amyrtæus, Egypt lost its liberties, and again found itself within the grasp of

<small>Herodotus,
lib. ii. 44.

B.C. 454.</small>

THE SUN-WORSHIPPERS. 223

ARTAXERXES, rightly named LONGIMANUS, whose outstretched arm made the nations tremble from the Hellespont and Nile to the Indus. The Persian king, with more humanity than we should have looked for from the conqueror, employed Thannyras and Pausiris, the sons, to govern as satraps those provinces which their fathers had lately held as rebels; Thannyras, the son of Inarus, governed that part to the west of the Nile called Libya (see Fig. 197); and Pausiris, the son of Amyrtæus, governed the rest of Egypt; while the Egyptians consoled their wounded vanity in living under a race of foreign kings by inventing a story that Cyrus had married a daughter of their king Hophra, and that Cambyses and his successors had therefore gained the kingdom not by conquest but by inheritance. These two native satraps were appointed to the government of Egypt, a few years after Judæa had in the same way been placed by the Persians under the rule of Ezra as high priest; and Mered, the son of Ezra, would seem to have married a sister of one or other of these Egyptian satraps.

Herodotus, lib. iii. 15.

Fig. 197.

Lib. iii. 2.

1 Chron. iv. 17, 18.

(33) The Persian sun-worship was at this time not unknown in Egypt. On a wall in the city of Alabastron we see carved what we must understand to be Thannyras, the governor of the province, worshipping the sun, not the Egyptian statue of Ra, but the sun itself, which is there called Adon-Ra, from the Hebrew title Adonai (see Fig. 198). Every ray of sunshine ends with a hand, to denote its active power over the world, and thus explains to

Burton's Excerpt. vi.

Fig. 198.

us why the King Artaxerxes was himself called Longimanus. His trembling subjects thought that his power was felt in almost every land on which the sun shone. The worshipper is styled within the ovals of his name (Fig. 197) *Pharaoh Thaomra, his name, successor of Adonra;* a name which seems meant for Thannyras, the son of Inarus. The bad style of the sculpture agrees with the fallen state of the nation. The false anatomy and want of simplicity in the human figure are what we look for when the people have lost their dignity of character. The shape of the head given to Thaomra, when in the form of a sphinx, is not that of the Theban kings, but that of the labouring class, with low forehead and forward mouth (see Fig. 199). Like the kings of Sais, he has no beard.

Fig. 199.

The artist at the same time lost his good taste and love of simplicity. In one case we see that the figure of the sun, under which the Theban king Oimenepthah I. is worshipping Amun-Ra, has had added to it a number of rays of sunshine, each ending in a hand; and this addition we may suppose was made in the reign of Artaxerxes (see Fig. 200). That the Egyptians did not refuse to copy the Persians is also seen in another name of their great god Amun-Ra. Many eastern nations are unable to sound the letter M; in its place they use a B. On a mummy from Memphis and on the sarcophagus of Amyrtæus we find the name of the god written Oben-Ra. This is moreover the very spelling used on a plate of ivory found among the ruins of Nineveh to which distant city

<small>Hartwell Museum.</small>

<small>British Museum.</small>

the Egyptian style of art had made its way two centuries earlier.

(34) On the death of Artaxerxes Longimanus, his son, XERXES II., governed Persia and its provinces for two months;

Fig. 200.

and then SOGDIANUS reigned for seven months. Sogdianus was put to death by his brother DARIUS NOTHUS, in whose favour Arxanes, satrap of Egypt, rebelled; not, however, to make the Egyptians independent, but only to make use of them in choosing a master for the Persian empire. The meddling tyranny of the satraps under Darius was very galling to the Egyptians, and kept alive the feelings of hatred which separated the conquered from the conquerors. Ostanes the Mede undertook to regulate the Egyptian worship and instruction in the chief temple of Memphis; and thus the god Pthah, who was their god of fire, was to be worshipped after the fashion of the Persian fire-worshippers. The foreigners whom Ostanes employed in this attack upon the religion of Egypt were Pammenes, and Maria, a learned Jewess who had written on chemistry, and Democritus of Abdera, the physician and philosopher, who had been educated by Persians and had embraced the Persian religion. Democritus, with his love of Eastern philosophy, had a great

Ctesias, ap. Photium. B.C. 423.

Syncelli Chronogr.

Diogenes Laertius.

respect for Egyptian studies; and though his chief pursuit in Egypt was natural science, yet he gained some knowledge of hieroglyphics, and wrote a work on the sacred writings of Meroë, as Upper Egypt was then named.

<small>Diod. Sic. lib. i. 98.</small>

Democritus lived in intimacy with the Egyptian priests during his five years' residence among them, and they considered him one of their best pupils in their favourite study of astrology. The priests never willingly wrote the names of these Persian kings on their monuments; and they thus lost the power of dating by means of the reign. On an inscription dated only "in the year ten," the want of a king's name, as well as the style of art, will almost prove that it was made under one of the Persian conquerors.

<small>Egypt. Inscrip. pl. 13.</small>

(35) During these years Egypt remained quiet under the weight of its heavy chains, but at the end of Darius's reign of nineteen years ARTAXERXES MNEMON came to the throne of Persia, when, fortunately for the Egyptians, his title was not undisputed. His brother Cyrus, who dwelt at Sardis, as satrap of Lydia, and held chief sway in Asia Minor, also claimed the kingdom; and hiring a large body of Greek mercenaries, he marched towards Babylon to assert his rights. Cyrus was defeated, and the ten thousand Greeks commanded by Xenophon made good the retreat which is immortalised by that historian. But though Artaxerxes thus kept his throne, the civil war had weakened his power; and the Egyptians, taking advantage of his trouble, threw off the yoke which they had groaned under for fifty-five years since the deaths of Inarus and Amyrtæus. An Egyptian, a native of Mendes, descended from the ancient race of kings, and bearing the names of Psammetichus and Nepherites, headed the rebellion, and seated himself on the throne of his ancestors. That all Egypt obeyed him we learn by finding near the cataracts at the southern frontier, a dedication in his name to Mandoo, the god of the city belonging to his family. He was saved from the power of Persia by the wars which arose among the satraps of the great king. Tissaphernes, who was the most powerful, and now satrap of Lydia, as successor to Cyrus, was loyal to

<small>B.C. 404.</small>

<small>Xenophon, Anabasis.</small>

<small>B.C. 401.</small>

<small>Diod. Sic. lib. xiv. 35.</small>

<small>B.C. 400.</small>

<small>H. Horeau, Panorama.</small>

Artaxerxes, and therefore hostile to Egypt. Tamos, the governor of Ionia, another of these satraps, who was in danger of punishment because he had joined the cause of Cyrus, put his younger children and his wealth on board the Persian fleet, and rashly sailed to the Egyptian king as to a friend, from the forces of Tissaphernes. But the avarice and ambition of the Egyptian were greater than his sense of friendship or justice; he thought Tamos could be of no further use to him, so he strangled his friend and the children, and seized the money and ships for his own use.

(36) NEPHERITES (see Fig. 201) is known to us only by the share which he bore in the war between the Spartans and the Persians. He sent, as his supplies, to help the former against the common enemy, one hundred triremes and five hundred thousand measures of wheat. This wheat, however, was lost; for the Egyptian transports carried it into the harbour of Rhodes, without knowing that the Rhodians had surrendered to Artaxerxes; and it was seized by Conon, the admiral of the Persian fleet. Nepherites of Mendes reigned six years, and though none then within the military age could remember their country's former freedom, though none but the aged could recollect the days of Inarus and Amyrtæus, yet he established his power on so firm a base, that Egypt remained independent under his successors for fifty-four years longer.

<small>Diod. Sic. lib. xiv. 79.</small>

<small>Manetho.</small>

Fig. 201.

(37) ACHORIS (see Fig. 202), who succeeded Nepherites, found his kingdom sheltered from the Persians by a new ally, who stood between him and the threatened danger. Evagoras of Salamis, copying the example of the Egyptians, had risen against the Persians, and driven them out of Cyprus and made himself king of that island. The forces of Artaxerxes had therefore to be first turned against Cyprus. To the support of the brave Evagoras the Tyrians sent their fleet, the neighbouring Arabs sent soldiers, and Achoris, in the tenth year of his reign, sent a large supply of corn and money, together with fifty ships of war. Evagoras, however, was beaten by the larger forces of the Persians, under the

<small>B.C. 394.</small>

<small>Diod. Sic. lib. xv. 3.</small>

Fig. 202.

command of Gaius, the son of Tamos, and lost several cities; and, leaving his son in command of the rest, he sailed for Egypt to consult with Achoris about the means of carrying on the war, and to beg for further help. Evagoras spent several months in Egypt, but was not able to obtain from Achoris such large supplies as he wished for. The next year, however, Gaius, the commander of the Persian fleet, deserted from Artaxerxes; and though his father Tamos had been basely murdered by Nepherites on a former desertion, yet his fear and hatred of Artaxerxes made him take the same steps, and seek the alliance of Achoris. Thus during a reign of thirteen years Achoris was able to keep the war at a distance, and in some measure to cultivate the arts of peace at home. Some additions were then made to the temple of Medinet Abou, on which his name is met with in the hieroglyphical inscriptions. His name is also found on the temple at Karnak.

<small>Wilkinson, Thebes.</small>

(38) After his death PSAMMUTHIS (see Fig. 203) reigned one year, NEPHERITES II. four months, and MUTHIS one year; all called of the dynasty of Mendes, on the east side of the Delta, either from making Mendes their capital, or from being descended from the race of priests of that city.

<small>Manetho.
B.C. 382.</small>

Fig. 203.

(39) After these short reigns NECTANEBO I. (see Fig. 204) of the city of Sebennytus gained the sovereign power; and in his reign the Persians again moved their forces to reduce the rebellious Egyptians to obedience. Artaxerxes Mnemon gave the command of the Persians to Pharnabazus, and that of the twenty thousand Greek mercenaries to Iphicrates of Athens; and when the troops were assembled at Acca they amounted to upwards of two hundred thousand men, and five hundred ships of war of all sizes, beside the transports. But the slow movements of the Persians left their enemies full time to prepare for defence. Nectanebo strengthened the fortresses by which the mouths of the Nile were guarded; he stopped up some channels by banks of earth and others by his ships, and drew trenches from the Lake of Menzaleh towards the Bitter Lakes,

<small>B.C. 380.
Diod. Sic.
lib. xv. 41.</small>

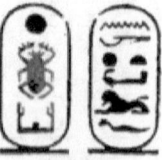

Fig. 204.

across the roads near Pelusium, by which Egypt could be entered by land. In short, he made the river impassable by mounds and the land by ditches, and when the Persian fleet arrived at Pelusium they found the place too strong for an attack; they could neither enter the river nor land the troops. Pharnabazus therefore withdrew his ships into deep water and sailed for the Mendesian mouth, in hopes of finding it less guarded.

(40) When the Persians again entered the Nile near Mendes, they found the coast, as they had expected, badly guarded; for Nectanebo had taken the greater part of his forces to Pelusium. Pharnabazus and Iphicrates landed a body of three thousand men, who routed an equal number of Egyptians, and then gained the fortress that guarded that mouth of the river. By this victory the Nile was opened to the fleet, and Egypt might have been again conquered; but it was saved by the quarrels between the Persian and Greek commanders. Iphicrates proposed that they should at once sail up the river, and boldly seize Memphis, which they heard was left with only half a garrison; but Pharnabazus would not move because the rest of the Persian forces had not arrived. Iphicrates then offered to sail up the Nile to Memphis with only the small body of well-disciplined Greeks which were with them at Mendes. But this proposal was still less agreeable to Pharnabazus; he feared that when Iphicrates and the Greeks had gained Memphis they might hold it on their own account, instead of giving it up to himself or another satrap of Artaxerxes. In this way was much valuable time wasted. In the meanwhile Nectanebo at Pelusium learned where the Persians had made good their landing; and accordingly he sent one body of troops to guard Memphis, while he gathered the rest of his army round Mendes. He there harassed the Persians in numerous skirmishes, and after a time routed them with great slaughter in the open field. In this way the spring was spent, the midsummer winds arose, the Nile began to overflow its banks, and the Persians had no choice but to leave a country where the husbandman was sailing over his fields in a boat.

(41) After this defeat of the Persians, Nectanebo was left in peace during the rest of his reign of eighteen years.

Under his government some few buildings were carried on in Egypt; his name is carved on the repairs or additions to the temples of Thebes; and we find him effacing in one place the name of the Ethiopian Tirhakah to make way for his own. He also dedicated a small temple to the goddess Athor, at Philæ, on the borders of Ethiopia. Nectanebo also added to the sculptures on the small temple of polished basalt, which was brought to Sais by Amasis, partly sculptured by Amyrtæus, and which remained unfinished when Herodotus saw it.

<small>Wilkinson, Thebes.</small>

(42) The peace with Persia left the country again open to Greek travellers. It was in this reign visited by Eudoxus, the astronomer, Chrysippus, the physician, and Plato, the still more famous Athenian philosopher. During the former war between Persia and Egypt, the Spartans had fought on the side of Artaxerxes, and the Athenians helped Inarus; but in this last invasion the Greek states had changed sides; and so, when these travellers from Athens came into Egypt, they found it necessary to bring with them friendly letters from Agesilaus king of Sparta to Nectanebo and the priests. Plato brought with him a cargo of olive oil, instead of money, to pay the expense of his journey. We can have no greater proof of the esteem in which the Egyptian schools were held than that these men, each at the head of his own branch of science, should have come to Egypt to finish their studies. Here Eudoxus, the earliest systematic astronomer among the Greeks, spent sixteen months, studying under the priests, and like them shaving his chin and eyebrows; and he may have learned from his tutor Ichonuphys, who was then lecturing at Heliopolis, the true length of the year and month, upon which he formed his octaëterid, a period of eight years or ninety-nine months. At Memphis, Eudoxus consulted the bull Apis as to his fortune; and the god in reply licked his cloak. This the priests in waiting told him meant that he would soon die. In Egypt Chrysippus may have learnt anatomy by the dissection of the human body, which the prejudices of the Greeks forbade him to study at home. Plato had been attending as a pupil on Socrates, and listening to his conversation on the immortality of the soul; but from the

<small>Diogenes Laertius, lib. viii. 90. Strabo, lib. xvii. Plutarch. in Solone.</small>

<small>Diogenes Laertius, viii. 90.</small>

priests of Heliopolis, which was as much a Jewish as an Egyptian city, where Moses planned the liberation of his countrymen, and near to where Jeremiah wrote his Lamentations for their downfall, we must believe that the Athenian philosopher gained new views of a future state of rewards and punishment. In Plato's writings we see Greek philosophy in its best form, united with some of the truths of the Old Testament, but not without many traces of Egyptian mysticism, and also with an Egyptian disregard for the marriage tie, which is very unworthy of a pupil of Socrates. Had Plato's philosophy died with himself, it would claim but little notice here; it is the writings of his successors that make us note its rise as important in the history of Egypt. Each future century we find Platonism becoming more mystical, or, if we may say so, more Egyptian and less Greek; we trace its changes through the writings of Jesus the son of Sirach, of Philo-Judæus, of the author of the book of Wisdom, and through the Christian writings of Athenagoras and Clemens, all of whom wrote in Egypt; and again when paganism made its last stand against Christianity it was in the schools of the Alexandrian Platonists.

Plato praises the Egyptian manufacturing industry as a chief peculiarity in their character; and while describing the Athenians as lovers of learning, he classes the Egyptians with the Phenicians as skilful in trade. But he speaks of them as curiously afraid of all novelty. The music never varied, and the priests when joining in the lamentations with the goddess Isis every year sang the same poem. Either by law, or by custom which is stronger than law, the painters and sculptors were forbidden to make any change in their figures; the works of art which were then being made he thought neither more beautiful, nor, as he adds, more ugly, than those which were called ten thousand years old. And by these works of the sculptors we may judge of the mind and habits of the rest of the people. They were imprisoned within the scheme of education by which they had been trained. There was a perfect union between the civil and the priestly powers, which as soon as the country was united under one sceptre made the government doubly despotic. The ruling class guided the thoughts and educated the minds of the nation;

De Republ. iv.

De Legibus, ii.

232 NECTANEBO I.—B.C. 379–362. [CHAP. V.

and thus the very learning which had so early raised the
Egyptians above their neighbours was now chiefly employed
to repress novelty and check improvement. The
poet Euripides is supposed to have accompanied
Plato on this journey. He fell ill while in
Egypt, but was cured by the priests, chiefly by the help of
sea-water.

<small>Diogenes Laertius, lib. iii. 6.</small>

(43) Changes, however, were slowly creeping into the
Egyptian opinions from the foreigners in the Delta; and one
of the most interesting related to the important doctrine of
life hereafter. The Egyptians had considered the resurrection of the body as the means necessary to life after death.
Accordingly they embalmed it with care; and their paintings
show us the spirit or soul, in form of a bird, again returning
to the mummy and putting life and breath into its mouth,
while the god Anubis is preparing to unwrap the bandages
(see Fig. 205). Without the body no future life could be

Fig. 205.

enjoyed. But we may suppose that in Heliopolis, as afterwards in Alexandria, a more spiritual opinion was held, and
the immortality of the soul and a future life were believed
in even without a resurrection of the body. Some were of
opinion that when the earthly body fell to the ground, an
angelic or spiritual body at once rose up to heaven without
waiting for a day of resurrection. The painter, distinguishing

the heavenly body by its blue colour and the earthly body by its red colour, represented this opinion on the mummy case (see Fig. 206); for the wealthy priest would prudently have

Fig. 206.

his body embalmed even when he was not sure that it was needed for his enjoyment of a future life. Both these opinions were known to the Jews; and while the Sadducees denied that there would be any resurrection, whether angel or spirit, the Pharisees acknowledged both. *Acts, xxiii. 8.*

(44) When Nectanebo died he was succeeded by TACHOS at the very time that Artaxerxes Mnemon was gathering together his forces for a fresh attack upon Egypt. Tachos sent an embassy to Sparta with a large sum of money to engage some Greek allies; and the Spartans appointed their king Agesilaus and a council of thirty to this service, with orders to raise a body of mercenaries by means of the Egyptian gold. When Agesilaus landed in Egypt the great officers of state came to meet him, and the people crowded down to the shore to get a sight of the general who had before defeated the Persians in their own country, and was now come to check their invasion of Egypt. But they saw a little old man of above seventy years of age seated on the grass by the sea side; and when the messengers from Tachos offered him the royal presents, he only accepted the plain food, and told them that they might take the sweetmeats and perfumes to the Helots who attended the army as slaves. Agesilaus had brought with him a thousand Spartans; and Tachos gave him the command of *Manetho. B.C. 362. Plutarch. Vit. Agesilai. Diod. Sic. lib. xv. 92.*

his ten thousand Greek mercenaries, while he put his son the young Nectanebo at the head of his eighty thousand Egyptians. His fleet of two hundred ships he intrusted to Chabrias the Athenian, who had entered his service without permission from his own state, as the Athenians were then fighting on the side of Persia. These large preparations, however, emptied the Egyptian treasury, and except from the regular crown rents on the land, and the voluntary gifts from the priests, Tachos had no means of filling it. Chabrias persuaded him to risk the unpopularity of laying on a tax, a measure of no difficulty in the free state of Athens, but a dangerous experiment in Egypt; and Tachos accordingly put a duty on the sale of corn. By the advice of Chabrias also, the king levied a sum of gold and silver upon some of his richer subjects under the name of a forced loan. The injustice, however, was in some measure lessened by the payment of interest; and at last the whole was repaid to them. Chabrias drew up his fleet within the Pelusiac branch of the river, where the Greek sailors under Psammetichus had made an intrenchment with a suitable sea beach; and the place afterwards bore the name of the Camps of Chabrias.

Aristoteles, De curâ reif., lib. ii.

Polyænus, Strateg. lib. iii. 2.

Pliny, lib. v. 14.

(45) Tachos did not wait to be attacked by the Persians, but he led his army into Palestine to meet them. He had refused to follow the wise advice of Agesilaus, who wished him to stay at home to guard his capital from enemies whether foreign or Egyptian, and to trust his armies to his generals; and he soon found out his mistake. While he was in Palestine with his army, and his son Nectanebo, whom he had made general of the Egyptian troops, was besieging some towns in Syria, the unpopularity of the Greek mercenaries and of the new tax raised the Egyptians in rebellion; and the prefect of Egypt, with the troops that were left behind to garrison the cities, declared the young Nectanebo king in the place of his father. When the news reached the army in Palestine the whole of the Egyptian troops, hardly needing the large promises with which they were bribed, declared in favour of their brethren at home, and they immediately marched to Egypt with young NECTANEBO, leaving Tachos in Palestine.

Diod. Sic. lib. xv. 92.

(46) While this was going forward, the Athenians, from a wish to please their friend Artaxerxes, had by a public vote recalled Chabrias from the command of the Egyptian fleet, and at the same time Tachos quarrelled with Agesilaus. In his anger he laughed at his small size, and quoted against him the fable, that when the mountain was in labour and the gods frightened, it brought forth a mouse. "You will soon find me a lion," said Agesilaus; and he left the king's service to join that of his rebellious son in Egypt. On this the kingdom was lost to Tachos; his subjects were in rebellion, and he had no mercenaries. He sent from Palestine to make terms with Artaxerxes, and then fled into Persia, feeling less in fear of the Persian armies than of a rebellious son. He gave up his independence in hopes of recovering his kingdom; and Artaxerxes, who wished to gain possession of Egypt, not to conquer Tachos, promised him his friendship and the help of the very army that had been employed against him. Fortunately, however, before the Persian army moved, Artaxerxes Mnemon died; and thus the Egyptians kept their freedom a few years longer.
Cornelius Nepos, Vit. Chabriæ. Athenæus, lib. xiv.
Diod. Sic. lib. xv. 92.

(47) We hear no more of the dethroned Tachos after his flight into Persia. He had hitherto lived a temperate life, but he gave himself up to Persian luxury after his fall from the throne. The foreign dishes did not agree with his health, and he very shortly died of a dysentery. He had reigned about two years.
Ælianus, lib. v. 1. Manetho.

(48) Nectanebo's first trouble was a serious rebellion which began at the city of Mendes, and was probably headed by one of the descendants of Nepherites, whose family had before reigned in that city. The king would have been defeated, had not Agesilaus the Spartan, who before fought for Tachos, been still engaged in the Egyptian service. The rebel from Mendes brought a large army into the field, and drove Nectanebo and Agesilaus to shut themselves up in the city of Tanis. He then sat down before the place for a regular siege, and he had drawn his trenches nearly round the city, when the Greeks sallied forth under the old Agesilaus, and led Nectanebo safely through the besieging army. After two or three other battles the Mendesian was wholly routed and the rebellion put down.
Plutarch. Vit. Agesilai.

(49) Agesilaus the Spartan deserved and received the thanks of Nectanebo for this service; but he refused his rewards, and he astonished the luxurious Egyptians as much by the plainness of his dress and diet, and the hardiness of his way of life, as by his skill and bravery in battle. He distributed among his followers the whole of the large gift of two hundred and twenty talents, which Nectanebo sent him when he was returning to Sparta. But Agesilaus never reached home alive. When he arrived at the port of Menelaus, between Egypt and Cyrene, he was seized with illness, and there he breathed his last. His body was covered with wax for want of honey, and thus carried to Sparta.

(50) Artaxerxes Ochus, the next king of Persia, soon renewed the war. In his first invasion he was unsuccessful, and he returned home laughed at by the Egyptians and his own allies. Of the latter, Cyprus, Phenicia, and Cilicia, taking advantage of his weakness, revolted and joined the Egyptians. Before the Persian king next moved his forces towards Egypt his first aim was to reconquer those states; for in losing them he lost his fleet and his best sailors. He got together from all parts of his large empire an army of three hundred thousand foot, thirty thousand horse, three hundred ships of war, and five hundred ships of burden. His other supplies were equally large. Every nation and city of Asia sent embassies with gifts, not only of food and other necessaries for the army, but of all such costly articles as trembling subjects would think agreeable to a haughty monarch who had called upon them for supplies. Theopompus the historian describes at length the beasts of burden laden with luxuries for the palate, the droves of oxen for slaughter, the little mountains of salted fish and meat, the volumes of books, the countless weapons of war, both Grecian and barbarian, the tents heavy with cloth of gold, the costly couches and carpets, the embroidered and scarlet robes, cups and vases of chased silver and wrought gold, and others ornamented with precious stones and of exquisite workmanship. Nothing among the most rare productions of the earth or the most valued achievements of art was forgotten in this tribute to a monarch marching to the conquest of a rebellious province.

Diod. Sic. lib. xvi. 40.

Longinus, sect. 43.

(51) Artaxerxes got possession of Sidon by the help of the treachery of Tennes, the chief citizen there; and, as a traitor can only be of use once, he then put him to death. On this first success all Phenicia surrendered to the Persians, and in the course of the year the greater part of Cyprus did the same. Then the Greek mercenaries joined the Persian army more readily, and the next year Ochus a second time led his forces towards Egypt. After some little delay from the sand-banks off the mouth of the Nile, the Persian land and sea forces at the same time reached Pelusium. Ochus himself accompanied his army, and encamped near this city, and placed his Greek mercenaries in the front. Nectanebo, on his part, had not been idle. He had fortified all the mouths of the Nile and the cities on his Arabian frontier, and had got together an army of twenty thousand Greek mercenaries, twenty thousand Libyans, and sixty thousand of the Egyptian militia. But he was ruined, as his father had been, by refusing to follow the advice of his Greek generals. He was at first too rash, and would not keep on the defensive; but having met with a trifling loss he was then too timid, and retreated with half his army to cover Memphis. Had he remained at his post, the Greeks would no doubt have guarded his kingdom; but he retreated, and the invading army was left at leisure to lay siege to Pelusium in due form. The Persians emptied the city moat by drawing off the water into other channels. They then brought up their machines on the dry ground, and with their battering-rams made a wide breach in the walls. The Greek garrison, however, was not easily discouraged; they again and again stopped up the breach by wooden beams; and it was only after they heard of the flight of Nectanebo that they made terms with the besiegers for their own safety. They gave up the city to the Persians on receiving a promise from Lacrates, the Greek commander in the Persian service, that they should be sent to Greece in safety. The Persian generals would have broken this promise; but Ochus supported Lacrates, and the garrison and citizens were treated kindly according to the agreement. In the same way, when the city of Bubastis was conquered, Ochus would allow no prisoners to be taken, but ordered the garrison and the in-

Diod. Sic. lib. xvi. 45.

B.C. 349.

Diod. Sic. lib. xvi. 47.

habitants to be equally well treated. This conduct had all the effect that he wished for; it at once disarmed the Egyptians, and left them at full leisure to quarrel with their Greek mercenaries. Most of the towns in the Delta then opened their gates to the Persians without a struggle.

(52) Amongst a people degraded by despotism a single battle usually decides the fate of the state. Nectanebo, who was at Memphis, seeing that he had lost all chance of saving his throne, thought only of his treasures, and fled hastily up the Nile with such valuables as he could take with him into Ethiopia, beyond the reach of the Persian arms.

Athenæus, lib. v, 13. According to another account, Nectanebo was taken prisoner by Ochus, and treated by him with great generosity and kindness; and, when dining at the table of his conqueror, he was led to remark that the proverbial magnificence of the Persian monarch even fell short of the cost and luxury which he had himself been used to, and that he had been ruined by his own wealth, and conquered by the moderation of Ochus.

(53) No sooner, however, was OCHUS master of the country than his conduct changed. He levelled the fortifications of all cities that he did not garrison;

Diod. Sic. lib. xvi. 51. he destroyed the temples, carried away the gold and silver, and only gave up the sacred records on receiving a heavy ransom for them from the priests. He copied

Ælianus, lib. iv. 8. Cambyses in making a wanton attack upon the religion and prejudices of his new subjects. When unsuccessful in his first invasion, the Egyptians, punning on his name, Artaxerxes Ochus, had called him Artaxerxes the Ass, and this was not forgotten. So taking up with their joke, he brought forward an ass as the patron deity of the Egyptians, and then slew their sacred bull Apis in sacrifice to the new god. But this insult to the Egyptian religion was neither forgotten nor forgiven. Soon after

Lib. vi. 8. Ochus returned to Persia he was stabbed by the slaves in his own service, and first to strike the blow was Bagoas, an Egyptian eunuch, who was urged to the deed by zeal for the bull Apis. He cut the king's body into pieces and threw it to the beasts, as Osiris had been treated by Typhon in the Egyptian mythology.

(54) Ochus had returned to Babylon laden with spoils, and leaving the satrap Pherendates to govern the country; and for the next seventeen years Egypt was a province of Persia. _{Diod. Sic. lib. xvi. 51.}

(55) Thus ended the kingdom of the Copts, if Lower Egypt still deserved that name. It was a country with several races of men; at least three languages were there spoken as native, and neither could now claim the superiority. The energies of the people seemed gone; they scarcely thought their political institutions worth guarding; while the land-holding soldiers, a terror only to their poorer neighbours, kept the arms in their own hands, and were equally unwilling to fight themselves and to allow the Greek mercenaries to fight for them. The superiority of the Greeks had humbled at the same time the valour and the patriotism of the Egyptians, whose skill in war was so little valued that they were even laughed at by the Persians.

(56) The death of Artaxerxes Ochus, and the accession of ARSES, and then of the unfortunate DARIUS CODOMANUS, made no change in the fate of the Egyptians. Egypt remained a province of Persia till Persia was conquered by the Greeks under Alexander. These last two hundred years, which in Egypt are dark with Persian tyranny and unsuccessful struggles for the nation's freedom, are the very years which embrace all that was most bright and glorious in Greek arts and letters. Athens, Sparta, and a few more little cities, had flourished in their noble rivalry. They had once for a moment acted together against the attacks of their common enemy the Persians. But when the growing strength of the monarchies around them called for union, the democracies were unable to unite, and therefore sunk half willingly under the king of Macedonia. Athenian liberty was cradled by Solon and crushed by Alexander. Between these two lived Æschylus, Pindar, Thucydides, Socrates, and Demosthenes. When Solon visited Egypt, Persia was preparing for the Egyptian war; and when Alexander entered Egypt he had already silenced the Athenian orators and was marching to the overthrow of the Persian monarchy.

CHAPTER VI.

EGYPT CONQUERED BY THE GREEKS. ALEXANDER THE GREAT. CLEOMENES. B.C. 332-323.

(1) Such was the unhappy state of Egypt when the young Alexander, succeeding his father Philip on the throne of Macedonia, got himself appointed general by the chief of the Greek states, and marched against Darius Codomanus at the head of the allied armies. It was not difficult to foresee the result. The Greeks had learned the weakness of the Persians by having been so often hired to fight for them. For a century past, every Persian army had had a body of ten or twenty thousand Greeks in the van, and without this guard the Persians were like a flock of sheep without the shepherd's dog. Those countries which had trusted to Greek mercenaries to defend them could hardly help falling when the Greek states united for their conquest.

(2) Alexander defeated the Persians under Darius in a great and memorable battle near the town of Issus, at the foot of the Taurus, at the pass which divides Syria from Asia Minor, and then, instead of marching upon Persia, he turned aside to the easier conquest of Egypt. In his way there he spent seven months on the siege of the wealthy city of Tyre, and he there punished with death every man capable of carrying arms, and made slaves of the rest. He was then stopped for some time before the little town of Gaza, where Batis, the brave governor, had the courage to close the gates against the Greek army. His angry fretfulness at being checked by so small a force was only equalled by his cruelty when he had overcome it; he tied Batis by the heels to his chariot, and dragged him round the walls of the city, as Achilles had dragged the body of Hector.

<small>Diod. Sic. lib. xvii.
Q. Curtius, lib. iv.
B.C. 332.</small>

(3) On the seventh day after leaving Gaza he reached Pelusium, the most easterly town in Egypt, after a march of

one hundred and seventy miles along the coast of the Mediterranean, through a parched glaring desert which forms the natural boundary of the country; while the fleet kept close to the shore to carry the stores for the army, as no fresh water is to be met with on the line of march. The Egyptians did not even try to hide their joy at his approach; they were bending very unwillingly under the heavy and hated yoke of Persia. The Persians had long been looked upon as their natural enemies, and in the pride of their success had added insults to the other evils of being governed by the satrap of a conqueror. They had not even gained the respect of the conquered by their warlike courage, for Egypt had in a great part been conquered and held by Greek mercenaries.

<small>Arrian. lib. iii.</small>
<small>Q. Curtius, lib. iv.</small>

(4) The Persian forces had been mostly withdrawn from the country by Sabaces, the satrap of Egypt, to be led against Alexander in Asia Minor, and had formed part of the army of Darius when he was beaten near the town of Issus, on the coast of Cilicia. The garrisons were not strong enough to guard the towns left in their charge; the Greek fleet easily overpowered the Egyptian fleet in the harbour of Pelusium, and the town opened its gates to Alexander. Here he left a garrison, and ordering his fleet to meet him at Memphis, he marched along the river's bank to Heliopolis. All the towns on his approach opened their gates to him. Mazakes, who had been left without an army as satrap of Egypt when Sabaces led the troops into Asia Minor, and who had heard of the shameful flight of Darius, of the death of Sabaces, and that Alexander was master of Phenicia, Syria, and the north of Arabia, had no choice but to yield up the fortified cities without a struggle. The Macedonian army crossed the Nile near Heliopolis, and then entered Memphis.

<small>Arrian. lib. iii.</small>

(5) Memphis had long been the chief city of all Egypt, even when not the seat of government. In earlier ages, when the warlike virtues of the Thebans had made Egypt the greatest kingdom in the world, Memphis and the lowland corn-fields of the Delta paid tribute to Thebes; but, with the improvements in navigation, the cities on the coast rose in wealth; the navigation of the Red Sea, though always dangerous, became less dreaded, and Thebes lost the toll on

VOL. I.

the carrying trade of the Nile. Wealth alone, however, would not have given the sovereignty to Lower Egypt, had not the Greek mercenaries been at hand to fight for those who would pay them. The kings of Sais had guarded their thrones with Greek shields; and it was on the rash but praiseworthy attempt of Amasis to lessen the power of these mercenaries that they joined Cambyses, and Egypt became a Persian province. In the struggles of the Egyptians to throw off the Persian yoke, we have seen little more than the Athenians and Spartans carrying on their old quarrels on the coasts and plains of the Delta; and the Athenians, who counted their losses by ships not by men, said that in their victories and defeats together Egypt had cost them two hundred triremes. Hence, when Alexander by his successes in Greece had put a stop to the feuds at home, the mercenaries of both parties flocked to his conquering standard, and he found himself on the throne of Upper and Lower Egypt without any struggle being made against him by the Egyptians. The Greek part of the population, who had been living in Egypt as foreigners, now found themselves masters. Egypt became at once a Greek kingdom, as though the blood and language of the people were changed at the conqueror's bidding. But the reader of these pages has seen that the change had been coming about slowly for several centuries.

<small>Ælianus, lib. v. 10.</small>

(6) Alexander's character as a triumphant general gains little from this easy conquest of an unwarlike country, and the overthrow of a crumbling monarchy. But as the founder of a new Macedonian state, and for his reuniting the scattered elements of society in Lower Egypt after the Persian conquest in the only form in which a government could be made to stand, he deserves to be placed among the least mischievous of conquerors. We trace his march, not by the ruin, misery, and anarchy which usually follow in the rear of an army, but by the building of new cities, the more certain administration of justice, the revival of trade, and the growth of learning. On reaching Memphis, his first care was to prove to the Egyptians that he was come to re-establish their ancient monarchy. He went in state to the temple of Apis, and sacrificed to the sacred bull, as the native kings had done at their coronations; and gained the good will

<small>Arrian. lib. iii.</small>

of the crowd by games and music, which were performed by skilful Greeks for their amusement. But though the temple of Pthah at Memphis, in which the state ceremonies were performed, had risen in beauty and importance by the repeated additions of the later kings who had fixed the seat of government in Lower Egypt, yet the Sun, or Amun-Ra, or Kneph-Ra, the god of Thebes, or Jupiter-Ammon, as he was called by the Greeks, was the god under whose spreading wings Egypt had seen its proudest days. Every Egyptian king had called himself "the son of the Sun;" those who had reigned at Thebes had boasted that they were "beloved by Amun-Ra;" and when Alexander ordered the ancient titles to be used towards himself, he wished to lay his offerings in the temple of this god, and to be acknowledged by the priests as his son. As a reader of Homer, and the pupil of Aristotle, he must have wished to see the wonders of "Egyptian Thebes," the proper place for this ceremony; and it could only have been because, as a general, he had not time for a march of five hundred miles, that he chose the nearer and less known temple of Kneph-Ra, in the Oasis of Ammon, one hundred and eighty miles from the coast.

(7) Accordingly, he floated down the river from Memphis to the sea, taking with him the light-armed troops and the royal band of knights-companions. When he reached Canopus, he sailed westward along the coast, and landed at Rhacotis, a small village on the spot where Alexandria now stands. Here he made no stay; but as he passed through it, he must have seen at a glance, for he was never there a second time, that the place was formed by nature to be a great harbour, and that with a little help from art it would be the port of all Egypt. The mouths of the Nile were too shallow for the ever increasing size of the merchant vessels which were then being built; and the engineers found the deeper water which was wanted between the village of Rhacotis and the little island of Pharos. It was all that he had seen and admired at Tyre, but it was on a larger scale and with deeper water. It was the very spot that he was in search of, in every way suitable for the Greek colony which he proposed to found as the best means of keeping Egypt in obedience. Even from before the time of Homer the island of Pharos

had given shelter to the Greek traders on that coast. He gave his orders to Dinocrates, the architect, to improve the harbour, and to lay down the plan of his new city; and we shall hereafter see that the success of the undertaking proved the wisdom both of the statesman and of the builder.

<small>Ammianus Marcellinus, lib. xxii.</small>

(8) From Rhacotis he marched along the coast to Paraetonium, a distance of about two hundred miles through the desert; and there, or on his way there, he was met by the ambassadors from Cyrene, who were sent with gifts to beg for peace, and to ask him to honour their city with a visit. Alexander graciously received the gifts of the Cyrenaeans, and promised them his friendship, but could not spare time to visit their city; and, without stopping, he turned southward to the oasis.

<small>Arrian. lib. iii.</small>
<small>Q. Curtius, lib. iv.</small>

(9) The Oasis of Ammon is the most northerly of the three oases of the Libyan desert. It is a green and shady valley in the midst of parched sand-hills, and is refreshed by a deep spring of water, which, as it is always of nearly the same heat, seems cool in the hot hours of the day and warm when the air is cool at night. This little stream, after flowing through the valley, is lost in the dry sands. The spot was a halting-place for caravans passing from Paraetonium to the next oasis. The priests of the temple carried on a small trade in sending to Lower Egypt a valuable salt, which from the name of the place was called salt of ammonia. It was probably manufactured from the soot of camel's dung, the usual fuel of the desert, where wood was far too scarce and too valuable to be burnt. In this oasis stood the temple of Amun-Ra. The figure of the god was that of a man having the head and horns of a ram; and the piety of the merchants, who left their treasures in the strong rooms of the temple while they rested their camels under the palm-trees, had loaded the statue with jewels. On holidays the priests carried the god about on their shoulders in a gilt barge, with silver dishes hanging from each side, while women and maidens followed singing his praises. Alexander, on his approach with his army, was met by the chief priest of the temple, who, whether willing or unwilling, had no choice

<small>Athenaeus, lib. ii. 25.</small>

<small>Q. Curtius, lib. iv.</small>

but to hail the conqueror of Egypt as "the son of Amun-Ra;" and having left his gifts before the altar, and gained the end for which he came, he returned the shortest way to Memphis. In the meantime Apollonides had marched at the head of another body of troops from Memphis to Elephantine, and had made himself master of the whole valley of the Nile below the cataracts. Arrian. lib. iii.

(10) Alexander (see Fig. 207) has been much laughed at by the Greeks for thus calling himself the son of Ammon; but it should be remembered that it was only among people who worshipped and built temples to their kings that, for reasons of state, he called himself a god; that he never was guilty of the folly of claiming such honours in Greece, or of his Greek soldiers; and that among his friends he always allowed his godhead to be made the subject of a good-humoured joke. In his graver moments he remarked that God is the father of us all, and that He makes the best men in a more peculiar manner His sons; and once, when wounded, he pointed out to the bystanders that his blood was like that of other mortals. Plutarch in Alexandro. Apophtheg- mata.

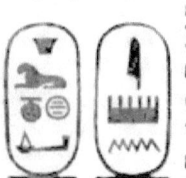

Fig. 207.

(11) At Memphis he received the ambassadors that came from Greece to wish him joy of his success; he reviewed his troops, and gave out his plans for the government of his new kingdom. He threw bridges of boats over the Nile at the ford below Memphis, and also over the several branches of the river. He divided the country into two *nomarchies* or judgeships, and to fill these two offices of *nomarchs* or chief judges, the highest civil offices in the kingdom, he chose Doloaspis and Petisis, two Egyptians. Their duty was to watch over the due administration of justice, one in Upper and the other in Lower Egypt, and perhaps to hear appeals from the lower judges. He left the garrisons in the command of his own Greek generals; Pantaleon commanded the counts, or knights-companions, who garrisoned Memphis, and Polemon was governor of Pelusium. These were the chief fortresses in the kingdom: Memphis overlooked the Delta, the navigation of the river, and the pass to Upper Egypt; Pelusium was Arrian. lib. iii.

the harbour for the ships of war, and the frontier town on the only side on which Egypt could be attacked. The other cities were given to other governors; Licidas commanded the mercenaries, Peucestes and Balacrus the other troops, Eugnostus was secretary, while Æschylus and Ephippus were left as overlookers, or perhaps, in the language of modern governments, as civil commissioners. Apollonius was made prefect of Libya, of which district Parætonium was the capital, and Cleomenes prefect of Arabia at Heroopolis, in guard of that frontier. Orders were given to all these generals that justice was to be administered by the Egyptian *nomarchs* according to the common law or ancient customs of the land. Petisis, however, either never entered upon his office or soon quitted it, and Doloaspis was left *nomarch* of all Egypt.

(12) This is perhaps the earliest instance that history has recorded of a conqueror governing a province according to its own laws, and allowing the religion of the conquered to remain as the established religion of the state; and the length of time that the Græco-Egyptian monarchy lasted, and the splendour with which it shone, prove the wisdom and humanity of the founder. This example has been copied, with equal success, in our own colonial and Indian governments; but we do not know whether Alexander had any example to guide his views, or whether his own good sense pointed out to him the folly of those who wished to make a people open not only their gates to the garrisons, but their minds to the religious opinions of the conquerors. At any rate the highest meed of praise is due to the statesman, whoever he may have been, who first taught the world this lesson of statesmanlike wisdom and religious humanity.

(13) Alexander sent into the Thebaid a body of seven thousand Samaritans, whose quarrels with the Jews made them wish to leave their own country. He gave them lands to cultivate on the banks of the Nile which had gone out of cultivation with the gradual decline of Upper Egypt; and he employed them to guard the province against invasion or rebellion. He did not stay in Egypt longer than was necessary to give these orders. He had found time to talk with Psammo, the philosopher of the greatest name then in Memphis; but though the buildings of Upper Egypt were unvisited, he

hastened towards the Euphrates to meet Darius. In his absence Egypt remained quiet and happy. Peucestes soon followed him to Babylon with some of the troops that had been left in Egypt; and Cleomenes, the governor of Heroopolis, was then made collector of the taxes and prefect of Egypt. Cleomenes was a bad man; he disobeyed the orders sent from Alexander on the Indus, and he seems to have forgotten the mild feelings which guided his master; yet upon the whole, after the galling yoke of the Persians, the Egyptians must have felt grateful for the blessings of justice and good government.

<small>Arrian. lib. vii.</small>

(14) At one time, when passing through the Thebaid in his barge on the Nile, Cleomenes was wrecked, and one of his children bitten by a crocodile. On this plea, he called together the priests, probably of Crocodilopolis, where this animal was held sacred, and told them that he was going to revenge himself upon the crocodiles by having them all caught and killed; and he was only bought off from carrying his threat into execution by the priests giving him all the treasure that they could get together. Alexander had left orders that the great market should be moved from Canopus to his new city of Alexandria, as soon as it should be ready to receive it. As the building went forward, the priests and rich traders of Canopus, in alarm at losing the advantages of their port, gave Cleomenes a large sum of money for leave to keep their market open. This sum he took, and when the building at Alexandria was finished he again came to Canopus, and because the traders would not or could not raise a second and larger sum, he carried Alexander's orders into execution, and closed the market of their city.

<small>Aristoteles, De curâ reif., lib. ii.</small>

(15) But instances such as these, of a public officer making use of dishonest means to increase the amount of the revenue which it was his duty to collect, might unfortunately be found even in countries which were for the most part enjoying the blessings of wise laws and good government; and it is not probable that, while Alexander was with the army in Persia, the acts of fraud and wrong should have been fewer in his own kingdom of Macedonia. The dishonesty of Cleomenes was indeed equally shown toward the Mace-

donians, by his wish to cheat the troops out of part of their pay. The pay of the soldiers was due on the first day of each month, but on that day he took care to be out of the way, and the soldiers were paid a few days later; and by doing the same on each following month, he at length changed the pay-day to the last day of the month, and cheated the army out of a whole month's pay.

(16) Another act for which Cleomenes was blamed was not so certainly wrong. One summer, when the harvest had been less plentiful than usual, he forbade the export of corn, which was a large part of the trade of Egypt, thereby lowering the price to the poor so far as they could afford to purchase such costly food, but injuring the landowners. On this, the heads of the provinces sent to him in alarm, to say that they should not be able to get in the usual amount of tribute; he therefore allowed the export as usual, but raised the duty; and he was reproached for receiving a larger revenue while the landowners were suffering from a smaller crop.

(17) At Ecbatana, the capital of Media, Alexander lost his friend Hephæstion, and in grief for his death he sent to Egypt to inquire of the oracle at the temple of Kneph, in the Oasis of Ammon, what honours he might pay to the deceased. The messengers brought him an answer, that he might declare Hephæstion a demigod, and order that he should be worshipped. Accordingly Alexander then sent a command to Cleomenes that he should build a temple to his lost favourite in his new city of Alexandria, and that the lighthouse which was to be built on the island of Pharos should be named after him; and as modern insurances against risks by sea usually begin with the words "In the name of God; Amen;" so all contracts between merchants in the port of Alexandria were to be written solemnly "In the name of Hephæstion." Feeling the difficulty of getting obeyed at the mouth of the Nile, while he was himself writing from the sources of the Indus, he added that if when he came to Egypt he found his wish carried into effect, he would pardon Cleomenes for those acts of misgovernment of which he had been accused, and for any others which might then come to his ears. It must remain doubtful with what feelings the priests gave their advice in

Arrian.
lib. vii.

favour of these commands that Hephæstion should be worshipped, or that Alexander himself should be called a god. They certainly never looked upon either of them as one of the creators of the world. They perhaps rather viewed them as canonised saints, as mediators between gods and men; and a Greek inscription on a votive slab, in which Alexander and Hephæstion are standing before the god Amun-Kneph, helps to explain this when it declares that Alexander is able to appease Olympic Jove. They ranked them perhaps with the four lesser gods of the dead whom they painted upon the funereal tablets as coming before the judge Osiris as advocates, and presenting to him an atoning sacrifice on behalf of every man on his death. Egypt. Inscript. 2nd Ser. 57.

(18) A somatophylax in the Macedonian army was no doubt at first, as the word means, one of the officers who had to answer for the king's safety; perhaps in modern language a colonel in the body-guards or household troops; but as, in unmixed monarchies, the faithful officer who was nearest the king's person, to whose watchfulness he trusted in the hour of danger, often found himself the adviser in matters of state, so, in the time of Alexander, the title of somatophylax was given to those generals on whose wisdom the king chiefly leaned, and by whose advice he was usually guided. Among these, and foremost in Alexander's love and esteem, was Ptolemy, the son of Lagus. Philip, the father of Alexander, had given Arsinoë, one of his relations, in marriage to Lagus; and her eldest son Ptolemy, born soon after the marriage, was always thought to be the king's son, though never so acknowledged. As he grew up, he was put into the highest offices by Philip, without raising in the young Alexander's mind the distrust which might have been felt if Ptolemy could have boasted that he was the elder brother. He earned the good opinion of Alexander by his military successes in Asia, and gained his gratitude by saving his life when he was in danger among the Oxydracæ, near the River Indus; and moreover, Alexander looked up to him as the historian whose literary powers and knowledge of military tactics were to hand down to the wonder of future ages those conquests of which he was an eye-witness. Arrian. lib. iii. Pausanias, lib. i. 6.

(19) Alexander's victories over Darius, and march to the River Indus, are no part of this history: it is enough to say that he died at Babylon eight years after he had entered Egypt; and his half-brother Philip Arridæus, a weak-minded unambitious young man, was declared by the generals assembled at Babylon to be his successor. His royal blood united more voices in the army in his favour than the warlike and statesmanlike character of any one of the rival generals. They were forced to be content with sharing the provinces between them as his lieutenants; some hoping to govern by their power over the weak mind of Arridæus, and others secretly meaning to make themselves independent.

<small>Q. Curtius, lib. x.
Justinus, lib. xiii.
B.C. 323.</small>

(20) In this weighty matter, Ptolemy showed the wisdom and judgment which had already gained him his high character. Though his military rank and skill were equal to those of any one of Alexander's generals, and his claim by birth perhaps equal to that of Arridæus, he was not one of those who aimed at the throne; nor did he even aim at the second place, but left to Perdiccas the regency, with the care of the king's person, in whose name that ambitious general vainly hoped to govern the whole of Alexander's conquests. But Ptolemy, more wisely measuring his strength with the several tasks, chose the province of Egypt, the province which, cut off as it was from the rest by sea and desert, was of all others the easiest to be held as an independent kingdom against the power of Perdiccas. When Egypt was given to Ptolemy by the council of generals, Cleomenes was at the same time and by the same power made second in command, and he governed Egypt for one year before Ptolemy's arrival, that being in name the first year of the reign of Philip Arridæus, or, according to the chronologer's mode of dating, the first year after Alexander's death.

<small>Arrian. ap. Photium, lib. x.</small>

(21) The death of Alexander is one of the great epochs from which the Greek historians count their years. Other kings have made the beginning of their reigns an epoch for history, but in the case of Alexander his death seemed to his countrymen more important than his conquests. He had been as unsuccessful in strengthening his own throne as he had been successful in overthrowing others. When his

active mind ceased to direct the united armies of Greece, Macedonia sunk to that rank as a state which it held before his wiser father raised it; but the kingdoms which he had overthrown did not again rise. It was at once seen that the great empires of the East, which had so long employed Greek mercenaries, were now wholly unable to throw off a yoke which had been riveted more by their own consent during the last two centuries than by Alexander's brilliant victories during a short reign of twelve years. Our history also at this time changes its character. Having been dug with the mummies out of the tombs, and put together like the pieces of a broken statue, it has wanted life and warmth. It has been far from performing that higher task, in which the historian has an advantage even over the moralist, of describing the action and pointing out its consequences; of showing how in nations, as in individuals, goodness and crime, wisdom and folly, are each followed by its own reward. But henceforth it will be less of an antiquarian inquiry, and we may hope to see more of men's good and evil passions, of their aims, their motives, and their feelings.

In the next four pages are set forth the three principal lists of the early kings of Thebes and Memphis before the time of Rameses II.; namely that of Eratosthenes, that of Manetho, and that of the tablet of Abydos. They show that Eratosthenes and the tablet agree in making Manetho's eighteenth dynasty follow immediately upon his twelfth; and that Eratosthenes places the builders of the pyramids at no earlier point of time before the great Theban kings than the foregoing pages do.

The chronological table which follows shows which kings reigned over part of Egypt, and which over the whole, and what little kingdoms sunk into others. The names before which a star (*) is placed, are those whose date is fixed by independent reasons, and by the help of which the other names are placed.

ERATOSTHENES. The Kings of Thebes from No. 12 to No. 30 [with notes to show the agreement with Manetho and the Tablet].	THE TABLET OF ABYDOS, With the addition of the First Two Kings, the Second Names, and the Wives of Two; and with the Translations of the Names.			MANETHO.	Names found in the Pyramids.
				XI. DYNASTY OF THEBES. 15 Kings unnamed. 16. Ammenemes I.	
12. Chnubus Gneurus, or Chryses, son of Chryses. [Noubkora.]	[B.C. 1600.]		Amunmai Thori or Gori I.	IV. DYNASTY OF MEMPHIS. 1. Soris. 2. Suphis of the Pyramid. 3. Suphis.	Chofo of the oldest Pyramid, the second in size.
13. Rauosis.			Osirtesen I. or Osiri-gesen.	XII. DYNASTY OF THEBES. 1. Geson Goses.	
14. Biyris.	Noubkora.		Amunmai Thori II.	4. Mencheres.	
				2. Ammenemes II.	Nef-Chofo of the largest Pyramid.
15. Saophis, [Suphis, or Chofo of Memphis.]	Meshora.		Osirtesen II.	5. Rhatases. 3. Sesostris. 6. Bicheres.	

16. Saophis II. [Sensuphis, or Nef-Chofo of Memphis.]	Meskora. [B.C. 1500.]	Osirtesen III.	Labaris. 5. Ammers.	· 7. Sobercheres. · 8. Thampthis.
17. Moscheres Heliodotus. [Meskora Osirtesen III.]		Amunmai Thori III. Laobra.	6. Ammenemes III.	V. DYNASTY OF MEMPHIS. 1. Othoes.
18. Musthis.		Scemiophra.	7. Queen Semiophris.	· 2. Phius.
19. Pammes Archondes.	Chebra. [B.C. 1425.]	Ames.	XVIII. DYNASTY OF THEBES. 1. Amosis. 2. Chebros.	· 3. Methusuphis.
20. Apappus the Great, reigned one hundred years. [Philops of Memphis.]	Sebekara, or Shogsueg-kara.	Amunothph I.	3. 4. Amenophthis. Amersis (perhaps his widow).	· 4. Phiops, lived 100 years.

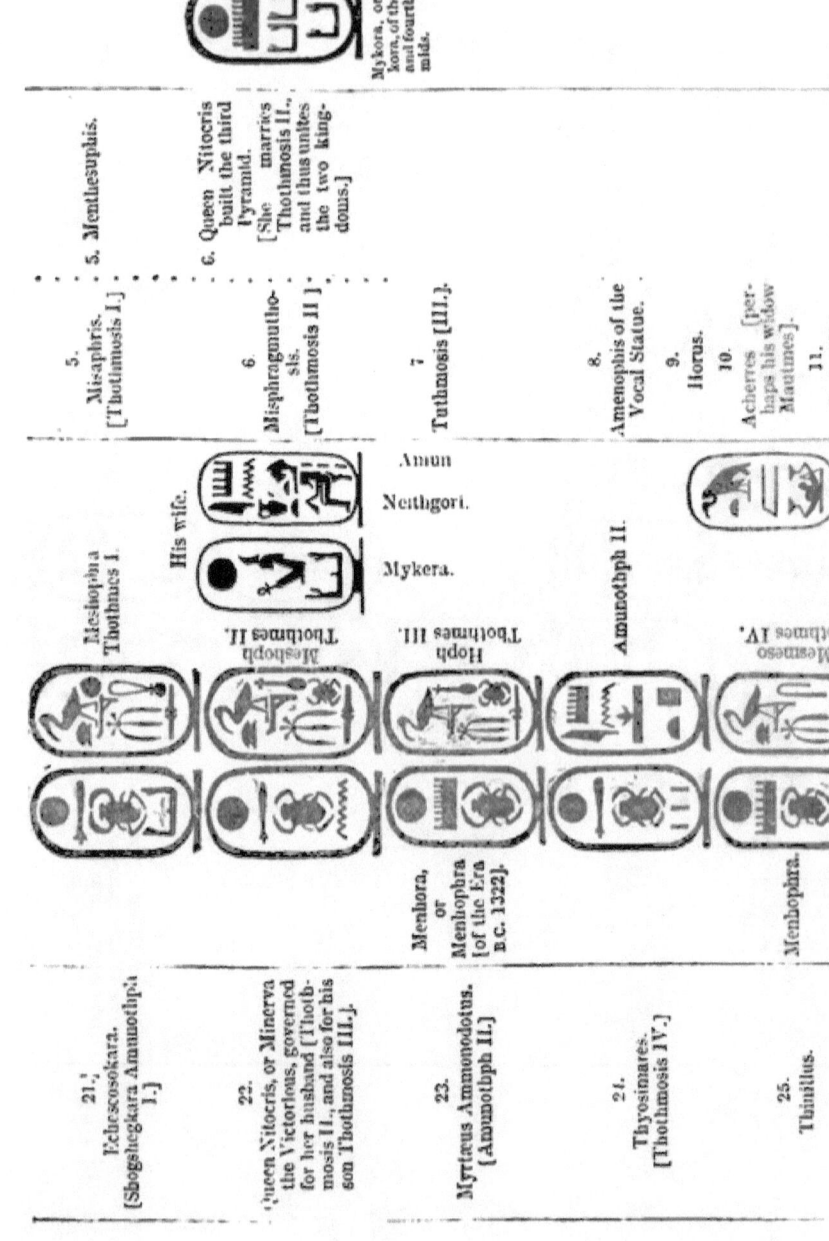

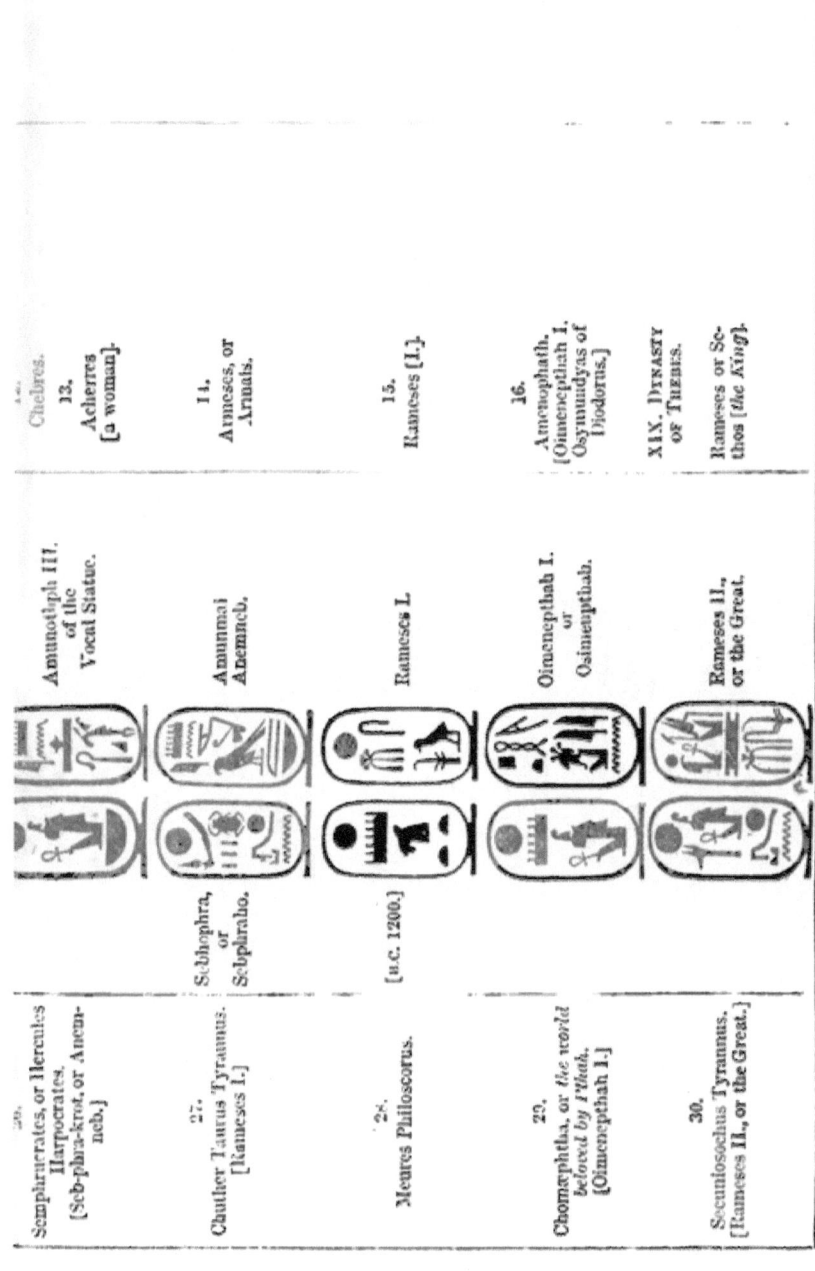

256 TABLE OF CHRONOLOGY.

B.C.	THEBES	THIS	HERACLEOPOLIS	MEMPHIS	SAIS	TANIS. XOIS. BUBASTIS.		B.C.
1700	15 Kings						Soris		
							Suphis		
							Sensuphis		
1600	Amunmai Thori I.					Mencheres			
	Osirtesen I.					Ratheris			
	Amunmai Thori II					Bicheres			
	Osirtesen II.					Sebercheres			
	Osirtesen III.					Thampsis			
1500	Amunmai Thori III.				Labaris	Othoes		Salatis	
	Sesmiophra					Phius		Beon	
	Amosis					Methusuphis		Apachnas	
	Chebros					Phiops		Apophis	
	Amunothph I.					Menthesuphis		Janias	
	Thothmosis I.					Nitocris		Asseth	
1400	Thothmosis II.							Joseph	
	*Thothmosis III.								
	Amunothph II.								
	Thothmosis IV.								
1300	Amunothph III.								Moses
	Amunmai Anemneb								
	Rameses I.								
	Oimenepthah I								
1200	Rameses II.								
	Pthahmen Tūmeiothph								Samson
	Oimenepthah II.								
	Osirtia Ramerer								
1100	Rameses III.								
	*Rameses IV.								

B.C.	ETHIOPIA			ELEPHANTINE
	Napata	Soleb	Sonker	
1700	. . . .	. . . .	. . . .	│││││
1600	. . . .	. . . .	. . . .	│││││
1500	. . . .	. . . .	. . . .	│││││
1400	. . . .	. . . .	. . . .	
1300	. . . .	. . . .	. . . .	
1200	. . . .	. . . .	. . . .	
1100	. . . .	. . . .	. . . .	

B.C.								B.C.
1000		Rameses V. Rameses VI. *Zerah = Rameses VII. Rameses VIII. Rameses IX. Rameses X.			Smendes Psusenes Nephelcheres	*Shishank Osorchon ——— ——— ——— Tacellothis	Solomon Rehoboam	1000
900		Ameses? Amunmai—? Ameses? ———?			Amenophthis Osochor Psinaches Pausennes	——— ——— ———		900
800	Sabacothph Sevechus *Tirhakah		Anysis Sethon	Bocchoris Ammeres	*Petubastes Osorchon Psammus Zeet		Hezekiah	800
700				Stephinathis Nechepsus Necho I. Psammetichus I. Necho II. Psammetichus II.			Josiah	700
600				*Hophra Amasis Psammenitus *Cambyses *Darius Mandotliph Xerxes			Zedekiah	600
500				Artaxerxes Inarus and Amyrtæus Xerxes II. Darius Artaxerxes Nepherites				500
400				Achoris Psammuthis; Nepherites; Muthis Nectanebo Tachus; Nectanebo II. Ochus; Arses; Darius Alexander *Ptolemy				400
300								300

Fig. 208.—Ptolemy Soter.

CHAPTER VII.

PTOLEMY SOTER, AS GOVERNOR UNDER PHILIP ARRIDÆUS, AND UNDER ALEXANDER ÆGUS, AND AS KING. B.C. 322-284.

(1) WHENEVER a man of ambition aims at raising himself by means of industry and ability to a higher rank in the world than that in which he was born, if he seeks to throw off his family and to break those ties by which he fancies he is held back, the opinion of the world as certainly chains him to the load that he wishes to rise from. Anybody with less good sense and knowledge of mankind than PTOLEMY would have called himself the natural son of Philip Amyntas, the king of Macedonia, and would have wished his relationship with Lagus to have been forgotten; but we may be sure that in

that case the name of Lagus would have been thrown at him as a reproach, and he more wisely took it as his title; instead of being ashamed of his father's name he ennobled it, and took care that his children and his children's children should be proud of being of the family of the Lagidæ. He was one of those who at the death of Alexander had raised their voices against giving the whole of the conquered countries to one king; he wished that they should have been shared equally among the generals as independent kingdoms; but in this he was overruled, and he accepted his government as the lieutenant of the youthful Philip Arridæus (see Fig. 209), though no doubt with the fixed purpose of making Egypt an independent kingdom. On reaching Memphis, the seat of his government, his whole thoughts were turned towards strengthening himself against Perdiccas, who hoped to be obeyed, in the name of his young and weak-minded king, by all his fellow generals.

Pausanias, lib. i. 6.

Fig. 209.

(2) The Greek and foreign mercenaries of which the army of Alexander was made up, and who were faithful to his memory and to his family, had little to guide them in the choice of which leader they should follow to his distant province, beside the thought of where they should be best treated; and Ptolemy's high character for wisdom, generosity, and warlike skill had gained many friends for him among the officers; they saw that the wealth of Egypt would put it in his power to reward those whose services were valuable to him; and hence crowds flocked to his standard. On reaching their provinces, the Greek soldiers, whether Spartans or Athenians, forgetting the glories of Thermopylæ and Marathon, and proud of their wider conquests under the late king, always called themselves Macedonians. They pleased themselves with the thought that the whole of the conquered countries were still governed by the brother of Alexander; and no one of his generals, in his wildest thoughts of ambition, whether aiming like Ptolemy at founding a kingdom, or like Perdiccas at the government of the world, was unwise enough to throw off the title of lieutenant to Philip Arridæus, and to forfeit the love of the Macedonian soldiers and his surest hold on their loyalty.

(3) The first act of Ptolemy was to put to death Cleomenes, who had been made receiver-general of the taxes by Alexander, and who had afterwards been made sub-governor of Egypt by the same council of generals which had made Ptolemy governor.' This may even have been called for by the dishonesty and crooked dealing which Cleomenes had been guilty of in getting in the taxes; but though the whole tenor of Ptolemy's life would seem to disprove the charge, we cannot but fear that he was in part led to this deed because he looked upon Cleomenes as the friend of Perdiccas, or because he could not trust him in his plans for making himself king of Egypt. Conquerors are seldom very nice about the steps which they take to gain the end in view, and though we shall be often called upon to praise the mildness with which Ptolemy used his power, we shall see that he was not much better than other kings in the means which he took to enlarge it.

(4) The first addition which he made to his kingdom was the little Dorian state of Cyrene and its sister cities, which had before asked for the friendship of Alexander, but was still free. It was being torn to pieces by the struggles of two parties for power, which ended in an appeal to arms; and the nobles were driven out to seek for help from Ptolemy. This was readily granted; he led them back in triumph into their city, and Cyrene became the prize of the conquering umpire, and was easily united to the Greek portion of Ptolemy's kingdom.

Diod. Sic. lib. xviii.

(5) In the second year after the death of Alexander, the funeral train set out from Babylon to carry the body of the conqueror to its place of burial. This sacred charge had been given to a general named Arridæus, who followed the chariot with a strong band of soldiers. In every city through which the funeral passed, the people came out in crowds to gaze upon the dazzling show, and to pay their last homage to the embalmed body of their king. Perdiccas had given orders that it should be carried to Æga, in Macedonia, the burial-place of Philip and his forefathers; for such was the love borne by the soldiers to Alexander, even after his death, that it was thought that the city which should have the honour of being his last resting-place would be the seat of

B.C. 321.

Pausanias, lib. i. 6; and Arrian, ap. Photium, lib. x.

government for the whole of his wide conquests. But Ptolemy had gained over Arridæus to favour his ambitious views; and when the funeral reached Syria he met it with an army which he led out of Egypt to honour and to guard the sacred prize. He then gave out that the body was to be buried in the Oasis of Ammon, in the temple of the god who had acknowledged Alexander as his son; but when the joint armies reached Memphis, they left it there, till the new city of Alexandria should be ready to receive it; and we shall soon see that Ptolemy, who never forgot to reward any one who had been of use to him, gave to Arridæus the earliest and greatest gift that he had in his power to give. Diod. Sic. lib. xviii. 26.

(6) Perdiccas, in the death of Cleomenes and the seizure of the body of Alexander, had seen quite enough proof that Ptolemy, though too wise to take the name of king, had in reality grasped the power; and he now led the Macedonian army against Egypt, to enforce obedience and to punish the rebellious lieutenant. He carried with him the two princes, Philip Arridæus, and the infant Alexander Ægus, the son of Alexander the Great, born after his father's death, both to ornament his army and to prove his right to issue orders over the provinces. At Pelusium he was met by Ptolemy, who had strengthened all his cities, and had left garrisons in them; and, when he laid siege to a small fortress near Pelusium, Ptolemy forced him to withdraw his troops, and to retire to his camp. At night, however, he left his trenches without any noise, and marched hastily towards Memphis, leaving the garrisoned towns in his rear. Pausanias, lib. i. 6. Diod. Sic. lib. xviii. 33.

(7) In this bold and as it would seem rash step, Perdiccas was badly supported by his generals. He was stern and overbearing in his manner; he never asked advice from a council of war; his highest officers were kept in the dark about to-morrow's march; he wished to be obeyed, without caring to be loved. Ptolemy, on the other hand, was just and mild to everybody; he always sought the advice of his generals, and listened to them as his equals; he was beloved alike by officers and soldiers. Perdiccas attempted to cross the Nile at the deep fords below Memphis. Part of his army passed the first ford, though the water was up to the men's

breasts. But they could not pass the second ford in the face of Ptolemy's army. After this check, whole bodies of men, headed by their generals, left their ranks; and among them Python, a general who had held the same rank under Alexander as Perdiccas himself, and who would no longer put up with his haughty commands. Upon this the disorder spread through the whole army, and Perdiccas soon fell by the hand of one of his own soldiers.

(8) On the death of their leader, all cause of war ceased. Ptolemy sent corn and cattle into the camp of the invading army, which then asked for orders from him who the day before had been their enemy. The princes Philip Arridæus and the young Alexander both fell into his hands; and he might then, as guardian in their name, have sent his orders over the whole of Alexander's conquests. But, by grasping at what was clearly out of his reach, he would have lost more friends and power than he would have gained; and when the Macedonian phalanx, whose voice was law to the rest of the army, asked his advice in the choice of a guardian for the two princes, he recommended to them Python and Arridæus; Python, who had just joined him, and had been the cause of the rout of the Macedonian army, and Arridæus, who had given up to him the body of Alexander.

(9) The Macedonian army, accordingly, chose Python and Arridæus as guardians, and as rulers with unlimited power over the whole of Alexander's conquests; but, though none of the Greek generals who now held Asia Minor, Syria, Babylonia, Thrace, or Egypt, dared to acknowledge it to the soldiers, yet in reality the power of the guardians was limited to the little kingdom of Macedonia. With the death of Perdiccas, and the withdrawal of his army, Phenicia and Cœle-Syria were left unguarded, and almost without a master; and Ptolemy, who had before been kept back by his wise forethought rather than by the moderation of his views, sent an army under the command of Nicanor, to conquer those countries. Jerusalem was the only place that held out against the Egyptian army; but Nicanor, says the historian Agatharcides, seeing that on every seventh day the garrison withdrew from the walls, chose that day for the assault, and thus gained the city.

<small>Josephus, contra Apionem. B.C. 320.</small>

(10) In the earlier times of Egyptian history, when navi-

gation was less easy, and when seas separated kingdoms instead of joining them, the Thebaid enjoyed, under the Coptic kings, the trading wealth which followed the stream of its great river, the longest piece of inland navigation then known; but with the improvement in navigation and shipbuilding, countries began to feel their strength in the timber of their forests and the number of their harbours; and, as timber and sea-coast were equally unknown in the Thebaid, that country fell as Lower Egypt rose; the wealth which before centered in Thebes was then found in the ports of the Delta, where the barges of the Nile met the ships of the Mediterranean. What used to be Egypt was an inland kingdom, bounded by the desert; but Egypt under Ptolemy was a country on the sea-coast. On the conquest of Phenicia and Cœle-Syria, he was master of the forest of Lebanon and Antilibanus, and stretched his coast from Cyrene to Antioch, a distance of twelve hundred miles, and aimed at making Egypt a naval power. After this time, we note the increase of the timber trade with Asia Minor, or Phœnicia, or Cyprus by finding mummy cases made of wood foreign to Egypt.

(11) The wise and mild plans which were laid down by Alexander for the government of Egypt when a province, were easily followed by Ptolemy when it became his own kingdom. The Greek soldiers lived in their garrisons or in Alexandria under the Macedonian laws; while the Egyptian laws were administered by their own priests, who were upheld in all the rights of their order and in their freedom from land-tax. The temples of Pthah, of Amun-Ra, and the other gods of the country were not only kept open, but were repaired and even built at the cost of the king; the religion of the people, and not that of their rulers, was made the established religion of the state. On the death of the god Apis, the sacred bull of Memphis, the chief of the animals which were kept and fed at the cost of the several cities, and who had died of old age soon after Ptolemy came to Egypt, he spent the sum of fifty talents, or eight thousand five hundred pounds, on its funeral; and the priests, who had not forgotten that Cambyses, their former conqueror, had wounded the Apis of his day with his own sword, must have been highly pleased with this mark of his care for them. The burial-

place for the bulls is an arched gallery tunnelled into the hill behind Memphis for more than two thousand feet, with a row of cells on each side of it. In every cell is a huge granite sarcophagus, within which were placed the earthly remains of a bull that had once been the Apis of its day, which after having for perhaps twenty years received the honours of a god, was there buried with more than kingly state.

The cell was then walled up, and ornamented on the outside with various tablets in honour of the deceased animal, which were placed in these dark passages by the piety of his worshippers (see Fig. 210). The priests of Thebes were now at liberty to cut out from their monuments the names of Mandoo-Ra or other usurping gods, and to restore that of Amun-Ra, which had been before cut out. They also rebuilt the inner room, or the holy of holies, in the great temple of Karnak. It had been overthrown by the Persians in wantonness, or in hatred of the Egyptian religion; and the priests now put upon it the name of Philip Arridæus, for whom Ptolemy was governing Egypt.

Fig. 210.

Wilkinson, Thebes.

(12) The Egyptians, who during the last two centuries had sometimes seen their temples plundered and their trade crushed by the grasping tyranny of the Persian satraps, and had at other times been almost as much hurt by their own vain struggles for freedom, now found themselves in the quiet enjoyment of good laws, with a prosperity which promised soon to equal that of the reigns of Necho or Amasis. It is true that they had not regained their independence and political liberty; that as compared with the Greeks they felt themselves an inferior race, and that they only enjoyed their civil rights during the pleasure of a Greek autocrat; but then it is to be remembered that the native rulers with whom Ptolemy was compared were the kings of Lower Egypt, who like himself were surrounded by Greek mercenaries, and who never rested their power on the broad base of national pride and love of country; and that nobody

could have hoped to see a Theban king arise to bring back the days of Thothmosis and Rameses. Thebes was every day sinking in wealth and strength; and its race of hereditary soldiers, proud in the recollection of former glory, who had after centuries of struggles been forced to receive laws from Memphis, perhaps yielded obedience to a Greek conqueror with less pain than to their own vassals of Lower Egypt.

(13) Ptolemy's government was in form nearly the same in Alexandria as in the rest of Egypt, but in reality it was wholly different. His sway over the Egyptians was supported by Greek force, but over the Greeks it rested on the broad base of public opinion. Every Greek had the privilege of bearing arms, and of meeting in the Gymnasium in public assembly, to explain a grievance and petition for its redress. The citizens and the soldiers were the same body of men; they at the same time held the force and had the spirit to use it. But they had no senate, no body of nobles, no political constitution which might save their freedom in after generations from the ambitious grasp of the sovereign, or from their own degeneracy. While claiming to be equal among themselves they were making themselves slaves; and though at present the government so entirely bore the stamp of their own will that they might fancy they enjoyed a democracy, yet history teaches us that the simple paternal form of government never fails to become sooner or later a cruel tyranny. The building of Alexandria must be held the master-stroke of policy by which Egypt was kept in obedience. Here, and afterwards in a few other cities, such as Ptolemais in the Thebaid and Parembole in Nubia, the Greeks lived without insulting or troubling the Egyptians, and by their numbers held the country like so many troops in garrison. It was a wise policy to make no greater change than necessary in the kingdom, and to leave the Egyptians under their own laws and magistrates, and in the enjoyment of their own religion; and yet it was necessary to have the country garrisoned with Greeks, whose presence in the old cities could not but be extremely galling to the Egyptians. This was done by means of these new Greek cities, where the power by which Egypt was governed was stronger by being united, and less hateful by being out of sight. Seldom

or never was so great a monarchy founded with so little force and so little crime.

(14) Ptolemy, however, did not attempt the difficult task of uniting the two races, and of treating the conquered and the conquerors as entitled to the same privileges, a task which modern European humanity has the credit of first attempting. From the time of Necho and Psammetichus, many of the Greeks who settled in Egypt intermarried with the natives, and very much laid aside their own habits; and sometimes their offspring, after a generation or two, became wholly Egyptian. By the Greek laws the children of these mixed marriages were declared to be barbarians, not Greeks but Egyptians, and were brought up accordingly. They left the worship of Jupiter and Juno for that of Isis and Osiris, and perhaps the more readily for the greater earnestness with which the Egyptian gods were worshipped. We now trace their descendants by the form of their skulls, even into the priestly families; and of one hundred mummies covered with hieroglyphics, taken up from the catacombs near Thebes, about twenty show an European origin, while of those from the tombs near Memphis, seventy out of every hundred have lost their Coptic peculiarities. It is easy to foresee that an important change would have been wrought in the character of the people and in their political institutions, if the Greek laws had been humane and wise enough to grant to the children of mixed marriages the privileges, the education, and thereby the moral feelings of the more favoured parent. Greek civilization, instead of struggling like a plant in foreign soil, would each generation have become more naturalised. This had been done by the Copts before the beginning of our history, if we are right in thinking that they were new-comers. They held all children equally legitimate; and though they marked the natives of the soil as a lower caste, yet they had brought all the nation to talk Coptic, and to receive the Coptic civilization. It was also done by the Arabs at the end of our history, who gave to all the nation the Arabic language and civilization. But it was not attempted by the Greeks; and, when we remember the fitness of the Greeks for founding colonies, and the ease with which the arts and customs of a conquering

Morton's Crania Ægyptiaca.

and more civilised people have spread and been received, it is not too much to suppose, if the Greek law of marriage had been altered by Ptolemy, that within three centuries above half the nation would have spoken the Greek language, and boasted of its Greek origin. This wise mixture of races had indeed been planned by Alexander, as was learned from the papers which he left behind him, Diod. Sic. lib. xviii. 4. But history then taught no lessons which needed the observation of centuries, and Ptolemy probably felt no necessity for interfering with these prejudices of his countrymen, nor could he have been aware that the permanency of his new kingdom could in any way depend upon the law of marriage.

(15) The building of the city of Alexandria, which was begun before the death of Alexander, was carried on briskly by Ptolemy, though many of the public works were only finished in the reign of his son. It was placed on a strip of land between the sea and the Lake Strabo, lib. xvii. Mareotis, where hitherto the ibis had walked at leisure, disturbed only by the few fishermen of the neighbouring village of Rhacotis. The citizens pleased themselves with remarking that its ground-plan was in the form of a soldier's cloak. The two main streets crossed one another at right angles in the middle of the city, which was thirty stadia or three miles long, and seven stadia broad; and the whole of the streets were wide enough for carriages. In front of the city was a long narrow island named Pharos, which in the piercing mind of Alexander only needed a little help from art to become the breakwater of a large harbour. Accordingly one end of the island of Pharos was joined to the mainland by a stone mole seven stadia or nearly three-quarters of a mile long, which from its length was called the Heptastadium. There were two breaks in the mole to let the water pass, without which perhaps the harbour might have become blocked up with sand; and bridges were thrown over these two passages, while the mouth of the harbour was between the mainland and the other end of the island. Most of the public buildings of the city fronted the harbour. Among these were the royal docks for building the ships of war; the Emporium or exchange, which had, by the favour of its founder, gained the privileges which before belonged

to the city of Canopus; and the Posideion, or temple of Neptune, which naturally had a place in a seaport town, where the Greek sailors might offer up their vows on setting sail, or perform them on their safe return from a long voyage. There also stood the burial-place for the Greek kings of Egypt, which was named the Soma, because it held "the body," as that of Alexander was from its importance called. The city was supplied with water from the Nile, which was led into large public cisterns built under the houses, with two or three stories of arches. On the other side of the Heptastadium, and on the outside of the city, were some more docks, and a ship-canal into the Lake Mareotis; on that side also was the Necropolis, or public burial-place for the city, with large underground catacombs regularly formed with a main passage and numerous side passages branching off from it and countless cells on each side of the passages. There were also for the amusement of the citizens a theatre, an amphitheatre, a gymnasium with a large *stoa* or portico, a stadium in which games were celebrated every fifth year, public groves or gardens, and a hippodrome for chariot races.

(16) Towering above all these buildings was the temple of Serapis, the god whose worship became so popular in the later ages of the Roman empire. The Egyptian god Osiris was at the same time the bearded Bacchus of the Greeks, who conquered India beyond the Ganges, and the god of the lower regions, who sat as judge while the actions of the dead were weighed before him in a pair of scales.

<small>Egyptian Inscriptions, plate 4.</small> He was afterwards divided into two persons; one of these was named Pthah-sokar Osiris, and the other Apis Osiris, or Osiri-Apis. The latter, who was called Serapis by the Greeks, was in this division of the persons made the husband of Isis and the judge of the dead; and it may have been for this reason that his temple was often on the outside of the city walls with the public burial-place. He is known by his having, beside the whip and crozier which are the two sceptres of Osiris, a bull's head, which shows his connection with Apis (see Fig. 211). He
<small>Eustathius, in Dionysio Alexandr.</small> was sometimes called by the Greeks the Sinopite Jupiter, a name which may mean Memphite Jupiter, from Sinopion, a hill near Memphis, as the other Osiris was named Pthah-sokar from Sakara, another hill in

the same neighbourhood. Or it may mean Pontic Jupiter, from Sinope, a city of Pontus, from whence Ptolemy is said to have brought a statue to ornament Alexandria, which when it arrived Manetho and Timotheus declared to be a Serapis. To receive this statue a new temple was built, which before it was finished was the largest building in the city. Osiris was also the god from whom the native kings traced their pedigree; and as, to spare the nation's wounded vanity, the Ptolemies were no longer to be counted as foreign conquerors, a new god was added to the mythology, who was given as another son to Osiris, and named Macedon, from whom the Macedonian kings were said to have sprung; and they were thus brought into the religion of the people. The Greeks readily took up the same story; and three reigns later, Satyrus traced the royal family of the Ptolemies from Bacchus or Osiris, through Hercules or Horus, and the kings of Macedonia.

Fig. 211.

Plutarch. De Iside et Osiride.

Diod. Sic. lib. i. 18.

Theophilus, Antioch. ii.

(17) But among the public buildings of Alexandria which were planned in the enlarged mind of Ptolemy, the one which chiefly calls for our notice, the one indeed to which the city owes its fairest fame, is the Museum or college of philosophy. Its chief room was a great hall, which was used as a lecture-room and common dining-room; it had a covered walk or portico all round the outside, and there was an *exhedra* or seat on which the philosophers sometimes sat in the open air. The professors or fellows of the college were supported by a public income. Its library soon became the largest in the world. It was open equally to those who read for the sake of knowledge and those who copied for the sake of gain; and it thus helped to make science, wisdom, lofty thoughts, and poetic beauties, those rare fruits of genius and industry, the common property of all that valued them. Ptolemy was himself an author; his history of Alexander's wars was highly praised by Arrian, in

Strabo, lib. xvii.

whose pages we now read much of it; his love of art was shown in the buildings of Alexandria; and those agreeable manners and that habit of rewarding skill and knowledge wherever he could find them, which had already brought to his army many of the bravest of Alexander's soldiers, were now equally successful in bringing to his court such painters and sculptors, such poets, historians, and mathematicians, as soon made the Museum one of the brightest spots in the known world. Fortunate indeed was Alexandria in having a sovereign who took such a true view of his own dignity as to encourage arts and letters as the means of making himself more respected at the head of a great commercial nation. Such an academy not only brings together a number of men of learning to direct the student, but its book-shelves are a storehouse of materials for future study, and it may be said to be surrounded with an atmosphere of knowledge, which makes tens of thousands better for the instruction which is delivered to a few hundreds in the class rooms. The arts and letters which Ptolemy then planted, did not perhaps bear their richest fruit till the reign of his son; but they took such good root that they continued to flourish under the last of his successors, unchoked by the vices and follies by which they were then surrounded.

(18) In return for the literature which Greece then gave to Egypt, she gained the knowledge of papyrus, a tall rush which grows wild near the sources of the Nile, and was then cultivated in the Egyptian marshes. Before that time books had been written on linen, wax, bark, or the leaves of trees; and public records on stone, brass, or lead; but the knowledge of papyrus was felt by all men of letters like the invention of printing in modern Europe. Books were then known by many for the first time, and very little else was afterwards used in Greece or Rome; for, when parchment was made, about two centuries later, it was too costly to be used as long as papyrus was within reach. Copies were multiplied on frail strips of this plant, and it was found that mere thoughts, when worth preserving, were less liable to be destroyed by time than temples and palaces of the hardest stone.

<small>Pliny,
lib. xiii. 21.</small>

(19) While Egypt under Ptolemy was thus enjoying the advantages of its insulated position, and was thereby at

leisure to cultivate the arts of peace, the other provinces were being harassed by the unceasing wars of Alexander's generals, who were aiming like Ptolemy at raising their own power. Many changes had taken place among them in the short space of eight years which had passed since the death of Alexander. Philip Arridæus, in whose name the provinces had been governed, had been put to death; Antigonus was master of Asia Minor with a kingdom more powerful though not so easily guarded as Egypt; Cassander held Macedonia, and had the care of the young Alexander Ægus (see Fig. 212), who was then called the heir to the whole of his father's wide conquests, and whose life, like that of Arridæus, was soon to end with his minority; Lysimachus was trying to form a kingdom in Thrace; and Seleucus had for a short time held Babylonia.

B.C. 315.

Diod. Sic. lib. xix.

Fig. 212.

(20) Ptolemy bore no part in the wars which brought about these changes, beyond being once or twice called upon to send troops to guard his province of Cœle-Syria. But Antigonus, in his ambitious efforts to stretch his power over the whole of the provinces, had by force or treachery driven Seleucus out of Babylon, and forced him to seek Egypt for safety, where Ptolemy received him with the kindness and good policy which had before gained so many friends. No arguments of Seleucus were wanting to persuade Ptolemy that Antigonus was aiming at universal conquest, and that his next attack would be upon Egypt. He therefore sent ambassadors to make treaties of alliance with Cassander and Lysimachus, who readily joined him against the common enemy.

(21) The large fleet and army which Antigonus got together for the invasion of Egypt proved his opinion of the strength and skill of Ptolemy. All Syria, except one or two cities, laid down its arms before him on his approach. But he found that the whole of the fleet had been already removed to the ports of Egypt, and he ordered Phenicia to furnish him with eight thousand ship-builders and carpenters, to build galleys from the forests of Lebanon and Antilibanus, and ordered Syria to send four hundred and fifty thousand medimni, or nearly three millions of bushels

B.C. 314.

of wheat, for the use of his army within the year. By these means he raised his fleet to two hundred and forty-three long galleys or ships of war.

(22) Ptolemy was for a short time called off from the war in Syria by a rising in Cyrene. The Cyrenæans, who clung to their Doric love of freedom, and were latterly smarting at its loss, had taken arms and were besieging the Egyptian, or as they would have called themselves the Macedonian garrison, who had shut themselves up in the citadel. He at first sent messengers to order the Cyrenæans to return to their duty; but his orders were not listened to; the rebels no doubt thought themselves safe, as his armies seemed more wanted on the eastern frontier; his messengers were put to death, and the siege of the citadel pushed forward with all possible speed. On this he sent a large land force, followed by a fleet, in order to crush the revolt at a single blow; and the ringleaders were brought to Alexandria in chains. Magas, a son of Queen Berenice and step-son of Ptolemy, was then made governor of Cyrene.

<small>B.C. 313.</small>

(23) When this trouble at home was put an end to, Ptolemy crossed over to Cyprus to punish the kings of the little states on that island for having joined Antigonus. For now that the fate of empires was to be settled by naval battles the friendship of Cyprus became very important to the neighbouring states. The island of Cyprus is one hundred and fifty miles long and seventy-five broad, or not much less than Lower Egypt. It has always been rich in corn and wine, and not less so in its mines and harbours. It had usually been divided into nine little states, each governed by a king having several cities under him. One of these cities was Citium, whence the island or its people had been known to the Jews and in the east by the name of Chittim. It had long shared the trade of the Mediterranean with the cities of Tyre and Sidon and Tarsus, and when those seaports fell under Babylon and Persia, Cyprus shared their fate. The large and safe harbours gave to this island a great value in the naval warfare between Egypt, Phœnicia, and Asia Minor. Alexander had given it as his opinion that the command of the sea went with the island of Cyprus. When he held Asia Minor he called Cyprus the key to Egypt; and with still greater

<small>Diod. Sic. lib. xvi. 42.</small>

<small>Arrian. lib. ii.</small>

reason might Ptolemy, looking from Egypt, think that island the key to Phenicia. Accordingly he landed there with so large a force that he met with no resistance. He added Cyprus to the rest of his dominions. He banished the kings, and made Nicocreon governor of the whole island. Diod. Sic. lib. xix.

(24) From Cyprus, Ptolemy landed with his army in Upper Syria, as the northern part of that country was called, while the part nearer to Palestine was called Cœle-Syria. Here he took the towns of Posideion and Potami-Caron, and then marching hastily into Asia Minor, he took Mallus, a city of Cilicia. Having rewarded his soldiers with the booty there seized, he again embarked and returned to Alexandria. This inroad seems to have been meant to draw off the enemy from Cœle-Syria; and it had the wished-for effect, for Demetrius, who commanded the forces of his father Antigonus in that quarter, marched northward to the relief of Cilicia; but he did not arrive there till Ptolemy's fleet was already under sail for Egypt.

(25) Ptolemy, on reaching Alexandria, set his army in motion towards Pelusium, on its way to Palestine. His forces were eighteen thousand foot and four thousand horse, part Macedonians, as the Greeks living in Egypt were always called, and part mercenaries, followed by a crowd of Egyptians, of whom some were armed for battle, and some were to take care of the baggage. There are in all ages some nations who are so much before others in warlike skill and courage, that no inequality of numbers can make up for it. Not that one Greek could overcome ten barbarians; but that a body of Greeks, if large enough to make an army, with a centre, wings, heavy-armed, light-armed, and cavalry, would never think it worth while to count the crowd of barbarians that might be led against them. The number wanted to make an army has changed with the art of war. In modern Europe it must be much larger, perhaps many times what was needed before gunpowder was used; but we may quote the battle of Marathon, and the retreat of the ten thousand under Xenophon, to prove that this number was enough with the Greeks. When Greeks fought against Greeks it is probable that the larger army would conquer, but ten thousand Greeks would beat any number of barbarians.

This will help us to understand the low state of discipline among the native Egyptians under Ptolemy. When measuring his strength against Demetrius he took no account of their number; he had twenty-two thousand Greeks and a crowd of Egyptians. He was met at Gaza by the young Demetrius with an army of eleven thousand foot and twenty-three hundred horse, followed by forty-three elephants, and a body of light-armed barbarians, who, like the Egyptians in the army of Ptolemy, were not counted. But the youthful courage of Demetrius was no match for the cool skill and larger army of Ptolemy; the elephants were easily stopped by iron hurdles, and the Egyptian army, after gaining a complete victory, entered Gaza, while Demetrius fled to Azotus. Ptolemy, in his victory, showed a generosity unknown in modern warfare; he not only gave leave to the conquered army to bury their dead, but sent back the whole of the royal baggage which had fallen into his hands, and also those personal friends of Demetrius who were found among the prisoners; that is to say, all those who wished to depart, as the larger part of these Greek armies were equally ready to fight on either side. He may have thought that, in this almost civil strife, as much was to be gained by acts of friendship as by arms; but this should in no wise lessen our praise of any such deed, which, like an oasis in the desert, is one of the refreshing spots on which the mind rests in the dry and often barren history of war.

<small>Diod. Sic. lib. xix.</small>

(26) By this victory the whole of Phenicia was again joined to Egypt, and Seleucus regained Babylonia. There, by following the example of Ptolemy in his good treatment of the people, and in leaving them their own laws and religion, he founded a monarchy, and gave his name to a race of kings which rivalled even the Lagidæ. He raised up again for a short time the throne of Nebuchadnezzar. But it was only for a short time. The Chaldees and Assyrians now yielded the first rank to the Greeks who had settled among them; and the Greeks were more numerous in the Syrian portion of his empire. Accordingly Seleucus built a new capital on the River Orontes, and named it Antioch, after his father. Babylon then yielded the same obedience to this new Greek city that Memphis paid to Alexandria. Assyria and Babylonia became subject provinces; and the successors

of Seleucus styled themselves not kings of Babylon but of Syria.

(27) When Antigonus, who was in Phrygia, on the other side of his kingdom, heard that his son Demetrius had been beaten at Gaza, he marched with all his forces to give battle to Ptolemy. He soon crossed Mount Taurus, the lofty range which divides Asia Minor from Syria and Mesopotamia, and joined his camp to that of his son in Upper Syria. But Ptolemy had gone through life without ever making a hazardous move; not indeed without ever suffering a loss, but without ever fighting a battle when its loss would have ruined him; and he did not choose to risk his kingdom against the far larger forces of Antigonus. Therefore, with the advice of his council of generals, he levelled the fortifications of Aca, Joppa, Samaria, and Gaza, and withdrew his forces and treasure into Egypt, leaving the desert between himself and the army of Antigonus.

(28) Antigonus could not safely attempt to march through the desert in the face of Ptolemy's army. He had therefore, first, either to conquer or gain the friendship of the Nabatæans, a warlike race of Arabs, who held the north of Arabia; and then he might march by Petra, Mount Sinai, and the coast of the Red Sea, without being in want of water for his army. The Nabatæans were the tribe at an earlier time called Edomites. But they lost that name when they carried it to the southern portion of Judæa, then called Idumæa; for when the Jews regained Idumæa they called these Edomites of the desert Nebaoth or Nabatæans. The Nabatæans professed neutrality between Antigonus and Ptolemy, the two contending powers; but the mild temper of Ptolemy had so far gained their friendship that the haughty Antigonus, though he did not refuse their pledges of peace, secretly made up his mind to conquer them.

(29) Petra, the city of the Nabatæans, is in a narrow valley between steep overhanging rocks, so difficult of approach that a handful of men could guard it against the largest army. Not more than two horsemen can ride abreast through the chasm in the rock by which it is entered from the east (see Fig. 213), while the other entrance from the west is down a hill-side too steep for a loaded camel. The eastern proverb reminds

Pliny, lib. vi. 32. Laborde's Travels.

us that "Water is the chief thing;" and a large stream within the valley, in addition to the strength of the fortress, made it

Fig. 213.

a favourite resting-place for caravans, which, whether they were coming from Tyre or Jerusalem, were forced to pass by this city in their way to the Incense Country of Arabia Felix, or to the Elanitic Gulf of the Red Sea, and for other caravans from Egypt to Dedan on the Persian Gulf. These warlike Arabs seem to have received a toll from the caravans, and they held their rocky fastness unconquered by the great nations which surrounded them. From its strength it had the Hebrew name of Mibzar, *the fortress*. Its temples and tombs were cut out of the live rock, and it was by the Jews also named Sela, *the rock*, and by the Greeks named Petra, from which last the country was sometimes called Arabia Petræa.

(30) Antigonus heard that the Nabatæans had left Petra less guarded than usual, and had gone to a neighbouring fair, probably to meet a caravan from the south, and to receive spices in exchange for the woollen goods from Tyre. He therefore sent forward four thousand light-armed foot and six hundred horse, who overpowered the guard and seized the city. The Arabs, when they heard of what had happened, returned in the night, surrounded the place, came upon the Greeks from above, by paths known only to themselves, and overcame them with such slaughter, that out of the four thousand six hundred men only fifty returned to Antigonus to tell the tale.

Diod. Sic. lib. xix.

(31) The Nabatæans then sent to Antigonus to complain of this crafty attack being made upon Petra after they had received from him a promise of friendship. He endeavoured to put them off their guard by disowning the acts of his general; he sent them home

Diod. Sic. lib. xix.

with promises of peace, but at the same time sent forward his son Demetrius, with four thousand horse and four thousand foot, to take revenge upon them, and again seize their city. But the Arabs were this time upon their guard; the nature of the place was as unfavourable to the Greek arms and warfare as it was favourable to the Arabs; and these eight thousand men, the flower of the army, under the brave Demetrius, were unable to force their way through the narrow pass into this remarkable city.

(32) Had Antigonus been master of the sea, he might perhaps have marched through the desert along the coast of the Mediterranean to Pelusium, with his fleet to wait upon his army, as Perdiccas had done. But without this, the only way that he could enter Egypt was through the neighbourhood of Petra, and then along the same path by which the Jews under Moses had come out; and the stop thus put upon the invasion of Egypt by this little city shows us the strength of Ptolemy's eastern frontier. Antigonus then led his army northward, leaving Egypt unattacked.

(33) This retreat was followed by a treaty of peace between these generals, by which it was agreed that each should keep the country that he then held; that Cassander should govern Macedonia until Alexander Ægus, the son of Alexander the Great, should be of age; that Lysimachus should keep Thrace, Ptolemy Egypt, and Antigonus Asia Minor and Palestine; and each wishing to be looked upon as the friend of the soldiers by whom his power was upheld, and the whole of these wide conquests kept in awe, added the very unnecessary article, that the Greeks living in each of these countries should be governed according to their own laws. B.C. 312.

(34) All the provinces held by these generals became more or less Greek kingdoms, yet in no one did so many Greeks settle as in Lower Egypt. Though the rest of Egypt was governed by Egyptian laws and judges, the city of Alexandria was under Macedonian law. It did not form part of the nome of Hermopolites, in which it was built. It scarcely formed a part of Egypt, but was a Greek state in its neighbourhood, holding the Egyptians in a state of slavery. In that city no Egyptian could live without feeling himself of a conquered race. He was not admitted to the privileges of Macedonian

citizenship; while they were at once granted to every Greek, and soon to every Jew, who would settle there. The same hieroglyphical word stood for Greek and for Lower Egyptian; Lycophron seems to speak of the Egyptian nation under the name of Macedonians; and whenever, during the reigns of the Ptolemies, the citizens of the capital of Egypt met in public assembly in the Gymnasium, they were addressed, "Ye men of Macedonia." Inasmuch as they were Macedonians, they were of course Dorians; and a woman, crowding to see the procession of Isis in the streets of Alexandria, when blamed for her talkativeness, would answer that there was no law against Dorians talking Doric.

<small>Vocabul. Hierog. No. 722.</small>

<small>Polybius, lib. xv.</small>

<small>Theocritus, Idyll. xv. 94.</small>

(35) By the treaty just spoken of, Ptolemy, in the thirteenth year after the death of Alexander, was left undisputed master of Egypt. During these years he had not only gained the love of the Egyptians and Alexandrians by his wise and just government, but had won their respect as a general by the skill with which he had kept the war at a distance. He had lost and won battles in Syria, in Asia Minor, in the island of Cyprus, and at sea; but since Perdiccas marched against him, before he had a force to defend himself with, no foreign army had drunk the sacred waters of the Nile.

<small>Diod. Sic. lib. xix.</small>

(36) It was under the government of Ptolemy that the wonders of Upper Egypt were first seen by any Greeks who had leisure, a love of knowledge, and enough of literature, to examine carefully and to describe what they saw. Loose and highly-coloured accounts of the wealth of Thebes had reached Greece even before the time of Homer, and again through Herodotus and other travellers in the Delta; but nothing was certainly known of it till it was visited by Hecatæus of Abdera, who, among other works, wrote a history of the Hyperborean or northern nations, and also a history or rather a description of Egypt, part of which we now read in the pages of Diodorus Siculus. When he travelled in Upper Egypt, Thebes, though still a populous city, was more thought of by the antiquary than by the statesman. Its wealth, however, was still great; and when, under the just government of Ptolemy, it was no longer

<small>Lib. ii. 47; lib. i. 46.</small>

necessary for the priests to hide their treasures, it was found that the temples still held the very large sum of three hundred talents of gold, and two thousand three hundred talents of silver, or above one million sterling, which had escaped the plundering hands of the Persian satraps. Many of the Theban tombs, which are sets of rooms tunnelled into the hills on the Libyan side of the Nile, had even then been opened to gratify the curiosity of the learned or the greediness of the conqueror. Forty-seven royal tombs were mentioned in the records of the priests, of which the entrances had been covered up with earth and hidden in the sloping sides of the hills, in the hope that they might remain undisturbed and unplundered, and might keep safe the embalmed bodies of the kings till they should rise again at the end of the world; and seventeen of these had already been found out and broken open. Hecatæus was told that the other tombs had been before destroyed; and we owe it perhaps to this mistake that they remained unopened for more than two thousand years longer, to reward the searches of modern travellers, and to unfold to us the history of their builders.

(37) The Memnonium, the great palace of Rameses II., was then standing; and though it had been plundered by the Persians, the building itself was unhurt. Its massive walls had scarcely felt the wear of the centuries which had rolled over them. Hecatæus measured its rooms, its courtyards, and its avenue of sphinxes; and by his measurements we can now distinguish its ruins from those of the other palaces of Thebes. One of its rooms, perhaps after the days of its builder, had been fitted up as a library, and held the histories and records of the priests; but the golden zodiac or circle on which were engraved the days of the year, with the stars which were seen to rise at sunrise and set at sunset, by which each day was known, had been taken away by Cambyses. Hecatæus also saw the three other palace-temples of Thebes, which we now call by the names of the villages in which they stand, namely, of Luxor, of Karnak, and of Medinet Abou. But the Greeks, in their accounts of Egypt, have sadly puzzled us by their careless alteration of names from similarity of sound. To Miamun Rameses they gave the common Greek name Memnon; and the city of Hiroth they called Heroöpolis, as if it meant *the city of*

heroes. The capital of Upper Egypt, which was called the city, as a capital is often called, or in Coptic, *Tape* or *Thabou*, they named Thebes, and in their mythology they confounded it with Thebes in Bœotia. The city of the god Kneph they called Canopus, and said it was so named after the pilot of Menelaus. The royal quarries of Toorah, opposite Memphis, so named from Ouro, *the king*, they called the Trojan Mountain. One of the oldest cities in Egypt, Stephanus Byzantinus. This, or, with the prefix for *city*, Abouthis, they called Abydos, and then said that it was colonised by Milesians from Abydos in Asia. In the same careless way have the Greeks given us an account of the Egyptian gods. They thought them the same as their own, though with new faces; and instead of describing their qualities, they have for the most part contented themselves with translating their names.

(38) If Ptolemy did not make his government as much feared by the half-armed Ethiopians as it was by the well-disciplined Europeans, it must have been because the Thebans wished to guard their own frontier rather than because his troops were always wanted against a more powerful enemy; but the inroads of the Ethiopians were so far from being checked that the country to the south of Thebes was unsafe for travellers, and no Greek was able to reach Syene and the lower cataracts during his reign. The trade through Ethiopia was wholly stopped, and the caravans went from Thebes to Cosseir, to meet the ships which brought the goods of Arabia and India from the opposite coast of the Red Sea.

(39) In the wars between Egypt and Asia Minor, in which Palestine had the misfortune to be the prize struggled for, and the debateable land on which the battles were fought, the Jews were often made to smart under the stern pride of Antigonus, and to rejoice at the milder temper of Josephus, Antiq. xii. 1. Ptolemy. The Egyptians of the Delta and the Jews had always been friends; and hence, when Ptolemy promised to treat the Jews with the same kindness as the Greeks, and more than the Egyptians, and held out all the rights of Macedonian citizenship to those who would settle in his rising city of Alexandria, he was followed by crowds of industrious traders, manufacturers, and men of letters. They chose to live in Egypt in peace and wealth,

rather than to stay in Palestine in the daily fear of having their houses sacked and burnt at every fresh quarrel between Ptolemy and Antigonus. In Alexandria, a suburb by the sea, on the east side of the city, was allotted for their use, which was afterwards included within the fortifications, and thus made a fifth ward. Here the genius of the Jewish nation for trade was for the first time fully shown. In their own country their laws had more particularly directed them towards agriculture, to which they have always seemed least fitted; but in Egypt, where the cultivation of the soil was so admirably understood by the natives, the Jews found a free course for their own skill in commerce. Josephus, in Apion. ii.

(40) With these conquests of Jerusalem the chain of Jewish genealogies in the Hebrew scriptures was brought to a close. The genealogy of the Levites, which had been added as part of the book of Nehemiah, and that of the sons of David, as part of the book of Chronicles, end at this time. One of the last among the Jews there mentioned removed into Egypt under the patronage of Ptolemy; namely, Hezekias, the heir to David's throne, who was not more looked up to for his rank than for his eloquence and knowledge; and with him came Mosollam, who was known for his bravery and skill as an archer. Hecataeus, who wrote a history of the Jews, gained his knowledge of the nation from the learned men who then followed Ptolemy into Egypt. He mentions Mosollam once riding out with a troop of soldiers, who as they rode were watching the flight of a bird that had been let loose by a soothsayer, to foretell what was going to happen; and Mosollam brought it down with an arrow from his bow, wittily remarking that, as it could not foresee its own death, it certainly knew nothing about the fortunes of the soldiers. Nehemiah, ch. xii.
1 Chron. ch. iii. 23
Josephus, in Apionem i. 22.

(41) No sooner was the peace agreed upon between the four generals, who were the most powerful kings in the known world, than Cassander, who held Macedonia, put to death both the Queen Roxana and her son, the young Alexander Ægus, then thirteen years old, in whose name these generals had each governed his kingdom with unlimited sway, and who was then of an age that the Diod. Sic. lib. xix.
B.C. 311.

soldiers, the givers of all power, were already planning to make him the real king of Macedonia, and of his father's wide conquests.

(42) The Macedonian phalanx, which formed the pride and sinews of every army, were equally held by their deep-rooted loyalty to the memory of Alexander, whether they were fighting for Ptolemy or for Antigonus, and equally thought that they were guarding a province for his heir; and it was through fear of loosening their hold upon the faithfulness of these their best troops that Ptolemy and his rivals alike chose to govern their kingdoms under the unpretending title of lieutenants of the king of Macedonia. Hence, upon the death of Alexander Ægus, there was a throne, or at least a state prison, left empty for a new claimant.

<small>Diod. Sic. lib. xx. 20.</small>

Polysperchon, an old general of Alexander's army, then thought that he saw a way to turn Cassander out of Macedonia, by the help of Hercules, the natural son of Alexander by Barce; and, having proclaimed him king, he led him with a strong army against Cassander. But Polysperchon wanted either courage or means for what he had undertaken, and he soon yielded to the bribes of Cassander, and put Hercules to death.

(43) The cities on the southern coast of Asia Minor yielded to Antigonus obedience as slight as the ties which held them to one another. The coast of Caria, Lycia, Pamphylia, and Cilicia had been occupied by Greek colonists, while the interior of the country was held by Asiatics. The two races and languages were in part mixed. The tomb of King Mausolus, sculptured by Scopas, showed that Greek taste was quite at home in Caria. Among the Lycians, sculpture, though less beautiful, was earlier; and their early use of the long vowels leads us to think that the Greek colonists in Asia may have been teachers to their countrymen in Athens in some of the arts of civilization. The cities of Pamphylia and Cilicia in their habits as in their situation were nearer the Syrians, and famous for their shipping. They all enjoyed a full share of the trade and piracy of those seas, and were a tempting prize to Ptolemy. The treaty of peace between the generals never lessened their jealousy nor wholly stopped the warfare; and the next year Ptolemy, finding that his troops could hardly keep their

<small>Lib. xx. 27.</small>

possessions in Cilicia, carried over an army in person to attack the forces of Antigonus in Lycia. He landed at Phaselis, the frontier town of Pamphylia, and having carried that by storm, he moved westward along the coast of Lycia. He made himself master of Xanthus, the capital, which was garrisoned by the troops of Antigonus; and then of Caunus, a strong place on the coast of Caria, with two citadels, one of which he gained by force and the other by surrender. He then sailed to the island of Cos, which he gained by the treachery of Ptolemy, the nephew of Antigonus, who held it for his uncle, but who went over to the Egyptian king with all his forces. By this success he gained the whole southern coast of Asia Minor.

(44) The brother and two children of Alexander having been in their turns, as we have seen, murdered by their guardians, Cleopatra, his sister, and Thessalonica, his niece, were alone left alive of the royal family of Macedonia. *Diod. Sic. lib. xx. 37. B.C. 308.* Almost every one of the generals had already courted a marriage with Cleopatra, which had either been refused by herself or hindered by his rivals; and lastly Ptolemy, now that by the death of her nephews she brought kingdoms, or the love of the Macedonian mercenaries, which was worth more than kingdoms, as her dower, sent to ask her hand in marriage. This offer was accepted by Cleopatra; but, on her journey from Sardis, the capital of Lydia, to Egypt, on her way to join her future husband, she was put to death by Antigonus. The niece was put to death a few years later. Thus every one who was of the family of Alexander paid the forfeit of life for that honour, and these two deaths ended the tragedy. An aristocracy does not arise or keep its place in all countries with equal ease or from the same causes. Families that had before been renowned were forgotten on the wide and brilliant spread of Greek power under Alexander in Europe, Asia, and Africa. The royal house of Macedon stood alone in its greatness. The officers which surrounded it, like Charlemagne's Knights, outshone all other nobles; and upon the death of his sister and niece the only princely families among the Greeks were those of the generals in Alexander's army.

(45) While Ptolemy was busy in helping the Greek cities of Asia to gain their liberty, Menelaus, his brother and

admiral, was almost driven out of Cyprus by Demetrius. On this Ptolemy got together his fleet, to the number of one hundred and forty long galleys and two hundred transports, manned with not less than ten thousand men, and sailed with them to the help of his brother. This fleet, under the command of Menelaus, was met by Demetrius with the fleet of Antigonus, consisting of one hundred and twelve long galleys and a number of transports; and the Egyptian fleet, which had hitherto been master of the sea, was beaten near the city of Salamis in Cyprus by the smaller fleet of Demetrius. This was the heaviest loss that had ever befallen Ptolemy. Eighty long galleys were sunk, and forty long galleys, with one hundred transports and eight thousand men, were taken prisoners. He could no longer hope to keep Cyprus, and he sailed hastily back to Egypt, leaving to Demetrius the garrisons of the island as his prisoners, all of whom were enrolled in the army of Antigonus, to the number of sixteen thousand foot and six hundred horse.

(46) This naval victory gave Demetrius the means of unburdening his proud mind of a debt of gratitude to his enemy; and accordingly, remembering what Ptolemy had done after the battle of Gaza, he sent back to Egypt, unasked for and unransomed, those prisoners who were of high rank, that is to say, the whole that had any choice about which side they fought for; and among them were Leontiscus, the son, and Menelaus, the brother, of Ptolemy (*vide Additions*, p. 428).

<small>Plutarch. Vit. Demet.</small>

<small>Justinus, lib. xv. 2.</small>

(47) Antigonus was overjoyed with the news of his son's victory. By lessening the power of Ptolemy, it had done much to smooth his own path to the sovereignty of Alexander's empire, which was then left without an heir; and he immediately took the title of king, and gave the same title to his son Demetrius. In this he was followed by Ptolemy and the other generals, but with this difference, that while Antigonus called himself sovereign of all the provinces, Ptolemy called himself sovereign of Egypt (see Fig. 214); and while Antigonus gained Syria and Cyprus, Ptolemy gained the friendship of every other kingdom and of every free city in Greece; they all looked upon him as their best ally against Antigonus, the common enemy.

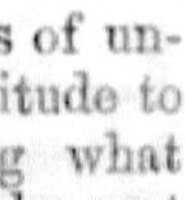

<small>Diod. Sic. lib. xx. 53. B.C. 306.</small>

Fig. 214.

(48) The next year Antigonus mustered his forces in Cœle-Syria, and got ready for a second attack upon Egypt. He had more than eighty thousand foot, accompanied with what was then the usual proportion of cavalry, namely, eight thousand horse, and eighty-three elephants. Demetrius brought with him from Cyprus the fleet of one hundred and fifty long galleys, and one hundred transports laden with stores and engines of war. With this fleet, to which Ptolemy after his late loss had no ships that he could oppose, Antigonus had no need to ask leave of the Arabs of the little city of Petra to march through their passes; but he led his army straight through the desert to Pelusium, while the ships of burden kept close to the shore with the stores. The pride of Antigonus would not let him follow the advice of the sailors, and wait eight days till the north winds of the spring equinox had passed; and by this haste many of his ships were wrecked on the coast, while others were driven into the Nile, and fell into the hands of Ptolemy. Antigonus himself, marching with the land forces, found all the strong places well guarded by the Egyptian army; and, being driven back at every point, discouraged by the loss of his ships and by seeing whole bodies of his troops go over to Ptolemy, he at last took the advice of his officers and led back his army to Syria, while Ptolemy returned to Alexandria, to employ those powers of mind in the works of peace which he had so successfully used in war.

<small>Diod. Sic. lib. xx. 73. B.C. 305.</small>

(49) Antigonus then turned the weight of his mighty kingdom against the little island of Rhodes, which, though in sight of the coast of Asia Minor, held itself independent of him, and in close friendship with Ptolemy. The Dorian island of Rhodes had from the earliest dawn of history held a high place among the states of Greece; and in all the arts of civilized life, in painting, sculpture, letters, and commerce, it had been lately rising in rank while the other free states had been falling. Its maritime laws were so highly thought of that they were copied by most other states, and being afterwards adopted into the Pandects of Justinian, they have in part become the law of modern Europe. It was the only state in which Greek liberty then kept its ground against the great empires of Alexander's successors.

(50) Against this little state Demetrius led two hundred

long galleys and one hundred and seventy transports, with more than forty thousand men. The Greek world looked on with deep interest while the veterans of Antigonus were again and again driven back from the walls of the blockaded city by its brave and virtuous citizens; who, while their houses were burning and their walls crumbling under the battering-ram, left the statues of Antigonus and Demetrius standing unhurt in the market-place, saved by their love of art and the remembrance of former kindness, which, with a true greatness of mind, they would not let the cruelties of the siege outweigh. The galleys of Ptolemy, though unable to keep at sea against the larger fleet of Demetrius, often forced their way into the harbour with the welcome supplies of corn. Month after month every stratagem and machine which the ingenuity of Demetrius could invent were tried and failed; and after the siege had lasted more than a year he was glad to find an excuse for withdrawing his troops; and the Rhodians in their joy hailed Ptolemy with the title of Soter, or *saviour*. This name he ever afterwards kept, though by the Greek writers he is more often called Ptolemy the son of Lagus. If we search the history of the world for a second instance of so small a state daring to withstand the armies of so mighty an empire, we shall perhaps not find any one more remarkable than that of the same island, when, seventeen hundred years afterwards, it again drew upon itself the eyes of the world, while it beat off the forces of the Ottoman empire under Mahomet II., and, standing like a rock in front of Christendom, it rolled back for years the tide of war, till its walls were at last crumbled to a heap of ruins by Solyman the Great, after a siege of many months.

(51) The next of Ptolemy's conquests was Cœle-Syria; and soon after this the wars between these successors of Alexander were put an end to by the death of Antigonus, whose overtowering ambition was among the chief causes of quarrel. This happened at the great battle of Ipsus, in Phrygia, where they all met, with above eighty thousand men in each army. Antigonus, king of Asia Minor, was accompanied by his son Demetrius, and by Pyrrhus, king of Epirus; and he was defeated by Ptolemy, king of Egypt, Seleucus, king of Babylon, Lysimachus, king

of Thrace, and Cassander, king of Macedonia; and the old man lost his life fighting bravely. After the battle Demetrius fled to Cyprus, and yielded to the terms of peace which were imposed on him by the four allied sovereigns. He sent his friend Pyrrhus as a hostage to Alexandria; and there this young king of Epirus soon gained the friendship of Ptolemy, and afterwards his stepdaughter in marriage. Ptolemy was thus left master of the whole of the southern coast of Asia Minor and Syria, indeed, of the whole coast of the eastern end of the Mediterranean, from the island of Cos on the north to Cyrene on the south. Plutarch. Vit. Pyrrhi.

(52) During these formidable wars with Antigonus, Ptolemy had never been troubled with any serious rising of the conquered Egyptians; and perhaps the wars may not have been without their use in strengthening his throne. The first danger to a successful conqueror is from the avarice and disappointment of his followers, who usually claim the kingdom as their booty, and who think themselves wronged and their past services forgotten if any limit is placed to their tyranny over the conquered. But these foreign wars may have taught the Alexandrians that Ptolemy was not strong enough to ill-treat the Egyptians, and may thus have saved him from the indiscretion of his friends and from their reproaches for ingratitude.

(53) In the late war the little Dorian island of Cos, on the coast of Asia Minor, fell, as we have seen, under the power of Ptolemy. This island was remarkable as being the first spot in Europe into which the manufacture of silk was introduced, which it probably gained when under the power of Persia before the overthrow of Darius. The luxury of the Egyptian ladies, who affected to be overheated by any clothing that could conceal their limbs, had long ago introduced a tight thin dress which neither our climate nor notions of modesty would allow, and for this dress silk, when it could be obtained, was much valued; and Pamphila of Cos had the glory of having woven webs so transparent that the Egyptian women were enabled to display their fair forms yet more openly by means of this clothing. Cos continued always in the power of the Ptolemies, who used it as a royal fortress, occasionally sending their treasures and their children there as to a place of safety from Aristoteles, Hist. Anim. v. 19.

Alexandrian rebellion; and there the silk manufacture flourished in secret for two or three centuries. When it ceased is unknown, as it was part of the merchants' craft to endeavour to keep each branch of trade to themselves, by concealing the channel through which they obtained their supply of goods; and many of the dresses which were sold in Rome under the emperors by the name of Coan robes may have been brought from the East through Alexandria.

(54) One of the most valuable gifts which Egypt owed to Ptolemy was its coinage. Even Thebes, "where treasures were largest in the houses," never was able to pass gold and silver from hand to hand without the trouble of weighing, and the doubt as to the fineness of the metal. The Greek merchants who crowded the markets of Canopus and Alexandria must have filled Lower Egypt with the coins of the cities from whence they came, all unlike one another in stamp and weight; but while every little city or even colony of Greece had its own coinage, Egypt had as yet very few coins of its own. We are even doubtful whether we know by sight those coined by the Persians. In the early years of Ptolemy's government Ptolemy had issued a very few coins bearing the names of the young kings in whose name he held the country, but he seems not to have coined any quantity of money till after he had himself taken the title of king. His coins are of gold, silver, and bronze, and are in a fine style of Greek workmanship. Those of gold and silver bear on one side the portrait of the king, without a beard, having the head bound with the royal diadem (see Fig. 215), which, unlike the high priestly crown

<small>B.C. 302.
Visconti,
Icon. Grec.</small>

Fig. 215.

of the native Egyptian kings, or the modern crown of gold and precious stones, is a plain riband tied in a bow behind.

On the other side they have the name of *Ptolemy Soter*, or *King Ptolemy*, with an eagle standing upon a thunderbolt, which was only another way of drawing the eagle and sun, the hieroglyphical characters for the title Pharaoh (see Fig. 216). As the Egyptian statues were most of them made in the neighbourhood of the quarries, so many of the silver and copper coins were made in the neighbourhood of the mines. These often bear the first two letters of the names of Paphos or Salamis or Citium, the chief cities of Cyprus, and they were no doubt engraved and struck in that island. The gold coins of Egypt were probably made in Alexandria. The coins are not of the same weight as those of Greece; but Ptolemy followed the Egyptian standard of weight, which was that to which the Jewish shekel was adjusted, and which was in use in the wealthy cities of Tyre and Sidon and Beryttus. The drachma weighs fifty-five grains, making the talent of silver worth about one hundred and fifty pounds sterling. His bronze coins have the head of Serapis or Jupiter in the place of that of the king (see Fig. 217), as is

Fig. 216.

Fig. 217.

also the case with those of his successors; but few of these bronze pieces bear any marks from which we can learn the reign in which they were coined. They are of better metal than those of other countries, as the bronze is free from lead and has more tin in it. The historian in his very agreeable labours should never lose sight of the coins. They teach us by their workmanship the state of the arts, and by their weight, number, and purity of metal, the wealth of the country. They also teach dates, titles, and the places where they were struck; and even in those cases where they seem to add little to what we learn from other sources, they are still the living witnesses to which we appeal, to prove the truth of the authors who have told us more.

(55) The art of engraving coins did not flourish alone in Alexandria; painters and sculptors flocked to Egypt to enjoy the favours of Ptolemy. Apelles, indeed, whose paintings were thought by those who had seen them to surpass any that had been before painted, or were likely to be painted, had quarrelled with Ptolemy, who had known him well when he was the friend and painter of Alexander. Once when he was at Alexandria, somebody wickedly told him that he was invited to dine at the royal table, and when Ptolemy asked who it was that had sent his unwelcome guest, Apelles drew the face of the mischief-maker on the wall, and he was known to all the court by the likeness.

<small>Pliny, lib. xxxv. 36.</small>

(56) It was perhaps at one of these dinners, at which Ptolemy enjoyed the society of the men of letters, or perhaps when visiting the philosophers in their schools, that he asked Euclid if he could not show him a shorter and easier way to the higher truths of mathematics than that by which he led the pupils in the Museum; and Euclid, as if to remind him of the royal roads of Persia, which ran by the side of the high-roads, but were kept clear and free for the king's own use, made him the well-known answer that there was no royal road to geometry.

<small>Proclus, Comm. ii. 4.</small>

(57) Ptolemy lived in easy familiarity with the learned men of Alexandria; and at another of these literary dinners, when Diodorus, the rhetorician, who was thought to have been the inventor of the Dilemma, was puzzled by a question put to him by Stilpo, the king in joke said that his name should be Cronus, a god who had been laughed at in the comedies. Indeed he was so teazed by Ptolemy for not being able to answer it, that he got up and left the room. He afterwards wrote a book upon the subject; but the ridicule was said to have embittered the rest of his life. This was the person against whom Callimachus some years later wrote a bitter epigram, beginning "Cronus is a wise man." Diodorus was of the

<small>Diogenes Laertius.</small>

Sceptical school of philosophy, which, though not far removed from the Cyrenaic school, was never popular in Alexandria. Among other paradoxes he used to deny the existence of motion. He argued that the motion was not in the place where the body moved from, nor in the place that the body moved to, and that accordingly it did not exist at all. Once he met with a violent fall, which put his shoulder out of joint, and he applied to Herophilus, the surgeon, to set it. Herophilus began by asking him where the fall took place, whether in the place where the shoulder was, or in the place where it fell to; but the smarting philosopher begged him to begin by setting his limb, and they would talk about the existence of motion afterwards.

<small>Sextus Empiricus, adv. Grammaticos, lib. i. 13.</small>

<small>Pyrrhonicæ Hypothes. lib. ii. 22.</small>

(58) Stilpo was at this time only on a visit to Ptolemy, for he had refused his offers of money and of a professorship in the Museum, and had chosen to remain at Megara, where he was the ornament of his birthplace. He had been banished from Athens for speaking against their gods, and for saying that the colossal Minerva was not the daughter of Jupiter but of Phidias the sculptor. His name as a philosopher stood so high that when Demetrius, in his late wars with Ptolemy, took the city of Megara by storm, the conqueror "bid spare the house of Stilpo, when temple and tower went to the ground;" and when Demetrius gave orders that Stilpo should be repaid for what he had lost in the siege, the philosopher proudly answered that he had lost nothing, for that he had no wealth but his learning.

<small>Diogenes Laertius.</small>

(59) The historian Theopompus of Chios then came to Alexandria, and wrote an account of the wars between the Egyptians and the Persians. It is now lost, but it contained at least the events from the successful invasion by Artaxerxes Longimanus till the unsuccessful invasion by Artaxerxes Mnemon.

<small>Photius, cod. clxxvi.</small>

<small>C. Nepos, Vit. Iphicr.</small>

(60) No men of learning in Alexandria were more famous than the physicians. Erasistratus of Cos had the credit of having once cured Antiochus, afterwards king of Syria. He was the grandson of Aristotle, and may be called the father of the science of anatomy; his writings are often quoted by Dioscorides. Antiochus in his

<small>Pliny, lib. xxix. 3.</small>

youth had fallen deeply in love with his young stepmother, and was pining away in silence and despair. Erasistratus found out the cause of his illness, which was straightway cured by Seleucus giving up his wife to his own son. This act strongly points out the changed opinions of the world in matters of right and wrong; for it was then thought the father's best title to the name of Nicator; he had before conquered his enemies, but he then conquered himself.

<small>Suidas.</small>

(61) Erasistratus was the first who thought that a knowledge of anatomy should be made a part of the healing art. Before his time surgery and medicine had been deemed one and the same; they had both been studied by the slow and uncertain steps of experience unguided by theory. Many a man who had been ill, whether through disease or wound, and had regained his health, thought it his duty to Esculapius and to his neighbours to write up in the temple of the god the nature of his ailings and the simples to which he fancied that he owed his cure. By copying these loose but well-meant inscriptions of medical cases, Hippocrates had, a century earlier, laid the foundations of the science; but nothing further was added to it till Erasistratus, setting at nought the prejudices in which he was born, began dissecting the human body in the schools of Alexandria. There the mixing together of Greeks and Egyptians had weakened those religious feelings of respect for the dead which are usually shocked by anatomy; and this study flourished from the low tone of the morality as much as from the encouragement which good sense should grant to every search for knowledge.

(62) Herophilus lived about the same time with Erasistratus, and was, like him, famous for his knowledge of the anatomy of man. But so hateful was this study in the eyes of many, that these anatomists were charged, by writers who ought to have known better, with the cruelty of cutting men open when alive. They had few followers in the hated use of the dissecting knife. It was from their writings that Galen borrowed the anatomical parts of his work; and thus it was to the dissections of these two great men helped indeed by opening the bodies of animals, that the world owed almost the whole of its knowledge of the anatomy of man, till the fifteenth century, when surgeons

<small>Celsus, lib. i.</small>

were again bold enough to face the outcry of the mob, and to study the human body with the knife.

(63) Hegesias of Cyrene was an early lecturer on philosophy at Alexandria. His short and broken sentences are laughed at by Cicero, yet he was so much listened to, when lecturing against the fear of death, and showing that in quitting life we leave behind us more pains than pleasures, that he was stopped by Ptolemy Soter, through fear of his causing self-murder among his hearers. He then wrote a book upon the same subject; for though the state watched over the public teaching, it took no notice of books; writing had not yet become the mightiest power on earth. The miseries, however, of this world, which he so eloquently and feelingly described in his lectures and writings, did not drive him to put an end to his own life. Cicero, Brutus. Tuscul. Quæst. l. 34.

(64) Philostephanus of Cyrene, the friend of Callimachus, was a naturalist who wrote upon fishes, and is the first we hear of who limited his studies to one branch of natural history. Athenæus, lib. viii.

(65) But Cyrene did not send all its great men to Alexandria. Plato had studied mathematics there under Theodorus, and it had a school of its own which gave its name to the Cyrenaic sect. The founder of this sect was Aristippus, the pupil of Socrates, who had missed the high honour of being present at his death. He was the first philosopher who took money from his pupils, and used to say that they valued their lessons more for having to pay for them; but he was blamed by his brethren for thus lowering the dignity of the teacher. He died several years before Ptolemy Soter came into Egypt. The Cyrenaic sect thought happiness, not goodness, was the end to be aimed at through life, and selfishness, rather than kindness to others, the right spring of men's actions. It would hardly be fair to take their opinions from the mouths of their enemies; and the dialogues of Socrates with their founder, as told to us by Xenophon, would prove a lower tone of morality than he is likely to have held. The wish for happiness and the philosophical love of self, which should lead to goodness, though a far worse rule of life than the love of goodness for its own sake, which is the groundwork of religion, was certainly far

better than unguided passion and the love of to-day's pleasure. But often as this unsafe rule has been set up for our guidance, there have always been found many to make use of it in a way not meant by the teacher. The Cyrenaic sect soon fell into the disrepute to which these principles were likely to lead it, and wholly ceased when Epicurus taught the same opinions more philosophically.

(66) Anniceris of Cyrene, though a follower of Aristippus, somewhat improved upon the low-toned philosophy of his master. He granted that there were many things worth our aim, which could not be brought within the narrow bounds of what is useful. He did not overlook friendship, kindness, honouring our parents, and serving our country; and he thought that a wise man would undertake many labours which would bring him no return in those pleasures which were alone thought happiness by Aristippus.

<small>Diogenes Laertius, lib. ii. 96.</small>

(67) The chair of philosophy at Cyrene was afterwards filled by Arete, the daughter of Aristippus; for books were costly, and reading by no means a cheap amusement, and such were the hindrances in the way of gaining knowledge, that few could be so well qualified to teach as the philosopher's daughter. She was followed after her death by her son Aristippus, who, having been brought up in his mother's lecture-room, was called, in order to distinguish him from his grandfather of the same name, Metrodidactus, or *mother-taught*. History has not told us whether he took the name himself in gratitude for the debt which he owed to this learned lady, or whether it was given him by his pupils; but in either case it was a sure way of giving to the mother the fame which was due to her for the education of her son; for no one could fail to ask who was the mother of Metrodidactus.

(68) Theodorus, one of the pupils of Metrodidactus, though at one time banished from Cyrene, rose to honour under Soter, and was sent by him as ambassador to Lysimachus. He was called the Atheist by his enemies, and the Divine by his friends, but we cannot now determine which title he best deserved. It was then usual to call those atheists who questioned the existence of the pagan gods; and we must not suppose that all who suffered under that reproach denied that the world was governed by a ruling providence. The dis-

believer in the false religion of the million is often the only real believer in a God. Theodorus was of the cold school of philosophy which was chiefly followed in Alexandria. It was earthly, lifeless, and unpoetical, arising from the successful cultivation of the physical sciences, not enough counteracted by the more ennobling pursuits of poetry and the fine arts. Hence, while commerce and the arts of production were carried to higher perfection than at any former time, and science was made greatly to assist in the supply of our bodily wants, the arts of civilisation, though by no means neglected, were cultivated without any lofty aim, or true knowledge of their dignity.

(69) Antiphilus, who was born in Egypt, and had studied painting under Ctesidemus, rose to high rank as a painter in Alexandria. Among his best-known pictures were the bearded Bacchus, the young Alexander, and Hippolytus, or rather his chariot-horses, frightened by the bull (see Fig. 218). His boy, blowing up a fire with his mouth, was much praised for the mouth of the boy, and for the light and shade of the room. His Ptolemy hunting was also highly thought of. Antiphilus showed a mean jealousy of Apelles, and accused him of joining in a plot against the king, for which Apelles narrowly escaped punishment; but when Ptolemy found that the charge was untrue, he sent the latter a gift of one hundred talents to make amends. The angry feelings of Apelles were by no means cooled by this gift, but they boiled over in his great picture of Calumny. On the right of the picture sat Ptolemy, holding out his hand to Calumny, who was coming up to him. On each side of the king stood a woman, who seemed meant for Ignorance and Suspicion. Calumny was a beautiful maiden, but with anger and deep-rooted malice in her face; in her left hand was a lighted torch, and with her right she was dragging along by the hair a young man, who was stretching forth his hands to heaven and calling upon the gods to bear witness that he was guiltless. Before her walked Envy, a pale, hollow-eyed diseased man, perhaps a portrait of the accuser; and behind were two women, Craft and Deceit, who were encouraging and supporting her. At a distance stood Repentance, in the ragged black garb of mourning, who was turning away her face for shame as Truth came up to her.

Pliny, xxxv. 37.

xxxv. 40.

Lucian. De Calumnia.

(70) Ptolemy Soter was plain in his manners, and scarcely surpassed his own generals in the costliness of his way of life. He often dined and slept at the houses of his friends; and his own house had so little of the palace, that he borrowed dishes and tables of his friends when

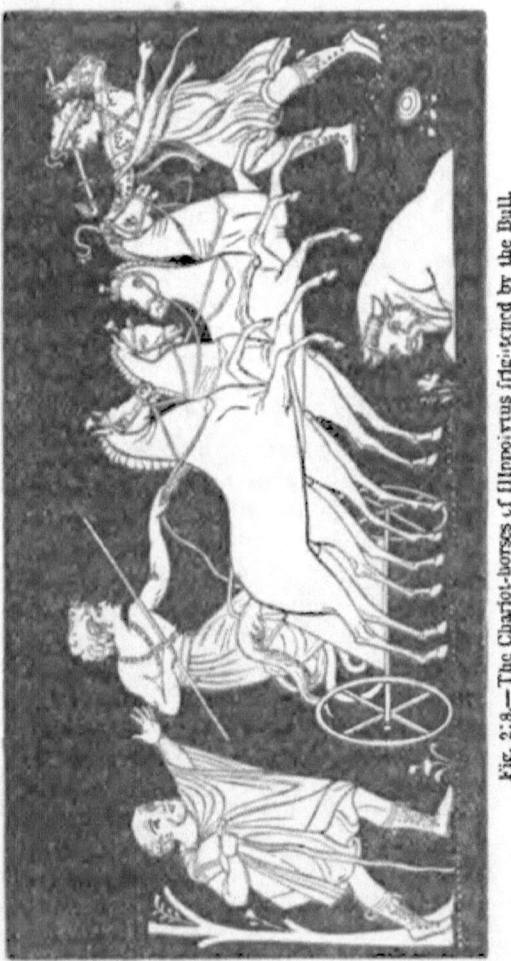

Fig. 248.—The Chariot-horses of Hippolytus frightened by the Bull.

Plutarch. Apophtheg- mata.

he asked any number of them to dine with him in return, saying that it was the part of a king to enrich others rather than to be rich himself. Before he took the title of king, he styled himself, and was styled by friendly states, by the simple name of Ptolemy the Macedonian; and during the whole of his reign he was as far from being overbearing in his behaviour as from being king-like in his dress and household. Once when he wished to laugh at a boasting antiquary, he asked him, what he knew could not be answered, who was the father of Peleus; and the other let his wit so far get the better of his prudence as in return to ask the king, who had perhaps never heard the name of his own grandfather, if he knew who was the father of Lagus. But Ptolemy took no further notice of this than to remark that if a king cannot bear rude answers he ought not to ask rude questions. Pausanias, lib. vi. 3; lib. x. 7.
Plutarch. De irâ cohibend.

(71) An answer which Ptolemy once made to a soothsayer might almost be taken as the proverb which had guided him through life. When his soldiers met with an anchor in one of their marches, and were disheartened on being told by the soothsayer that it was a proof that they ought to stop where they then were, the king restored their courage by remarking, that an anchor was an omen of safety, not of delay. Appian. Syriac. 56.

(72) Ptolemy's first children were by Thais, the noted courtezan, but they were not thought legitimate. Leontiscus, the eldest, we hear of, fighting bravely against Demetrius; of the second, named Lagus, after his grandfather, we hear nothing. Athenæus, lib. xiii. 5.
Justinus, lib. xv. 2.

(73) He then married Eurydice, the daughter of Antipater, by whom he had several children. The eldest son, Ptolemy, was named Ceraunus, *the Thunderer*, and was banished by his father from Alexandria. In his distress he fled to Seleucus, by whom he was kindly received; but after the death of Ptolemy Soter he basely plotted against Seleucus and put him to death. He then defeated in battle Antigonus, the son of Demetrius, and got possession of Macedonia for a short time. He married his half-sister Arsinoë, and put her children to death; and was soon afterwards put to death himself by the Gauls, who were either fighting against him or were mercenaries in his own army. Pausanias, lib. i. 6; lib. i. 16.
Memnon, ap. Photium.

(74) Another son of Ptolemy and Eurydice was put to

death by Ptolemy Philadelphus, for plotting against his
throne, to which, as the elder brother, he might
have thought himself the best entitled.

<small>Pausanias, lib. i. 7.</small>

(75) Their daughter Lysandra married Agathocles, the son
of Lysimachus; but when Agathocles was put to
death by his father, she fled to Egypt with her
children, and put herself under Ptolemy's care.

<small>Lib. i. 9, 10.</small>

(76) Ptolemy then, as we have seen, asked in marriage
the hand of Cleopatra, the sister of Alexander; but
on her death he married Berenice, a lady who had
come into Egypt with Eurydice, and had formed part of her

<small>Lib. i. 6.</small>

Fig. 219.—Berenice Soter.

household. She was the widow of a man named Philip; and
she had by her first husband a son named Magas,
whom Ptolemy made governor of Cyrene, and a
daughter, Antigone, whom Ptolemy gave in marriage to Pyrrhus, when that young king was living in
Alexandria as hostage for Demetrius.

<small>Plutarch. Vit. Pyrrhi.</small>

(77) Berenice's mildness and goodness of heart were useful
in softening her husband's severity. Once when
Ptolemy was unbending his mind at a game of dice
with her, one of his officers came up to his side, and
began to read over to him a list of criminals who had been

<small>Ælian. Var. Hist. xiv. 43.</small>

condemned to death, with their crimes, and to ask his pleasure on each. Ptolemy continued playing, and gave very little attention to the unhappy tale; but Berenice's feelings overcame the softness of her character, and she took the paper out of the officer's hand, and would not let him finish reading it, saying it was very unbecoming in the king to treat the matter so lightly, as if he thought no more of the loss of a life than the loss of a throw.

(78) With Berenice Ptolemy spent the rest of his years without anything to trouble the happiness of his family. He saw their elder son Ptolemy, whom we must call by the name which he took late in life, Philadelphus, grow up everything that he could wish him to be; and, moved alike by his love for the mother and by the good qualities of the son, he chose him as his successor on the throne, instead of his eldest son Ptolemy Ceraunus, who had shown, by every act in his life, his unfitness for the trust.

(79) His daughter Arsinoë married Lysimachus in his old age, and urged him against his son Agathocles, the husband of her own sister. She afterwards married her half-brother Ptolemy Ceraunus; and lastly we shall see her the wife of her brother Philadelphus. Pausanias, lib. i. 10. Justinus, lib. xvii. 2.

(80) Argæus, the youngest son of Ptolemy, was put to death by Philadelphus, on a charge of treason. Pausanias, lib. i. 7.

(81) Of his youngest daughter Philotera we know nothing, except that her brother Philadelphus afterwards named a city on the coast of the Red Sea after her. Strabo, lib. 15.

(82) After the last battle with Demetrius, Ptolemy had regained the island of Cyprus and Cœle-Syria, including Judæa; and his throne became stronger as his life drew to an end. With a wisdom rare in kings and conquerors, he had never let his ambition pass his means; he never aimed at universal power; and he was led, both by his kind feelings and wise policy, to befriend all those states which like his own were threatened by that mad ambition in others.

(83) His history of Alexander's wars is lost, and we therefore cannot judge of his merits as an author; but we may still point out with pleasure how much his people gained

from his love of letters; though indeed we do not need the example of Ptolemy to show that learning and philosophy are as much in place, and find as wide a field of usefulness, in governing a kingdom as in the employments of the teacher, the lawyer, or the physician, who so often claim them as their own.

(84) His last public act, in the thirty-eighth year of his reign, was ordered by the same forbearance which had governed every part of his life. Feeling the weight of years press heavily upon him, that he was less able than formerly to bear the duties of his office, and wishing to see his son firmly seated on the throne, he laid aside his diadem and his title, and, without consulting either the army or the capital, proclaimed Ptolemy, his son by Berenice, king, and contented himself with the modest rank of somatophylax, or satrap, to his successor. He had used his power so justly that he was not afraid to lay it down; and he has taught us how little of true greatness there is in rank, by showing how much more there is in resigning it. This is perhaps the most successful instance known of a king, who had been used to be obeyed by armies and by nations, willingly giving up his power when he found his bodily strength no longer equal to it. Charles V. gave up the empire in disappointment, and hid himself in a monastery to avoid the sight of anything which could remind him of his former greatness. Diocletian, who, more like a philosopher, did not refuse to hear news from the world of politics which he had left, had his last days embittered and his life shortened by witnessing the misconduct of his successors. But Ptolemy Soter had the happiness of having a son willing to follow in the track which he had laid down for him, and of living to see the wisdom of his own laws proved by the well-being of the kingdom under his successor.

<small>Justinus, lib. xvi. 2.</small>

(85) But while we are watching the success of Ptolemy's plans, and the rise of this Greek monarchy at Alexandria, we cannot help being pained with the thought that the Copts of Upper Egypt are forgotten, and asking whether it would not have been still better to have raised Thebes to the place which it once held, and to have recalled the days of Rameses, instead of trying what might seem the hopeless task, to plant Greek arts in Africa. But a review of this history

will show that, as far as human forethought can judge, this could not have been done. A people whose religious opinions were fixed against all change, like the pillars upon which they were carved, and whose philosophy had not noticed that men's minds were made to move forward, had no choice but to be left behind and trampled on, as their more active neighbours marched onwards in the path of improvement. If Thebes had fallen only on the conquest by Cambyses, if the rebellions against the Persians had been those of Copts throwing off their chains and struggling for freedom, we might have hoped to have seen Egypt, on the fall of Darius, again rise under kings of the blood and language of the people; and we should have thought the gilded and half-hid chains of the Ptolemies were little better than the heavy yoke of the Persians. This, however, is very far from having been the case. We first see the kings of Lower Egypt guarding their thrones at Sais by Greek soldiers; and then, that every struggle of Inarus, of Nectanebo, and of Tachos, against the Persians, was only made by the courage and arms of Greeks hired in the Delta by Egyptian gold. During the three hundred years before Alexander was hailed by Egypt as its deliverer, scarcely once had the Copts, trusting to their own courage, stood up in arms against either Persians or Greeks; and the country was only then conquered without a battle, because the power and arms were already in the hands of the Greeks; because in the mixed races of the Delta the Greeks were so far the strongest, though not the most numerous, that a Greek kingdom rose there with the same ease, and for the same reasons, that an Arab kingdom rose in the same place nine centuries later. Moral worth, national pride, love of country, and the better feelings of clanship, are the chief grounds upon which a great people can be raised. These feelings are closely allied to self-denial, or a willingness on the part of each man to give up much for the good of the whole. By this, chiefly, public monuments are built, and citizens stand by one another in battle; and these feelings were certainly strong in Upper Egypt in the days of its greatness. But, when the throne was moved to Lower Egypt, when the kingdom was governed by the kings of Sais, and even afterwards, when it was struggling against the Persians, these virtues were wanting, and they trusted to foreign hirelings in their struggle for freedom. The Delta was peopled by three races of men, Copts, Greeks, and Phenicians, or Arabs; and even before the sceptre was given to the Greeks by Alexander's conquests we have seen that the Copts had lost the virtues needed to hold it.

An Egyptian landowner holding his sceptre and his staff of inheritance.

Fig. 220.— Ptolemy II. and his first Wife.

CHAPTER VIII.

PTOLEMY PHILADELPHUS.   B.C. 284-246.

(1) FEW princes ever mounted a throne with such fair prospects before them as the second PTOLEMY (see Fig. 221).

Fig. 221.

He was born in Cos, an island on the coast of Caria, which the Ptolemies kept as a family fortress, safe from Egyptian rebellion and Alexandrian rudeness, and, while their fleets were masters of the sea, safe from foreign armies. He had been brought up with great care, and being a younger son was not spoilt by that flattery which in all courts is so freely offered to the heir. He first studied letters and philosophy under Philetas of Cos, an author of some elegies and epigrams now lost; and as he grew up he found himself surrounded by the philosophers and writers

Suidas.

with whom his father mixed on the easiest terms of friendship. During the long reign of Ptolemy Soter the people had been made happy by wise and good laws, trade had flourished, the cities had grown rich, and the fortresses had been strengthened. The troops were well trained, their loyalty undoubted, and the Egyptians, instead of being distrusted as slaves, were enrolled in a phalanx, armed and disciplined like the Macedonians. The population of the country was counted at seven millions. Alexandria, the capital of the kingdom, was not only the largest trading city in the world, but was one of the most favoured seats of learning. It surely must have been easy to foresee that the prince then mounting the throne, even if but slightly gifted with virtues, would give his name to a reign which could not be otherwise than remarkable in the history of Egypt. But Philadelphus, though like his father he was not free from the vices of his times and of his rank, had more of wisdom than is usually the lot of kings; and though we cannot but see that he was only watering the plants and gathering the fruit where his father had planted, and that like Lorenzo de' Medici he has received the praise for reaping the harvest which is due to his father for his wisdom in sowing the seed, yet we must at the same time acknowledge that Philadelphus was a successor worthy of Ptolemy Soter. He may have been in the twenty third year of his age when his father gave up to him the cares and honours of royalty.

Diod. Sic. lib. i. 31.

(2) The first act of his reign, or rather the last of his father's reign, was the proclamation, or the ceremony of showing the new king to the troops and people. All that was dazzling, all that was costly or curious, all that the wealth of Egypt could buy or the gratitude of the provinces could give, was brought forth to grace this religious show, which, as we learn from the sculptures in the old tombs, was copied rather from the triumphs of Rameses and Thothmosis than from anything that had been seen in Greece.

(3) The procession began with the pomp of Osiris, at the head of which were the Sileni, in scarlet and purple cloaks, who opened the way through the crowd. Twenty satyrs followed on each side of the road, bearing torches; and then Victories with golden wings,

Athenaeus, lib. v.

clothed in skins, each with a golden staff six cubits long, twined round with ivy. An altar was carried next, covered with golden ivy-leaves, with a garland of golden vine-leaves tied with white ribands; and this was followed by a hundred and twenty boys in scarlet frocks, carrying bowls of crocus, myrrh, and frankincense, which made the air fragrant with the scent. Then came forty dancing satyrs crowned with golden ivy-leaves, with their naked bodies stained with gay colours, each carrying a crown of vine-leaves and gold; then two Sileni in scarlet cloaks and white boots, one having the hat and wand of Mercury and the other a trumpet; and between them walked a man, six feet high, in tragic dress and mask, meant for the year, carrying a golden cornucopia. He was followed by a tall and beautiful woman, meant for the Lustrum of five years, carrying in one hand a crown and in the other a palm-branch. Then came an altar, and a troop of satyrs in gold and scarlet, carrying golden wine-vases and drinking-cups.

(4) Then came Philiscus, the poet, the priest of Osiris, with all the servants of the god; then the Delphic tripods, the prizes which were to be given in the wrestling matches; that for the boys was nine cubits high, and that for the men twelve cubits high. Next came a four-wheeled car, fourteen cubits long and eight wide, drawn along by one hundred and eighty men, on which was the statue of Osiris, fifteen feet high, pouring wine out of a golden vase, and having a scarlet frock down to his feet, with a yellow transparent robe over it, and over all a scarlet cloak. Before the statue was a large golden bowl, and a tripod with bowls of incense on it. Over the whole was an awning of ivy and vine-leaves; and in the same chariot were the priests and priestesses of the god.

(5) This was followed by a smaller chariot drawn by sixty men, in which was the statue of Isis in a robe of yellow and gold. Then came a chariot full of grapes, and another with a large cask of wine, which was poured out on the road as the procession moved on, and at which the eager crowd filled their jugs and drinking-cups. Then came another band of satyrs and Sileni, and more chariots of wine; then eighty Delphic vases of silver, and Panathenaic and other vases; and sixteen hundred dancing boys in white frocks and

golden crowns; then a number of beautiful pictures; and a chariot carrying a grove of trees, out of which flew pigeons and doves, so tied that they might be easily caught by the crowd.

(6) On another chariot, drawn by an elephant, came Osiris, as he returned from his Indian conquests. He was followed by twenty-four chariots drawn by elephants, sixty drawn by goats, twelve by some kind of stags, seven by gazelles, four by wild asses, fifteen by buffaloes, eight by ostriches, and seven by stags of some other kind. Then came chariots loaded with the tributes of the conquered nations; men of Ethiopia carrying six hundred elephants' teeth; sixty huntsmen leading two thousand four hundred dogs; and one hundred and fifty men carrying trees, in the branches of which were tied parrots and other beautiful birds. Next walked the foreign animals, Ethiopian and Arabian sheep, Brahmin bulls, a white bear, leopards, panthers, boars, a camelopard, and a rhinoceros; proving to the wondering crowd the variety and strangeness of the countries that owned their monarch's sway.

Athenæus, lib. v.

(7) In another chariot was seen Bacchus running away from Juno, and flying to the altar of Rhea. After that came the statues of Alexander and Ptolemy Soter crowned with gold and ivy; by the side of Ptolemy stood the statues of Virtue, of the god Chem, and of the city of Corinth; and he was followed by female statues of the conquered cities of Ionia, Greece, Asia Minor, and Persia, and the statues of other gods. Then came crowds of singers and cymbal-players, and two thousand bulls with gilt horns, crowns, and breastplates.

(8) Then came Amun-Ra and other gods; and the statue of Alexander between Victory and the goddess Neith, in a chariot drawn by elephants; then a number of thrones of ivory and gold; on one was a golden crown, on another a golden cornucopia, and on the throne of Ptolemy Soter was a crown worth ten thousand *aurei*, or nearly six thousand pounds sterling; then three thousand two hundred golden crowns, twenty golden shields, sixty-four suits of golden armour; and the whole was closed with forty waggons of silver vessels, twenty of golden vessels, eighty of costly Eastern scents, and fifty-seven thousand six hundred foot soldiers, and twenty-three thousand two hundred horse. The

procession began moving by torchlight before day broke in the morning, and the sun set in the evening before it had all passed.

(9) It went through the streets of Alexandria to the royal tents on the outside of the city, where, as in the procession, everything that was costly in art, or scarce in nature, was brought together in honour of the day. At the public games, as a kind of tax or coronation money, twenty golden crowns were given to Ptolemy Soter, twenty-three to Berenice, and twenty to their son the new king, beside other costly gifts; and two thousand two hundred and thirty-nine talents, or three hundred and fifty thousand pounds, were spent on the amusements of the day. For the account of this curious procession we are indebted to Callixenes of Rhodes, who was then travelling in Egypt, and who wrote a history of Alexandria.

(10) Ptolemy Soter lived two years after he had withdrawn himself from the cares of government; and the weight of his name was not without its use in adding steadiness to the throne of his successor. Instead of parcelling out his wide provinces among his sons as so many kingdoms, he had given them all to one son, and that not the eldest; and on his death the jealousy of those who had been disinherited and disappointed broke out in rebellion.

<small>Porphyrius, ap. Scalig.</small>

(11) In reviewing the history of past ages, we place ourselves in thought, at each century, on that spot of the earth on which the historians of the time lived; and from that spot, as from a height, we look over the other kingdoms of the world as far countries, about which we know nothing but what is known at the place where we then stand. Thus, in the time of Moses, we live in Egypt and in the desert; in the reign of Solomon at Jerusalem; in the time of Pericles at Athens; and in the reigns of Ptolemy Soter and Philadelphus at Alexandria. But knowing, as we must know, of the after greatness of Rome, and that in a few ages we shall have to stand on the capitol, and hear news from the distant province of Egypt, it is with peculiar interest that we hear for the first time that the bravery and rising power of the Romans had forced themselves into the notice of Philadelphus. Pyrrhus, the king of Epirus, had been beaten by the Romans and driven out of Italy; and the king of Egypt thought it not beneath him to send an ambassador to the senate, to wish them joy of their

<small>Livy, Epit. xiv. B.C. 274.</small>

success, and to make a treaty of peace with the republic.
The embassy, as we might suppose, was received in Rome with great joy; and three ambassadors, two of the proud name of Fabius, with Quintus Ogulnius, were sent back to seal the treaty. Philadelphus gave them some costly gifts, probably those usually given to ambassadors; but Rome was then young, her citizens had not yet made gold the end for which they lived, and the ambassadors returned the gifts, for they could receive nothing beyond the thanks of the senate for having done their duty. This treaty was never broken; and in the war which broke out in the middle of this reign between Rome and Carthage, usually called the first Punic war, when the Carthaginians sent to Alexandria to beg for a loan of two thousand talents, Philadelphus refused it, saying that he would help them against his enemies, but not against his friends.

<small>Valerius Max. iv. 3.</small>
<small>Dion Cassius, Frag. 147.</small>
<small>Appian. Sicul. l.</small>

(12) The sea was not then a high road between distant nations, and such was the complete separation which a few leagues of water placed between the Greek and Roman world, that while each was shaken to its foundation, the one by the quarrels between Alexander's successors, and the other by the Punic war, neither felt or joined in the struggles of the other. From that time forward, however, we find Egypt in alliance with Rome. But we also find that they were day by day changing place with one another; Egypt soon began to sink, while Rome was rising in power; Egypt soon received help from her stronger ally, and at last became a province of the Roman empire.

(13) At the time of this embassy, when Greek arts were nearly unknown to the Romans, the ambassadors must have seen much that was new to them, and much that was worth copying; and three years afterwards, when one of them, Quintus Ogulnius, together with Caius Fabius Pictor, were chosen consuls, they coined silver for the first time in Rome. With them begins the series of consular denarii, which throws such light on Roman history.

<small>Pliny, lib. xxxiii. 13.</small>
<small>B.C. 269.</small>

(14) About the middle of this reign, Berenice, the mother of the king, died; and it was most likely then that Philadelphus began to date from the beginning of his own reign; he had before gone on like his father, dating

<small>B.C. 266.</small>

from the beginning of his father's reign. In the year after her death the great feast of Osiris, in the month of Mesore, was celebrated at Alexandria with more than usual pomp by the Queen Arsinoë. Venus, or Isis, had just raised Berenice to heaven; and Arsinoë, in return, showed her gratitude by the sums of money spent on the feast of Osiris, or Adonis, as he was sometimes called by the Greeks. Theocritus, who was there, wrote a poem on the day, and tells us of the crowds in the streets, of the queen's gifts to the temple, and of the beautiful tapestries, on which were woven the figures of the god and goddess breathing as if alive; and he has given a free translation of the Maneros, the national poem, in which the priests each year consoled the goddess Isis for the death of Osiris, which was sung through the streets of Alexandria by a Greek girl in the procession. _{Theocritus, Idyll. 15.}

(15) One of the chief troubles in the reign of Philadelphus was the revolt of Cyrene. The government of that part of Africa had been entrusted to Magas, the half-brother of the king, a son of Berenice by her former husband. Berenice, who had been successful in setting aside Ceraunus to make room for her son Philadelphus on the throne of Egypt, has even been said to have favoured the rebellious and ungrateful efforts of her elder son Magas, to make himself king of Cyrene. Magas, without waiting till the large armies of Egypt were drawn together to crush his little state, marched hastily towards Alexandria, in the hopes of being joined by some of the restless thousands of that crowded city. But he was quickly recalled to Cyrene by the news of the rising of the Marmaridæ, the race of Libyan herdsmen that had been driven back from the coast by the Greek settlers who founded Cyrene. Philadelphus then led his army along the coast against the rebels; but he was, in the same way, stopped by the fear of treachery among his own Gallic mercenaries. _{Pausanias, lib. i. 7. B.C. 265.}

(16) More than a century before this time, the Celts, or Gauls, had found their own forests too crowded for their way of life, and moving southward, had overrun the fair plains of the north of Italy, and nearly crushed imperial Rome in the cradle, in the time of Nectanebo I. Other bands of these fierce barbarians had wandered as far as Greece, and tried their wild and unarmed courage against

the spears of the Macedonian phalanx. But the large armies which were called out by the quarrels of Alexander's successors could not be raised without the help of barbarians, and in these ranks the Gauls found the pay and plunder for which they had left their own forests. Thus we meet with them in the armies of Egypt, of Macedonia, and of Asia Minor; and in this last country they afterwards settled, and gave their own name to the province of Galatia. Philadelphus had reason to believe that four thousand of these Gauls, who formed part of the army which he was leading against Cyrene, were secretly plotting against him. Therefore, with a measured cruelty which the use of foreign mercenaries could alone have taught him, he led back his army to the marshes of the Delta, and, entrapping the four thousand distrusted Gauls in one of the small islands, he hemmed them in between the water and the spears of the phalanx, and they all died miserably, by famine, by drowning, or by the sword.

(17) Magas had married Apime, the daughter of Antiochus Soter, king of Syria; and he sent to his father-in-law to beg him to march upon Cœle-Syria and Palestine, to call off the army of Philadelphus from Cyrene. But Philadelphus did not wait for this attack; his armies moved before Antiochus was ready, and, by a successful inroad upon Syria, he prevented any relief being sent to Magas.

(18) After the war between the brothers had lasted some years, Magas made an offer of peace, which was to be sealed by betrothing his only child Berenice to the son of Philadelphus. To this offer Philadelphus yielded, as by the death of Magas, who was already worn out by luxury and disease, Cyrene would then fall to his own son. Magas, indeed, died before the marriage took place; but, notwithstanding the efforts made by his widow to break the agreement, the treaty was kept, and on this marriage Cyrene again formed part of the kingdom of Egypt.

<small>Justinus, lib. xxvi. 3.</small>

<small>B.C. 256.</small>

(19) The king's massacre of the four thousand Gauls belongs to a class of crimes which men are sadly little shocked at. Wrong-doing on so large a scale seldom meets with punishment; and therefore we sometimes forget that it deserves it. But the black spot upon the character of Philadelphus, which all the blaze of science and letters by which

he was surrounded cannot make us overlook, is the death of two of his brothers. A son of Eurydice, who might perhaps have thought that he was robbed of the throne of Egypt by his younger brother, and who was unsuccessful in raising the island of Cyprus in rebellion, and a younger brother, Argæus, who was also charged with joining in a plot, both lost their lives by his orders. Well might the historians believe that the name of Philadelphus, which he took to show his love for a sister, was given him as a reproach for the murder of two brothers and the war of many years against a third. Pausanias, lib. i. 7.

(20) It was only in the beginning of this reign, after Egypt had been for more than fifty years under the rule of the Macedonians, that murders and robberies, the crimes which usually follow in the train of war and conquest, were brought to an end. Before this reign no Greek was ever known to have reached Elephantine and Syene since Herodotus made his hasty tour in the Thebaid; and during much of the last reign no part of Upper Egypt was safe for a Greek traveller, if he were alone, or if he quitted the high road. The peasants, whose feelings of hatred we can hardly wonder at, waylaid the stragglers, and, Egyptian-like, as the Greeks said, or slave-like, as it would be wiser to say, often put them to death in cold blood. But a long course of good government had at last quieted the whole country and left room for further improvements by Philadelphus. Diod. Sic. lib. i. 37. Theocritus, Idyll. xv. 48.

(21) Among other buildings, Philadelphus raised a temple in Alexandria to the honour of his father and mother, and placed in it their statues, made of ivory and gold, and ordered that they should be worshipped like the gods and other kings of the country. He also built a temple to Ceres and Proserpine, and then the Eleusinian mysteries were taught in Alexandria to the few who were willing and worthy to be admitted, and who could be trusted with the secret rites. The south-east quarter of the city, in which this temple stood, was called the Eleusinis; and here the troop of maidens were to be seen carrying the sacred basket through the streets and singing hymns in honour of the goddess; while they charged all profane persons who met the pro-

cession to keep their eyes upon the ground, lest they should see the basket and the priestesses, who were too pure for them to look upon.

(22) In this reign was finished the lighthouse on the island of Pharos, as a guide to ships when entering the harbour of Alexandria by night. It was built by the architect Sostratus, and it was dedicated "to the gods Soteres," as Soter and Berenice were called in all public writings. They were henceforth to be the gods of the port and of its shipping, as Hephæstion had before been by order of Alexander the Great. The building of the royal burial-place in Alexandria, which had been begun by Ptolemy Soter, was also finished, and then Philadelphus removed the sacred body of Alexander from Memphis, where it had for the time been left, to this city, which the conqueror had himself planned, and which was now to be made a holy spot by his embalmed remains. Hither pilgrims came to the hero's tomb, and bowed before the golden sarcophagus in which his body was placed. But more active travellers often climbed to the roof of the temple of Pan, in the middle of the city, and there looked round on the space between the Lake Mareotis and the sea. They observed it covered with temples, and houses, and streets, and gardens, they noted the palaces of the Bruchium, the canal bringing barges from the Nile, the lighthouse on the island, and the ships in the harbour, and then could they most truly say they had seen the monument of Alexander the Great.

<small>Strabo, lib. xvii.</small>

<small>Pausanias, lib. i. 7.</small>

(23) The navigation of the Red Sea, along which the wind blows hard from the north for nine months in the year, was found so dangerous by the little vessels from the south of Arabia, that they always chose the most southerly port in which they could meet the Egyptian buyers. The merchants with their bales of goods found a journey on camels through the desert, where the path is marked only by the skeletons of the animals that have died upon the route, less costly than a coasting voyage. Hence, when Philadelphus had made the whole of Upper Egypt to the cataracts as quiet and safe as the Delta, he made a new port on the rocky coast of the Red Sea, nearly two hundred miles to the south of Cosseir, and named it Berenice, after his

<small>Diod. Sic. lib. i.</small>

<small>Pliny. lib. vi. 26.</small>

mother. It was called the Troglodytic Berenice, to distinguish it from other cities of the same name. He also built four public inns or watering-houses, where the caravans might find water for the camels and shelter from the noonday sun, on their twelve days' journey through the desert from Coptos on the Nile to this new port. He also rebuilt and at the same time renamed, the old port of Cosseir, or Ænum, as it was before called, and named it Philotera, after his younger sister. By this route and by the coasting vessels on the Red Sea Philadelphus hoped to regain part of the trade that the country had lost by the disturbed and rebellious state of Ethiopia, which very much separated Egypt from the gold mines. The trade which thus passed down the Nile from Syene, from Berenice, and from Philotera, paid a toll or duty at the custom-house station of Phylake, a little below Lycopolis, on the west bank of the river, where a guard of soldiers was encamped; and this station gradually grew into a town. Strabo, lib. xvii. Agatharcides, ap. Photium.

(24) The route before spoken of, from Coptos to Berenice, passed near the emerald mines, on the mountain range of red granite and porphyry which runs about thirty miles from the sea. This part of the range was called Mount Smaragdus, now Mount Zabarah, and the precious stones, of brightest clearest green, received their name from the mountain. They were found in veins of micaceous schist, and their number and value repaid the labour of three or four hundred miners. The ruins of two small towns still mark the dwelling-places of the workmen; while the Roman, Greek, and Egyptian styles of architecture in the temples fix the ages in which the mines were worked for emeralds or the quarries for porphyry and *Breccia verde*. Cailliaud, Voyage à l'Oasis.

(25) In the number of ports which were then growing into the rank of cities, we see full proof of the great trade of Egypt at that time; and we may form some opinion of the profit which was gained from the trade of the Red Sea from the report of Clitarchus to Alexander, that the people of one of the islands would give a talent of gold for a horse, so plentiful with them was gold, and so scarce the useful animals of Europe; and one of the three towns named after the late queen, on that coast, was known by the name of the Nubian or Golden Berenice, Pliny, lib. vi. 36. Lib. vi. 34.

from the large supply of gold which was dug from the mines in the neighbourhood. This was the port of the Nubian gold mines, perhaps the town before called Ophir by Solomon's Tyrian sailors, and not many miles from that now named Souakin.

(26) Philadelphus also built a city on the sands at the head of the Red Sea, near where Suez now stands, and named it Arsinoë, after his sister; and he again opened the canal which Necho II. and Darius had begun, by which ships were to pass from the Nile to this city on the Red Sea. This canal began in the Pelusiac branch of the river, a little above the city of Bubastis, and, passing by the city of Thoum or Patumus, was carried to the Lower Bitter Lakes in the reign of Darius. Thus far it was thirty-seven miles long. From thence Philadelphus wished to carry it forward to the Red Sea, near the town of Arsinoë, and moreover cleared it from the sands which soon overwhelmed it and choked it up whenever it was neglected by the government. But his undertaking was stopped by the engineers finding the waters of the canal several feet lower than the level of the Red Sea; and that if finished it would become a salt-water canal, which could neither water the fields nor give drink to the cities in the valley. He also built a third city of the name of Berenice, called the Berenice Epidires, at the very mouth of the Red Sea on a point of land where Abyssinia is hardly more than fifteen miles from the opposite coast of Arabia. This naming of cities after his mother and sisters was no idle compliment; they probably received the crown revenues of those cities for their maintenance. We know that this was the case with the revenues of the Arsinoite nome, and that it was so with the city at the head of the Red Sea is made probable by its name changing with that of the queen. In this reign it was named Arsinoë and afterwards Cleopatris.

(27) With a view further to increase the trade with the East, Philadelphus sent Dionysius on an expedition overland to India, to gain a knowledge of the country and of its means and wants. He went by the way of the Caspian Sea through Bactria, in the line of

Alexander's march. He dwelt there, at the court of the sovereign, soon after the time that Megasthenes was there; and he wrote a report of what he saw and learned. But it is sad to find, in our search for what is valuable in the history of past times, that while the deeds of conquerors who have laid waste the world, and the freaks of tyrants who have made nations unhappy, are recorded with careful accuracy, the discovery of useful arts, and the spread of the most valuable branches of commerce, are often unnoticed or forgotten. The information gained on this interesting journey of discovery is wholly lost. But by the help of such scientific travellers many valuable foreign plants were brought Pliny, lib. xii. 31, 37. into the valley of the Nile during this and the following reigns; and some of the gums and scents of Arabia were successfully cultivated there for several centuries.

(28) In latitude 17°, separated from the Golden Berenice by one of the forests of Ethiopia, was the new city of Ptolemais, which, however, was little more than a post from which the hunting parties went out to catch elephants for the armies of Egypt. Philadelphus tried to command, to persuade, and to bribe the neighbouring tribes not to kill these elephants for food, but they Agatharcides, ap. Photium. refused all treaty with him; these zealous huntsmen answered that, if he offered them the kingdom of Egypt with all its wealth, they would not give up the pleasure of catching and eating elephants. The Ethiopian forests, however, were able to supply the Egyptian armies with about one elephant for every thousand men, which was the number then thought best in the Greek military tactics. Hieronymus in Dan. xi. Asia had been the only country from which the armies had been supplied with elephants before Philadelphus brought them from Ethiopia.

(29) The temple of Isis among the palm-groves in Philæ, a rocky island in the Nile near the cataracts of Syene, was begun in this reign, though not finished Wilkinson, Thebes. till some reigns later (see Fig. 222). It is still the wonder of travellers, and by its size and style Denon, pl. 70, 71, 72. proves the wealth and good taste of the priests. But its ornaments are not so simple as those of the older temples; and the capitals of its columns are varied by the fullblown papyrus flower of several sizes, its half-opened buds, its

closed buds, and its leaves (see Figs. 223—227), and by palm-branches (see Fig. 228). It seems to have been built on the site of an older temple, which may have been overthrown by the Persians. The priests of lower rank lived in twelve small cells, only ten feet deep, ranged along the right-hand side of the courtyard, while the chief priest dwelt in the larger rooms on the opposite side of the same court. But when the outer courtyard was afterwards built, there was added on its right side a row of fifteen rather larger cells for a further number of priests, who with the former passed their

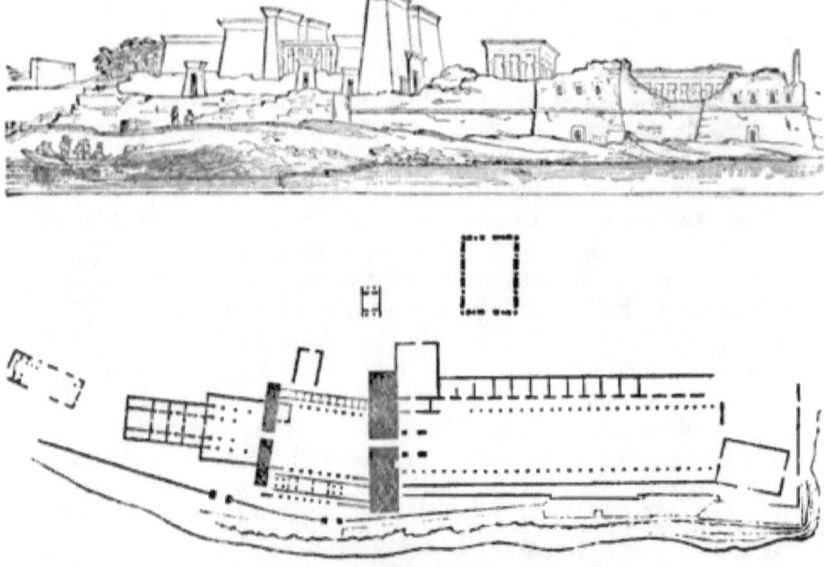

Fig. 222.

lives in the worship of the Trinity of the place, Isis, Osiris, and their son Horus. This island of Philæ is the most beautiful spot in Egypt; where the bend of the river just above the cataracts forms a quiet lake surrounded on all sides by fantastic cliffs of red granite. Its name is a corruption from Abou-lakh, *the city of the frontier.* This temple was one of the places in which Osiris was said to be buried; and here the priests every day made use of three hundred and sixty sacred vessels, as they poured out three hundred and sixty libations of milk in his honour,

Diod. Sic. lib. i. 22.

and in token of their grief for his sufferings. No oath was so binding as that sworn in the name of Him that lies buried in Philæ. None but priests were allowed to set foot on this sacred island, and one of their duties was to throw a piece of gold once a year into the river in order to purchase of it its annual blessing of a bountiful overflow. The gold was usually in the form of a ring, and hence perhaps the Venetians borrowed their custom of wedding the

Seneca, Nat. Quæst. lib. iv.

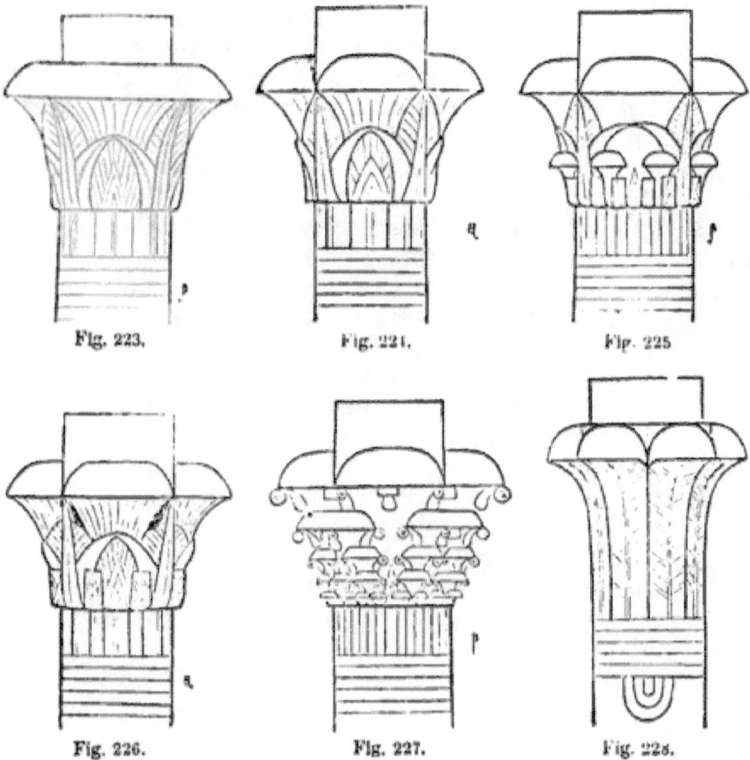

Fig. 223.   Fig. 224.   Fig. 225.

Fig. 226.   Fig. 227.   Fig. 228.

Adriatic. The statues of the goddess in the temple were all meant for portraits of the Queen Arsinoë. The priests who dwelt in the cells within the courtyards of the temples, of which we see the remains in this temple at Philæ, were there confined for life to the service of the altar by the double force of religion and the stone walls.

Manetho, Apotelesm. i. 235.

They were called Ophtho, or persons *dedicated*, and by the Greeks Catochoi, or persons *confined*, of which last our Latin name, a religious *recluse*, is the translation. These pagans

Fig. 229.

gave us the first example of a monastic life and our name for it. They showed their zeal for their gods by the amount of want which they were able to endure. Cleanliness and change of linen were luxuries which they thought it right to shun, and they added to their discomfort by cutting their flesh from time to time with knives. They thought that sitting upon the ground in idleness, with the knees up to the chin, was one of the first of religious duties. In this posture they are often represented in their statues (see Fig. 229).

(30) The Museum of Alexandria held at this time the highest rank among the Greek schools, whether for poetry, mathematics, astronomy, or medicine, the four branches into which it was divided. Its library soon held two hundred thousand rolls of papyrus; which, however, could hardly have been equal to ten thousand printed volumes. Many of these were bought by Philadelphus in Athens and Rhodes; and his copy of Aristotle's works was bought of the philosopher Nileus, who had been a hearer of that great man, and afterwards inherited his books through Theophrastus, to whom they had been left by Aristotle. The books in the Museum were of course all Greek; the Greeks did not study foreign languages, and thought the Egyptian writings barbarous.

<small>Josephus, Antiq. xii. 2.</small>

<small>Athenaus, lib. i. 2.</small>

<small>Strabo, lib. xiii.</small>

(31) In the last reign Demetrius Phalereus had been at the head of this library, who, after ruling Athens with great praise, was banished from his country, and fled to Ptolemy Soter, under whom he consoled himself for the loss of power in the enjoyment of literary leisure. He was at the same time the most learned and the most polished of orators. He brought learning from the closet into the forum; and, by the soft turn which he gave to public speaking, made that sweet and lovely which had before been grave and severe.

<small>Hieronym. in Dan. xi.</small>

<small>Cicero, Brutus.</small>

Cicero thought him the great master in the art of speaking, and seems to have taken him as the model upon which he wished to form his own style. He wrote upon philosophy, history, government, and poetry; but the only one of his works which has reached our time is his treatise on elocution; and the careful thought which he there gives to the choice of words and to the form of a sentence, and even the parts of a sentence, shows the value then set upon style. Indeed, he seems rather to have charmed his hearers by the softness of his words, than to have roused them to noble deeds by the strength of his thoughts. He not only advised Ptolemy Soter what books he should buy, but which he should read, and he chiefly recommended those on government and policy; and it is alike to the credit of the king and of the librarian, that he put before him books which, from their praise of freedom and hatred of tyrants, few persons would even speak of in the presence of a king. But Demetrius had also been consulted by Soter about the choice of a successor, and had given his opinion that the crown ought to be left to his eldest son, and that wars would arise between his children if it were not so left; hence we can hardly wonder that, on the death of Soter, Demetrius should have lost his place at the head of the Museum, and been ordered to leave Alexandria. He died, as courtiers say, in disgrace; and he was buried near Diospolis, in the Busirite nome of the Delta. According to one account he was put to death by the bite of an asp, in obedience to the new king's orders.
Suidas.
Plutarch, Regum apophtheg.
Diogenes Laertius, lib. v.
Cicero, pro Rabirio.

(32) Soon after this we find Zenodotus of Ephesus filling the office of librarian to the Museum. He was a poet, who, with others, had been employed by Soter in the education of his children. He is also known as the first of those Alexandrian critics who turned their thoughts towards mending the text of Homer, and to whom we are indebted for the tolerably correct state of the great poet's works, which had become faulty through the carelessness of the copiers. Zenodotus was soon followed by other critics in this task of editing Homer. But their labours were not approved of by all; and when Aratus asked Timon which he thought the best edition of
Suidas.
Diogenes in Timone.

the poet, the philosopher shrewdly answered, "That which has been least corrected."

(33) At the head of the mathematical school was Euclid; who is, however, less known to us by what his pupils have said of him than by his own invaluable work on geometry. This is one of the few of the scientific writings of the ancients that are still in use among us. The discoveries of the man of science are made use of by his successor, and the discoverer perhaps loses part of his reward when his writings are passed by, after they have served us as a stepping-stone to mount by. If he wishes his works to live with those of the poet and orator, he must, like them, cultivate those beauties of style which are fitted to his matter. Euclid did so; and the Elements have been for more than two thousand years the model for all writers on geometry. He begins at the beginning, and leads the learner, step by step, from the simplest propositions, called axioms, which rest upon metaphysical rather than mathematical proof, to high geometrical truths. The mind is indeed sometimes wearied by being made to stop at every single step in the path, and wishes with Ptolemy Soter for a shorter road; but upon the whole Euclid's neatness and clearness have never been equalled. The writings of Hippocrates, Eudoxus, Leon, Theatetus, and others, from which the Elements were very much taken, are now lost, and their names hardly known; while the writings of Euclid, from their style and manner, will be read as long as geometry is studied.

<small>Proclus, Comm. ii. 4.</small>

(34) Ctesibius at the same time ranked equally high in mixed mathematics, although his name is now little known; he wrote on the theory of hydrostatics, and was the inventor of several water-engines, an application of mathematics which was much called for by the artificial irrigation of Egypt. He also invented that useful instrument the water-clock, or hour-glass, to supply the place of the sun-dial after sunset; and by these and other inventions, he rose from being the son of a barber in Alexandria to hold a high rank in the scientific world. The water-clock, in order to be useful, had to be adjusted to the common sun-dial. And as this divided the daylight into twelve hours, long hours in summer

<small>Athenæus, lib. ix.
Pliny, lib. vii. 34.
Vitruvius, lib. ix. 9.</small>

and short hours in winter, it required not a little skill in Ctesibius, to make his hours of the corresponding uneven lengths.

(35) Among the best known of the men of letters who came to Alexandria to enjoy the patronage of Philadelphus was Theocritus. He was born or at least brought up at Syracuse. Many of his poems are now lost; but his pastoral poems, though too rough for the polished taste of Quintilian, and perhaps more like nature than we wish any works of imitative art to be, have always been looked upon as the model of that kind of poetry. If his shepherds do not speak the language of courtiers, they have at least a rustic propriety which makes us admire the manners and thoughts of the peasant. He repaid the bounty of the king in the way most agreeable to him; he speaks of him as one

Idyll. xiv. 60.

> to freemen kind,
> Wise, fond of books and love, of generous mind;
> Knows well his friend, but better knows his foe;
> Scatters his wealth; when asked he ne'er says No,
> But gives as kings should give.

Theocritus boasted that he would in an undying poem place him in the rank of the demigods; and, writing with the Pyramids and the Memnonium before his eyes, assured him that generosity toward the poets would do more to make his name live for ever than any building that he could raise. The muse of Theocritus is wholly Sicilian; he has drawn no pictures from the country to which he had removed. He hardly mentions Egypt; when he writes to please himself his free thoughts wander over the hills and plains of Sicily; when he writes through gratitude, they are imprisoned in the court of Alexandria.

(36) In a back street of Alexandria, in a part of the city named Eleusinis, near the temple of Ceres and Proserpine, lived the poet Callimachus, earning his livelihood by teaching. *Suidas.* But the writer of the Hymns could not long dwell so near the court of Philadelphus unknown and unhonoured. He was made professor of poetry in the Museum, and even now repays the king and patron for what he then received. He was a man of great industry, and wrote in prose and in all kinds of verse; but of these only a

few hymns and epigrams have come down to our time. Egypt seems to have been the birthplace of the mournful elegy, and Callimachus was the chief of the elegiac poets. He was born at Cyrene; and though from the language in which he wrote his thoughts are mostly Greek, yet he did not forget the place of his birth. He calls upon Apollo by the name of Carneus, because, after Sparta and Thera, Cyrene was his chosen seat. He paints Latona, weary and in pain in the island of Delos, as leaning against a palm-tree, by the side of the River Inopus, which, sinking into the ground, was to rise again in Egypt, near the cataracts of Syene; and prettily pointing to Philadelphus, he makes Apollo, yet unborn, ask his mother not to give birth to him in the island of Cos, because that island was already chosen as the birthplace of another god, the child of the gods Soteres, who would be the copy of his father, and under whose diadem both Egypt and the islands would be proud to be governed by a Macedonian.

Hymn to Apollo.
Hymn to Delos.

(37) The poet Philætas, who had been the first tutor of Philadelphus, was in elegy second only to Callimachus; but Quintilian (while advising us about books, to read much but not many) does not rank him among the few first-rate poets by whom the student should form his taste; and his works are now lost. He was small and thin in person, and it was jokingly said of him that he wore leaden soles to his shoes lest he should be blown away by the wind. But in losing his poetry we have perhaps lost the point of the joke. While these three, Theocritus, Callimachus, and Philætas, were writing in Alexandria, the Museum was certainly the chief seat of the muses. Athens itself could boast of no such poet but Menander, with whom Attic literature ended; and him Philadelphus earnestly invited to his court. He sent a ship to Greece on purpose to fetch him; but neither this honour nor the promised salary could make him quit his mother-country and the schools of Athens; and in the time of Pausanias his tomb was still visited by the scholar on the road to the Piræus, and his statue was still seen in the theatre.

Quintilian, lib. x. 1.

Ælianus, lib. ix. 14.

Pliny, lib. vii. 31.

(38) Strato, the pupil of Theophrastus, though chiefly known for his writings on physics, was also a writer on many

branches of knowledge. He was one of the men of learning who had taken part in the education of Philadelphus; and the king showed his gratitude to his teacher by making him a present of eighty talents, or twelve thousand pounds sterling. He was for eighteen years at the head of one of the Alexandrian schools.

<small>Diogenes Laertius, lib. v. 58.</small>

(39) Timocharis, the astronomer, made some of his observations at Alexandria in the last reign, and continued them through half of this reign. He began a catalogue of the fixed stars, with their latitudes and their longitudes measured from the equinoctial point; by the help of which Hipparchus, one hundred and fifty years afterwards, made the great discovery that the equinoctial point had moved. He has left an observation of the place of Venus, on the seventeenth day of the month of Mesore, in the thirteenth year of this reign, which by the modern tables of the planets is known to have been on the eighth day of October, B.C. 272; from which we learn that the first year of Philadelphus ended in November, B.C. 284, and the first year of Ptolemy Soter ended in November, B.C. 322; thus fixing the chronology of these reigns with a certainty which leaves nothing to be wished for.

<small>Ptolemæi Syntax. Mag. lib. vii. 3.</small>

<small>Dr. Young, Astron. Col.</small>

(40) Aristillus also made observations of the same kind at Alexandria. Few of them have been handed down to us, but they were made use of by Hipparchus.

<small>Ptolemæi Syntax. Mag. lib. vii. 3.</small>

(41) Aristarchus, the astronomer of Samos, most likely came to Alexandria in the last reign, as some of his observations were made in the very beginning of the reign of Philadelphus. He is the first astronomer who is known to have taken the true view of the solar system. He said that the sun was the centre round which the earth moved in a circle; and, as if he had foreseen that even in after ages we should hardly be able to measure the distance of the fixed stars, he said that the earth's yearly path bore no greater proportion to the hollow globe of the heavens in which the stars were set, than the point without size in the centre of a circle does to its circumference. But the work in which he proved these great truths, or perhaps threw out these happy guesses, is lost; and the astro-

<small>Lib. iii. 2.</small>

<small>Archimedes ap. Wallis.</small>

nomers who followed him clung to the old belief that the earth was the centre round which the sun moved. The only writings of Aristarchus which now remain are his short work on the distances and magnitude of the sun and moon, in which the error in his results arises from the want of good observations rather than from any mistake in his mathematical principles.

(42) Aratus, who was born in Cilicia, is sometimes counted among the Pleiades, or seven stars of Alexandria. Suidas. Tzetzes in Lycophronte. His Phænomena is a short astronomical poem, without life or feeling, which scarcely aims at any of the grace or flow of poetry. It describes the planets and the constellations one by one, and tells us what stars are seen in the head, feet, and other parts of each figure; and then the seasons, and the stars seen at night at each time of the year. When maps were little known, it must have been of great use, in giving to learners who wished to know the names of the stars that knowledge which we now gain from globes; and its being in verse made it the more easy to remember. The value which the ancients set upon this poem is curiously shown by the number of Latin translations which were made from it. Cicero in his early youth, before he was known as an orator or philosopher, perhaps before he himself knew in which path of letters he was soon to take the lead, translated this poem; and it is not a little proof of the high place which Cicero's writings held in the opinions of those with whom he lived, that this is perhaps the only copy of school-boy's verses which has come down to us from the ancients. The next translation is by Germanicus Cæsar, whose early death and many good qualities have thrown such a bright light upon his name. He shone as a general, as an orator, and as an author; but his Greek comedies, his Latin orations, and his poem on Augustus, are lost, while his translation of Aratus is all that is left, to prove that this high name in literature was not given to him for his political virtues alone. Lastly, Avienus, a writer in the reign of Diocletian, or perhaps of Theodosius, has left a rugged unpolished translation of this much-valued poem.

Amor. i. 15. Aratus, the poet of the heavens, will be read, says Ovid, as long as the sun and moon shall shine. But mathematics and astronomy are as much opposed to poetry as prose is to verse. Poetry gives us pleasure by its grace and ease, while science leads to knowledge by laborious and often painful steps. Poetry places pictures before the eye, not arguments before the mind, and moves the heart and feelings rather than exercises the head. With a more happy choice of his subject, Aratus might perhaps have gained the honour which Ovid thought him entitled to.

(43) Sosibius was one of the rhetoricians of the Museum who lived upon the bounty of Philadelphus. The king, wishing to laugh at his habit of verbal criticism, once told his treasurer to refuse his salary, and say that it had been already paid. Sosibius complained to the king, and the book of receipts was sent for, in which Philadelphus found the names of Soter, Sosigines, Bion, and Apollonius, and showing to the critic one syllable of his name in each of those words, said that putting them together, they must be taken as the receipt for his salary. *Athenæus, lib. xi. 12.*

(44) Other authors wrote on lighter matters. Apollodorus Gelöus, the physician, addressed to Philadelphus a volume of advice as to which Greek wines were best fitted for his royal palate. The Italian and Sicilian were then unknown in Egypt, and those of the Thebaid were wholly beneath his notice, while the vine had as yet hardly been planted in the neighbourhood of Alexandria. He particularly praised the Naspercenite wine from the southern banks of the Black Sea, the Oretic from the island of Eubœa; the Œneatic from Locris; the Leucadian from the island of Leucas; and the Ambraciote from Epirus. But above all these he placed the Peparethian wine from the island of Peparethus, a wine which of course did not please the many, as this experienced taster acknowledges that nobody is likely to have a true relish for it till after six years' acquaintance. *Lib. xi. 472.* *Pliny, lib. xiv. 9.*

(45) Such were the Greek authors who basked in the sunshine of royal favour at Alexandria; who could have told us, if they had thought it worth their while, all that we now wish to know of the trade, religion, language, and early history of Egypt. But they thought that the barbarians were not worth the notice of men who called themselves Macedonians. Philadelphus, however, thought otherwise; and by his command Manetho, an Egyptian, wrote in Greek a history of Egypt, copied from the hiero- *Syncellus.*

glyphical writing on the temples, and he dedicated it to the king. We know it only in the quotations of Josephus and Julius Africanus; and what we have is little more than a list of kings' names. He was a priest of Heliopolis, which had been even from the time of Moses the great seat of Egyptian learning, and was so still for those branches of learning which were not cultivated by the Greeks of Alexandria. Josephus quotes him as a pagan, and therefore disinterested witness to the truth of the Jewish history; and from the high value which we set upon everything that throws light upon the Old Testament, nobody can read without feelings of deep interest the Egyptian, and therefore, of course, unfavourable, history of the Jews under Moses. The correctness of Manetho's list of kings, which runs back for fifteen hundred years, is shown by our finding the names agree with every Egyptian inscription with which they can be compared. But what little there is in it beyond the names would seem to be built on rather uncertain tradition. Besides his history, Manetho has left us a work on astrology, called Apotelesmatica, or *Events*, a work of which there seems no reason to doubt the genuineness. It is a poem in hexameter verse, in good Greek, addressed to King Ptolemy, in which he calls not only upon Apollo and the Muse, but, like a true Egyptian, upon Hermes, from whose darkly worded writings he had gained his knowledge. He says that the king's greatness might have been foretold from the places of Mars and the Sun at the time of his birth, and that his marriage with his sister Arsinoë arose from the places of Venus and Saturn at the same time. But while we smile at this being said as the result of astronomical calculations, we must remember that for centuries afterwards, almost in our own time, the science of judicial astrology was made a branch of astronomy, and that the fault lay rather in the age than in the man; and we have the pain of thinking that, while many of the valuable writings by Manetho are lost, the copiers and readers of manuscripts have carefully saved for us this nearly worthless poem on astrology.

Manetho, Apotelesm. Lib. ii.
(46) Petosiris was another writer on astrology and astronomy, who was highly praised by his friend Manetho; and his calculations on the distances of the sun and planets are quoted by Pliny. His works are lost;

but his name calls for our notice, as he must have been a native Egyptian, and a priest. Like Manetho, he also wrote on the calculation of nativities; and the later Greek astrologers, when what they had foretold did not come to pass, were wont to lay the blame on Petosiris. The priests were believed to possess these and other supernatural powers; and to help their claims to be believed many of them practised ventriloquism, or the art of speaking from the stomach without moving the lips.

<small>Anthologia Græca, lib. ii. 6.</small>

<small>Isaiah, xliv. 25. &c. ap. LXX.</small>

(47) Timosthenes, the admiral under Philadelphus, must not be forgotten in this list of authors; for though his verses to Apollo were little worth notice, his voyages of discovery, and his work in ten books on harbours, placed him in the first rank among geographers.

<small>Strabo, lib. ix. 421.</small>

(48) Colotes, a pupil and follower of Epicurus, dedicated to Philadelphus a work of which the very title proves the nature of his philosophy, and how soon the rules of his master had fitted themselves to the habits of the sensualist. Its title was, "That it is impossible even to support life according to the philosophical rules of any but the Epicureans." It was a good deal read and talked about; and three hundred years afterwards Plutarch thought it not a waste of time to write against it at some length. The moral philosophy of the Museum was by no means of that pure and lofty tone which raises the character of its followers; the science of morals did not there flourish equally with those of mathematics and physics; and hereafter we shall be able to trace in the unfortunate political state of the Alexandrians a frivolity and a want of morality which was the natural growth of this unhealthy plant.

<small>Plutarch, in Colotem.</small>

(49) At a time when books were few, and far too dear to be within reach of the many, and indeed when the number of those who could read must have been small, other means were of course taken to meet the thirst after knowledge; and the chief of these were the public readings in the Theatre. This was not overlooked by Philadelphus, who employed Hegesias to read Herodotus, and Hermophantus to read Homer, the earliest historian and the earliest poet, the two authors who had taken deepest root in the minds of the Greeks. These public readings, which

<small>Athenæus, lib. xiv. 3.</small>

were common throughout Greece and its colonies, had not a little effect on the authors. Books were then written for the ear rather than for the eye, to be listened to rather than to be read, and this was one among the causes of Greek elegance and simplicity of style.

(50) Among others who were brought to Alexandria by the fame of Philadelphus's bounty was Zoilus, the grammarian, whose ill-natured criticism on Homer's poems had earned for him the name of Homeromastix, or *the scourge of Homer*. He read his criticisms to Philadelphus, who was so much displeased with his carping and unfair manner of finding fault, that he even refused to relieve him when in distress. The king told him, that while hundreds had earned a livelihood by pointing out the beauties of the Iliad and Odyssey in their public readings, surely one person who was so much wiser might be able to live by pointing out the faults. With the ill-natured Zoilus we may mention the licentious Sotades, who gave his name to a species of poetry peculiar in its measure and pauses, and also in its want of decency. But his writings are lost, having been of course thrown aside the sooner for the impurity with which they were tainted.

<small>Vitruvius, lib. vii. præfat.</small>

<small>Quintilian, lib. 1. 5.</small>

(51) Timon, a tragic poet, was also one of the visitors to this court; but, as he was more fond of eating and drinking than of philosophy, we need not wonder at our knowing nothing of his tragedies, or at his not being made a professor by Philadelphus. But he took his revenge on the better-fed philosophers of the court, in a poem in which he calls them literary fighting-cocks, who were being fattened by the king, and were always quarrelling in the coops of the Museum.

<small>Diogenes Laertius.
Athenæus, lib. l. 19.</small>

(52) The Alexandrian men of science and letters maintained themselves, some few by fees received from their pupils, others as professors holding salaries in the Museum, and others by civil employments under the government. There was little to encourage in them the feelings of noble pride or independence. The first rank in Alexandria was held by the civil and military servants of the crown, who enjoyed the lucrative employments of receiving the taxes, hearing the lawsuits by appeal, and repressing rebellions.

With these men the philosophers mixed, not as equals, but partaking of their wealth and luxuries, and paying their score with wit and conversation. There were no landholders in the city, as the soil of the country was owned by Egyptians; and the wealthy trading classes, of all nations and languages, could bestow little patronage on Greek learning, and therefore little independence on its professors.

(53) Philadelphus was not less fond of paintings and statues than of books; and he seems to have joined the Achaian league as much for the sake of the pictures which Aratus, its general, was in the habit of sending to him, as for political reasons. Aratus, the chief of Sicyon, was an acknowledged judge of paintings, and Sicyon was then the first school of Greece. The pieces which he sent to Philadelphus were mostly those of Pamphilus, the master, and of Melanthius, the fellow-pupil, of Apelles. Pamphilus was famed for his perspective; and he is said to have received from every pupil the large sum of ten talents, or fifteen hundred pounds, a year. His best-known pieces were, Ulysses in his ship, and the victory of the Athenians near the town of Phlius; but we are not told whether either of these were sent to Philadelphus. It was through Pamphilus that, at first in Sicyon, and afterwards throughout all Greece, drawing was taught to boys as part of a liberal education. Neacles also painted for Aratus; and we might almost suppose that it was as a gift to the king of Egypt that he painted his Sea-fight between the Egyptians and the Persians, in which the painter shows us that it was fought within the mouth of the Nile by making a crocodile bite at an ass drinking on the shore.

_{Plutarch. Aratus.}

_{Pliny, lib. xxxv. 36.}

_{Lib. xxxv. 40.}

(54) Helena, the daughter of Timon, was a painter of some note at this time, at Alexandria; but the only piece of hers known to us by name is the Battle of Issus, which three hundred years afterwards was hung up by Vespasian in the Temple of Peace at Rome. We must wonder at a woman choosing to paint the horrors and pains of a battle-piece; but, as we are not told what point of time was chosen, we may hope that it was after the battle, when Alexander, in his tent, raised up from their knees the wife and lovely daughter of Darius, who had been found among the prisoners. As for the Egyptians, they

_{Ptolemæus, ap. Photium.}

330 PTOLEMY PHILADELPHUS—B.C. 284-246. [CHAP. VIII.

showed no taste in painting. Their method of drawing the human figure mathematically by means of squares (see Fig. 230), which was not unsuitable in working a statue sixty feet high, checked all flights of genius; and it afterwards destroyed Greek art, when the Greek painters were idle enough to use it.

<small>Petronius Arbit. Sat.</small>

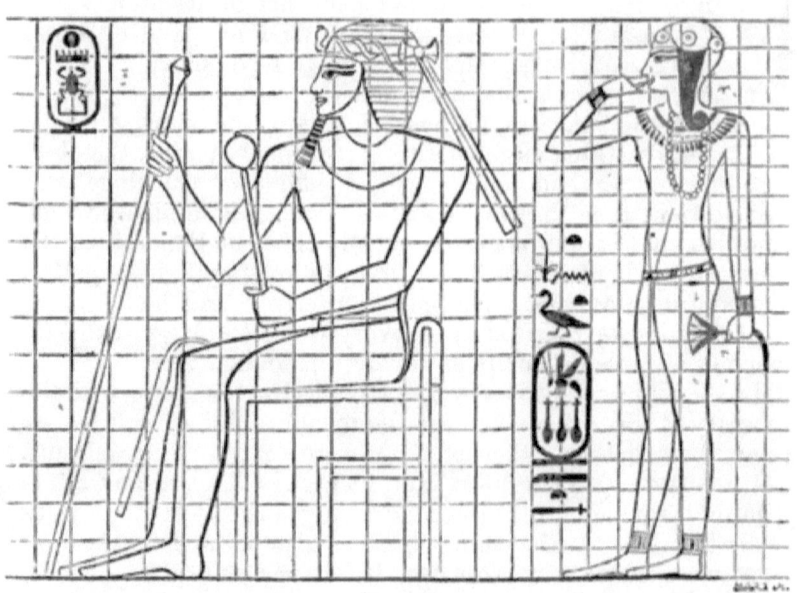

Fig. 230.

(55) We hear but little of the statues and sculptures made for Philadelphus; but we cannot help remarking, that, while the public places of Athens were filled with the statues of the great and good men who had deserved well of their country, the statues which were most common in Alexandria were those of Cline, a favourite damsel, who filled the office of cupbearer to the king.

<small>Athenæus, lib. x. 7.</small>

(56) The favour shown to the Jews by Ptolemy Soter was not withdrawn by his son. He even bought from his own soldiers and freed from slavery one hundred and twenty thousand men of that nation, who were scattered over Egypt. He paid for each, out of the royal

<small>Josephus, Antiq. xii. 2.</small>

treasury, one hundred and twenty drachmas, or about three pounds, to those of his subjects who held them either by right of war or by purchase. In fixing the amount of the ransom, the king would seem to have been guided by his Jewish advisers, as this is exactly equal to thirty shekels, the sum fixed by the Jewish law as the price of a slave. The Jews who lived in Lower Egypt, in the enjoyment of civil and religious liberty, looked upon that country as their home. They had already a Greek translation of either the whole or some part of their sacred writings, which had been made for those whose families had been for so many generations in Egypt, that they could not read the language of their forefathers. But they now hoped, by means of the king's friendship and the weight which his wishes must carry with them, to have a Greek translation of the Bible which should bear the stamp of authority.

(57) Accordingly, to please them Philadelphus sent Aristæus, a man whose wisdom had gained his friendship, and Andræus, a captain of the guard, both of them Greek Jews, with costly gifts to Eleazer, the high priest of Jerusalem, and asked him to employ learned and fit men to make a Greek translation of the Bible for the library at Alexandria. Eleazer named seventy elders to undertake the task, who held their first sitting on the business at the king's dinner-table; when Menedemus, the Socratic philosopher, the pupil of Plato, was also present, who had been sent to Philadelphus as ambassador from Eubœa. The translators then divided the work among themselves; and when each had finished his task it was laid before a meeting of the seventy, and then published by authority. Thus was said to have been made the Greek translation of the Old Testament, which, from the number of the translators, we now call the Septuagint; but a doubt is thrown upon the whole story by the fables which have been mingled with it to give authority to the translation.

(58) The difference of style in the several books proves that it was the work of many writers, and perhaps of different times. It bears in every part the strongest marks of the country in which it was written. It contains many Egyptian words, and gives the Coptic names for the Egyptian towns. In the book of Zechariah the translator's knowledge of

Ch. xiv. 18.

the climate leads him to omit the threat against the Israelites in Egypt that they shall have no rain if they come not up to Jerusalem to the feast. There are at the same time ample traces of the language from which it was taken, and even of the characters in which the original was written. Occasional mistakes arise from one Hebrew letter being like another; which prove that they were the square characters now in use, and that there were no vowel points. The chief disagreement between the original and the translation is in the chronology, which the translators very improperly undertook to correct, in order to make it better agree with Egyptian history and the more advanced state of Alexandrian science. They made the Exodus of Moses only forty years more modern; but they shortened the residence of Jacob's children in Egypt by one hundred and seventy-five years, allowing to it only the more probable space of two hundred and fifty-five years. They thus made the great Jewish epoch, the migration of Abraham out of Chaldæa, two hundred and fifteen years more modern, and then they thought it necessary to make such a large addition to the age of the world as the history of science and civilisation, and the state of Egypt at the time of Abraham, seemed to call for. Accordingly, they added to the genealogies of the patriarchs neither more nor less than a whole Egyptian cycle of fourteen hundred and sixty years, or five hundred and eighty between Adam and Noah, and eight hundred and eighty between Noah and Abraham, though in so doing they carelessly made Methuselah outlive the Flood. Again when they say that the city of On, which Ezekiel by the addition of a single letter calls Aven, or *vanity*, was Heliopolis, we are inclined to think that they are purposely misleading us. On was probably the old name of Onion, where the Israelites, even in the time of Isaiah, were carrying on a temple-service, to the horror of their brethren in Jerusalem; and Ezekiel called it Aven, or *vanity*, to join Isaiah in the blame of such doings. To relieve the Jewish town of Onion from this reproach, the Greek translators said that On and Aven meant Heliopolis.

1 Kings, ch. vi. 1.
Exodus, ch. xii. 40.

(59) The Alexandrian Jews did not venture to write in Greek letters the sacred word Jehovah; in its place they called the Almighty by the name of The Lord. It will be enough

to quote three passages from this translation, to show how, by a refinement of criticism, they often found more meaning in their Scriptures than ever entered the minds of the writers. Thus when the Psalmist, speaking of the power of Jehovah, says, with a truly Eastern figure, *He maketh the winds his messengers, and the lightning his servants;* these translators change the sentence into a philosophical description of the spiritual nature of angelic beings, and say, *He maketh his angels into spirits, and his servants into a flame of fire.* Again, when Isaiah describes the Spirit of the Lord, as a spirit of wisdom and understanding, a spirit of counsel and might, a spirit of knowledge and godly fear, the Greek Jews considered these six spirits as angelic beings, and added a spirit of piety, to complete the mystic number of seven, which with the Almighty afterwards made the Ogdoad of the Gnostics. Again, when the Hebrew text, in opposition to the polytheism with which the Jews were surrounded, says, *Jehovah is our God, Jehovah alone,* the translators turn it to contradict the Egyptian doctrine of a plurality of persons in the unity of the Godhead, by which the priests now said that their numerous divinities only made one God; and in the Alexandrian Greek this text, says, *The Lord our God is one Lord.*

Psalm, civ. 4.

Ch. xi. 2.

Deuteron. ch. vi. 4.

(60) By this translation the Bible became known for the first time to the Greek philosophers. We do not indeed hear that they immediately read it or noticed it, we do not find it quoted till after the spread of Christianity; but it had a silent effect on their opinions, which we trace in the new school of Platonists soon afterwards rising in Alexandria. From a few words in the poems of Callimachus, he indeed would seem to have read it as soon as it was published. More just views of the Creator, and of man's duties, were thence gained by many philosophers; and we must class among the great steps in the history of civilization, indeed, as a forerunner of Christianity, this spread of Jewish opinions among the Pagans. The story of the seventy translators may not have been true; but this number of elders proves the importance of the Jews who had settled in Egypt. Hitherto Jerusalem had been the only city in which the Jews held a Great Sanhedrim, or council of seventy, while in other cities, whether in Judæa

Maimonides, De Synedr. 1

or in the Dispersion, there were smaller Sanhedrims of twenty-five elders only. Thus in their Sanhedrim, in their Scriptures, and fifty years afterwards in their temple, the Jews of Egypt claimed an equal rank with their brethren of Judæa. But the use of a translation of the Law and the Prophets was far from pleasing to the Jews of Judæa; it widened the breach between the Hebrews and the Hellenists. The former declared that its publica-

<small>Scaliger, Emendatio Temporum, cap. vii.</small>

tion was marked by a supernatural darkness, which overspread the whole earth for three days; and among the twenty-five fast days in the Jewish calendar, the eighth day of Thebeth was kept by one half of the nation as a day of mourning for the other half's crime of using a Greek translation of the Bible.

(61) When Aratus of Sicyon first laid a plot to free his country from its tyrant, who reigned by the help of the king of Macedonia, he sent to Philadelphus to beg for money. He naturally looked to the king of Egypt for help when entering upon a struggle against their common rival; but the king seems to have thought the plans of this young man too wild to be countenanced.

<small>Plutarch. Aratus.</small>

Aratus, however, soon raised Sicyon to a level with the first states of Greece, and made himself leader of the Achaian league, under which band and name the Greeks were then struggling for freedom against Macedonia; and when, by his courage and success, he had shown himself worthy of the proud name which was afterwards given him, of the Last of the Greeks, Philadelphus, like other patrons, gave him the help which he less needed. Aratus, as we have seen, bought his friendship with pictures, the gifts of all others the most welcome; and when he went to Egypt, Philadelphus gave him one hundred and fifty talents, or nine thousand pounds, and joined the Achaian league, on the agreement that in carrying on the war by sea and land they should obey the orders from Alexandria.

(62) The friendship of Philadelphus, indeed, was courted by all the neighbouring states; the little island of Delos set up its statue to him; and the cities of Greece vied with one another in doing him honour. The Athenians named one of the tribes of their city, and also one of their public lecture-rooms, by his

<small>Inscript. Letronne, Recherches. Pausanias, lib. i. 6, 17.</small>

name; and two hundred years afterwards, when Cicero and his friend Atticus were learning wisdom and eloquence from the lips of Antiochus in Athens, it was in the Gymnasium of Ptolemy. Cicero, De fin. v. 1.

(63) Philadelphus, when young, had married Arsinoë, the daughter of Lysimachus of Thrace, by whom he had three children, Ptolemy, who succeeded him, Lysimachus, and Berenice; but, having found that his wife was intriguing with Amyntas, and with his physician Chrysippus of Rhodes, he put these two to death, and banished the Queen Arsinoë to Coptos in the Thebaid. Scholiast in Theocrito, xvii. 128.

(64) He then took Arsinoë, his own sister, as the partner of his throne. She had married first the old Lysimachus, king of Thrace, and then Ceraunus, her half-brother, when he was king of Macedonia. As they were not children of the same mother, this second marriage was neither illegal nor improper in Macedonia; but her third marriage with Philadelphus could only be justified by the laws of Egypt, their adopted country. They were both past the middle age, and whether Philadelphus looked upon her as his wife or not, at any rate they had no children. Her own children by Lysimachus had been put to death by Ceraunus, and she readily adopted those of her brother with all the kindness of a mother. She was a woman of an enlarged mind; her husband and her step-children alike valued her; and Eratosthenes showed his opinion of her learning and strong sense by giving the name of Arsinoë to one of his works, which perhaps a modern writer would have named Tabletalk. This seeming marriage, however, between brother and sister did not escape blame with the Greeks of Alexandria. The poet Sotades, whose verses were as licentious as his life, wrote some coarse lines against the queen, for which he was forced to fly from Egypt, and being overtaken at sea he was wrapped up in lead and thrown overboard. Athenæus, lib. vii. 1.

Lib. xiv. 4.

(65) In the Egyptian inscriptions Ptolemy and Arsinoë are always called the brother gods; on the coins they are called Adelphi, *the brothers;* and afterwards the king took the name of Philadelphus, or *sister-loving,* by which he is now usually known. In the first half of his reign Philadelphus dated his coins from the year that his father came to the throne; and it was not till the nineteenth year of his

reign, soon after the death of his mother, that he made an era of his own, and dated his coins by the year of his own reign. The wealth of the country is well shown by the great size of those most in use, which were, in gold, the *tetra-stater*, or piece of eight drachms, and in silver, the *tetra-drachma*, or piece of four drachms, while Greece had hardly seen a piece of gold larger than the single *stater*. In Alexandrian accounts also the unit of money was the silver didrachm, and thus double that in use among the merchants of Greece. Among the coins is one with the heads of Soter and Philadelphus on the one side, and the head of Berenice, the wife of the one and mother of the other, on the other side (see Fig. 231). This we may suppose to have been

<small>Exodus, xxx. 13. ap. LXX. Horapollo, I. 11.</small>

<small>Visconti, Icon. Grec.</small>

Fig. 231.

struck during the first two years of his reign, in the lifetime of his father. Another bears on one side the heads of Ptolemy Soter and Berenice, with the title of "*the gods*," and on the other side the heads of Philadelphus and his wife Arsinoë, with the title of "*the brothers*" (see Fig. 232).

Fig. 232.

This was struck after the death of his parents. A third was struck by the king, after his second marriage, in honour of his queen and sister. On the one side is the head of the queen, and on the other is the name of "*Arsinoë the brother-loving*," with the cornucopia, or horn of Amalthea, an emblem borrowed by the queens of Egypt from the goddess Amalthea, the wife of the Libyan Ammon (see Fig. 233). This also was struck after his second marriage. *Diod. Sic lib. iii. 67.*

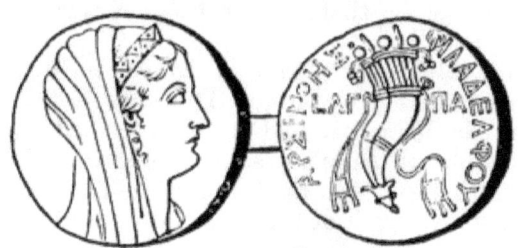

Fig. 233.

(66) On the death of Arsinoë, Philadelphus built a tomb for her in Alexandria, called the Arsinoëum, and set up in front of it an obelisk eighty cubits high, which had been made by King Nectanebo, but had been left plain, without carving. Satyrus, the architect, had the charge of moving it. He dug a canal to it as it lay upon the ground, and moved two heavily laden barges under it. The burdens were then taken out of the barges, and as they floated higher they raised the obelisk off the ground. He then found it a task as great or greater to set it up in its place; and this Greek engineer must surely have looked back with wonder on the labour and knowledge of mechanics which must have been used in setting up the obelisks, colossal statues, and pyramids, which he saw scattered over the country. This obelisk now ornaments the cathedral of the Popes on the Vatican hill at Rome. *Pliny, lib. xxxvi. 14.*

(67) Satyrus, or Satyrius, wrote a treatise on precious stones, and he also carved on them with great skill; but his works are known only in the following lines, which were written by Diodorus on his portrait of Arsinoë cut in crystal:— *Lib. xxxvii.*

> E'en Zeuxis had been proud to trace
>   The lines within this pebble seen;
> Satyrius here hath carved the face
>   Of fair Arsinoë, Egypt's queen;
> But such her beauty, sweetness, grace,
>   The copy falls far short, I ween,

Anthologia Graeca, iv. 18.

As, however, the museums of Europe contain two beautiful cameos cut on sardonyx, one with the heads of Philadelphus and his first wife Arsinoë (see Fig. 220), and the other with the heads of the same king and his second wife Arsinoë, it is not impossible that one or both of them may be the work of Satyrius.

(68) Philadelphus is also said to have listened to the whimsical proposal of Dinochares, the architect, to build a vaulted room of loadstone in the temple of Arsinoë, so that an iron statue of the queen should hang in the air between the floor and the roof. But the death of the king and of the architect took place before this was tried. He set up there, however, her statue, six feet high, carved out of a most remarkable block of topaz, which had been presented to his mother by Philemon, the prefect of the Troglodytic coast in the last reign.

<small>Pliny.
lib. xxxiv.
42.</small>

<small>Lib. xxxvii.
32.</small>

(69) Philadelphus lived in peace with Ergamenes, king of Meroë, or Upper Ethiopia, who, while seeking for a knowledge of philosophy and the arts of life from his Greek neighbours, seems also to have gained a love of despotism and a dislike of that control with which the priests of Ethiopia and Egypt had always limited the power of their kings. The king of Meroë had hitherto reigned like Amunothph or Thothmosis of old, as the head of the priesthood, supported and controlled by the priestly aristocracy by which he was surrounded. But he longed for the absolute power of Philadelphus. Accordingly, he surrounded the golden temple with a chosen body of troops, and put the whole of the priests to death; and from that time he governed Ethiopia as an autocrat. But with the loss of their liberties the Ethiopians lost the wish to guard the throne; by grasping at more power their sovereign lost what he already possessed; and in the next reign their country was conquered by Egypt.

<small>Diod. Sic.
lib. iii. 6.</small>

(70) The wars between Philadelphus and his great neighbour Antiochus Theos seem not to have been carried on very actively, though they did not wholly cease till Philadelphus offered as a bribe his daughter Berenice, with a large sum of money under the name of a dower. Antiochus was already married to Laodice,

<small>Hieronym.
in Dan. xi.</small>

whom he loved dearly, and by whom he had two children, Seleucus and Antiochus; but political ambition had deadened the feelings of his heart, and he agreed to declare this first marriage void and his two sons illegitimate, and that his children, if any should be born to him by Berenice, should inherit the throne of Babylon and the east. Philadelphus, with an equal want of feeling, and disregarding the consequences of such a marriage, led his daughter to Pelusium on her journey to her betrothed husband, and sent with her so large a sum of gold and silver that he was nicknamed the "dower-giver."

(71) The peace between the two countries lasted as long as Philadelphus lived, and was strengthened by kindnesses which each did to the other. Ptolemy, when in Syria, was much struck by the beauty of a statue of Diana, and begged it of Antiochus as an ornament for Alexandria. But as soon as the statue reached Egypt, Arsinoë fell dangerously ill, and she dreamed that the goddess came by night, and told her that the illness was sent to her for the wrong done to the statue by her husband; and accordingly it was sent back with many gifts to the temple from which it had been brought. Libanius, Orat. xi.

(72) While Berenice and her husband lived at Antioch, Philadelphus kindly sent there from time to time water from the sacred Nile for her use, as the Egyptians believed that none other was so wholesome. Antiochus, when ill, sent to Alexandria for a physician; and Cleombrotus of Cos accordingly went, by command of Ptolemy, to Syria. He was successful in curing the king, and on his return he received from Philadelphus a present of one hundred talents, or fifteen thousand pounds, as a fee for his journey. Polybius, ap. Athenaeum.
Pliny, lib. vii. 37.

(73) Philadelphus was of a weak frame of body, and had delicate health; and, though a lover of learning beyond other kings of his time, he also surpassed them in his unmeasured luxury and love of pleasure. He had many mistresses, Egyptian as well as Greek, and the names of some of them have been handed down to us. He often boasted that he had found out the way to live for ever; but, like other free-livers, he was sometimes, by the gout in his feet, made to acknow- Strabo, lib. xvii.
Athenaeus, lib. xiii. 5.
Lib. xii. 9.

ledge that he was only a man, and indeed to wish that he could change places with the beggar whom he saw from his palace windows, eating the garbage on the banks of the Nile with an appetite which he had long wanted. It was during illness that he found most time for reading, and his mind most open to the truths of philosophy; and he chiefly wooed the Muses when ill health left him at leisure from his other courtships. He had a fleet of eight hundred state barges, with gilt prows and poops and scarlet awnings upon the decks, which were used in the royal processions and religious shows, and which usually lay in dock at Schedia, on the Canopic River, five-and-twenty miles from Alexandria. He was no doubt in part withheld from war by this luxurious love of ease; but his reign taught the world the new lesson, that an ambitious monarch may gratify his wish for praise, and gain the admiration of surrounding nations, as much by cultivating the blessed arts of peace as by plunging his people into the miseries of war.

Ælianus, v. II. iv. 15.

Applan. Præfat.

Strabo, lib. xvii.

(74) He reigned over Egypt, with the neighbouring parts of Arabia; also over Libya, Phenicia, Cœle-Syria, part of Ethiopia, Pamphylia, Cilicia, Lycia, Caria, Cyprus, and the isles of the Cyclades. The island of Rhodes, and many of the cities of Greece, were bound to him by the closest ties of friendship, for past help and for the hope of future. The wealthy cities of Tyre and Sidon did homage to him, as before to his father, by putting his crowned head upon their coins. The forces of Egypt reached the very large number of two hundred thousand foot and twenty thousand horse, two thousand chariots, four hundred Ethiopian elephants, fifteen hundred ships of war, and one thousand transports. Of this large force, it is not likely that even one fourth should have been Greeks; the rest must have been Egyptians and **Syrians**, with some Gauls. The body of chariots, though still forming part of the force furnished for military service by the Theban tenants of the crown, was of no use against modern science; and the other Egyptian troops, though now chiefly armed and disciplined like Greeks, were very much below the Macedonian phalanx in real strength. The galleys also,

Theocritus, Idyll. xvii.

Hieronym. in Dan. xi.

though no doubt under the guidance and skill of Greeks and Phenicians, were in part manned by Egyptians, whose inland habits wholly unfitted them for the sea, and whose religious prejudices made them feel the pressing for the navy as a heavy grievance.

(75) These large forces were maintained by a yearly income equally large, of fourteen thousand eight hundred talents, or two millions and a quarter of pounds sterling, beside the tax on corn, which was taken in kind, of a million and a half of artabas, or about five millions of bushels. To this wealth we may add a mass of gold, silver, and other valuable stores in the treasury, which Appian.
Præf. 10. were boastfully reckoned at the unheard-of sum of seven hundred and forty thousand talents, or above one hundred million pounds sterling.

(76) The trade down the Nile was larger than it had ever been before; the coasting trade on the Mediterranean was new; the people were rich and happy; justice was administered to the Egyptians according to their own laws, and to the Greeks of Alexandria according to the Macedonian laws; the navy commanded the whole of the eastern half of the Mediterranean; the schools and library had risen to a great height upon the wise plans of Ptolemy Soter; in every point of view Alexandria was the chief city in the world. Athens had no poets or other writers during this century equal in merit to those who ennobled the Museum. Philadelphus, by joining to the greatness and good government of his father the costly splendour and pomp of an eastern monarch, so drew the eyes of after ages Philo,
De Mose. upon his reign that his name passed into a proverb; if any work of art was remarkable for its good taste or costliness, it was called Philadelphian; even history and chronology were set at nought, and we sometimes find poets of a century later counted among the Pleiades of Alexandria in the reign of Philadelphus.

(77) It is true that many of these advantages were forced in the hotbed of royal patronage; that the navy was built in the harbours of Phenicia and Asia Minor; and that the men of letters who then drew upon themselves the eyes of the world were only Greek settlers, whose writings could have done little to raise the character of the native Copts. But

the Ptolemies, in raising this building of their own, were not at the same time crushing another. Their splendid monarchy had not been built on the ruins of freedom; and even if the Greek settlers in the Delta had formed themselves into a free state, we can hardly believe that the Egyptians would have been so well treated as they were by this military despotism. From the temples which were built or enlarged in Upper Egypt, and from the beauty of the hieroglyphical inscriptions, we find that even the native arts were more flourishing than they had ever been since the fall of the kings of Thebes; and we may almost look upon the conquest of Egypt by the Greeks, and its remaining under the Ptolemies, as a blessing to the people of Upper Egypt.

(78) Philadelphus died in the thirty-eighth year of his reign, and perhaps the sixty-first of his age. He left the kingdom as powerful and more wealthy than when it came to him from his father; and he had the happiness of having a son who would carry on, even for the third generation, the wise plans of the first Ptolemy.

Porphyrius ap. Scalig.

Fig. 234.—Small votive Pyramid.

CHAPTER IX.

PTOLEMY EUERGETES, PTOLEMY PHILOPATOR, AND PTOLEMY EPIPHANES. B.C. 246—180.

(1) PTOLEMY, the eldest son of Philadelphus (see Fig. 235), succeeded his father on the throne of Egypt, and Justinus. after a short time took the lib. xxvii. 1 name of EUERGETES. He began B.C. 246. his reign with a Syrian war; for no sooner was Philadelphus dead, than Antiochus, who had married Berenice only because it was one of the articles of the treaty with Egypt, sent her away, together with her young son. Antiochus then recalled his first wife Laodice, and she, distrusting her changeable husband, had him at once murdered to secure the throne to her own children. Seleucus, the eldest, seized the throne of Syria; and, urged on by his mother, sent a body of men after Berenice, with orders to put her to death, together with her son, who by the articles of marriage had been made heir to the throne.

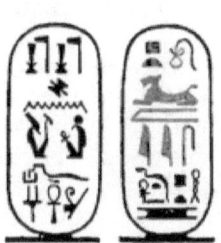

Fig. 235.

(2) The cities of Asia Minor hastily sent help to the queen and her son, while Ptolemy Euergetes, her brother, who had just come to the throne of Egypt, marched without loss of time into Syria. But it was too late to save them; they were both put to death by the soldiers of Seleucus. Many of the cities, moved by hatred of their king's cruelty, opened their gates to the army of Euergetes; and, had he not been recalled to Egypt by troubles at home, he would soon have been master of the whole of the Hieronym. in Dan. xi. kingdom of Seleucus. As it was he had marched beyond the Euphrates, had left an Egyptian army in Seleucia, the capital of Syria, and had gained a large part of Asia Minor. On his march homeward, he laid his gifts upon the altar in the Temple of Jerusalem, and Josephus, in Apion. ii. there returned thanks to Heaven for his victories. He had been taught to bow the knee to the crowds of

Greek and Egyptian gods; and, as Palestine was part of his kingdom, it seemed quite natural to add the God of the Jews to the list.

(3) From the middle of the reign of Philadelphus till the fifth year of this reign, for twenty-two years, the Romans had been struggling with the Carthaginians for their very being, Eutropius, in the first Punic war, which they had just brought lib. iii. 1. to a close; and on hearing of Ptolemy's war in Syria B.C. 232. they sent to Egypt with friendly offers of help. But their ambassadors did not reach Alexandria before peace was made, and they were sent home with many thanks.

(4) It was while the king was with the army upon this Callima- Assyrian war that his Queen Berenice in Egypt, chus, ap. sacrificing a bull to the gods, vowed that if they Catullum. brought her husband safe home she would cut off her beautiful tresses, and hang them up in the temple as a thank-offering. Euergetes soon after returned a conqueror, and the queen's locks were yielded up to the knife, while the whole court praised her heroism. Conon, the astronomer, was then busy in noting the places of the fixed stars; and grouping together into a constellation a cluster which the earlier astronomers had left unnamed, between the Bear, the Lion, the Virgin and Boötes, he marked it out on his globe, and gave it to the world as the new constellation of the Hair of Berenice. Callimachus took the hint from the courtly astronomer, and, in a poem which we know only in the translation by Catullus, he makes the hair swear by the head from which it was cut off, that it was against its will that it left the queen, and was raised to the skies; but what could it do against the force of steel? The poet and the astronomer have here been of use to one another; the constellation of Coma Berenices is known to hundreds who have not read Callimachus or Catullus, but it is from the poet that we learn why the queen's locks were set among the stars. Berenice was still young, and she may have been beautiful; Epigram. at any rate the poets said she was. Callimachus, in 55. one of his epigrams, adds her as a fourth to the number of the Graces, and moreover tells us that—

> In Berenice's form and face
> We've all that gives the Graces grace.

Another courtly poet, perhaps Posidippus, mistakes her statue for that of Venus, and says:— Anthologia Græca, iv. 3.

> This statue's a Venus;—Oh, no;
> 'Tis the Queen Berenice, I see;
> But which it's most like of the two
> I doubt whether all would agree.

(5) No sooner had Euergetes reached home than Seleucus in his turn marched upon Egypt, and sent for his brother, Antiochus Hierax, to bring up his forces and to join him. Justinus, lib. xxvii. 2. But before Antiochus could come up the army of Seleucus was already beaten; and Antiochus, instead of helping his brother in his distress, strove to rob him of his crown. Instead of leading his army against Euergetes, he marched upon Seleucus, and by the help of his Gallic mercenaries beat him in battle. But the traitor was himself soon afterwards beaten by Eumenes, king of Bithynia, who had entered Syria in the hope that it would fall an easy prey into his hands after being torn to pieces by a civil war. Antiochus, after the rout of his army, fled to Egypt, believing that he should meet with kinder treatment from Euergetes, his enemy, than after his late treachery he could hope for from his own brother. But he was ordered by Euergetes to be closely guarded, and when he afterwards made his escape he lost his life in his flight by unknown hands.

(6) The king, in his late attack upon Seleucus, had carried off a large booty of forty thousand talents of silver, and, what he seems to have valued even more Hieronym. in Dan. xi. than that treasure, two thousand five hundred vases and statues of the gods, many of which either really were, or were said to be, those carried away from Egypt by Cambyses nearly three hundred years before. These were replaced in the temples of Upper Egypt with great pomp; and the priests, in gratitude for the care which he had thus shown for the religion and temples of the country, then gave him the name of Euergetes, or the *benefactor*, by which we have been already calling him. In Alexander the Egyptians had seen a deliverer from the Persian yoke, and a humane conqueror, who left them their customs and their religion. In Ptolemy Soter they had a brave and just king, who kept war at a distance, and by his wise laws laid the foundation of

the future greatness of his family, of Alexandria, and of his kingdom. In Philadelphus they had also a Greek king whose love of learning and of show dazzled the eyes of the people, and whose court at Alexandria had carried away from Athens the honour of being the favoured seat of the Muses. But Euergetes was born in Egypt, and though perhaps the least of these great kings, in the eyes of the priests he must have ranked at their head. He seems to have thought more of conquering Ethiopia than Assyria; and he was the only one of the Ptolemies who is known to have honoured the once great city of Thebes with a visit. He enriched the temples, and sacrificed to the gods of the country, not through policy but through choice; and when during the minority of his grandson, the priests and temples were again flourishing, they showed their gratitude by saying that the young king acted in obedience to the will of the god Euergetes.

Rosetta Stone.

(7) In the ninth year of this reign Ptolemy and his wife lost a daughter, who had been named after her mother Berenice. Her death happened at the time that the priests were assembled at Canopus from all parts of Egypt on their yearly visit to the king; and they at once decreed that the young princess should be made a goddess, and that the usual divine honours should be paid to her in the temples as to the other gods of the country. And at the same time, with a view to paying divine honours more worthily to the king and queen, the gods Euergetæ, they separated a number of priests from the four existing orders, and made a fifth order of priests, who were to be named the priests of the Euergetæ, and were to be employed in celebrating their festivals. The priests then assembled further ordered that the decree to this effect should be carved on a tablet in hieroglyphics, in common Egyptian writing, and in Greek, and should be set up in all the principal temples in Egypt. One very complete copy of this decree in hieroglyphics and in Greek has lately been found in the neighbourhood of Tanis; and it would have furnished us with the wished-for key to reading the hieroglyphics, had we not already gained that key from the Rosetta Stone, a decree in three characters written in the reign of this king's grandson.

At this time the city of Canopus, situated on the coast

about fifteen miles from Alexandria, was the religious capital of the country, at least so far as the priesthood looked to the king for support. The priestly senators, when meeting there, must have been more under Greek influence than if they met at Thebes or Memphis. And accordingly we learn from this decree of Canopus, compared with a second imperfect copy of the same, that the Greek is the original and the hieroglyphics the translation. Moreover Greek discoveries in science could not have been unknown in Canopus; and Timocharis, who in the last reign measured the longitude of the stars from the equinoctial point, cannot but have given exactness to the belief, that had long floated unsteadily in the popular mind, that the Egyptian civil year of three hundred and sixty-five days was too short, and that the natural year was about a quarter of a day longer than the civil year then in use. This correction the priests at Canopus now proposed to introduce into the religious calendar, so that the summer festivals should not get moved into the winter, nor the winter festivals into the summer, as had formerly been the case. On the ninth year of the reign the first of Payni fell on our 18th of July, when the Dogstar rose heliacally and the Nile began to rise, and the priests decreed, that whereas the civil first of Payni would every fourth year fall one day earlier in the natural year, yet the religious first of Payni should remain fixed to the rising of the Dogstar, and thus each of the feasts be always celebrated in its own season. This great improvement of adding an intercalary day every fourth year was at this time limited to the priestly calendar, by which the religious festivals were regulated; it was not yet introduced into the civil calendar, and thus Euergetes lost the honour which the priests proposed for him, of having amended and made perfect what they called the "arrangement of the seasons and the disposition of the pole."

Burton's Excerpt. Hierogl.

(8) Euergetes enlarged the great temple at Thebes, which is now called the temple of Karnak, on the walls of which we see him handing an offering to his father and mother, the brother-gods. In one place he is in a Greek dress, which is not common on the Ptolemaic buildings, as most of the Greek kings are carved upon the walls in the dress of the country. The early kings had often

Wilkinson, Thebes.

shown their piety to a temple by enlarging the sacred area and adding a new wall and gateway in front of the former; and this custom Euergetes followed at Karnak (see Fig. 236).* As these grand stone sculptured gateways belonged to a wall of unbaked bricks, which has long since crumbled to pieces, they now stand apart like so many triumphal arches. He also added a portico with beautiful columns to the temple at Hibe in the Great Oasis, and he began a small temple at Esne, or Latopolis, where he is drawn upon the walls in the act of striking down the chiefs of the conquered nations, Inscript. Letronne, Recherches. and is followed by a tame lion. He built a temple to Osiris at Canopus, on the mouth of the Nile; for, notwithstanding the large number of Greeks and strangers who had settled there, the ancient religion was not yet driven out of the Delta; and he dedicated it to the god in a Greek inscription on a plate of gold, in the names of himself and Berenice, whom he called his wife and sister. She is also called the king's sister in many of the hieroglyphical inscriptions, as are many of the other queens of the Ptolemies who were not so related to their husbands. This custom, though it took its rise in the Egyptian mythology, must have been strengthened by the marriages of Philadelphus and some of his successors with their sisters. In the hieroglyphical inscriptions he is usually called "beloved by Pthah," the god of Memphis, an addition to his name which was used by most of his successors.

Fig. 236.

(9) During this century the Greek artists in Egypt, as indeed elsewhere, adopted in their style an affectation of antiquity, which unless seen through would make us think their statues older than they really are. They sometimes set a stiff beard upon a face without expression, or arranged the hair of the head in an old-fashioned manner, and while making the drapery fly out in a direction opposed to that of the figure, gave to it formal zigzag lines, which could only

* *Vide Additions*, p. 429.

be proper if it were hanging down in quiet. At other times, while they gave to the human figure all the truth to which their art had then reached, they yet gave to the drapery these stiff zigzag forms. Such is the style of art in a figure of Mercury which was brought from Canopus, and may have been made at this time (see Fig. 237). No habit of mind would have been more improving to the Alexandrian character than a respect for antiquity; but this respect ought to be shown in a noble rivalry, in trying to surpass those who have gone before us, and not, as in this manner, by copying their faults. Hieroglyphics seem to have flourished in their more ancient style and forms under the generous patronage of the Ptolemies. In the time of the Egyptian kings of Lower Egypt, we find new grammatical endings to the nouns, and more letters used to spell each word than under the kings of Thebes; but, on comparing the hieroglyphics of the Ptolemies with the others, we find that in these and some other points they are more like the older writings, under the kings of Thebes, than the newer, under the kings of Sais.

Fig. 237.

(10) But, while the Egyptians were flattered, and no doubt raised in moral worth by their monarch's taking up the religious feelings of the country, and throwing aside some of the Greek habits of his father and grandfather, Euergetes was sowing the seeds of a greater change than he could himself have been aware of. It was by Greek arms and arts of war that Egypt then held its place among nations; and we shall see in the coming reigns, that while the court became more Asiatic and less European, the army and government did not remain unchanged.

(11) Euergetes, finding himself at peace with all his neigh-

bours on the coasts of the Mediterranean, then turned his arms towards the south. In preparation for this war he added a body of five hundred Greek cavalry to his army; and he clothed one hundred of them, horses as well as men, in thick linen cloth against the arrows of the enemy, so that no part of the horses could be seen but their eyes. He easily conquered the tribes of Ethiopia, whose wild courage was but a weak barrier to the arms and discipline of the Greeks; and made himself for the moment master of part of highlands of Abyssinia, the country of the Hexumitæ. The range of mountains which follows the Egyptian coast of the Red Sea divides in about latitude 15°, and a branch turns westward. On the north side of this range rises the River Astaborus, which reaches the Nile above the fifth cataract, and forms one side of the island of Meroë. On the south side of the same high district rises the Blue River, which reaches the Nile above the sixth cataract, and forms another side of Meroë. The Hexumitæ, who dwelt on this mountain district and the neighbouring coast, were of a different race from the Arabs of Ethiopia. They were more Jewish in language and religion. Their civilization reached them, not from Egypt, from which they were separated by wilder tribes, but from the opposite coast of Arabia. To the ports of the Hexumitæ the ships of Solomon and Hiram sailed, in their way to the more distant places on the African coast. This district Euergetes conquered, and at Adule, a port in latitude 15°, he set up a large chair or throne of white marble, on which he recounted his victories in a Greek inscription. But not content with his real conquests, which reached from the Hellespont to the Euphrates, he added, like Rameses, that he had conquered Thrace, Persia, Media, and Bactria. He thus teaches us that monumental inscriptions, though read with difficulty, do not always tell the truth. This was the most southerly spot to which the kings of Egypt ever sent an army. But they kept no hold on the country. Distance had placed it not only beyond their power, but almost beyond their knowledge; and two hundred years afterwards, when the geographer Strabo was making inquiries about that part of Arabia, as it was called, he was told of this monument as set up by the hero Sesostris, to whom it was usual to give the credit of so many wonderful works.

(12) Since Cœle-Syria and Judæa were by the first Ptolemy made a province of Egypt, the Jews had lived in unbroken tranquillity, and with very little loss of freedom. The kings of Egypt had allowed them to govern themselves, to live under their own laws, and choose their own high-priest; but they required of them the payment to Alexandria of a yearly tribute. Part of this was the sacred poll-tax of half a shekel, or about eight-pence for every male above the age of twenty, which by the Mosaic law they had previously paid for the service of the Temple. This is called in the Gospels the Didrachms; though the Alexandrian translators of the Bible, altering the sum, either through mistake or on purpose, have made it in the Greek Pentateuch only half a didrachm, or about fourpence. This yearly tribute from the Temple the high-priest of Jerusalem had been usually allowed to collect and farm; but in the latter end of this reign, the high-priest Onias, a weak and covetous old man, refused to send to Alexandria the twenty talents, or three thousand pounds, at which it was then valued. When Euergetes sent Athenion as ambassador to claim it, and even threatened to send a body of troops to fetch it, still the tribute was not paid; notwithstanding the fright of the Jews, the priest would not part with his money.

Exodus, ch. xxx. 13.

Matt. xvii. 24.

Josephus, Antiq. xii. 3.

(13) On this, Joseph, the nephew of Onias, set out for Egypt, to try and turn away the king's anger. He went to Memphis, and met Euergetes riding in his chariot with the queen and Athenion, the ambassador. The king, when he knew him, begged him to get into the chariot and sit with him; and Joseph made himself so agreeable that he was lodged in the palace at Memphis, and dined every day at the royal table. While he was at Memphis the revenues of the provinces for the coming year were put up to auction; and the farmers bid eight thousand talents, or one million two hundred thousand pounds, for the taxes of Cœle-Syria, Phenicia, and Samaria. Joseph then bid double that sum, and when he was asked what security he could give, he play-fully said that he was sure that Euergetes and the queen would willingly become bound for his honesty; and the king

was so much pleased with him, that the office was at once given to him, and he held it for twenty-two years.

(14) Euergetes did not forget his allies in Greece, but continued the yearly payment to Aratus, the general of the Achaian league, to support a power which held the Macedonians in check; and when the Spartans under Cleomenes tried to overthrow the power of the Achaians, Euergetes would not help them. He naturally thought that they wished to throw off their dependence on Alexandria, and he might perhaps have had the wisdom to see that if the Grecian states quarrelled among themselves they could no longer withstand the armies of Macedonia. But Cleomenes, while struggling to raise his little kingdom to its former rank among the states of Greece, was not so unwise as to break the Egyptian treaty, and to throw himself into the power of his more dangerous neighbour, Antigonus, king of Macedonia; and, when Antigonus marched upon the Peloponnesus, Cleomenes routed his army at the isthmus of Corinth. Antigonus, however, afterwards passed the isthmus, and beat the Spartans before the walls of Argos. Cleomenes then sent to Egypt for help in money; but the distrust felt by Euergetes was not yet removed, and the money was not granted till he had sent his mother and children to Alexandria, as hostages for his good faith. With the gold of Egypt he raised an army of twenty thousand men; but he was soon afterwards beaten at Sellasia by Antigonus with thirty thousand; and the whole of the Peloponnesus, weakened by the jealousy of its states, then fell under the power of the Macedonians. Upon this defeat, Cleomenes sailed for Alexandria, and there he was kindly received by Euergetes, who then saw how mistaken he had been in distrusting this brave Spartan; and the king gave him twenty-four talents, or four thousand pounds a year for his maintenance in Egypt, till he should be sent back to Greece with a fleet and army to regain his throne.

Plutarch. Cleomenes.

(15) Among the men of letters who at this time taught in the Alexandrian schools was Aristophanes, the grammarian, who afterwards held the office of head of the Museum. At one of the public sittings, at which the king was to hear the poems and other writings of the pupils read, and, by the help of seven men of letters who sat

Suidas.
Vitruvius, lib. vii. praef.

with him as judges, was to give away honours and rewards to the best authors, one of the chairs was empty, one of the judges happened not to be there. The king asked who should be called up to fill his place; and, after thinking over the matter, the six judges fixed upon Aristophanes, who had made himself known to them by being seen daily studying in the public library. When the reading was over, the king, the public, and the six other judges, were agreed upon which was the best piece of writing; but Aristophanes was bold enough to think otherwise, and he was able, by means of his great reading, to find the book in the library from which the pupil had copied the greater part of his work. The king was much struck with this proof of his learning, and soon afterwards made him keeper of the library which he had already so well used. Aristophanes followed Zenodotus in his critical efforts to mend the text of Homer's poems. He also invented the several marks by which grammarians now distinguish the length and tone of a syllable and the breathing of a vowel, Arcadius, ap. Villoison Epist. Vinarienses. that is, the marks for long and short, and the accents and aspirate. The last two, after his time, were always placed over Greek words, and are still used in printed books; the marks for long and short syllables are only used in works of prosody.

(16) Eratosthenes of Cyrene, the inventor of astronomical geography, was at this time at the head of the mathematical school. He was the first who fixed the place of a city upon the earth by the help of astronomy, or by means of its latitude, which he learned from the length of the sun's shadow at noon on the equinoctial days (see Fig. 238). This observation he named the Theory of Shadows. Nor was that all; for nothing is denied to well-directed labour. By his Theory of Shadows he learned that the earth is Pliny, lib. vi. 34. Cleomedes De Mundo. Strabo, lib. i. a ball, and his next aim was to determine its size. He knew that at noon on the longest day the sun throws no shadow at Syene. He had learned by measurement that Syene was due south of Alexandria, and at a distance of five thousand *stadia*. He therefore measured the sun's shadow at noon on the longest day in his own study in Alexandria, and thus found that if a circle were drawn round the world, these two cities

were distant by a fiftieth part of that circle (see Fig. 239). This gave him the measure of the earth's circumference. Had a traveller from Alexandria, through Ethiopia, through Meroë, passing by the unknown sources of the Nile, been able to cross the unheard-of lands and seas beyond, and thence to come round by the equally unknown north, through the Hyperborean nations, the Euxine Sea, and Rhodes again to Alexandria, Eratosthenes would have told him that he had travelled over fifty times five thousand *stadia*. With this knowledge, he lessened the mistakes in maps, which, before his time, had been drawn without any help from astronomy, and in which the distances in miles had been mostly laid down by days' journeys or by measuring along the crooked roads. By these great strides of science he justly earned the name of Surveyor of the World.

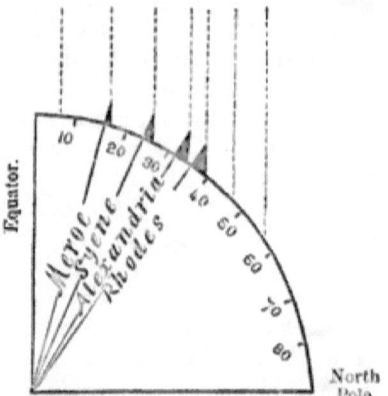

Fig. 238.—Latitude measured on the equinoctial day.

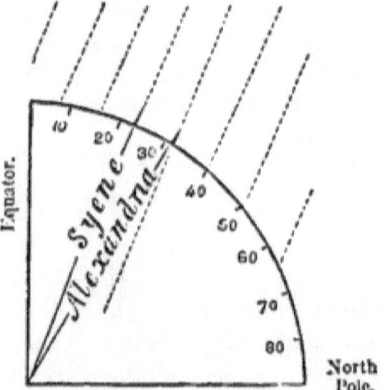

Fig. 239.—The Earth measured on the longest day.

Ptolemy, lib. i.

By measuring the sun's shadow, at the same place, on the longest and on the shortest day in the year, he learned the obliquity of the ecliptic, which he fixed at more than 23° 50', and less than 23° 52' 30". But in pure mathematics he did not rank so high. Hipparchus said of him that he wrote mathematically about geography and geographically about mathematics; indeed, Hipparchus in his Commentaries on the Geography of Eratosthenes, in many

Strabo, lib. i.

places defended the old maps against his too bold changes. Eratosthenes was a man of such unbounded knowledge, and so nearly at the head of every branch of learning, that, as in philosophy he was called a *second* Plato, and was spoken of in the same way in many other sciences, he was jokingly called Beta, or *Number Two*.

(17) As a poet, Eratosthenes, like the rest of the Alexandrian school, was critically and coldly correct; Longinus considers his little poem of Erigone faultless, but equally free from high excellence. His longest work now remaining is a description of the constellations. He also wrote a history of Egypt, to correct the errors, or to explain the omissions of Manetho; but as he could not, like Manetho, read the sculptured records for himself, when they disagree we must prefer the authority of the native historian. But nevertheless the small remains of his history are of some use to us; for, while Manetho's lists only give us the separate dynasties of the several cities, without saying which king reigned over all Egypt and which was under the sceptre of another, Eratosthenes means to give us a straightforward list of the kings of Thebes only.

Sect. xxxiii.

(18) But what most strikes us with wonder and regret is, that these two writers, Manetho, an Egyptian priest who wrote in Greek, Eratosthenes, a Greek who understood something of Egyptian, neither of them took the trouble to lay open to their readers the peculiarities of the hieroglyphics. Through all these reigns, the titles and praises of the Ptolemies were carved upon the temples in the sacred characters. These two histories were translated from the same inscriptions. We even now read the names of the kings which they mention carved on the statues and temples; and yet the language of the hieroglyphics still remained unknown beyond the class of priests; such was the want of curiosity on the part of the Greek grammarians of Alexandria. Such we may add was their want of respect for the philosophy of the Egyptians; and we need no stronger proof that the philosophers of the Museum had hitherto borrowed none of the doctrines of the priests, though we shall find them freely adopted after the rise of Christianity.

(19) Lycon of Troas was another settler in Alexandria.

He followed Strato, whom we have before spoken of, as the head of one of the schools in the Museum. He was very successful in bringing up the young men, who needed, he used to say, modesty and the love of praise, as a horse needs bridle and spur. His eloquence was so pleasing that he was wittily called Glycon, or *the sweet*.

<small>Diogenes Laertius.</small>

(20) Carneades of Cyrene at the same time held a high place among philosophers; but as he had removed to Athens, where he was at the head of a school, and was even sent to Rome as the ambassador of the Athenians, we must not claim the whole honour of him for the Ptolemies under whom he was born. It is therefore enough to say of him that, though a follower of Plato, he made such changes in the opinions of the Academy, by not wholly throwing off the evidence of the senses, that his school was called the New Academy.

<small>Cicero, Acad. iv. 45. B.C. 222.</small>

(21) Apollonius, who was born at Alexandria, but is commonly called Apollonius Rhodius, because he passed many years of his life at Rhodes, had been, like Eratosthenes, a hearer of Callimachus. His only work which we now know is his Argonautics, a poem on the voyage of Jason to Colchis in search of the golden fleece. It is a regular epic poem, in imitation of Homer; and, like other imitations, it wants the interest which hangs upon the reality of manners and story in the Iliad. Aristophanes and his pupil Aristarchus, the great critics of the day, with whose judgment few dared to disagree, and who had perhaps quarrelled with the poet, declared that it was not poetry; and after that, the most that Quintilian would say for it was that it ought not to be overlooked, and that it never falls below mediocrity. It is not wanting in graceful expressions and well-turned sentences, but it possesses no depth of feeling or happy boldness of thought, and Longinus dismisses it with the cold praise of being free from fault.

<small>Suidas.</small>

<small>Quintilian, lib. x. 1.</small>

(22) His master Callimachus showed his dislike of his young rival by hurling against him a reproachful poem, in which he speaks of him under the name of an Ibis. This is now lost, but it was copied by Ovid in his poem of the same name; and from the Roman

<small>Suidas. Callimachus.</small>

we can gather something of the dark and learned style in which Callimachus threw out his biting reproaches. We do not know from what this quarrel arose, but it seems to have been the cause of Apollonius leaving Alexandria. He removed to Rhodes, where he taught in the schools during all the reign of Philopator, till he was recalled by Epiphanes, and made librarian of the Museum in his old age, on the death of Eratosthenes.

(23) Lycophron, the tragic writer, lived about this time at Alexandria, and was one of the seven men of letters sometimes called the Alexandrian Pleiades, though writers are not agreed upon the names which fill up the list. His tragedies are all lost, and the only work of his which we now have is the dark and muddy poem of Aleandra, or Cassandra, of which the lines most striking to the historian are those in which the prophetess foretells the coming greatness of Rome; "that the children of Æneas will raise the crown upon their spears, and seize the sceptres of sea and land." Lycophron was the friend of Menedemus and Aratus; and it is not easy to believe that these lines were written before the overthrow of Hannibal in Italy, and of the Greek phalanx at Cynocephalæ, or that one who was a man in the reign of Philadelphus should have foreseen the triumph of the Roman arms. These words may have been a later addition to the poem, to improve the prophecy. Suidas.
Line 1227.
Diogenes Laertius.

(24) Conon, one of the greatest of the Alexandrian astronomers, has left no writings for us to judge of his merits by, though they were thought highly of, and made great use of, by his successors. He worked both as an observer and an inquirer, mapping out the heavens by his observations, and collecting the accounts of the eclipses which had been before observed in Egypt. He was the friend of Archimedes of Syracuse, to whom he sent his problems, and from whom he received that great geometrician's writings in return. Seneca, Quæst. vii. 3.
Archimedes, passim.

(25) Apollonius of Perga came to Alexandria in this reign, to study mathematics under the pupils of Euclid. He is well known for his work on conic sections, or the several curves which are made by cutting a cone; and he may be called the founder of this study. The Greek mathematicians sought after knowledge for its own sake, and, unlike ourselves,

followed up those branches of their studies which, like conic sections, led to no end that could in the narrow sense be called useful, with the same zeal that they did other branches out of which sprung the great practical truths of mechanics, astronomy, and geography. They found reward enough in the enlargement of their minds and in the beauty of the truth learnt. Alexandrian science gained in loftiness of tone what its poetry and philosophy wanted. Thus the properties of the ellipse, the hyperbola, and the parabola, continued to be studied by after mathematicians; but no use was made of this knowledge till nearly two thousand years later, when Kepler crowned the labours of Apollonius with the great discovery that the paths of the planets round the sun were conic sections. The Egyptians, however, made great use of mathematical knowledge, particularly in the irrigation of their fields; and Archimedes of Syracuse, who came to Alexandria about this time to study under Conon, did the country a real service by his invention of the *cochlea*, or screw-pump. The more distant fields of the valley of the Nile, rising above the level of the inundation, have to be watered artificially by pumping out of the canals into ditches at a higher level. For this work Archimedes proposed a spiral tube, twisting round an axis, which was to be put in motion either by the hand or by the force of the stream out of which it was to pump; and this was found so convenient that it soon became the machine most in use throughout Egypt for irrigation.

<small>Archimedes. Quadr. Parab.</small>

<small>Diod. Sic. lib. v. 37, and l. 34.</small>

(26) But while we are dazzled by the brilliancy of these clusters of men of letters and science who graced the court of Alexandria, we must not shut our eyes to those faults which are always found in works called forth rather by the fostering warmth of royal pensions than by a love of knowledge in the people. The well-fed and well-paid philosophers of the Museum were not likely to overtake the mighty men of Athens in its best days, who had studied and taught without any pension from the government, without taking any fee from their pupils; who were urged forward towards excellence by the love of knowledge and of honour; who had no other aim than that of being useful to their hearers, and looked for no reward beyond their love and esteem.

(27) Books may, if we please, be divided into works of

industry and works of taste. Among the first we may place mathematics, criticism, and compilations; among the second we ought to find poetry and oratory. Works of industry and care may be found in many ages and in many countries; they may even be written at the command of a sovereign; but those which have gained the praise of all mankind for their pure taste and richness of thought seem to have ripened only on those spots and in those times at which the mind of man, from causes perhaps too deep for our search, has been able to burst forth with more than usual strength. When we review the writings of the Alexandrian authors we are forced to acknowledge that they are most of them of the former class; we may say of them all, what Ovid said of Callimachus, that they are more to be admired for their Amor. i. xv. industry and art than for their taste and genius; most of the poets are forgotten, while we even now look back to Alexandria as the cradle of geometry, geography, astronomy, anatomy, and criticism.

(28) In oratory Alexandria made no attempts whatever; it is a branch of literature not likely to flourish under a despotic monarchy. In Athens it fell with the loss of liberty, and Demetrius Phalereus was the last of the real Athenian orators. After his time the orations were declamations written carefully in the study, and coldly spoken in the school for the instruction of the pupils, and wholly wanting in fire and genius; and the Alexandrian men of letters forbore to copy Greece in its lifeless harangues. For the same reasons the Alexandrians were not successful in history. A species of writing, which a despot requires to be false and flattering, is little likely to flourish; and hence the only historians of the Museum were chronologists, antiquaries, and writers of travels. Those sciences which give to man a command over matter have usually flourished when called for by the wants of trade, wealth, or luxury; but writings of which the aim is to lead men to what is good by showing them that it is within their reach, to keep them from what is low by making them think highly of what they might be, writings which enchain the reader and give one man a power over the minds of others, can have no place among those who feel themselves already crushed beneath the more real chains of military power.

(29) The coins of Euergetes bear the name of "*Ptolemy the king*," round the head on the one side, with no title by which they can be known from the other kings of the same name (see Fig. 240). But his portrait is known from his Phenician coins. In the same way the

Visconti, Icon. Grec.

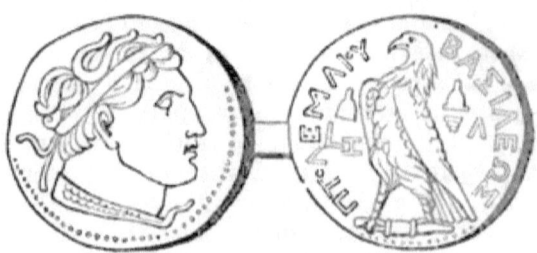

Fig. 240.

coins of his queen have only the name of "*Berenice the queen*" (see Fig. 241), but they are known from those of the later queens by the beauty of the workmanship, which soon fell far below that of the first Ptolemies.

Fig. 241.

(30) Euergetes had married his cousin Berenice, who, like the other queens of Egypt, is sometimes called Cleopatra; by her he left two sons, Ptolemy and Magas, to the eldest of whom he left his kingdom, after a reign of twenty-five years of unclouded prosperity. Egypt was during this reign at the very height of its power and wealth. It had seen three kings, who, though not equally great men, not equally fit to found a monarchy or to raise the literature of a people, were equally successful in the parts which they had undertaken. Euergetes left to his son a

Porphyrius, ap. Scalig.

kingdom perhaps as large as the world had ever seen under one sceptre; and though many of his boasted victories were like letters written in the sand, of which the traces were soon lost, yet he was by far the greatest monarch of his day. We may be sure that in these prosperous reigns life and property were safe, and justice was administered fairly by judges who were independent of the crown; as even centuries afterwards we find that it was part of a judge's oath on taking office, that, if he were ordered by the king to do what was wrong, he would not obey him. But here the bright pages in the history of the Ptolemies end. Though trade and agriculture still enriched the country, though arts and letters did not quit Alexandria, we have from this time forward to mark the growth of only vice and luxury, and to measure the wisdom of Ptolemy Soter by the length of time that his laws and institutions were able to bear up against the misrule and folly of his descendants. Plutarchi Apophtheg- mata.

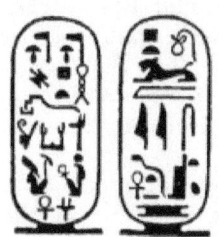

Fig. 242.

(31) PTOLEMY (see Fig. 242), the eldest son of Euergetes, inherited the crown of his forefathers, but none of the great qualities by which they had won and guarded it. He was then about thirty-four years old. His first act was to call together his council, and to ask their advice about putting to death his mother Berenice and his brother Magas. Their crime was the being too much liked by the army; and the council was called upon to say whether it would be safe to have them killed. Cleomenes, the banished king of Sparta, who was one of the council, alone raised his voice against their murder, and wisely said that the throne would be still safer if there were more brothers to stand between the king and the daring hopes of a traitor. The minister Sosibius, on the other hand, said that the mercenaries could not be trusted while Magas was alive; but Cleomenes remarked to him, that more than three thousand of them were Peloponnesians, and that they would follow him sooner than they would Magas. Berenice and Magas were, however, put to death; but the speech of Cleomenes was not forgotten. If his popularity with the Plutarch. Cleomenes. Polybius, lib. v. B.C. 221.

mercenaries could secure their allegiance, he could, when he chose, make them rebel; from that time he was treated rather as a prisoner than as a friend, and he lost all chance of being helped to regain his kingdom.

(32) Nothing is known of the death of Euergetes, the late king, and there is no proof that it was by unfair means. But when his son began a cruel and wicked reign by putting to death his mother and brother, and by taking the name of Philopator, or *father-loving*, the world seems to have thought that he was the murderer of his father, and had taken this name to throw a cloak over the deed.

(33) The task of the historian would be more agreeable if he always had to point out how crime and goodness were followed by their just rewards; but unfortunately history is not free from acts of successful wickedness. By this murder of his brother, and by the minority both of Antiochus, king of Syria, and of Philip, king of Macedonia, Philopator found himself safe from enemies either at home or abroad, and he gave himself up to a life of thoughtlessness and pleasure. The army and fleet were left to go to ruin, and the foreign provinces, which had hitherto been looked upon as the bulwarks of Egypt, were only half guarded; but the throne rested on the virtues of his forefathers, and it was not till his death that it was found to have been undermined by his own vices.

(34) Egypt had been governed by kings of more than usual wisdom for above one hundred years, and was at the very height of its power when Philopator came to the throne. He found himself master of Ethiopia, Cyrene, Phenicia, Cœle-Syria, part of Upper Syria, Cyprus, Rhodes, the cities along the coast of Asia Minor from Pamphylia to Lysimachia, and the cities of Ænos and Maronea in Thrace. The unwilling obedience of distant provinces usually costs more than it is worth; but many of these possessions across the Mediterranean had put themselves willingly into the power of his predecessors for the sake of their protection, and they cost little more than a message to warn off invaders. Egypt was the greatest naval power in the world, having the command of the sea and the whole of the coast at the eastern end of the Mediterranean. But on the death of Euergetes the happiness of the people came to an

Polybius, lib. v.

end. In a despotic monarchy, where so much rests upon the good qualities of the king, we can hardly hope to find a longer course of good government than we have seen at Alexandria. The flatterers and pleasures which are brought to the court by the greatness and wealth of each king in his turn must at last poison the heart and turn the head of a son; and thus it was with Philopator.

(35) The first trouble which arose from his loose and vicious habits was an attempt made upon his life by Cleomenes, who found the palace in Alexandria had now become a prison. The Spartan took advantage of the king's being at Canopus to escape from his guards, and to raise a riot in Alexandria; but not being able to gain the citadel, and seeing that disgrace and death must follow upon the failure of this mad undertaking, he stabbed himself with his own dagger.

(36) The kingdom of Syria, after being humbled by Ptolemy Euergetes, had risen lately under the able rule of Antiochus, son of Seleucus Callinicus. His energy and courage soon recovered from Egypt the provinces that Syria had before lost, and afterwards gained for him the name of Antiochus the Great. He made himself master of the city of Damascus by a stratagem. When encamped near this place he invited the neighbouring chiefs to a sumptuous entertainment, which threw off his guard Dinon, the general who held the city for Ptolemy. The danger of an attack did not seem very threatening while the king was feasting with his friends. But while the guests were eating and drinking, the troops were getting under arms; and the young Antiochus left the supper to storm the walls of Damascus. He carried the place that night by assault. Polyænus, Stratagem. lib. iv. 15.

(37) Soon after this, Seleucia, the capital, on the Orontes, twelve miles from Antioch, which had been taken by Euergetes, was retaken by Antiochus, or rather given up to him by the treachery of the garrison. Polybius, lib. v.
Theodotus also, the Alexandrian governor of Cœle-Syria, delivered up to him that province; and Antiochus marched southward, and had taken Tyre and Ptolemais before the Egyptian army could be brought into the field. There he gained forty ships of war, of which twenty were decked

vessels with four banks of oars, and the others smaller. He then marched towards Egypt, and on his way learned that Ptolemy was at Memphis. On his arrival at Pelusium he found that the place was strongly guarded, and that the garrison had opened the flood-gates from the neighbouring lake, and thereby spoiled the fresh water of all the neighbourhood; he therefore did not lay siege to that city, but seized many of the open towns on the east side of the Nile.

(38) On this, Philopator roused himself from his idleness, and got together his forces against the coming danger. He had a royal guard of three thousand men under Eurylochus of Magnesia; two thousand peltastæ under Socrates of Bœotia; the phalanx of twenty-five thousand men under Andromachus and Ptolemy, the son of Thaseas; eight thousand mercenaries under Phoxidas; the horse of the royal guard, the African horse, and the Egyptian horse, in all three thousand men, under Polycrates; the Greek and foreign horse, who were two thousand highly disciplined men, under Echecrates of Thessaly; three thousand Cretans under Cnopias of Alorus; three thousand Africans, armed like Macedonians, under Ammonius of Barce; the Egyptian phalanx of twenty thousand men under Sosibius the king's chief adviser; and lastly, four thousand Gauls and Thracians under Dionysius of Thrace. There were in all seventy-three thousand men and seventy-three elephants, or one elephant to every thousand men, which was the number usually allowed to the armies about this time. But before this army reached Pelusium, Antiochus had led back his forces to winter in Seleucia.

(39) The next spring Antiochus again marched towards Egypt with an army of seventy-two thousand foot, six thousand horse, and one hundred and two elephants. Philopator led his whole forces to the frontier to oppose his march, and met the Syrian army near the village of Raphia, a hundred miles to the east of Pelusium, the border town between Egypt and Palestine. Arsinoë, his queen and sister, rode with him on horseback through the ranks, and called upon the soldiers to fight for their wives and children. At first the Egyptians seemed in danger of being beaten. As the armies approached one another the Ethiopian elephants

trembled at the very smell of the Indian elephants, and shrunk from engaging with beasts so much larger than themselves. On the charge the left wing of each army was routed, as was often the case among the Greeks, when, from too great a trust in the shield, every soldier kept moving to the right, and thus left the left wing uncovered. But before the end of the day the invading army was defeated; and though some of the Egyptian officers treacherously left their posts, and carried their troops over to Antiochus, yet the Syrian army was wholly routed, and Arsinoë enjoyed the knowledge and the praise of having been the chief cause of her husband's success. The king in gratitude sacrificed to the gods the unusual offering of four elephants. Plutarch. Solert. Animal.

(40) By this victory Philopator regained Cœle-Syria, and there he spent three months; he then made a hasty, and, if we judge his reasons rightly, we must add, a disgraceful treaty with the enemy, that he might the sooner get back to his life of ease. The slothful Maccabees, lib. iii. vices of the king saved the nation from the evils of war. Before going home he passed through Jerusalem, where he gave thanks and sacrificed to God in the Temple of the Jews; and, being struck with the beauty of the building, asked to be shown into the inner room, in which were kept the ark of the covenant, Aaron's rod that budded, and the golden pot of manna, with the tables of the covenant. The priests told him of their law, by which every stranger, every Jew, and every priest but the high priest, was forbidden to pass beyond the second veil; but Philopator roughly answered that he was not bound by the Jewish laws, and ordered them to lead him into the holy of holies. The city was thrown into alarm by this unheard-of wickedness; the streets were filled with men and women in despair; the air was rent with shrieks and cries, and the priests prayed to Jehovah to guard His own temple from the stain. The king's mind, however, was not to be changed; the refusal of the priests only strengthened his wish, and all struggle was useless while the court of the Temple was filled with Greek soldiers. But the prayer of the priests was heard; the king, says the Jewish historian, fell to the ground in a fit, like a reed broken by the wind, and was carried out speechless by his friends and generals.

(41) On his return to Egypt, he showed his hatred of the nation by his treatment of the Jews in Alexandria. He made a law, that they should lose the rank of Macedonians, and be enrolled among the class of Egyptians. He ordered them to have their bodies marked with pricks, in the form of an ivy-leaf, in honour of Bacchus; and those who refused to have this done were outlawed, or forbidden to enter the courts of justice. The king himself had an ivy-leaf marked with pricks upon his forehead, from which he received the nickname of Gallus. This custom of marking the body had been forbidden in the Levitical law; it was not known among the Copts, but must always have been in use among the Lower Egyptians. It was used by the Arab prisoners of Rameses, and is used by the Egyptian Arabs of the present day.

<small>Etymologicon Magnum.</small>
<small>Levit. xix. 28.</small>
<small>Lane's Egypt.</small>

(42) He ordered the Jews to sacrifice on the pagan altars, and many of them were sent up to Alexandria to be punished for rebelling against his decree. Their resolution, however, or, as their historian asserts, a miracle from heaven, changed the king's mind. They expected to be trampled to death in the hippodrome by furious elephants; but after some delay they were released unhurt. The history of their escape, however, is more melancholy than the history of their danger. We read with painful interest, not without some satisfaction, the account of brave men suffering for conscience sake. But when these persecuted Jews become persecutors in their turn, our feelings towards them are wholly changed. No sooner did the persecution cease than they turned with pharisaical cruelty against their weaker brethren who had yielded to the storm; and they put to death three hundred of their countrymen, who in the hour of danger had yielded to the threats of punishment, and complied with the idolatrous ceremonies required of them.

<small>Maccabees, lib. iii.</small>

(43) The Egyptians, who, when the Persians were conquered by Alexander, could neither help nor hinder the Greek army, and who, when they formed part of the troops under the first Ptolemy, were uncounted and unvalued, had by this time been armed and disciplined like Greeks; and in the battle of Raphia the Egyptian phalanx had shown

itself not an unworthy rival of the Macedonians. By this
success in war, and by their hatred of their vicious
and cruel king, the Egyptians were now for the <small>Polybius, lib. v.</small>
first time encouraged to take arms against the
Greek government. The Egyptian phalanx murmured
against their Greek officers, and claimed their right to be
under an Egyptian general. But history has told us nothing
more of the rebellion than that it was successfully put down;
much as the Greeks were lowered in warlike courage by the
wealth and luxury of Egypt, much as the Egyptians were
raised by the Macedonian arms, the Greeks were still by far
the better soldiers.

(44) The ships built by Philopator do not raise his navy
in our opinion, for they were more remarkable for their huge
unwieldy size, their luxurious and costly furniture, than for
their fitness for war. One was four hundred and
twenty feet long and fifty-seven feet wide, with forty <small>Athenaeus, lib. v. 8.</small>
banks of oars. The longest oars were fifty-seven
feet long, and weighted with lead at the handles that they
might be the more easily moved. This huge ship was to be
rowed by four thousand rowers, its sails were to be shifted
by four hundred sailors, and three thousand soldiers were to
stand in ranks upon deck. There were seven beaks in front,
by which it was to strike and sink the ships of the enemy.
The royal barge in which the king and court moved on the
quiet waters of the Nile, was nearly as large as this ship of
war. It was three hundred and thirty feet long, and forty-
five feet wide; it was fitted up with state rooms and private
rooms, and was nearly sixty feet high to the top of
the royal awning. A third ship, which even sur- <small>Lib. v. 10.</small>
passed these in its fittings and ornaments, was given to
Philopator by Hiero, king of Syracuse. It was built under
the care of Archimedes, and its timbers would have made
sixty triremes. Beside baths, and rooms for pleasures of all
kinds, it had a library, and astronomical instruments, not
only for navigation, as in modern ships, but for study, as in
an observatory. It was a ship of war, and had eight towers,
from each of which stones were to be thrown at the enemy by
six men. Its machines, like modern cannons, could throw
stones of three hundred pounds weight, and arrows of eighteen
feet in length. It had four anchors of wood, and eight of

iron. It was called the ship of Syracuse, but after it had been given to Philopator it was known by the name of the ship of Alexandria.

(45) In the second year of Philopator's reign the Romans began that long and doubtful war with Hannibal, called the second Punic war, and in the twelfth year of this reign they sent ambassadors to renew their treaty of peace with Egypt. They sent as their gifts robes of purple for Philopator and Arsinoë, and for Philopator a chair of ivory and gold, which was the usual gift of the republic to friendly kings. The Alexandrians kept upon good terms both with the Romans and the Carthaginians during the whole of the Punic wars.

<small>Livy, lib. xxvii. 4.</small>
<small>B.C. 210.</small>

(46) When the city of Rhodes, which had long been joined in close friendship with Egypt, was shaken by an earthquake that threw down the colossal statue of Apollo, together with a large part of the city walls and docks, Philopator was not behind the other friendly kings and states in his gifts and help. He sent to his brave allies a large sum of silver and copper, with corn, timber, and hemp.

<small>Polybius, lib. v.</small>

(47) On the birth of his son and heir, ambassadors crowded to Alexandria with gifts and messages of joy. But they were all thrown into the shade by Hyrcanus, the son of Joseph, who was sent from Jerusalem by his father, and who brought to the king one hundred boys and one hundred girls, each carrying a talent of silver.

<small>Josephus, Ant. xii. 4.</small>
<small>B.C. 209.</small>

(48) Philopator soon after the birth of this his only child, employed Philammon, at the bidding of his mistress, to put to death his queen and sister Arsinoë, or Eurydice, as she is sometimes called. He had already forgotten his rank and his name, ennobled by the virtues of three generations, and had given up his days and nights to vice and riot. He kept in his pay several fools or laughing-stocks, as they were then called, who were the chosen companions of his meals; and he was the first who brought eunuchs into the court of Alexandria. His mistress Agathoclea, her brother Agathocles, and their mother Œnanthe, held him bound by those chains which clever, worthless, and selfish favourites throw around the mind of a weak and debauched

<small>Justinus, lib. xxx. 1.</small>
<small>Athenæus, lib. vi. 12.</small>
<small>Justinus, lib. xxx. 1.</small>

king. Agathocles, who never left his side, was his adviser in matters of business or pleasure, and governed alike the army, the courts of justice, and the women. Thus was spent a reign of seventeen years, during which the king had never but once, when he met Antiochus in battle, roused himself from his life of sloth.

(49) The misconduct and vices of Agathocles raised such an outcry against him, that Philopator, without giving up the pleasure of his favourite's company, was forced to take away from him the charge of receiving the taxes. Polybius, De Virtut. xv. That high post was then given to Tlepolemus, a young man, whose strength of body and warlike courage had made him the darling of the soldiers. Another charge given to Tlepolemus was that of watching over the supply and price of corn Polybius, lib. xv. in Alexandria. The wisest statesmen of old thought it part of a king's duty to take care that the people were fed, and seem never to have found out that it would be better done if the people were left to take care of themselves. They thought it moreover a piece of wise policy, or at any rate of clever king-craft, to keep down the price of food in the capital at the cost of the rest of the kingdom, and even sometimes to give a monthly fixed measure of corn to each citizen. By such means as these the crowd of poor and restless citizens who swell the mob of every capital, was larger in Alexandria than it otherwise would have been; and the danger of riot, which it was meant to lessen, was every year increased.

(50) Sosibius had made himself more hated than Agathocles; he had been the king's ready tool in all his murders. He had been stained, or at least reproached, with the murder of Lysimachus, the son De Virtut. xv. of Philadelphus; then of Magas, the son of Euergetes, and Berenice, the widow of Euergetes; of Cleomenes, the Spartan; and lastly, of Arsinoë, the wife of Philopator. For these crimes Sosibius was forced by the soldiers to give up to Tlepolemus the king's ring, or what in De Virtut. xvi. modern language would be called the great seal of the kingdom, the badge of office by which Egypt was governed; but the world soon saw that a body of luxurious mercenaries were as little able to choose a wise statesman as the king had been.

(51) With all his vices, Philopator had yet inherited the love of letters which has thrown so bright a light around the whole of the family; and to his other luxuries he sometimes added that of the society of the learned men of the Museum. When one of the professorships was empty, he wrote to Athens, and invited to Alexandria Sphærus, who had been the pupil of Zeno. One day when Sphærus was dining with the king, he said that a wise man should never guess, but only say what he knows. Philopator, wishing to tease him, ordered some waxen pomegranates to be handed to him, and when Sphærus bit one of them, he laughed at him for guessing that it was real fruit. But the Stoic answered that there are many cases in which our actions must be guided by what seems probable. None of the works of Sphærus have come down to us.

<small>Diogenes Laertius, lib. vii. 177.</small>

(52) Eratosthenes, of whom we have before spoken, was librarian of the Museum during this reign; and Ptolemy, the son of Agesarchus, then wrote his history of Alexandria, a work now lost. It was not, however, from their want of accuracy that these Alexandrian historians have been allowed to perish. None but a few scholars will turn aside from the cares and pleasures of life, from earning their livelihood, or even from the amusements of idleness, to read books written without life or feeling. Had these historians been so fortunate as to have been witnesses of a series of great and good actions, or had they been warmed with a love for their fellow-creatures, or had they had an aim after what was noble, or even had their pages contained a clear picture of the manners and customs of their times, the world would not have let them die.

<small>Suidas.</small>
<small>Athenæus, lib. x. 7.</small>

(53) The want of moral feeling in Alexandria was poorly supplied by the respect for talent. Philopator built there a shrine or temple to Homer, in which he placed a sitting figure of the poet, and round it seven worshippers, meant for the seven cities which claimed the honour of giving him birth. Had Homer himself worshipped in such temples, and had his thoughts been raised by no more lofty views, he would not have left us an Iliad or an Odyssey. In Upper Egypt there was no such want of religious earnestness; there the priests placed the name of

<small>Ælianus, V. H. xiii. 22.</small>

Philopator upon a small temple near Medinet Abou, dedicated to Amun-Ra and the goddess Athor; his name is also seen upon the temple at Karnak, and on the additions to the sculptures on the temple of Thoth at Pselcis in Ethiopia, between the first and second cataracts. Further than this the Ptolemies hardly aimed at holding the valley of the Nile southward. From this place the gold mines could be reached through the desert; and the country further south was of no value.

Wilkinson, Thebes.

Fig. 243.

(54) Some of this king's coins bear the name of "*Ptolemy Philopator*" (see Fig. 243), while those of the queen have her name, "*Arsinoë Philopator*," around the head (see Fig. 244). They are of a good style of art. He was also sometimes named Eupator; and it was under that name that the people of Paphos set up a monument to him in the temple of Venus.

Visconti, Icon. Grec. Josephus, Ant. xii. 3. Letronne, Recherches.

Fig. 244.

(55) The first three Ptolemies had been loved by their subjects and feared by their enemies; but Philopator, though his power was still acknowledged abroad, had by his vices

and cruelty made himself hated at home, and had undermined the foundations of the government. He began his reign like an eastern despot; instead of looking to his brother as a friend for help and strength, he distrusted him as a rival, and had him put to death. He employed the ministers of his vicious pleasures in the high offices of government; and, instead of philosophers and men of learning, he brought eunuchs into the palace as the companions of his son. He died worn out with disease in the seven-
<small>Porphyrius ap. Scalig.</small> teenth year of his reign and about the fifty-first of his age, leaving the fabric of the monarchy tottering with weakness; and thus in the pages of history the vices of Philopator and the wisdom of Soter teach nearly the same lesson.

(56) On the death of Philopator his son was only five years
<small>Justinus, lib. xxx. 2.</small> old. The minister Agathocles, who had ruled over the country with unbounded power, endeavoured by
<small>B.C. 204.</small> the help of his sister Agathoclea and the other mistresses of the late king to keep his death secret; so that while the women seized the money and jewels of the palace, he might have time to take such steps as would secure his own power over the kingdom. But the secret could not be long kept, and Agathocles called together the citizens of Alexandria to tell them of the death of Philopator, and to show them their young king.

(57) He went to the meeting, followed by his sister Agathoclea and the young Ptolemy,
<small>Polybius, lib. xv.</small> afterwards called Epiphanes (see Fig. 245). He began his speech, "Ye men of Macedonia," as this mixed body of Greeks and Jews was always called. He wiped his eyes with his chlamys in well-feigned grief, and showed them the new king, who had been trusted, he said, by his father to the motherly care of Agathoclea and to their loyalty. He then accused Tlepolemus of aiming at the throne, and brought forward a creature of his own to prove the truth of the charge. But his voice was soon drowned in the loud murmurs of the citizens; they had smarted too long under his tyranny, and

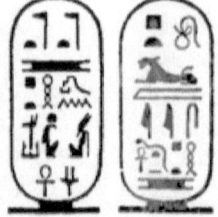

Fig. 245.

were too well acquainted with his falsehoods, to listen to anything that he could say against his rival. Besides, Tlepolemus had the charge of supplying Alexandria with corn, a duty which was more likely to gain friends than the pandering to the vices of their hated tyrant. Agathocles soon saw that his life was in danger, and he left the meeting and returned to the palace, in doubt whether he should seek for safety in flight, or boldly seize the power which he was craftily aiming at, and rid himself of his enemies by their murder.

(58) While he was wasting these precious minutes in doubt, the streets were filled with groups of men and of boys, who always formed a part of the mobs of Alexandria. They sullenly, but loudly, gave vent to their hatred of the minister; and if they had but found a leader they would have been in rebellion. In a little while the crowd moved off to the tents of the Macedonians, to learn their feelings on the matter, and then to the quarters of the mercenaries, both of which were close to the palace, and the mixed mob of armed and unarmed men soon told the fatal news, that the soldiers were as angry as the citizens. But they were still without a leader; they sent messengers to Tlepolemus, who was not in Alexandria, and he promised that he would soon be there; but perhaps he no more knew what to do than his guilty rival.

(59) Agathocles, in his doubt, did nothing; he sat down to supper with his friends, perhaps hoping that the storm might blow over of itself, perhaps trusting to chance and to the strong walls of the palace. His mother Œnanthe ran to the temple of Ceres and Proserpine, and sat down before the altar in tears, believing that the sanctuary of the temple would be her best safeguard; as if the laws of God, which had never bound her, would bind her enemies. It was a festal day, and the women in the temple, who knew nothing of the storm which had risen in the forum within these few hours, came forward to comfort her; but she answered them with curses; she knew that she was hated and would soon be despised, and she added the savage prayer, that they might have to eat their own children. The riot did not lessen at sunset. Men, women, and boys were moving through the streets all night with torches. The crowds were greatest in the stadium and in the theatre of Bacchus, but most noisy in

front of the palace. Agathocles was awakened by the noise, and in his fright ran to the bedroom of the young Ptolemy; and, distrusting the palace walls, hid himself, with his own family, the king, and two or three guards, in the underground passage which led from the palace to the theatre.

(60) The night, however, passed off without any violence; but at daybreak the murmurs became louder, and the thousands in the palace-yard called for the young king. By that time the Greek soldiers joined the mob, and then the guards within were no longer to be feared. The gates were soon burst open, and the palace searched. The mob rushed through the halls and lobbies, and learning where the king had fled, hastened to the underground passage. It was guarded by three doors of iron grating; but when the first was beaten in, Aristomenes was sent out to offer terms of surrender. Agathocles was willing to give up the young king, his misused power, his ill-gotten wealth and estates; he asked only for his life. But this was sternly refused, and a shout was raised to kill the messenger; and Aristomenes, the best of the ministers, whose only fault was the being a friend of Agathocles, and the having named his little daughter Agathoclea, would certainly have been killed upon the spot, if somebody had not reminded them that they wanted to send back an answer.

(61) Agathocles, seeing that he could hold out no longer, then gave up the little king, who was set upon a horse, and led away to the stadium amid the shouts of the crowd. There they seated him on the throne, and while he was crying at being surrounded by strange faces, the mob loudly called for revenge on the guilty ministers. Sosibius, the somatophylax, the son of the former general of that name, seeing no other way of stopping the fury of the mob and the child's sobs, asked him if the enemies of his mother and of his throne should be given up to the people. The child of course answered "yes," without understanding what was meant; and on that they let Sosibius take him to his own house to be out of the uproar. Agathocles was soon led out bound, and was stabbed by those who two days before would have felt honoured by a look from him. Agathoclea and her sister were then brought out, and lastly Œnanthe their mother was dragged away from the altar of Ceres and

Proserpine. Some bit them, some struck them with sticks, some tore their eyes out; as each fell down her body was torn to pieces, and her limbs scattered among the crowd; to such lengths of madness and angry cruelty was the Alexandrian mob sometimes driven. In the meanwhile some of the women called to mind that Philammon, who had been employed in the murder of Arsinoë, had within those three days come to Alexandria, and they made a rush at his house. The doors quickly gave way before their blows, and he was killed upon the spot by clubs and stones; his little son was strangled by these raging mothers, and his wife dragged naked into the street, and there torn to pieces. Thus died Agathocles and all his family; and the care of the young king then fell to Sosibius, the son of the late minister of that name, and to Aristomenes, who had already gained a high character for wisdom and firmness.

(62) While Egypt was thus without a government, Philip of Macedonia and Antiochus of Syria agreed to divide the foreign provinces between them; and Antiochus marched against Cœle-Syria and Phœnicia. *Justinus, lib. xxxi. 1.* The guardians of the young Ptolemy sent against him an army under Scopas, the Ætolian, who was at first successful, but was afterwards beaten by Antiochus at Paneas in the valley of the Jordan, three and twenty miles above the Lake of Tiberias, and driven back into Egypt. *Polybius, Legat. 72.* In these battles the Jews, who had not forgotten the ill-treatment that they had received from Philopator, joined Antiochus, after having been under the government of Egypt for exactly one hundred years; and in return Antiochus released Jerusalem from all taxes for three years, and afterwards from one *Josephus, Antiq. xii. 3. B.C. 202.* third of the taxes, and he sent a large sum of money for the service of the temple, and released the elders, priests, scribes, and singing men from all taxes for the future.

(63) The Alexandrian statesmen had latterly shown themselves in their foreign policy very unworthy pupils of Ptolemy Soter and Philadelphus, who had both ably trimmed the balance of power between the several successors of Alexander. But even had they been wiser, they could hardly, before the end of the second Punic war, have foreseen that the Romans would soon be their most dangerous enemies. The overthrow

of Hannibal, however, might perhaps have opened their eyes; but it was then too late; Egypt was too weak to form an alliance with Macedonia or Syria against the Romans. About this time the Romans sent ambassadors to Alexandria, to tell the king that they had conquered Hannibal, and brought to a close the second Punic war, and to thank him for the friendship of the Egyptians during that long and doubtful struggle of eighteen years, when so many of their nearer neighbours had joined the enemy. They begged that if the senate felt called upon to undertake a war against Philip, who, though no friend to the Egyptians, had not yet taken arms against them, it might cause no breach in the friendship between the king of Egypt and the Romans. In answer to this embassy, the Alexandrians, rushing to their own destruction, sent to Rome a message, which was meant to place the kingdom wholly in the hands of the senate. It was to beg them to undertake the guardianship of the young Ptolemy, and the defence of the kingdom against Philip and Antiochus during his childhood.

_{Livy, lib. xxxi. 2. B.C. 201.}

_{Justinus, lib. xxx. 2.}

(64) The Romans, in return, gave the wished-for answer; they sent ambassadors to Antiochus and Philip, to order them to make no attack upon Egypt, on pain of falling under the displeasure of the senate; and they sent Marcus Lepidus to Alexandria, to accept the offered prize, and to govern the foreign affairs of the kingdom, under the modest name of tutor to the young king. This high honour was afterwards mentioned by Lepidus, with pride, upon the coins struck when he was consul, in the eighteenth year of this reign (see Fig. 246). They have the city of

_{Eckhel, vol. v. 123.}

Fig. 246.

Alexandria on the one side, and on the other the title of "Tutor to the king," with the figure of the Roman in his

toga, putting the diadem on the head of the young Ptolemy, afterwards known by the name of PTOLEMY EPIPHANES.

(65) The haughty orders of the senate at first had very little weight with the two kings. Antiochus conquered Phenicia and Coele-Syria; and he was then met by a second message from the senate, who no longer spoke in the name of their ward, the young king of Egypt, but ordered him to give up to the Roman people the states which he had seized, and which belonged, they said, to the Romans by the right of war. On this, Antiochus made peace with Egypt by a treaty, in which he betrothed his daughter Cleopatra to the young Ptolemy, and added the disputed provinces of Phenicia and Coele-Syria as a dower, which were to be given up to Egypt when the king was old enough to be married. Justinus, lib. xxxi. 1. Hieronym. in Dan. xi. B.C. 198.

(66) Philip marched against Athens and the other states of Greece which had heretofore held themselves independent and in alliance with Egypt; and, when the Athenian embassy came to Alexandria to beg for the usual help, Ptolemy's ministers felt themselves so much in the power of the senate, that they sent to Rome to ask whether they should help their old friends the Athenians against Philip, the common enemy, or whether they should leave it to the Romans to help them. And these haughty republicans, who wished all their allies to forget the use of arms, who valued their friends not for their strength but for their obedience, sent them word that the senate did not wish them to help the Athenians, and that the Roman people would take care of their own allies. Livy, lib. xxxi. 9.

(67) If we now look back for two centuries, to the time when Egypt fought its battles against the Persians and guarded its coasts by the help of Greek arms, we remark that from that time it sunk till it became a province of Macedonia; and we cannot fail to see that the Greek kingdom of Egypt was in its turn at this time falling by the same steps by which it had then risen, and that it was already in reality, though not yet in name, a Roman province. But while, during this second fall, the Alexandrians looked upon the proud but unlettered Romans only as friends, as allies, who asked for no pay, who took no reward, who fought only for

ambition and for the glory of their country, we cannot but remark, and with sorrow for the cause of arts and letters, that in their former fall the Egyptians had only seen the elegant and learned Greeks in the light of mean hirelings who looked only for their pay, and who fought with equal pleasure on either side, with little thought about the justice of the cause, or their country's greatness. The Roman soldier would have been shocked at hearing the cry for quarter in his mother tongue; but the Spartan and the Athenian were used to it. Many are the virtues which the Romans gained with their strict feelings of clanship or pride of country, and which the Greeks lost, after the time of Alexander, by becoming philosophic citizens of the world.

(68) Soon after this, the battle of Cynocephalæ in Thessaly was fought between Philip and the Romans, in which the Romans lost only seven hundred men, while as many as eight thousand Macedonians were left dead upon the field. This battle, though only between Rome and Macedonia, must not be passed unnoticed in the history of Egypt, where the troops were armed and disciplined like Macedonians, as it was the first time that the world had seen the Macedonian phalanx routed and in flight before any troops not so armed.

<small>Polybius, lib. xvii. B.C. 197.</small>

(69) The phalanx was a body of spearsmen, in such close array that each man filled a space of only one square yard. The spear was seven yards long, and, when held in both hands, its point was five yards in front of the soldier's breast. There were sixteen ranks of these men, and when the first five ranks lowered their spears the point of the fifth spear was one yard in front of the foremost rank. The Romans, on the other hand, fought in open ranks, with one yard between each, or each man filled a space of four square yards, and in a charge would have to meet ten Macedonian spears. But then the Roman soldiers went into battle with much higher feelings than those of the Greeks. In Rome, arms were trusted only to the citizens, to those who had a country to love, a home to guard, and who had some share in making the laws which they were called upon to obey. But the Greek armies of Macedonia, Egypt, and Syria, were made up either of natives who bowed their necks in slavery, or of

mercenaries who made war their trade and rioted in its lawlessness, both of whom felt that they had little to gain from victory, and nothing to lose by a change of masters. Moreover, the warlike skill of the Romans was far greater than any that had yet been brought against the Greeks. It had lately been improved in their wars with Hannibal, the great master of that science. They saw that the phalanx could use its whole strength only on a plain; that a wood, a bog, a hill, or a river, were difficulties which this close body of men could not always overcome. A charge or a retreat equally lessened its force; the phalanx was meant to stand the charge of others. The Romans, therefore, chose their own time and their own ground; they loosened their ranks and widened their front, avoided the charge, and attacked the Greeks at the side and in the rear; and the fatal discovery was at last made, that the Macedonian phalanx was not unconquerable, and that closed ranks were only strong against barbarians. This news must have been heard by every statesman of Egypt and the East with alarm; the Romans were now their equals, and were soon to be their masters.

(70) But to return to Egypt. It was, as we have seen, a country governed by men of a foreign race. Neither the poor who tilled the land, nor the rich who owned the estates, had any share in the government. They had no public duty except to pay taxes to their Greek masters, who walked among them as superior beings, marked out for fitness to rule by greater skill in the arts both of war and peace. The Greeks by their arms, or rather by their military discipline, had enforced obedience for one hundred and fifty years; and as they had at the same time checked lawless violence, made life and property safe, and left industry to enjoy a large share of its own earnings, this obedience had been for the most part granted to them willingly. They had even trusted the Egyptians with arms. But none are able to command unless they are at the same time able to obey. The Alexandrians were now almost in rebellion against their young king and his ministers; and the Greek government no longer gave the usual advantages in return for the obedience which it tyrannically enforced. Anarchy and confusion increased each year during the childhood of the fifth Ptolemy, to whom Alexandrian flattery gave the title of

Rosetta Stone.

Epiphanes, or *The Illustrious*. The Egyptian phalanx had in the last reign shown signs of disobedience, and at length it broke out in open rebellion. The discontented party strengthened themselves in the Busirite nome, in the middle of the Delta, and fortified the city of Lycopolis against the government; and a large supply of arms and warlike stores which they there got together proved the length of time that they had been preparing for resistance. The royal troops laid siege to the city in due form; they surrounded it with mounds and ditches, they dammed up the bed of the river on each side of it; and, being helped by a rise in the Nile, which was that year greater than usual, they forced the rebels to surrender, on the king's promise that they should be spared. But Ptolemy was not bound by promises; he was as false and cruel as he was weak; the rebels were punished; and many of the troubles in his reign arose from his discontented subjects not being able to rely upon his word.

<small>Polybius. Virtut. xx.</small>

(71) The rich island of Cyprus also, which had been left by Philopator under the command of Polycrates, showed some signs of wishing to throw off the Egyptian yoke. But Polycrates was true to his trust; and though the king's ministers were almost too weak either to help the faithful or punish the treacherous, he not only saved the island for the minor, but, when he gave up his government to Ptolemy of Megalopolis, he brought to the royal treasury at Alexandria a large sum from the revenues of his province. By this faithful conduct he gained great weight in the Alexandrian councils, till, corrupted by the poisonous habits of the place, he gave way to luxury and vice.

<small>Polybius. Hist. xvii. Virtut. xix.</small>

(72) About the same time Scopas, who had lately led back to Alexandria his Ætolian mercenaries, so far showed signs of discontent and disobedience that the minister Aristomenes began to suspect him of planning resistance to the government. Scopas was greedy of money; nothing would satisfy his avarice. The other Greek generals of his rank received while in the Egyptian service a *mina* or fifty shillings a day, under the name of mess-money, beyond the usual military pay; and Scopas claimed and received for his services the large sum of ten minæ or twenty-five pounds

<small>Virtut. xiii.</small>

sterling a day for mess-money. But even this did not content him. Aristomenes observed that he was collecting his friends for some secret purpose, and in frequent consultation with them. He therefore summoned him to the king's presence, and being prepared for his refusal he sent a large force to fetch him. Fearing that the mercenaries might support their general, Aristomenes had even ordered out the elephants and prepared for battle. But as the blow came upon Scopas unexpectedly no resistance was made, and he was brought prisoner to the palace. Aristomenes, however, did not immediately venture to punish him, but wisely summoned the Ætolian ambassadors and the chiefs of the mercenaries to his trial; and, as they made no objection, he then had him poisoned in prison.

Hist. xvii.

(73) No sooner was this rebellion crushed than the council took into consideration the propriety of declaring the king's minority at an end, as the best means of re-establishing the royal authority; and they thereupon determined shortly to celebrate his Anacleteria, or the grand ceremony of exhibiting him to the people as their monarch, though he wanted some years of the legal age; and accordingly, in the ninth year of his reign, the young king was crowned with great pomp at Memphis, the ancient capital of the kingdom.

B.C. 196.

(74) On this occasion he came to Memphis by barge, in grand state, where he was met by the priests of Upper and Lower Egypt, and crowned in the temple of Pthah with the double crown called Pschent, the crown of the two provinces. After the ceremony the priests made the decree in honour of the king, which is carved on the stone known by the name of the Rosetta Stone, in the British Museum. Ptolemy is there styled king of Upper and Lower Egypt, son of the gods Philopatores, approved by Pthah, to whom Ra has given victory, a living image of Amun, son of Ra, Ptolemy immortal, beloved by Pthah, god Epiphanes most gracious. In the date of the decree we are told the names of the priests of Alexander, of the gods Soteres, of the gods Adelphi, of the gods Euergetæ, of the gods Philopatores, of the god Epiphanes himself, of Berenice Euergetis, of Arsinoë Philadelphus, and of Arsinoë Philopator. The preamble mentions with gratitude the services

Rosetta Stone.

of the king, or rather of his wise minister Aristomenes; and the enactment orders that the statue of the king shall be worshipped in every temple of Egypt, and be carried out in the processions with those of the gods of the country; and lastly, that the decree shall be carved at the foot of every statue of the king, in sacred, in common, and in Greek writing. It is to this stone, with its three kinds of letters, and to the skill and industry of Dr. Young, that we now owe our knowledge of hieroglyphics. The Greeks of Alexandria, and after them the Romans, who might have learned how to read this kind of writing if they had wished, seem never to have taken the trouble; it fell into disuse on the rise of Christianity in Egypt; and it was left for an Englishman to unravel the hidden meaning after it had been forgotten for nearly thirteen centuries.

Young's Hierogl. Discov.

(75) The preamble of this decree tells us that during the minority of the king the taxes were lessened; the crown debtors were forgiven; those who were found in prison charged with crimes against the state were released; the allowance from government for upholding the splendour of the temples was continued, as was the rent from the glebe or land belonging to the priests; the firstfruits, or rather the coronation money, a tax paid by the priests to the king on the year of his coming to the throne, which was by custom allowed to be less than what the law ordered, was not increased; the priests were relieved from the heavy burden of making a yearly voyage to do homage at Alexandria; there was a stop put to the pressing of men for the navy, which had been felt as a great cruelty by an inland people whose habits and religion alike made them hate the sea; and this was a boon which was the more easily granted, as the navy of Alexandria, which was built in foreign dockyards and steered by foreign pilots, had very much fallen off in the reign of Philopator. The duties on linen cloth, which was the chief manufacture of the kingdom, and, after corn, the chief article exported, were lessened; the priests, who manufactured linen for the king's own use, probably for the clothing of the army, and the sails for the navy, were not called upon for so large a part of what they made as before; and the royalties on the other linen manufactures, and the duties on the samples or patterns, both of which seem to have been

Rosetta Stone.

unpaid for the whole of the eight years of the minority, were wisely forgiven. All the temples of Egypt, and that of Apis at Memphis, in particular, were enriched by his gifts; in which pious works, in grateful remembrance of their former benefactor, and with a marked slight towards Philopator, they said that he was following the wishes of his grandfather the god Euergetes. From this decree we gain some little insight into the means by which the taxes were raised under the Ptolemies; and we also learn that they were so new and foreign from the habits of the people that they had no Egyptian word by which they could speak of them, and therefore borrowed the Greek word *Syntaxes*, as we have since done.

(76) History gives us many examples of kings who like Epiphanes gained great praise for the mildness and weakness of the government during their minorities. Aristomenes, the minister who had governed Egypt for Epiphanes, fully deserved that trust. While the young king looked up to him as a father, the country was well governed, and his orders obeyed; but as he grew older his good feelings were weakened by the pleasures which usually beset youth and royalty. The companions of his vices gained that power over his mind which Aristomenes lost, and it was not long before this wise tutor and counsellor was got rid of. The king, weary perhaps with last night's debauchery, had one day fallen asleep when he should have been listening to the speech of a foreign ambassador. Aristomenes gently shook him and awoke him. His flatterers, when alone with him, urged him to take this as an affront. If, said they, it was right to blame the king for falling asleep when worn out with business and the cares of state, it should have been done in private, and not in the face of the whole court. So Aristomenes was put to death by being ordered to drink poison. Epiphanes then lost that love of his people which the wisdom of the minister had gained for him; and he governed the kingdom with the cruelty of a tyrant, rather than with the legal power of a king. Even Aristonicus, his favourite eunuch, who was of the same age as himself, and had been brought up as his playfellow, passed him in the manly virtues of his age, and earned the praise of

<small>Diod. Sic. Excerpt. 291.</small>

<small>Plutarch. De adulator.</small>

<small>Diod. Sic. Excerpt. 297.</small>

<small>Polybius, Virtut. xx.</small>

the country for setting him a good example, and checking him in his career of vice.

(77) In the thirteenth year of his reign, when the young king reached the age of eighteen, Antiochus the Great sent his daughter Cleopatra into Egypt, and the marriage, which had been agreed upon six years before, was then carried into effect; and the provinces of Cœle-Syria, Phenicia, and Judæa, which had been promised as a dower, were, in form at least, handed over to the generals of Epiphanes. Cleopatra was a woman of strong mind and enlarged understanding; and Antiochus hoped that, by means of the power which she would have over the weaker mind of Epiphanes, he should gain more than he lost by giving up Cœle-Syria and Phenicia. But she acted the part of a wife and queen, and instead of betraying her husband into the hands of her father, she was throughout the reign his wisest and best counsellor.

Hieronym. in Dan. xi. B.C. 192.

(78) Antiochus seems never to have given up his hold upon the provinces which had been promised as the dower; and the peace between the two countries, which had been kept during the six years after Cleopatra had been betrothed, was broken as soon as she was married. The war was still going on between Antiochus and the Romans; and Epiphanes soon sent to Rome a thousand pounds weight of gold, and twenty thousand pounds of silver, to help the republic against their common enemy. But the Romans neither hired mercenaries nor fought as such, the thirst for gold had not yet become the strongest feeling in the senate, and they sent back the money to Alexandria with many thanks.

Livy, lib. xxxvi. 4. B.C. 191.

(79) In the twentieth year of his reign Epiphanes was troubled by a second serious rebellion of the Egyptians. Polycrates marched against them at the head of the Greek troops; and, as he brought with him a superior force, and the king's promise of a free pardon to all who should return to their obedience, the rebels yielded to necessity and laid down their arms. The leaders of the rebellion, Athinis, Pausiras, Chesuphus, and Irobashtus, whose Coptic names prove that this was a struggle on the part of the Egyptians to throw off the Greek yoke, were brought before the king at Sais. Epiphanes, in whose youthful heart

Polybius, Virtut. xx.

REBELLION OF THE EGYPTIANS.

were joined the cruelty and cowardice of a tyrant, who had not even shown himself to the army during the danger, was now eager to act the conqueror; and, in spite of the promises of safety on which these brave Copts had laid down their arms, he had them tied to his chariot wheels, and copying the vices of men whose virtues he could not even understand, like Achilles and Alexander, he dragged them living round the city walls, and then ordered them to be put to death. He then led the army to Naucratis, which was the port of Sais, and there he embarked on the Nile for Alexandria, and taking with him a further body of mercenaries, which Aristonicus had just brought from Greece, he entered the city in triumph.

(80) Ptolemy of Megalopolis, the new governor of Cyprus, copied his predecessor Polycrates in his wise and careful management. His chief aim was to keep the province quiet, and his next to collect the taxes. *Virtut. xxvii.* He was at first distrusted by the Alexandrian council for the large sum of money which he had got together and kept within his own power; but when he sent it all home to the empty treasury, they were as much pleased as they were surprised.

(81) Apollonius, whom we have spoken of in the reign of Euergetes, and who had been teaching at Rhodes during the reign of Philopator, was recalled to *Suidas.* Alexandria in the beginning of this reign, and made librarian of the Museum on the death of Eratosthenes. But he did not long enjoy that honour. He was already old, and shortly died at the age of ninety.

(82) The coins of this king are known by the glory or rays of sun which surround his head, and which agrees with his name Epiphanes, *illustrious*, or, as it *Visconti, Icon. Grec.* is written in the hieroglyphics, "light bearing." On the other side is the cornucopia between two stars, with the name of "*King Ptolemy*" (see Fig. 247). No temples, and few additions to temples, seem to have been built in Upper Egypt during this reign, which began and ended in rebellion. We find, however, a Greek inscription at Philæ, of "King Ptolemy and Queen Cleopatra, gods *Hierogl. plate 65.* Epiphanes, and Ptolemy their son, to Asclepius," a god whom the Egyptians called Imothph, the son of Pthah.

(83) Cyprus and Cyrene were nearly all that were left to Egypt of its foreign provinces. The cities of Greece, which

had of their own wish put themselves under Egypt for help against their nearer neighbours, now looked to Rome for that help; part of Asia Minor was under Seleucus, the son of

Fig. 247.

Antiochus the Great; Cœle-Syria and Phenicia, which had been given up to Epiphanes, had been again soon lost; and the Jews, who in all former wars had sided with the kings of Egypt, as being not only the stronger but the milder rulers, now joined Seleucus. The ease with which the wide-spreading provinces of this once mighty empire fell off from the decayed trunk, almost without a shake, showed how the whole had been upheld by the warlike skill of its kings, rather than by any deep-rooted hold in the habits of the people. The trunk indeed was never strong enough for its branches; and, instead of wondering that the handful of Greeks in Alexandria, on whom the power rested, lost those wide provinces, we should rather wonder that they were ever able to hold them.

(84) After the death of Antiochus the Great, Ptolemy again proposed to enforce his rights over Cœle-Syria, which he had given up only in the weakness of his Hieronym. in Dan. xi. minority; and he is said to have been asked by one of his generals, how he should be able to pay for the large forces which he was getting together for that purpose; and he playfully answered, that his treasure was in the number of his friends. But his joke was taken in earnest; they were afraid of new taxes and fresh levies on their estates; and means were easily taken to Porphyrius, ap. Scalig. poison him. He died in the twenty-ninth year of his age, after a reign of twenty-four years; leaving the navy unmanned, the army in disobedience, the treasury

empty, and the whole framework of government out of order.

(85) Just before his death he had sent to the Achaians to offer to send ten galleys to join their fleet; and Polybius, the historian, to whom we owe so much of our knowledge of these reigns, although he had not yet reached the age called for by the Greek law, was sent by the Achaians as one of the ambassadors, with his father, to return thanks; but before they had quitted their own country they were stopped by the news of the death of the Epiphanes.

<small>Polybius, Legat. 57.</small>

(86) Those who took away the life of the king seem to have had no thoughts of mending the form of government, nor any plan by which they might lessen the power of his successor. It was only one of those outbreaks of private vengeance which have often happened in unmixed monarchies, where men are taught that the only way to check the king's tyranny is by his murder; and the little notice that was taken of it by the people proves their want of public virtue as well as of political wisdom.

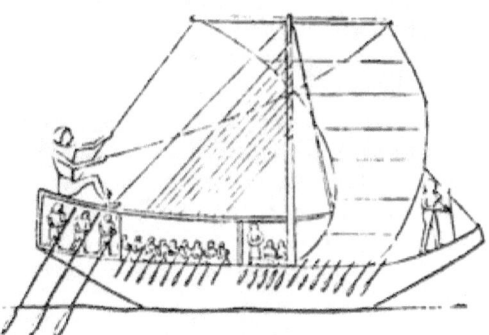

Fig. 248.—Ship on the Nile.

CHAPTER X.

PTOLEMY PHILOMETOR AND PTOLEMY EUERGETES II.
B.C. 180—116.

(1) At the beginning of the last reign the Alexandrians had sadly felt the want of a natural guardian to the

<small>Porphyrius,
ap. Scalig.
B.C. 180.</small> young king, and they were now glad to copy the customs of the conquered Egyptians. Epiphanes had left behind him two sons, each named Ptolemy, and a daughter named Cleopatra; and the elder son, though still a child, mounted the throne under the able guardianship of his mother Cleopatra, and took the very suitable name of PHILOMETOR, or *mother-loving* (see Fig. 249). The mother governed the kingdom for seven years as regent during the minority of her son.

(2) When Philometor reached his fourteenth year, the age at which his minority ceased, <small>Polybius, Legat. 78. B.C. 173.</small> the Anacleteria, or ceremony of his coronation, was celebrated with great pomp. Ambassadors from several foreign states were sent to Egypt to wish the king joy, to do honour to the day, and to renew the <small>Livy, lib xlii. 6. 2 Maccabees, iv. 21.</small> treaties of peace with him; Caius Valerius and four others were sent from Rome; Apollonius, the son of Mnestheus, was sent from Judæa; and we may regret with Polybius that he himself was not able to form part of the embassy then sent from the Achaians, that he might have seen the costly and curious ceremony and given us an account of it.

Fig. 249.

(3) While Cleopatra lived, she had been able to keep her <small>Hieronym. in Dan. xi.</small> son at peace with her brother Antiochus Epiphanes, and to guide the vessel of the state with a steady hand. But upon her death, Lenæus and the eunuch Eulaius, who then had the care of the young king, sought to reconquer Cœle-Syria; and they embroiled the country in a war, at a time when weakness and decay might have been

seen in every part of the army and navy, and when there was the greatest need of peace. Cœle-Syria and Phenicia had been given to Ptolemy Epiphanes as his wife's dower; but, when Philometor seemed too weak to grasp them, Antiochus denied that his father had ever made such a treaty, and got ready to march against Egypt, as the easiest way to guard Cœle-Syria. Polybius, Legat. 82.

(4) By this time the statesmen of Egypt ought to have learned the mistake in their foreign policy. By widening their frontier they always weakened it. They should have fortified the passes between the Red Sea and the Mediterranean, not cities in Asia. When Antiochus entered Egypt he was met at Pelusium by the army of Philometor, which he at once routed in a pitched battle. The whole of Egypt was then in his power; he marched upon Memphis with a small force, and seized it without having to strike a blow, helped perhaps by the plea that he was acting on behalf of his nephew Ptolemy Philometor, who then fell into his hands. Hieronym. in Dan. xi.

(5) On this, the younger Ptolemy, the brother of Philometor, who was with his sister Cleopatra in Alexandria, and was about fifteen years old, declared himself king, and sent ambassadors to Rome to ask for help against Antiochus; and taking the name of the most popular of his forefathers, he called himself EUERGETES (see Fig. 250). He is, however, better known in history as Ptolemy Physcon, or *bloated*, a nickname which was afterwards given to him when he had grown fat and unwieldy from the diseases of luxury.

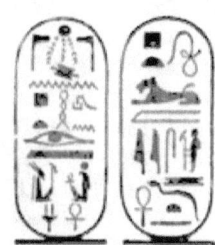

Fig. 250.

Porphyrius, ap. Scaliz.

B.C. 170.

Livy, lib. xliv. 19.

(6) Comanus and Cineas were the chief advisers of the young Euergetes; and in their alarm they proposed to send the foreign ambassadors to meet the invader on his march from Memphis, and to plead for peace. This task the ambassadors kindly undertook. There were then in Alexandria two embassies from the Achaians, one to renew the treaty of peace, and one to settle the terms of the coming wrestling match. There were there three embassies from Athens, one with gifts from the city, one about the Polybius, Legat. 81.

Panathenaic games, and one about the celebration of the mysteries, of which the last two were sacred embassies. There was also an embassy from Miletus, and one from Clazomenæ. On the day of their arrival at Memphis, Antiochus feasted these numerous ambassadors in grand state, and on the next day gave them an audience. But their arguments for peace carried no weight with him; and he denied that his father Antiochus the Great had ever given Cœle-Syria as a dower with his daughter Cleopatra to Epiphanes. To gain time, he promised the ambassadors that he would give them an answer as soon as his own ambassadors returned from Alexandria; and in the meanwhile he carried his army down the Nile to Naucratis, and thence marched to the capital to begin the siege.

(7) Antiochus, however, was defeated in his first assault upon Alexandria; and finding that he should not soon be able to bring the siege to an end, he sent off an embassy to Rome with a hundred and fifty talents of gold, fifty as a present to the senate under the name of a crown, and the rest to be divided among the states of Greece, whose help he might need. At the same time also an embassy from the Rhodians arrived in the port of Alexandria, to attempt to restore peace to the country of their old allies. Antiochus received the Rhodian ambassadors in his tent, but would not listen to the long speech with which they threatened him, and shortly told them that he came as the friend of his elder nephew, the young Philometor, and if the Alexandrians wished for peace they should open the gates to their rightful king. Antiochus was, however, defeated in all his assaults on the city, and he at last withdrew his army and returned to Syria. He left Euergetes king of the Greeks at Alexandria, and Philometor at Memphis king of the rest of Egypt. But he kept Pelusium, where he placed a strong garrison, that he might be able easily to re-enter Egypt whenever he chose.

Polybius, Legat. 83.

Legat. 84.

Livy, lib. xlv. 11.

(8) Ptolemy Macron, the Alexandrian governor of Cyprus, added to the troubles of the country by giving up his island to Antiochus. But he met with the usual fate of traitors, he was badly rewarded; and when he complained of his treatment, he was called a traitor by the very men who had gained by his treachery, and he

2 Maccabees, x. 13.

poisoned himself in the bitterness of his grief. Little as we know of his name, the historian can still point to it to prove the folly of wickedness. Antiochus, like most invaders, carried off whatever treasure fell into his hands. Egypt was a sponge which had not lately been squeezed, and his court and even his own dinner-table then shone with a blaze of silver and gold unknown in Syria before the inroad into Egypt. _{Athenæus, lib. v. 5.}

(9) By these acts, and by the garrison left in Pelusium, the eyes of Philometor were opened, and he saw that his uncle had not entered Egypt for his sake, but to make it a province of Syria, after it had been weakened by civil war. He therefore wisely forgave his rebellious brother and sister in Alexandria, and sent offers of peace to them; and it was agreed that the two Ptolemies should reign together, and turn their forces against the common enemy. It was most likely at this time, and as a part of this treaty, that Philometor married his sister Cleopatra; a marriage which, however much it may shock our feelings of right, was not forbidden either by the law or custom of the country. It was mainly by her advice and persuasion that the quarrel between the two brothers was for the time healed. _{Livy, lib. xlv. 11.}

(10) On this treaty between the brothers the year was called the twelfth of Ptolemy Philometor and the first of Ptolemy Euergetes, and the public deeds of the kingdom were so dated. _{Porphyrius, ap. Scalig. B.C. 169.}

(11) The next year Antiochus Epiphanes again entered Egypt, claiming the island of Cyprus and the country round Pelusium as the price of his forbearance; and on his marching forward, Memphis a second time opened its gates to him without a battle. He came down by slow marches towards Alexandria, and crossed the canal at Leucine, four miles from the city. There he was met by the Roman ambassadors, who ordered him to quit the country. On his hesitating, Popilius, who was one of them, drew a circle round him on the sand with his stick, and told him that, if he crossed that line without promising to leave Egypt at once, it should be taken as a declaration of war against Rome. On this threat Antiochus again quitted Egypt, and the brothers sent ambassadors to Rome to thank the senate for their _{Livy, lib. xlv. 12.} _{Lib. xlv. 12.}

help, and to acknowledge that they owed more to the Roman people than they did to the gods or to their forefathers.

(12) The treaty made on this occasion between Philometor and Antiochus was written by Heraclides Lembus, the son of Scrapion, a native of Oxyrynchus, who wrote on the succession of the philosophers in the several Greek schools, and other works on philosophy, but whose chief work was a history named the Lembeutic History. It is the natural policy of despotic monarchs to employ men of letters and science in the offices of government. Soldiers may rebel, nobles and men of wealth may be too independent, but men of letters without money, if they consent to be employed, can only obey. Moreover, when a literary education was enjoyed by few, neither kings nor statesmen had knowledge enough to write their own state papers, and they employed for this purpose some of the philosophers and grammarians who hung about the court. This task was not thought important enough to be usually mentioned in the lives of men whose fame rested on more lasting works, and hence we do not often know by whom it was performed.

<small>Suidas. Diogenes Laertius, v. 64.</small>

(13) Four years afterwards Antiochus Epiphanes died; and the Jews of Judæa, who had been for some time struggling for liberty, then gained a short rest for their unhappy country. Judas Maccabeus had raised his countrymen in rebellion against the foreigners, he had defeated the Syrian forces in several battles, and was at last able to purify the temple and re-establish the service there as of old. He therefore sent to the Jews of Egypt to ask them to join their Hebrew brethren in celebrating the Feast of Tabernacles on that great occasion.

<small>B.C. 164. 1 Maccabees, iv. 5.</small>

<small>2 Maccabees, i. 10.</small>

(14) The unhappy quarrels between the Egyptian kings soon broke out again; and, as the party of Euergetes was the stronger, Philometor was driven from his kingdom, and he fled to Rome for safety and for help. He entered the city privately, and took up his lodgings in the house of one of his own subjects, a painter of Alexandria. His pride led him to refuse the offers of better entertainment which were made to him by Demetrius, the nephew of Antiochus, who like himself was hoping to regain

<small>Livy, lib. xlvi. 21.</small>

his kingdom by the help of the Romans. The kings of Egypt and Syria, the two greatest kingdoms in the world, were at the same time asking to be heard at the bar of the Roman senate, and were claiming the thrones of their fathers at the hands of men who could make and unmake kings at their pleasure.

(15) As soon as the senate heard that Philometor was in Rome, they lodged him at the cost of the state in a manner becoming his high rank, and soon sent him back to Egypt, with orders that Euergetes should reign in Cyrene, and that the rest of the kingdom should belong to Philometor. This happened in the seventeenth year of Philometor and the sixth of Euergetes, which was the last year that was named after the two kings. Cassius Longinus, who was next year consul at Rome, was most likely among the ambassadors who replaced Philometor on the throne; for he put the Ptolemaic eagle and thunderbolt on his coins, as though to claim the sovereignty of Egypt for the senate. *Livy, lib. xlvi. 22. Porphyrius, ap. Scalig. B.C. 164. Eckhel, vol. v. 167.*

(16) To these orders Euergetes was forced to yield; but the next year he went himself to Rome to complain to the senate that they had made a very unfair division of the kingdom, and to beg that they would add the island of Cyprus to his share. After hearing the ambassadors from Philometor, who were sent to plead on the other side, the senate granted the prayer of Euergetes, and sent ambassadors to Cyprus, with orders to hand that island over to Euergetes, and to make use of the fleets and armies of the republic if these orders were disobeyed. *Livy, lib. xlvi. 32. Polybius, Legat. 113.*

(17) Euergetes, during his stay in Rome, if we may believe Plutarch, made an offer of marriage to Cornelia, the mother of the Gracchi; but this offer of a throne could not make the high-minded matron quit her children and her country. *Plutarch, Gracchus.*

(18) He left Italy with the Roman ambassadors, and in passing through Greece he raised a large body of mercenaries to help him to wrest Cyprus from his brother, as it would seem that the governor, faithful to his charge, would not listen to the commands of Rome. But the ambassadors had been told to conquer Cyprus, if necessary, with the arms of the republic only, and they therefore made Euergetes disband his levies. They sailed for *Polybius, Legat. 115.*

Alexandria to enforce their orders upon Philometor, and sent Euergetes home to Cyrene. Philometor received the Roman ambassadors with all due honours; he sometimes gave them fair promises, and sometimes put them off till another day; and tried to spin out the time without saying either yes or no to the message from the senate. Euergetes sent to Alexandria to ask if they had gained their point; but though they threatened to return to Rome if they were not at once obeyed, Philometor, by his kind treatment and still kinder words, kept them more than forty days longer at Alexandria.

(19) At last the Roman ambassadors left Egypt, and on their way home they went to Cyrene, to let Euergetes know that his brother had disobeyed the orders of the senate, and would not give up Cyprus; and Euergetes then sent two ambassadors to Rome to beg them to revenge their affronted dignity and to enforce their orders by arms. The senate of course declared the peace with Egypt at an end, and ordered the ambassadors from Philometor to quit Rome within five days, and sent their own ambassadors to Cyrene to tell Euergetes of their decree.
_{Polybius, Legat. 116.}
_{Legat. 117.}

(20) But while this was going on, the state of Cyrene had risen in arms against Euergetes; his vices and cruelty had made him hated, they had gained for him the nicknames of Kakergetes, or *mischief-maker*, and Physcon, or *bloated*; and while wishing to gain Cyprus he was in danger of losing his own kingdom. When he marched against the rebels he was beaten and wounded, either in the battle or by an attack upon his life afterwards, and his success was for some time doubtful. When he had at last put down this rising he sailed for Rome, to urge his complaints against Philometor, upon whom he laid the blame of the late rebellion, and to ask for help. The senate, after hearing both sides, sent a small fleet with Euergetes, not large enough to put him on the throne of Cyprus, but gave him, what they had before refused, leave to levy an army of his own, and to enlist their allies in Greece and Asia as mercenaries under his standard.
_{Legat. 115.}
_{Legat. 132.}

(21) The Roman troops seem not to have helped Euergetes; but he landed in Cyprus with his own mercenaries, and was there met by Philometor, who had brought over the Egyptian army in person. Euergetes, however,
_{Virtut. xxxi.}

was beaten in several battles, he was soon forced to shut himself up in the city of Lapitho, and at last to lay down his arms before his elder brother.

(22) If Philometor had upon this put his brother to death, the deed would have seemed almost blameless after the family murders at which we have already shuddered in this history. But, with a goodness of heart which is rarely met with in the history of kings, and which, if we looked up to merit as much as we do to success, would throw the warlike virtues of his forefathers into the shade, he a second time forgave his brother all that had passed, he replaced him on the throne of Cyrene, and promised to give him his daughter in marriage. We are not told whether the firmness and forgiving mildness of Philometor had turned the Roman senate in his favour, but their troops seemed wanted in other quarters; at any rate they left off trying to enforce their decree; Philometor kept Cyprus, and sent to Euergetes a yearly gift of corn from Alexandria.

Diod. Sic. Excerpt. 334.

(23) At a time when so few great events cross the stage, we must not let the fall of Macedonia pass unnoticed, nor fail to point out the rapid rise of Rome. We have seen the conquests in Europe, Asia, and Africa, by Macedonian valour under Alexander the Great, and on his death the Egyptian and other great kingdoms founded by his generals. We have since seen the Macedonian phalanx routed at Cynocephalæ, and lastly, in this reign, Macedonia was conquered by the Romans, the king led in triumph to Rome, and, in the insulting decree of the senate, the people declared free. But the Macedonians had never learned to govern themselves. The feelings which in a commonwealth would be pride of country, in a monarchy are entwined round the throne, as in an army round the standard, and when these are lost they are not easily regained. At any rate we never again meet with Macedonia on the page of history.

(24) About the same time the Romans entered on the third Punic war, and on the Achaian war; and before the end of this reign the city of Carthage, and the Achaian league, or the free states of Greece, both sunk under their victorious arms. But these conquests were not won with equal ease, nor with equal glory to the Roman generals; and while Mummius is never spoken of without blame for having

warred against art, and overthrown Corinth with its temples, statues, and pictures, the younger Scipio, who warred against commerce, is praised for having burned to the very ground the trading city of Carthage.

(25) During the wars in Syria between Philometor and Antiochus Epiphanes, at the beginning of this reign, the Jews were divided into two parties, one favouring the Egyptians and one the Syrians. At last the Syrian party drove their enemies out of Jerusalem; and Onias, the high-priest, with a large body of Jews, fled to Egypt. There they were well received by Philometor, who allowed them to dwell in the neighbourhood of Heliopolis, perhaps on the very spot which had been given to their forefathers when they entered Egypt under Jacob; and he gave them leave to build a temple and ordain priests for themselves. Onias built his temple at On or Onion, a city about twenty-three miles from Memphis, once the capital of the district of Heliopolis. It was on the site of an old Egyptian temple of the goddess Pasht, which had fallen into disuse and decay; most likely that very temple in which the wife of Joseph upwards of twelve centuries earlier had worshipped with her father Poti-phera, the priest and governor of that city. It was built after the model of the temple of Jerusalem, and though by the Jewish law there was to be no second temple, yet Onias defended himself by quoting some words of prophecy as if written by Isaiah, saying that in that day there shall be an altar to the Lord in the midst of the land of Egypt. The building of this temple, and the celebrating the Jewish feasts there, as in rivalry to the temple of Jerusalem, were a never-failing cause of quarrel between the Hebrew and the Greek Jews. One party or the other altered the words of the Bible to make it speak their own opinions about it. The Hebrew Bible now says that the new temple was in the City of Destruction, and the Greek Bible says that it was in the City of Righteousness. The leaders of the Greek party wished the Jews to throw aside the character of strangers and foreign traders, to be at home and to become owners of the soil. "Hate not laborious work," says the son of Sirach; "neither husbandry, which the Most High hath ordained."

THE JEWS AND THE SAMARITANS.

(26) About the same time the Jews brought before Ptolemy, as a judge, their quarrel with the Samaritans, as to whether, according to the law of Moses, the temple ought to have been built at Jerusalem, or on Mount Gerizim, where the Samaritans built their temple, or on Mount Ebal, where the Hebrew Bible says that it should be built; and as to which nation had altered their copies of the Bible in the twenty-seventh chapter of Deuteronomy. This dispute had lately been the cause of riots and rebellion. Ptolemy seems to have decided the question for political reasons, and to please his own subjects the Alexandrian Jews; and without listening to the arguments as to what the law ordered, he was content with the proof that the temple had stood at Jerusalem for above eight hundred years, and he put to death the two Samaritan pleaders, who had probably been guilty of some outrage against the Jews in zeal for Mount Gerizim, and for which they might then have been on their trial. *Josephus, Antiq. xiii. 3, 4. Deut. xxvii. 4. Josh. viii. 30. Deuteron. xxvii. 12. ch. xi. 29.*

(27) Onias, the high-priest, was much esteemed by Philometor, and bore high offices in the government; as also did Dositheus, another Jew, who had been very useful in helping the king to crush a rebellion. Dositheus called himself a priest and a Levite, though his title to that honour seems to have been doubted by his countrymen. He had brought with him into Egypt the book of Esther, written in Greek, which he said had been translated out of the Hebrew in Jerusalem by Lysimachus. It contained some additions not in our Bible. But as he did not publish the Hebrew, these chapters were viewed rather distrustfully. They were, however, added to the Greek Bible; and, as the Hebrew has never been brought forward, we now place them among the doubtful books of the Apocrypha. *Josephus, in Apion. ii. Esther, ch. xi. 1. B.C. 177.*

(28) Since the Ptolemies had found themselves too weak to hold Ethiopia, they had placed a body of soldiers on the border of the two countries, to guard Egypt from the inroads of the enemy. This station, twelve miles to the south of Syene, had by degrees grown into a city, and was called Parembole, or *The Camp;* and, as most of the soldiers were Greek mercenaries, it was natural *Inscript. Letronne, Recherches.*

that the temple which Philometor built there should be dedicated in the Greek language. Of the temples hitherto built by the Ptolemies, in the Egyptian cities, every one seems to have had the king's name and titles, and its dedication to the gods, carved on its massive portico in hieroglyphics; but this was in a Greek city, and it was dedicated to Isis and Serapis, on behalf of Philometor and his queen, in a Greek inscription.

(29) Philometor also built a temple at Antæopolis (see Fig. 251) to Antæus, a god of whom we know nothing but that he gave his name to the city; and another to Aroëris at Ombos; and in the same way he carved the dedications on the porticoes in the Greek language. This custom became

Fig. 251.

common after that time, and proves both the lessened weight which the native Egyptians bore in the state, and that the kings had forgotten the wise rules of Ptolemy Soter, in regard to the religious feelings of the people. They must have been greatly shocked by this use of foreign writing in the place of the old characters of the country, which, from having been used in the temples, even for ages beyond the reach of history, had at last been called sacred. In the temple at Antæopolis we note a marked change in the style of building. The screen in front of the great portico is almost removed by having a doorway made in it between every pair of columns. This may have been done to meet some change in the manner in which the ceremonies under the portico were to be performed. A second change, that of having fewer columns in front, was more a matter of taste, except so far as these newer temples were smaller than the old temples. Oimenepthah's temple at Rebek and Rameses II.'s Memnonium have each a row of ten columns under the portico; Rameses III.'s temple at Medinet Abou has eight columns, and this temple by Philometor has a row of only six columns under the portico. In Greece, on the other hand, the older temples had a front of only four columns, the newer of six columns, and afterwards some had a front of eight columns.

(30) It is to this reign, also, that we seem to owe the great temple at Apollinopolis Magna (see Fig. 252), although it was not finished till one or two reigns later. It is one of the largest and least ruined of the Egyptian temples. Its front is formed of two huge square towers, with sloping sides, between which is the narrow doorway, the only opening in its massive walls. Through this the worshipper entered a spacious courtyard or cloister, where he found shade from

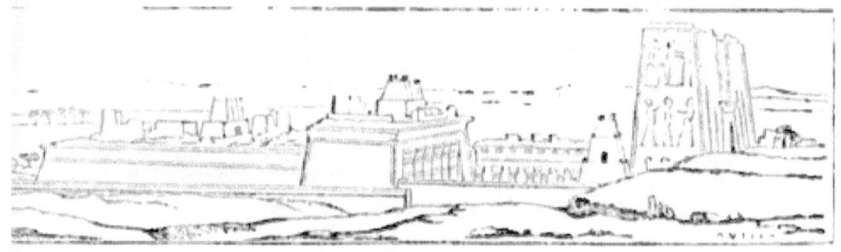

Fig. 252.

the sun under a covered walk on either side. In front is the lofty portico with six large columns, the entrance to the body of the building. This last is flat-roofed, and far lower than the grand portico, which hid it from the eyes of the crowd in the courtyard. The staircases in the towers are narrow. The sacred rooms within were small and dark, with only a glimmering flame here and there before an altar, except when lighted up with the blaze of lamps on a feast-day (see Plan Fig. 253 and Elevation Fig. 254). As a castle it must have had great strength; from the top and loopholes of the two towers, stones and darts might be hurled at the enemy; and as it was in the hands of the Egyptians, it is the strongest proof that they were either not distrusted or not feared by their Greek rulers. The city of Apollinopolis stands on a grand and lofty situation, overlooking the river and the valley; and this proud temple, rising over all, can only have been planned by military skill as a fortress to command the whole.

(31) At this time the Greeks in Egypt were beginning to follow the custom of their Egyptian brethren, to take upon themselves monastic vows, and to shut themselves up in the

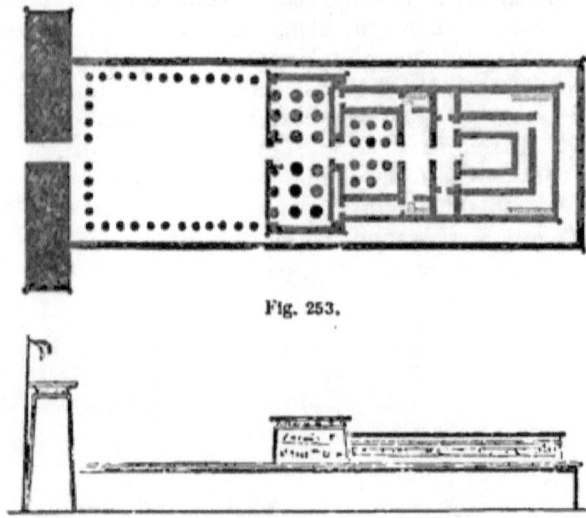

Fig. 253.

Fig. 254.

temples in religious idleness. But these foreigners were looked upon with jealousy by the Egyptian monks as intruders on their endowments, they were not members of the priestly families; and we meet with a petition addressed to Philometor by Ptolemy, the son of Glaucias, a monk in the temple of Serapis at Memphis, who styles himself a Macedonian, in which he begs as a reward for his having lived there as a religious recluse for fifteen years that his younger brother may receive an appointment as an officer in the army. In a second and third petition he complains that his cell had been violently entered by his brethren and himself illtreated because he was a Greek; and he reminds the king that last year when the king visited the Serapium he had addressed the same petition to him through the bars of his window.

<small>Boekh's Corpus Inscript. Cardl. Mai. Auctores Classici, v. 350.</small>

(32) From the report made to the king upon the monk's petition above mentioned we learn the amount of a junior officer's pay in a favourite cohort of Greeks stationed in Memphis. The young man was promised three artabas, or nine bushels of wheat and one hundred and fifty pieces of brass per month, and one hundred pieces of brass in place of each artaba of wheat not given to him. Thus his monthly pay was equal to about fourteen bushels of wheat. If the pieces of brass were of the largest size, or of two ounces and a quarter each, the bushel of wheat was worth about fifteen shillings; but if, as is more probable, the piece of brass was of the smallest size, the didrachm or quarter of an ounce, then the bushel of wheat was worth about eighteen pence.

(33) The priests in the temples of Egypt were maintained, partly by their own estates, and partly by the offerings of the pious; and we still possess a deed of sale made in this reign by the Theban priests, of one half of a third of their collections for the dead who had been buried in Thynabunum, the Libyan suburb of Thebes. This sixth share of the collections consisted of seven or eight families of slaves; the price of it was four hundred pieces of brass; the bargain was made in the presence of sixteen witnesses, whose names are given; and the deed was registered and signed by a public notary in the city of Thebes. The custom of giving offerings to the priests for the good of the dead would seem to have been a cause of some wealth to the temples, and must have been common even in the time of Moses. It was <small>Deuteron. ch. xxvi. 14.</small> one among the many Egyptian customs forbidden by the Hebrew law, and it continued in use from a very early time till long after the time of this deed. It is still common in China.

(34) From the deed of sale we also gain some knowledge of the state of slavery in Egypt. The names of the slaves and of their fathers are Coptic, and in some cases borrowed from the names of the gods; hence the slaves were probably of the same religion, and spoke nearly the same language as their masters. They sunk into that low state, rather by their own want of mind than by their masters' power. In each case the slave was joined in the same lot with his children; and the low price of four hundred pieces of brass, perhaps about eighty shillings, for eight families, or even if

it be meant for the half of eight families, proves that they were of the nature of serfs, and that the master either by law or custom could have had no power of cruelly overworking them. On the other hand, in the reign of Philadelphus, the prisoners taken in battle, who might be treated with greater severity, were ransomed at sixty shillings each. We see by the monuments that there were also a few negroes in the same unhappy state of slavery. They were probably not treated much worse than the lowest class of those born on the soil, but they were much more valuable. Other slaves of the Berber race were brought in coasting vessels from Opone, on the incense coast, near to the island of Dioscorides, and there they were purchased for Egypt. The morality of ancient nations was sadly lowered by this practice of owning slaves. The master degraded himself as well as the slave; and while a man's wealth arose from illtreating his poorer brethren, it was natural to remark that a rich man would not easily enter the kingdom of heaven.

<small>Arrian! Periplus.</small>

(35) Aristarchus, who had been the tutor of Euergetes II., and of a son of Philomotor, was one of the ornaments of this reign. He had been a pupil of Aristophanes, the grammarian, and had then studied under Crates at Pergamus, the rival school to Alexandria. He died at Cyprus, whither he probably withdrew himself on the death of Philometor. He was chiefly known for his critical writings, in which his opinions of poetry were thought so just that few dared to disagree with them; and his name soon became proverbial for a critic. Aristarchus had also the good fortune to be listened to in his lecture-room by one whose name is far more known than those of his two royal pupils. Moschus of Syracuse, the pastoral poet, was one of his hearers; but his fame must not be claimed for Alexandria; he can hardly have learned from the critic that just taste by which he joined softness and sweetness to the rude plainness of the Doric muse. Indeed in this he only followed his young friend Bion, whose death he so beautifully bewails, and from whose poems he generously owns that he learned so much. It may be as well to add, that the lines in which he says that Theocritus, who had been dead above one hundred years, joined with him in his sorrow for the death

<small>Suidas.</small>

of Bion, are later additions not found in the early manuscripts of his poems.

(36) From our slight acquaintance with Bion's life we are left in doubt whether he accompanied his friend Moschus to the court of Alexandria; but it is probable that he did. In his beautiful lamentation for the death of Adonis we have an imitation of the melancholy chant of the Egyptians, named *maneros*, which they sang through the streets in the procession on the feast of Isis, when the crowd joined in the chorus "Ah, hapless Isis, Osiris is no more." The tale has been a good deal changed by the Sicilian muse of Bion, but in the boar which killed Adonis, we have the wicked Typhon, the Hippopotamus, as carved on the monuments; we have also the wound in the thigh, and the consolations of the priests, who every year ended their mournful song with advising the goddess to reserve her sorrow for another year, when on the return of the festival the same lament would be again celebrated. The whole poem has a depth and earnestness of feeling which is truly Egyptian, but which was very little known in Alexandria.

(37) To the Alexandrian grammarians, and more particularly to Aristophanes, Aristarchus, and their pupil Ammonius, we are indebted for our present copies of Homer. These critics acted like modern editors, each publishing an edition, or rather writing out a copy, which was then recopied in the Museum as often as called for by the demands of the purchasers of books. Aristophanes left perhaps only one such copy or edition, while Aristarchus, in his efforts to correct the text of the great epic poet, made several such copies. These were in the hands of the later scholiasts, who appealed to them as their authority, and ventured to make no further alterations; we therefore now read the Iliad and Odyssey nearly as left by these Alexandrian critics. They no doubt took some liberties in altering the spelling and smoothing the lines; and though we should value most highly a copy in the rougher form in which it came into their hands, yet on the whole we must be great gainers by their labours. They divided the Iliad and Odyssey into twenty-four books each, and corrected the faulty metres; but one of their chief tasks was to set aside, or put a mark

<small>Scholiast. in Iliad. x. 397, &c.</small>

<small>Plutarch. Vita Homeri.</small>

against, those more modern lines which had crept into the ancient poems. It had been usual to call every old verse Homer's or Homeric, and these it was the business of the critic to mark as not genuine. Aristarchus was jocosely said to have called those lines spurious which he did not like; but everything that we can learn of him leads us to believe that he executed his task with judgment. From these men sprang the school of Alexandrian grammarians, who for several centuries continued their minute and often unprofitable studies in verbal criticism, and always looked back to Aristarchus as their head, as the philosophers did to Plato or Aristotle. Very few of them cultivated the highest branch of criticism, that of tracing the methods by which a great author produced his beauties and gave excellence to his writings. Some few of them wrote on the second branch, that of explaining his thoughts when time had thrown a shade over the meaning of his words. But most of them busied themselves on the lowest criticism, that of comparing the manuscripts to determine what words he wrote; and they were in search for blunders in the copy as much as for beauties in the work.

<small>Cicero, Epist. iii. 11.</small>

(38) It was not by the critics and grammarians alone that the text of the ancient authors was altered and made modern. Every copier uses not only his eye but his judgment, and if he sees in the manuscript before him a word which he does not quite understand, he is tempted to change it for one which in his opinion makes sense. In this way those writers that were most popular and most often copied would be the most altered. The orators and tragedians of Athens were left with the peculiarities that belong to the age and country in which they wrote; but the Æolic digamma was removed out of Homer, and the drinking songs of old Anacreon appeared in a dress not unsuited for the supper tables of Alexandria.

(39) These were the palmy days of criticism. Never before or since have critics held so high a place in literature. The world was called upon to worship and do honour to the poet, but chiefly that it might admire the skill of the critic who could name the several sources of his beauties. The critic now ranked higher than a priest at the foot of Mount Parnassus. Homer was lifted to the skies that the critic

might stand on a raised pedestal among the Muses. Such seems to be the meaning of the figures on the upper part of the well-known sculpture called the Apotheosis of Homer (see Fig. 255). It was made in this reign; and at the foot Ptolemy and his mother, in the Bartoli, Admiranda Rom. Antiq.

Fig. 255.

characters of Time and the World, are crowning the statue of the poet, in the presence of ten worshippers, who represent the literary excellences which shine forth in his poems. The figures of the Iliad and Odyssey kneel beside his seat, and the frogs and mice creep under his footstool, showing that the latter mock-heroic poem was already written and called the work of Homer.

(40) It has sometimes been made a question how far the poet and orator have been helped forward and guided by the rules of the critic; and at other times it has been thought

that the more tender flowers of literature have rather been
choked by this weed which entwines itself round them.
But history seems to teach us that neither of these opinions
is true. While Aristarchus was writing there were no poets
in Alexandria to be bound down by his laws, no orators to be
tamed by the fear of his lashes, and, on the other hand, none
wrote at his bidding, or rose to any real height by the narrow
steps by which he meant them to climb. It would seem as
if the fires of genius and of liberty had burned out together,
as if the vices which were already tainting the manners of
the Alexandrians had also poisoned their literary taste.
The golden age of poetry had passed before the brazen age
of criticism began. The critics wrote at a time when the
schools of literature would have been still more barren
without them.

(41) Another pupil of Aristarchus was Pamphilus, the
Alexandrian physician, who wrote on plants and
their uses, both in agriculture and medicine. But
Galen speaks very slightingly of him, and says that
he ran after fabulous stories of wonderful cures,
and that he trusted as much to the power of Egyptian charms
and amulets as to the medicinal properties of the herbs that
he wrote about. Pamphilus used to employ incantations to
increase the effect of his medicines; and to add to the weight
of his opinions he said they were taken from the writings of
Thrice-great Hermes.

<small>Suidas. De Simpli- cibus, lib. vi. proem.</small>

(42) Nicander, the poet and physician, is also claimed by
Alexandria, though part of his renown was shed
upon Pergamus, where he lived for some years
under King Attalus. He has left a poem in quaint
and learned phrase, on poisons, and the poisonous
bites and stings of animals, and on their remedies. Before
this time Aratus had written an astronomical poem, and
Manetho an astrological poem; and thus, in the place of
poetry, we now only meet with science put into verse, without earnestness or feeling, or any aim after purity and
loftiness of thought. Nor did these scientific poets pay
much attention to style; they did not seem aware that their
writings were works of art, and that, like paintings and
sculpture, they would be little valued unless the worth of the
form were greater than that of the substance.

<small>Tzetzes in Lycophronte. Suidas.</small>

(43) But by far the greatest man in Alexandria at this time was Hipparchus, the father of mathematical astronomy. Aristillus and Timocharis had before made a few observations on the fixed stars, but Hipparchus was the first to form a catalogue of any size. His great observations were made with a fixed armillary sphere, or rather a fixed instrument having a plane parallel to the equator, and a gnomon parallel to the earth's pole. If he was the inventor of this instrument, it was at least made upon principles known to Eratosthenes, and contained in his Theory of Shadows. With this instrument he noted the hour of the equinoctial day on which the sun shone equally upon the top and the bottom of the equatorial plane; that hour was the time of the equinox. By making many such observations he learned the length of the year, which he found was less than three hundred and sixty-five days and a quarter. He found that the four quarters of the year were not of equal length. He also made the great discovery of the precession of the equinox, or that the sidereal year, which is measured by the stars, was not of the same length as the common year, which is measured by the seasons. Thus he found that the star *Spica Virginis*, which in the time of Timocharis had been eight degrees before the equinoctial point, was then only six degrees before it. Hence he said that the precession of the equinox was not less than one degree in a century, and added, that it was not along the equator, but along the ecliptic. He was a man of great industry, and unwearied in his search after truth; and he left a name that was not equalled by that of any astronomer in the fifteen centuries which followed. But these astronomical discoveries about the length of the year were not received by the unenlightened; in some minds they clashed with religious opinions. The priests in the temple of Amun kept a lamp always burning before the altar of their god; and they had observed or fancied that its never-ceasing flame consumed every year less oil than it had in the past year. Hence they declared that the years were always growing shorter; and the doctrines of the priests give way very slowly before the calculations of the man of science.

Ptolemy, lib. iii. iv. vi.

Plutarch. De Oraculis.

(44) Hero, the pupil of Ctesibius, ranked very high as a

mathematician and mechanic. He has left a work which treats upon several branches of mechanics; on making warlike machines for throwing stones and arrows; and on automatons, or figures which were made to move, as if alive, by machinery under the floor. His chief work is on pneumatics, on making forcing pumps and fountains by the force of the air. Among other clever toys he made birds which sang, or at least uttered one note, by the air being driven

Fig. 256.

by water out of a close vessel through small pipes. Other playthings were moved by the force of air rarified by heat; and one to which the modern discovery of the steam-engine has given a value which it was by no means worthy of, was moved by the force of steam (see Fig. 256). The steam was raised by a fire placed under one vessel, and thence driven into a second vessel through a hole in the axis on which it was to turn, and rushed out of it through two holes in the line of its tangents; so that the force of the steam made the second vessel turn round in the opposite direction.

(45) The portrait of the king is known from those coins which bear the name of "*King Ptolemy, the mother-loving god*" (see Fig. 257). The eagle on the other side of the coins has a palm branch on its wing or by its side, which may be supposed to mean that they

Visconti, Icon. Grec.

Fig. 257.

were struck in the island of Cyprus. We have not before met with the title of "*god*," on the coins of the Ptolemies; but, as every one of them had been so named in the hieroglyphical inscriptions, it can scarcely be called new. The word among the pagans never had the high and awful meaning that it bears among those who worship the one Ruler of the world; and it was further lowered by being given not only to departed heroes, but to living priests, and even kings far worse than Philometor.

(46) When Philometor quitted the island of Cyprus after beating his brother in battle, he left Archias as governor, who entered into a plot to give it up to Demetrius, king of Syria, for the sum of five hundred talents. But the plot was found out, and the traitor then put an end to his own life, to escape from punishment and self-reproach. By this treachery of Demetrius, Philometor was made his enemy, and he joined Attalus, king of Pergamus, and Ariarathes, king of Cappadocia, in setting up Alexander Balas as a pretender to the throne of Syria, who beat Demetrius in battle, and put him to death. Philometor two years afterwards gave his elder daughter Cleopatra in marriage to Alexander, and led her himself to Ptolemais, or Acre, where the marriage was celebrated with great pomp. Polybius, De Virtut. xxxi. Justinus, lib. xxxv. 1. 1 Maccabees, ch. x.

(47) But even in Ptolemais, the city in which Alexander had been so covered with favours, Philometor was near falling under the treachery of his new son-in-law. He learned that a plot had been formed against his life by Ammonius, and he wrote to Alexander to beg that the traitor might be given up to justice. But Alexander acknowledged the plot as his own, and refused to give up his servant. On this, Philometor recalled his daughter and turned against Alexander the forces which he had led into Syria to uphold him. He then sent to the young Demetrius, afterwards called Nicator, the son of his late enemy, to offer him the throne and wife which he had lately given to Alexander Balas; and Demetrius was equally pleased with the two offers. Philometor then entered Antioch at the head of his army, and there he was proclaimed by the citizens king of Asia and Egypt; but, with a forbearance then very uncommon, he called together the council of the people, and refused the crown, and persuaded them to receive Demetrius as their king. Josephus, Antiq. xiii. 8.

(48) Alexander Balas and Demetrius Nicator each in his

turn acknowledged his debt to the king of Egypt by putting the Ptolemaic eagle on his coins, and adjusting them to the Egyptian standard of weight; and in this they were afterwards followed by Antiochus, the son of Demetrius. The Romans, on the other hand, sometimes used the same eagle in boast of their power over Egypt; but we cannot be mistaken in what was meant by these Syrian kings, who none of them, when their coins were struck, were seated safely on the throne. With them, as with some of the Greek cities of Asia Minor, the use of the Egyptian eagle on the coins was an act of homage.

<small>Numismata Pembroch.</small>

(49) Philometor and Demetrius, as soon as the latter was acknowledged king at Antioch, then marched against Alexander, routed his army, and drove him into Arabia. But in this battle Philometor's horse was frightened by the braying of an elephant, and threw the king into the ranks of the enemy, and he was taken up covered with wounds. He lay speechless for five days, and the surgeons then endeavoured to cut out a piece of the broken bone from his skull. He died under the operation; but not before the head of Alexander had been brought to him as the proof of his victory.

<small>Livy, Epit. lii. Josephus, Antiq. xiii. 8.</small>

(50) Thus fell Ptolemy Philometor, the last of the Ptolemies to whom history can point with pleasure. He was in the forty-second year of his age. His reign began in trouble; before he reached the years of manhood the country had been overrun by foreigners, and torn to pieces by civil war; but he left the kingdom stronger than he found it—a praise which he alone can share with Ptolemy Soter. He was alike brave and mild; he was the only one of the race who fell in battle, and the only one whose hands were unstained with civil blood. At an age and in a country when poison and the dagger were too often the means by which the king's authority was upheld, when goodness was little valued, and when conquests were thought the only measure of greatness, he spared the life of a brother taken in battle, he refused the crown of Syria when offered to him; and not only no one of his friends or kinsmen, but no citizen of Alexandria was put to death during the whole of his reign. We find grateful

<small>Polybius, De Virtut. xxxi.</small>

<small>Inscript. Letronne, Recherches.</small>

inscriptions to his honour at the city of Citium in Cyprus, in the island of Therae, and at Methone in Argolis.

(51) Philometor had reigned thirty-five years in all; eleven years alone, partly while under age, then six years jointly with his brother Euergetes II., and eighteen more alone while his brother reigned in Cyrene. He married his sister Cleopatra, and left her a widow with two daughters, each named Cleopatra. The elder daughter we have seen offered to Euergetes, then married to Alexander Balas, and lastly to Demetrius. The younger daughter, afterwards known by the name of Cleopatra Cocce, was still in the care of her mother. He had most likely had three sons. One perhaps had been the pupil of Aristarchus, and died before his father; as the little elegy by Antipater of Sidon, which is addressed to the dead child, on the grief of his father and mother, would seem to be meant for a son of Philometor. A second son we shall see murdered by his uncle, and find a third living in Syria with his brother-in-law Demetrius. Porphyrius, ap. Scalig.
Anthologia Graeca, iii. 7.

(52) On the death of Philometor, his widow, Cleopatra, and some of the chief men of Alexandria proclaimed his young son king, most likely under the name of Ptolemy Eupator; but Euergetes, whose claim was favoured by the mob, marched from Cyrene to Alexandria to seize the crown of Egypt. Onias, the Jew, defended the city for Cleopatra; but a peace was soon made by the help of Thermus, the Roman ambassador, who was thought to have been bribed by Euergetes, and on this the gates of Alexandria were opened; and it was agreed that Euergetes should be king, and marry Cleopatra, his sister and his brother's widow. We may take it for granted that one article of the treaty was that her son should reign on the death of his uncle, or perhaps jointly with him; but Euergetes, forgetting that he owed his own life to Philometor, and disregarding the Romans, who were a party to the treaty, had the boy put to death in the day of the marriage. We find an inscription in the island of Cyprus in honour of this young king the god Eupator, the son of the gods Philometores, showing that in that important Justin. lib. xxxviii. 8. B.C. 145.
MS. of Anastasy, ap. Young.
Josephus, in Apion. ii.
Justinus, lib. xxxviii. 8.
Trans. R. Soc. Lit. 2nd Ser.

part of the kingdom his claim to the throne had been at once acknowledged.

(53) The Alexandrians, after the vices and murders of former kings, could not have been much struck by the behaviour of Euergetes towards his family; but he was not less cruel towards his people. Alexandria, which he had entered peaceably, was handed over to the unbridled cruelty of the mercenaries, and blood flowed in every street. The anger of Euergetes fell more particularly on the Jews for the help which they had given to Cleopatra, and he threatened them with utter destruction. The threat was not carried into execution; but such was the Jews' alarm, that they celebrated a yearly festival in Alexandria for several hundred years, in thankfulness for their escape from it. The population of the city, which was made up of Jews, and Greeks of all nations, who looked upon it less as a home than as a place of trade in which they could follow their callings with the greatest gain, seemed to quit Alexandria as easily as they had come there under Ptolemy Soter; and Euergetes, who was afraid that he should soon be left to reign over a wilderness, made new laws in favour of trade and of strangers who would settle there.

<small>Josephus, in Apion. ii.</small>

(54) In his brother's lifetime, Euergetes had never laid aside his claim to the throne of Egypt, but had only yielded to the commands of Rome and to his brother's forces; and he now numbered the years of his reign from his former seizing of Alexandria. He had reigned six years with his brother, and then eighteen years in Cyrene, and he therefore called the first year of his real reign the twenty-fifth.

<small>Porphyrius, ap. Scalig.</small>

(55) In the next year he went to Memphis to be crowned; and, while the pomps and rites were there being performed, his queen and sister bore him a son, whom, from the place, and to please the people, he named Memphites. But his queen was already in disgrace; and some of those very friends who on his brother's death had marched with him against Alexandria were publicly put to death for speaking ill of his mistress Irene. He soon afterwards put away his wife and married her younger daughter, his niece Cleopatra Cocce; and for this and other acts against his family and his

<small>Diod. Sic. De Virtut. 354.</small>

<small>Justinus, lib. xxxviii. 8.</small>

people he lived hated by everybody. But the divorced Cleopatra was allowed to keep her title; and, as she was the widow of the late king, she held a rank in the state before the wife of the reigning king. Thus the small temple of Athor, in the island of Philæ (see Fig. 258), was dedicated to the goddess in the name of

Young's Hierogl. pl. 64.

Fig. 258.

King Ptolemy and Queen Cleopatra, his sister, and Queen Cleopatra his wife, the gods Euergetæ.

(56) The Roman senate, however, felt its authority slighted by this murder of the young Eupator and divorce of Cleopatra, both of whom were living under its protection. The late ambassador, Thermus, by whose folly or treachery Euergetes had been enabled to crush his rivals and gain the sovereign power, was, on his return to Rome, called to account for his conduct. Cato, the Censor, in one of his great speeches, accused him of having

Aulus Gellius, lib. xvii. 9.

been seduced from his duty by the love of Egyptian gold, and of having betrayed the queen to the bribes of Euergetes; and he loudly demanded his punishment accordingly. In the meanwhile, Scipio Africanus the younger and two other Roman ambassadors were sent by the senate to see that the kingdom of their ally was peaceably settled. Euergetes went to meet Scipio with great pomp, and received him with all the honours due to his rank; and the whole city followed him in crowds through the streets, eager to catch a sight of the conqueror of Carthage, of the greatest man who had been seen in Alexandria, of one who by his virtues and his triumphs had added a new glory even to the name of Scipio. He brought with him as his friend and companion, in the case of a modern ambassador we should say, as his chaplain, the philosopher Panætius, the chief of the Stoics, who had gained a great name for his three books on the Duty of Man, which were afterwards copied by Cicero.

Justinus, lib. xxxviii. 8.

Cicero, Acad. iv. 2. De Officiis, lib. iii. 2.

(57) Euergetes showed them over the palace and the treasury; and, though the Romans had already begun to run the down-hill race of luxury, in which the Egyptians were so far ahead of them, yet Scipio, who held to the old fashions and plain manners of the republic, was not dazzled by mere gold and purple. But the trade of Alexandria, the natural harbour, the forest of masts, and the lighthouse—the only one in the world—surpassed anything that his well-stored mind had looked for. He went by boat to Memphis, and saw the rich crops on either bank, and the easy navigation of the Nile, in which the boats were sailing up the river by the force of the wind and floating down by the force of the stream. The villages on the river side were large and thickly set, built of course of unburnt bricks, but each on a raised mound to keep it above the autumnal inundation, and each in the bosom of its own grove of palm-trees. The crowded population was well fed and well clothed. The Roman statesman saw that nothing was wanting but a good government to make Egypt what it used to be, the greatest kingdom in the world.

Diod. Sic. Legat. 32.

(58) Scipio went no higher than Memphis; the buildings of Upper Egypt, the oldest and the largest in the world,

could not draw him to Thebes, a city whose trade had fallen off, where the deposits of bullion in the temples had lessened, and whose linen manufacture had moved towards the Delta. Had this great statesman been a Greek, he would perhaps have gone on to this city, famous alike in history and in poetry; but as it was, Scipio and his friends then sailed for Cyprus, Syria, and the other provinces or kingdoms under the power of Rome, to finish this tour of inspection.

(59) The kind treatment shown to these and other Romans is also proved by an inscription set up in the island of Delos by Lucius and Caius Pedius, in gratitude to this king. It is on a monument dedicated to Apollo and Diana; but they have not told us whether they were visitors, or whether they were employed in the service of Euergetes. Inscript. Letronne, Recherches.

(60) For some time past the Jews, taking advantage of the weakness of Egypt and Syria, had been struggling to make themselves free; and, at the beginning of this reign Simon Maccabæus, the high priest, sent an embassy to Rome, with a shield of gold weighing one thousand *minæ*, as a present, to get their independence acknowledged by the Romans. On this the senate made a treaty of alliance with the family of the Maccabees, and, using the high tone of command to which they had for some time past been accustomed, they wrote to Euergetes and the king of Syria, ordering them not to make war upon their friends the Jews. But in an after decree the Romans recognised the close friendship and the trading intercourse between Egypt and Judæa; and when they declared that they would protect the Jews in their right to levy custom-house duties, they made an exception in favour of the Egyptian trade. The people of Judæa in these struggles were glad to forget the jealousy which had separated them from their brethren in Egypt, and the old quarrel between the Hebrews and the Hellenists; the Sanhedrim of Jerusalem wrote to the Sanhedrim of Alexandria, telling them that they were going to keep the Feast of Tabernacles in solemn thanksgiving to the Almighty for their deliverance, and begging for the benefit of their prayers. 1 Maccabees, ch. xiv. xv. B.C. 143.
Josephus, Antiq. xiv. 10.
2 Maccabees, ch. i. 7.

(61) The Jews, however, of Judæa, on their gaining their

former place as a nation, did not, as before, carry forward the chain of history in their sacred books. While they had been under the yoke of the Babylonians, the Persians, and the Syrians, their language had undergone some changes; and when the Hebrew of the Old Testament was no longer the spoken language, they perhaps thought it unworthy of them to write in any other. At any rate, it is to their Greek brethren in Egypt that we are indebted for the history of the bravery of the Maccabees. Jason of Cyrene wrote the history of the Maccabees, and of the Jewish wars against Antiochus Epiphanes and his son Antiochus Eupator. This work, which was in five books, is lost, and we now read only the short history which was drawn from it by some unknown Greek writer, which, with the letter from the Jews of Judæa to their brethren of Egypt, forms the second book of Maccabees.

<small>2 Maccabees, ch. ii. 23.</small>

(62) In the list of Alexandrian authors, we must not forget to mention Jesus, the son of Sirach, who came into Egypt in this reign, and translated into Greek the Hebrew work of his grandfather Jesus, which is named the Book of Wisdom, or Ecclesiasticus. It is written in imitation of the Proverbs of Solomon; and though its pithy sayings fall far short of the wisdom and lofty thoughts which crowd every line of that earlier work, yet it will always be read with profit and pleasure. In this book we see the earliest example that we now possess of a Jewish writer borrowing from the Greek philosophers; though how far the Greek thoughts were part of the original Hebrew may be doubted, because the work was left unfinished by Jesus the grandfather, and completed by the Alexandrian translator, his grandson. Hereafter we shall see the Alexandrian Jews engrafting on the Jewish theology more and more of the Platonic opinions, which very well suited the serious earnestness of their character, and which had a most remarkable effect in making their writings and opinions more fitted to spread into the pagan schools.

<small>Old Test. Apocrypha. B.C. 132.</small>

(63) This and other writings of the Alexandrian Jews were by them added to the list of sacred books which together made their Greek Bible; but they were never acknowledged at Jerusalem. The Hebrew books of the law and the prophets had been first gathered together by Nehemiah,

after the return of the Jews from Babylon; but his library had been broken up during the Syrian wars. These Hebrew books, with some few which had since been written, were again got together by Judas Maccabæus; and after his time very little more seems to have been added to them, though the Alexandrian Jews continued to add new books to their Greek Bible, while cultivating the Platonic philosophy with a success which made a change in their religious opinions. It was in Alexandria, and very much by the help of the Jews, that Eastern and Western opinions now met. Each made some change in the other, and on the union of the two, Alexandria gave to the world a new form of philosophy.

^{2 Maccabees, ch. ii. 13, 14.}

(64) The vices and cruelty of Euergetes called for more than usual skill in the minister to keep down the angry feelings of the people. This skill was found in the general Hierax, who was one of those men whose popular manners, habits of business, and knowledge of war, make them rise over every difficulty in times of trouble. On him rested the whole weight of the government; his wise measures in part made up for the vices of his master; and, when the treasure of the state had been turned to the king's pleasures, and the soldiers were murmuring for want of pay, Hierax brought forward his own money to quiet the rebellion. But at last the people could bear their grievances no longer; the soldiers without pay, instead of guarding the throne, were its greatest enemies, and the mob rose in Alexandria, set fire to the palace, and Euergetes was forced to leave the city and withdraw to Cyprus.

^{Diod. Sic. De Virtut. 361.}

^{Livy, Epit. 59.}

(65) The Alexandrians, when free from their tyrant, sent for Cleopatra, his sister and divorced queen, and set her upon the throne. Her son by Philometor, in whose name she had before claimed the throne, had been put to death by Euergetes; Memphites, one of her sons by Euergetes, was with his father in the island of Cyprus; and this cruel monster, fearing that his first wife Cleopatra and her advisers might make use of his son's name to strengthen her throne, had the child at once put to death. The birthday of Cleopatra was at hand, and it was to be celebrated in Alexandria with the usual pomp; and Euergetes, putting the head, hands, and feet of his son Memphites into a box, sent it to Alexandria by a messenger, who had orders

^{Diod. Sic. De Virtut. 374.}

to deliver it to Cleopatra in the midst of the feast, when the nobles and ambassadors were making their accustomed gifts. The grief of Cleopatra was only equalled by the anger of the Alexandrians, who the more readily armed themselves under Marsyas to defend the queen against the invasion threatened by Euergetes.

(66) The queen's forces shortly marched against the army of Euergetes that was entering Egypt under the command of Hegelochus; but the Egyptian army was beaten on the Syrian frontier. Marsyas was sent prisoner to Euergetes; and the king then showed the only act of mercy which can be mentioned to his praise, and spared the life of a prisoner whom he thought he could make use of. Cleopatra then sent to Syria, to her son-in-law Demetrius, to ask for help, which was at first readily granted; but Demetrius was soon called home again by a rising in Antioch. But great indeed must be the cruelty which a people will not bear from their own king rather than call in a foreign master to relieve them. Among the various feelings by which men are governed, few are stronger than the wish for national independence; hence the return of the hated and revengeful Euergetes was not dreaded so much by the Alexandrians as the being made a province of Syria. Cleopatra received no help from Demetrius, but she lost the love of her people by asking for it, and she was soon forced to fly from Alexandria. She put her treasures on board a ship and joined her son Ptolemy and her son-in-law Demetrius in Syria, while Euergetes regained his throne. As soon as Euergetes was again master of Egypt, it was his turn to be revenged upon Demetrius; and he brought forward Zabbineus, a young Egyptian, the son of Protarchus, a merchant, and sent him into Syria with an army to claim the throne under the name of Alexander, the adopted son of Antiochus. Alexander easily conquered and then put to death Demetrius, but when he found that he really was king of Syria, he would no longer receive orders from Egypt; and Euergetes found that the same plots and forces were then wanted to put down this puppet, which he had before used to set him up. He began by making peace with his sister Cleopatra, who was again allowed to return to Egypt; and we find her name joined with those of Euergetes and

Justinus, lib. xxxix. 1.

Trogus, prol. xxxix.

Inscript. Letronne, Recherches.

his second queen in one of the public acts of the priests. He then sent an army and his daughter Tryphæna in marriage to Antiochus Grypus, one of the sons of Demetrius, who gladly received his help, and conquered Alexander and gained the throne of his father.

(67) We possess a curious inscription upon an obelisk that once stood in the island of Philæ, recording, as one of the grievances that the villagers smarted under, the necessity of finding supplies for the troops on their marches, and also for all the government messengers and public servants, or those who claimed to travel as such. The cost of this grievance was probably greater at Philæ than in other places, because the traveller was there stopped in his voyage by the cataracts on the Nile, and he had to be supplied with labourers to carry his luggage where the navigation was interrupted. Accordingly the priests at Philæ petitioned the king that their temple might be relieved from this heavy and vexatious charge, which they said lessened their power of rightly performing their appointed sacrifices; and they further begged to be allowed to set up a monument to record the grant which they hoped for. Euergetes granted the priests' prayer, and accordingly they set up a small obelisk; and the petition and the king's answer were carved on the base. The courteous and respectful manner in which the king's secretary writes to the priests is a proof that the Egyptians were not altogether illtreated by their Greek rulers. Inscript. Letronne.

(68) The gold mines near the Nubian or Golden Berenice, though not so rich as they used to be, were worked with full activity by the unhappy prisoners, criminals, and slaves, who were there condemned to labour in gangs under the lash of their taskmasters. Men and women alike, even old men and children, each at such work as his overstretched strength was equal to, were imprisoned in these caverns tunnelled under the sea or into the side of the mountain; and there by torchlight they suffered the cruel tortures of their overseers without having power to make their groans heard above ground. No lot upon earth could be more wretched than that of these unhappy men; to all of them death would have been thought a boon. Seldom has the love of gold had more cruelty to answer for than in the Egyptian mines. Agatharcides, ap. Photium.

(69) The survey of the coast of the Red Sea, which was undertaken in this or the last reign, did not reach beyond the northern half of that sea. It was made by Agatharcides, who, when the philosopher Heracleides Lembus filled the office of secretary to the government under Philometor, had been his scribe and reader. Agatharcides gives a curious account of the half-savage people on these coasts, and of the more remarkable animals and products of the country. He was a most judicious historian, and gave a better guess than many at the true cause of why there was most water in the Nile in the driest season of the year; which was a subject of never-ceasing inquiry with the travellers and writers on physics. Thales said that its waters were held back at its mouths by the Etesian winds, which blow from the north during the summer months; and Democritus of Abdera said that these winds carried heavy rain-clouds to Ethiopia; whereas the north winds do not begin to blow till the Nile has risen, and the river has returned to its usual size before the winds cease. Anaxagoras, who was followed by Euripides, the poet, thought that the large supply of water came from the melting of snow in Ethiopia. Ephorus thought that there were deep springs in the river's bed, which gushed forth with greater force in summer than in winter. Herodotus and Œnopides both thought that the river was in its natural state when the country was overflowed; and the former said that its waters were lessened in winter by the attraction of the sun, then over southern Ethiopia; and the latter said that as the earth grew cool, the waters were sucked into its pores. The sources of the Nile were and still are, hid by the barbarism of the tribes on its banks; but by this time the Egyptians had learned that two large streams, which we call the White Nile and the Blue Nile, unite to form this great river; and Hapimou, the Nile-god, is now sculptured with two vases, from which he pours out his water. Travellers had reached the region of tropical rains; and Agatharcides said that the overflow in Egypt arose from the rains in Upper Ethiopia. But the Abys-

Diod. Sic. lib. i. 38–41.

Fig. 259.

sinian rains begin to fall at midsummer, too late to cause the inundation in Egypt; and therefore the truth seems after all to lie with the priests of Memphis, who said the Nile rises on the other side of the equator, and the rain falling in what was winter on that side of the globe made the Nile overflow in the Egyptian summer.

(70) The trade of the Egyptians had given them very little knowledge of geography. Indeed the whole trade of the ancients was carried on by buying goods from their nearest neighbours on one side, and selling them to those on the other side of them. Long voyages were unknown; and, though the trading wealth of Egypt had mainly arisen from carrying the merchandise of India and Arabia Felix from the ports on the Red Sea to the ports on the Mediterranean, the Egyptians seemed to have gained no knowledge of the countries from which these goods came. They bought them of the Arab traders, who came to Cosseir and the Troglodytic Berenice from the opposite coast; the Arabs had probably bought them from the caravans that had carried them across the desert from the Persian Gulf; and that these land journeys across the desert were both easier and cheaper than a coasting voyage we have before learned, from Philadelphus thinking it worth while to build watering and resting-houses in the desert between Coptos and Berenice, to save the coasting voyage of about equal length between Berenice and Cosseir. India seems to have been only known to the Greeks as a country that by sea was to be reached by the way of the Euphrates and the Persian Gulf; and though Scylax had, by the orders of Darius, dropped down the River Indus, coasted Arabia, and thence reached the Red Sea, this voyage was either forgotten or disbelieved, and in the time of the Ptolemies it seems probable that nobody thought that India could be reached by sea from Egypt. Arrian indeed thought that the difficulty of carrying water in their small ships, with large crews of rowers, was alone great enough to stop a voyage of such a length along a desert coast that could not supply them with fresh water. The long voyages of Solomon and Necho had been limited to coasting Africa; the voyage of Alexander the Great had been from the Indus to the Persian Gulf; hence

Agatharcides, ap. Photium.

Nearchus, Periplus.

* *Strabo, lib. ii.*

it was that the court of Euergetes was startled by the strange news that the Arabian guards on the coast of the Red Sea had found a man in a boat by himself, who could not speak Coptic, but who they afterwards found was an Indian, who had sailed straight from India, and had lost his shipmates. He was willing to show any one the route by which he had sailed; and Eudoxus of Cyzicus in Asia Minor came to Alexandria to persuade Euergetes to give him the command of a vessel for this voyage of discovery. A vessel was given him; and though he was but badly fitted out he reached a country which he called India by sea, and brought back a cargo of spices and precious stones. He wrote an account of the coasts which he visited, and it was made use of by Pliny. But it is more than probable the unknown country called India, which Eudoxus visited, was on the west coast of Africa. Abyssinia was often called India by the ancients.

(71) In these attempts at maritime discovery, and efforts after a cheaper means of obtaining the Indian products, the Greek sailors of Euergetes made a settlement in the island of Dioscorides, now called Socotara, in the Indian Ocean, forty leagues eastward of the coast of Africa; and there they met the trading vessels from India and Ceylon. This little island continued a Greek colony for upwards of seven centuries, and Greek was the only language spoken there till it fell under the Arabs in the twilight of history, when all the European possessions in Africa were overthrown. But the art of navigation was so far unknown that but little use was made of this voyage; the goods of India, which were all costly and of small weight, were still for the most part carried across the desert on camels' backs; and we may remark that at a later period hardly more than twenty small vessels ever went to India in one year during the reigns of the Ptolemies, and that it was not till Egypt was a province of Rome that the trade-winds across the Arabian Sea were found out by Hippalus, a pilot in the Indian trade. The voyage was little known in the time of Pliny; even the learned Propertius seems to have thought that the silk was a native of Arabia; and Palmyra and Petra, the two chief cities in the desert, whose whole wealth rested and whose very being hung upon their being watering-places for

these caravans, were still wealthy cities in the second century of our era, when the voyage by the Arabian Sea became for the first time easier and cheaper than the journeys across the desert.

(72) Euergetes had been a pupil of Aristobulus, a learned Jew, a writer of the Peripatetic sect of philosophers, one who had made his learning respected by the pagans from his success in cultivating their philosophy; and also of Aristarchus, the grammarian, the editor of Homer; and though the king had given himself up to the lowest pleasures, yet he held with his crown that love of letters and of learning which had ennobled his forefathers. He was himself an author, and like Ptolemy Soter wrote his Memorabilia, or an account of what he had seen most remarkable in his lifetime. We may suppose that his writings were not of a very high order; they were quoted by Athenæus, who wrote in the reign of Marcus Aurelius; but we learn little else from them than the names of the mistresses of Ptolemy Philadelphus, and that a flock of pheasants was kept in the palace of Alexandria. He also wrote a commentary on Homer, of which we know nothing. When busy upon literature he would allow his companions to argue with him till midnight on a point of history or a verse of poetry; but not one of them ever uttered a word against his tyranny, or argued in favour of a less cruel treatment of his enemies.

<small>2 Maccabees, i. 10. Clem. Alex. Strom. i. Athenæus, lib. ii. 84. Lib. xiii. 5. Lib. xiv. 20. Lib. ii. 58. Plutarch. De adulator.</small>

(73) In this reign the schools of Alexandria, though not holding the rank which they had gained under Philadelphus, were still highly thought of. The king still gave public salaries to the professors; and Panaretus, who had been a pupil of the philosopher Arcesilaus, received the very large sum of twelve talents, or two thousand pounds a year. Sositheus, and his rival, the younger Homer, the tragic poets of this reign, have even been called two of the Pleiades of Alexandria; but that was a title given to many authors of very different times, and to some of very little merit. Such indeed was the want of merit among the poets of Alexandria, that many of their names would have been unknown to posterity had they not been saved in the pages of the critics and grammarians.

<small>Suidas.</small>

(74) But, unfortunately, the larger number of the men of letters had in the late wars taken part with Philometor against the cruel and luxurious Euergetes.

<small>Athenæus, lib. iv. 29.</small>

Hence when the streets of Alexandria were flowing with the blood of those whom he called his enemies, crowds of learned men left Egypt, and were driven to earn a livelihood by teaching in the cities to which they then fled. They were all Greeks, and few of them had been born in Alexandria. They had been brought there by the wealth of the country and the favour of the sovereign; and they now withdrew when these advantages were taken away from them. The isles and coasts of the Mediterranean were so filled with grammarians, philosophers, geometers, musicians, schoolmasters, painters, and physicians, from Alexandria, that the cruelty of Euergetes II., like the taking of Constantinople by the Turks, may be said to have spread learning by the ill-treatment of its professors.

(75) The city which was then rising highest in arts and letters was Pergamus in Asia Minor, which under Eumenes and Attalus was almost taking the place which Alexandria had before held. Its library already held two hundred thousand volumes, and raised a jealousy in the mind of Euergetes. Not content with buying books and adding to the size of his own library, he wished to lessen the libraries of his rivals; and, nettled at the number of volumes which Eumenes had got together at Pergamus, he made a law, forbidding the export of the Egyptian papyrus on which they were written. On this the copiers employed by Eumenes wrote their books upon sheepskins, which were called *charta pergamena*, or parchment, from the name of the city in which they were written. Thus our own two words, parchment, from *Pergamus*, and paper, from *papyrus*, remain as monuments of the rivalry in book-collecting between the two kings.

<small>Pliny, lib. xiii. 21.</small>

(76) But even money and the commands of kings could not procure faultless copies of the books wanted; Galen, who lived in Pergamus under the Antonines, complains woefully of the treatment which authors had received from these hasty copiers; and such were the prices given for books that the copiers often ventured to put forth false writings to supply the demand

<small>Galen, in Hippocrat. ii. De nat. homin.</small>

of the purchasers. Alexandria in this and the following centuries, was the birthplace of many literary forgeries, which have puzzled the learned in modern days. Posidonius, a Stoic philosopher who wrote a history of the wars of this and the last reign in continuation of Polybius, was believed to be the author of a volume of speeches in accusation of Demosthenes, written in the names of the Athenian orators. Aristobulus, the king's tutor, in his Commentary on the Laws of Moses, was a bold forger of lines which he brings forward as from the Greek poets, in order to persuade the Greeks that their early writers borrowed much from the Hebrew Scriptures. Such are the lines declaring the seventh day to be holy, which he says are from Homer and Hesiod. The Apostle Paul would seem to have been misled by one of his forgeries when he quotes the words of Aratus, "For we are also His offspring." In Aratus those words refer to Jupiter; it is Aristobulus who first makes them point to God. At this time, perhaps, were written those prophetic words which now form part of Lycophron's poem, which proclaim the greatness of Rome, and that "the children of Æneas would hold the sceptre of sea and land."

<small>Suidas.</small>

<small>Eusebius Præp. Evang. xiii. 12.</small>

<small>Acts, xvii. 28.</small>

(77) Euergetes was so bloated with disease that his body was nearly six feet round, and he was made weak and slothful by this weight of flesh. He walked with a crutch, and wore a loose robe like a woman's, which reached to his feet and hands. He gave himself up very much to eating and drinking, and on the year that he was chosen priest of Apollo by the Cyrenæans, he showed his pleasure at the honour by a memorable feast which he gave in a costly manner to all those who had before filled that office. He had reigned six years with his brother, then eighteen years in Cyrene, and lastly twenty-nine years after the death of his brother, and he died in the fifty-fourth year of his reign, and perhaps the sixty-ninth of his age. He left a widow, Cleopatra Cocce; two sons, Ptolemy and Ptolemy Alexander; and three daughters, Cleopatra, married to her elder brother, Tryphæna, married to Antiochus Grypus, and Selene, unmarried; and also a natural son, Ptolemy Apion, to whom by will he left

<small>Athenæus, lib. xii. 12.</small>

<small>Porphyrius, ap. Scalig.</small>

the kingdom of Cyrene; while he left the kingdom of Egypt to his widow and one of his sons, giving her the power of choosing which should be her colleague.

<small>Justinus, lib. xxxix. 3.</small>

The first Euergetes earned and deserved the name, which was sadly disgraced by the second; but such was the fame of Egypt's greatness, that the titles of its kings were copied in nearly every Greek kingdom. We meet with the flattering names of Soter, Philadelphus, Euergetes, and the rest, on the coins of Syria, Parthia, Cappadocia, Paphlagonia, Pontus, Bactria, and Bithynia; while that of Euergetes, *the benefactor*, was at last used as another name for a tyrant.

<small>Luke, ch. xxii. 25.</small>

(78) It was during the reigns of Philometor and Euergetes II. that the earliest of the Hebrew Inscriptions at the foot of Mount Serbal, to which we can give a date, were written. The Jews living in Lower Egypt had naturally for several centuries been in the habit of making a pious pilgrimage to the Holy Mount, the Mount of God, which their history had pointed out as the spot where the Law was delivered to Moses. When they arrived there they usually cut a votive inscription on the rock. This custom had certainly begun before Genesis x. 30 was written, as then the mountain had already gained the name of "Sephar, [or *written*,] the mountain which was of old." The writer of the Book of Job had probably visited the Holy Mountain about the time of the Jews' return from Captivity in Babylon. He points to these Inscriptions, and gives to the mountain the same name in Chap. xix. 23, saying:—

> Oh that my words were now written!
> Oh that they were imprinted on [Mount] Sephar!
> That with an iron pen and a leaden hammer,
> They were chiselled into the rock for ever!

In Numbers xxxiii. 23, the name of the mountain is written Shephar; and the geographical minuteness of that chapter quite fixes on Serbal the honour of being the mountain spoken of. It is in Wady Mokatteb, or *the sculptured valley*, on the Egyptian side of Mount Serbal, that the most legible of the inscriptions are found.

These are short sentences, called votive Peace offerings and Memorial offerings, usually containing a prayer to Jehovah for unhappy Jerusalem. To most of them we can fix no date. But some few pray for relief from an enemy whom it was not safe to name openly; written perhaps while Antiochus Epiphanes was master of Egypt as well as of Judea. It was probably after his death, when in Egypt at least, a Jew might speak boldly, that one pilgrim adds the prayer "Slaughter, O Jehovah, Syria." Then we have a burst of inscriptions by men thankful that the city has broken free from a wicked people; and for a time they have a more hopeful tone. (See Fig. 260.) These latter writings

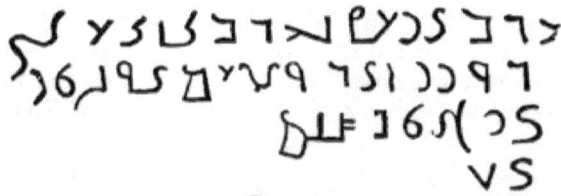

Fig. 260.

clearly belong to the time of the Maccabee revolt. The pilgrims had each travelled two hundred miles from the neighbourhood of Onion, or three hundred miles from Alexandria, and the same distance back again. Some came with camels, and some with horses. We must suppose them to have been men of substance, tradesmen and merchants, feeling warmly for the country of their fathers; and though the inscriptions profess to give no historic information, yet we learn from them that there had been for several centuries a colony of prosperous Jews in Lower Egypt, that they had always considered Serbal as the Holy Mountain spoken of in the Book of Exodus; and we further learn the forms of the Hebrew letters which they used.

ADDITIONS.

Page 171, line 23.

When a writer at this early period of the world's history shows much knowledge of a foreign country, we may be sure that he had visited it. Books of travels had not yet been written. Hence to the Greek travellers mentioned above, we

428   SILVER COIN OF DEMETRIUS.

may add the Hebrew poet, the writer of the Book of Job. He had seen the buffalo, which the Egyptians kept for its flesh and milk, but could not teach to plough in a furrow (xxxix. 10), and the river-horse lying in the water under the leaves of the lotus (xl. 21), and the Egyptian conjurors playing with the crocodile (iii. 8, Hebr.), and he had examined that animal's hide (xli. 15). He had seen the ostrich outrunning the horseman in the Nubian desert (xxxix. 18), and the workmen let down by cords into the Nubian gold mines (xxviii. 4–6). He had reached Nubia, not by the Nile, but by the caravan route through Arabia (vi. 19); and in passing had gathered mineral oil from the oil-mountain, from which the petroleum flows, near the head of the Red Sea (xxix. 6); and had seen the writing on Mount Serbal in Sinai, "with an iron pen and a leaden hammer chiselled into the rock for ever" (xix. 23, 24). This Hebrew poet's descriptions prove the places visited; and the time of his writing is known by his quoting from earlier writers and being quoted by a later.

Page 284, line 27.

Among other coins belonging to the island of Cyprus, we have one which seems to have been struck for Demetrius. It is of silver, and it weighs about eleven grains. On one side it bears a bearded head, with the lion's skin helmet of Alexander's successors. On the other side is a ram lying down. Beneath the ram are

De Luynes, Numism. Cypriote.

two Greek letters, "E Y," for Evagoras, the nation's hero, a former king of Salamis, and around it are five Cypriote letters, which, under De Luynes's guidance may be read from right to left as Salamis. The letters in front of the head may be read as Demetrius (see Fig.). The statues and other sculptured works of art, which have been found in the island, show a remarkable variety of styles: Egyptian, Phœnician, Assyrian, Greek, and native Cypriote, bearing proof of the various races which at times had ruled in the island. The Cypriote inscriptions have not yet been deciphered, nor is the language understood.

Page 348, *line* 9.

One of these gateways, now in ruins, near the great temple of Karnak, deserves particular mention from the double use which has been made of its stones. It stands on the south side of the temple, on the road towards a smaller temple built by Ptolemy Philadelphus, and on that part of the road which, by the direction which it takes, may be said to belong to Ptolemy's temple, rather than to the old temple of Karnak. This ruined gateway bears on the face of it the hieroglyphics sculptured by Amunothph III.; but many of the fallen stones bear on the back the name of the sun-worshipping Haomra. This has been thought to show that the sun-worshipper lived before the time of Amunothph III., whereas in our history he stands as the satrap Thannyras, governing Egypt for the Persian king, Artaxerxes Longimanus, many centuries later. The difficulty can be explained only by supposing that these stones, after having been first used by Amunothph III. for a gateway, had been used a second time by the sun-worshipper; and thirdly, that the priests, under the Ptolemies, being at liberty, as we have seen, to restore the monumental honours to their right owners, had begun to rebuild Amunothph's gateway on the road to Ptolemy's temple, and had left it unfinished, to puzzle us and instruct us by its two sets of hieroglyphics.

Page 230, *line* 34.

Ichonuphys's knowledge of astronomy soon bore good fruit, when in B.C. 357 a reform of the Calendar was attempted by the introduction of an intercalary day every fourth year. How far it was adopted throughout Egypt we do not know; probably not very generally; but an inscription at El Khargeh in the Great Oasis tells us that in that province it continued in use for four hundred years, that is, long after the same reform was again attempted at Canopus in B.C. 238, and even after the same reform was successfully introduced by the order of Augustus in B.C. 25. This inscription is dated by two calendars; at the beginning by the Julian Augustan calendar, which in B.C. 25 fixed the moving new year's day at the 29th of August; and at the end by another calendar, which had fixed it at the 20th of November. The difference between the two is 83 days, which, when multiplied by 4, gives us 332, as the number of years by which the one calendar was older than the other. Thus to Iconuphys belongs the honour of proposing what is known by the name of the Julian Calendar, as is proved by an inscription of A.D. 68 in the emperor Galba's reign.

<small>Boeckh, 4957.</small>

END OF VOLUME FIRST.

<small>LONDON : PRINTED BY WM. CLOWES AND SONS, LIMITED, STAMFORD STREET AND CHARING CROSS.</small>

www.ingramcontent.com/pod-product-compliance
Lightning Source LLC
Chambersburg PA
CBHW022107300426
44117CB00007B/624